Introduction to
Modern Statistics

THE MACMILLAN COMPANY
NEW YORK · CHICAGO
DALLAS · ATLANTA · SAN FRANCISCO
LONDON · MANILA
IN CANADA
BRETT-MACMILLAN LTD.
GALT, ONTARIO

Introduction to

Modern Statistics

WITH APPLICATIONS TO BUSINESS AND ECONOMICS

WERNER Z. HIRSCH
WASHINGTON UNIVERSITY

New York

THE MACMILLAN COMPANY

Library of Congress catalog card number: 57-5774

To
My Parents

The black-letter man may be the man of the present, but the man of the future is the man of statistics and the master of economics.

JUSTICE OLIVER WENDELL HOLMES

Preface

The necessity for equipping students of business and economics with a basic knowledge of statistical methods is widely recognized. However, there is considerable divergence as to character and purpose among the courses offered to fulfill this need.

In many institutions, it is impractical to assume that students enter the introductory course in statistics with sufficient knowledge of mathematics to master statistical theory. Under such circumstances the instructor faces two choices. He may limit his material to descriptive statistics for the most part, and present whatever inductive techniques are to be offered in the form of instructions and formulas that the student can follow but not understand. The alternative is to present modern methods of inference in such a way that a student who has had only high school algebra and geometry can grasp the reasoning underlying the formulas, even though he may not be able to derive them mathematically.

The latter approach can be intellectually more satisfying to both student and teacher. This will be especially true when the purpose of the course is to equip the future businessman and economist not only with a sound understanding of a number of important statistical techniques, coupled with a degree of proficiency in applying them, but also with a realistic appraisal of the role of modern statistical methods in the process of scientific decision making.

This is the point of view from which this book has been written. Concepts are introduced by concrete examples rather than in the abstract. The reasoning underlying a given method for solving a problem is then presented in relation to the example. Mathematical rigor has been sacrificed to some degree to ease the assimilation of major ideas, and the exposition is occasionally interrupted by bits of material in a lighter vein, in the hope that students will find that statistics is neither too difficult nor too tedious.

The book is arranged primarily to meet the needs of schools of business and departments of economics that offer a three- or four-unit introductory statistics course. In order to provide flexibility, slightly more material is included than will commonly be covered in such a course. For instance, the instructor who has only one three-unit course may wish to omit a discussion of binomial distribution, confidence interval estimation of percentages, and decisions about the significance of a difference between percentages, i.e., Chapters IX, X and XII. The rest of the material is self-contained and the omission of these three chapters will not be confusing. When using this book for a more general statistics course, as in the case of students primarily interested in the social sciences, index numbers and the time series analysis, i.e., Chapters XIII, XV and XVI could be omitted. The text could also be used for two successive three-unit courses of elementary statistics for students in business and economics, supplemented by additional reading on one or more of the following subjects: multiple regression and correlation analysis, analysis of variance, statistical control, and sampling methods. In addition, it is hoped that the book will prove helpful to those who are no longer in college.

I wish to express my gratitude to Professor Robert Ferber who gave generously of his time to read the entire manuscript. His critical discussion of substantive and expository points and his numerous suggestions were invaluable. My thanks also go to Norman Rasmussen of the International Business Machines Corporation for most valuable advice in connection with Chapter XIX. I am also indebted to many of my colleagues and former students for their helpful criticisms. To Mrs. Mary Hoekel go my thanks for technical assistance. I am indebted to Professor Sir Ronald A. Fisher, Cambridge, and to Messrs. Oliver and Boyd Ltd., Edinbourgh, for permission to reprint Appendix Table II from Fisher, *Statistical Methods for Research Workers;* and to Professor Fisher, Dr. Frank Yates, Rothamsted, and to Messrs. Oliver and Boyd Ltd., for permission to reprint portions of appendix Tables IV and VIII from *Statistical Tables for Biological, Agricultural, and Medical Research.* To all other persons and organizations who granted permission to reprint charts, tables or drawings, as acknowledged in the proper locations, I also wish to express my sincere appreciation.

No formal word of appreciation can be sufficient to thank my wife. My children also deserve gratitude for trying to keep quiet. As one of them put it: "Sh-sh—Daddy is making book!"

Responsibility for all errors and imperfections is, of course, mine.

W. Z. H.

Contents

lation and determination. Which came first, the hen or the egg? Adjusting for lost degrees of freedom. Is there a significant relationship? How close is the relationship in the population? Is the regression coefficient significant? What is the confidence interval of prediction? A larger sample. This method can be useful. Coding—a worksaver.

Trend. Periodic variations. Cycle. Irregular variations. All components.
Edit of annual data. Where to start and where to end? Methods of measuring trend. The graphic "freehand" fit. The semiaverage fit. The moving average fit. The least squares fit. An example. Trends in aggregates. Testing for curvilinearity. Not all things are odd. Converting annual trend data into monthly ones. The trend may not be linear— parabola. A curvilinear trend can become linear—logarithmic straight line. A warning.
Edit of monthly data. An example of seasonal rhythm. Simple average method. Ratio to moving average method. Applying the seasonal index. Seasonal computations by electronics.
Cyclical variations as a residual. The National Bureau's method of measuring typical cyclical behavior.

Introduction to
Modern Statistics

I

Introduction

Statistical thinking will one day be as necessary for efficient citizenship as the ability to read and write.

H. G. WELLS

What does the average person associate with the word "statistics"? The figure measurements of his favorite movie actress, the data on highway accidents last New Year's week end, or perhaps the old quotation, "There are lies, damned lies, and statistics"?

To most people, statistics mean numerical data—figures. But that there is also a field of knowledge called statistics, and that it is legitimately concerned with much more than tabulating sets of numbers, is not so widely known.

There are two branches of the subject of statistics. One, descriptive statistics, is concerned with collecting, tabulating, analyzing, interpreting, and presenting numerical data. The other, inductive statistics, is a set of intellectual tools, based upon the mathematical theory of probability, which enables us to use partial or limited numerical information for producing generalizations, estimates, predictions, and decisions in such a way that the fallibility of the conclusions can be assessed.

To illustrate, collection of information on the death rate of one million people of various ages in the United States during the period 1930–40 and the presentation of these data in the form of the *Commissioners' 1941 Standard Ordinary Mortality Table* are examples of descriptive work in statistics. The numerical data can be interpreted to show that of those persons included in the survey and forty-seven years of age 1 per cent passed away before the age of forty-eight.

1

These conclusions are by and large descriptive, as they do not go beyond the data and phenomenon at hand. However, the use to which this mortality table is put by life insurance companies goes much further. These data are used extensively to predict the future: the likelihood of death at a certain age. Largely upon such predictions, insurance companies base their premiums. This is inductive statistics.

Cartoon by George Lichty reproduced by permission of the Chicago Sun-Times Syndicate.

"It's rather comforting at a time like this, Bessie, to know that statistics show women are better drivers than men."

It should be clear that inductive statistics cannot reliably predict a single phenomenon such as whether one *particular* policyholder will die next year. But it can tell us with a stated reliability and precision the number of men, let us say, of age forty-five who died in the United States in the year under consideration. To the extent that conditions do not change, we could also estimate the number of men of that age group who will die next year in the United States.

By means of inductive statistics inferences can be drawn from sample data to show, for instance, the percentage of unemployment, as well as the total number of unemployed. With its help we can decide with a known risk of being wrong whether this January's unemployment is above or below that of last January. Also, it can aid in estimating people's preferences for certain radio and television programs; and, as a further example, it makes possible decisions at a known or assessable risk about changes in the quality and performance of specified production and marketing processes. These are but a few examples of the numerous areas to which modern statistics is applied.

The gamblers of the seventeenth century were largely responsible for the early development of probability theory. These gamblers were seeking a system of calculating odds. While it is easy to figure out the probability of throwing a six-spot on a die (1/6, if the die is honest), games of chance often involve much more complicated probabilities. For example, we might wish to calculate the probability of being dealt a full house in a card game, and it is easy to see that it takes some real thinking to find the answer. The laws of probability began to be discovered as far back as the first half of the seventeenth century, with such men as Galileo, Pascal, de Méré, Fermat, and Cardano (an inveterate gambler himself) participating in the early work. These early beginnings resulted in a theory of probability that is still being expanded and refined by mathematicians and forms the basis of modern statistics.

Since the methods of statistics are mathematical, at least in their origin, the reader who has little mathematical training may wonder whether he can ever expect to master the subject. It is certainly true that one cannot be a competent professional statistician or make new contributions to the theory and set of tools available for solving statistical problems without mathematical facility. However, one need not be a professional to learn enough statistics for dealing with some of the more common empirical problems in economics and business. Descriptive statistics, for one thing, requires little mathematics. Inductive statistics, the field that offers the powerful tools of scientific decision-making and estimation on the basis of sample data which economists and businessmen are finding extremely useful, requires a little more mathematics. Nevertheless it is the contention of this book that the reader who lacks mathematical training can acquire a working knowledge of the basic techniques of inductive statistics. More important, he can gain an intuitive comprehension of the reasoning underlying the methods and formulas he is using. He can learn enough to solve by himself simpler problems with the techniques he has acquired, to recognize those problems for which methods have been worked out and which he may master through further study, and to know those for which he needs the help of a competent professional statistician. Most important perhaps, he can acquaint himself with the tremendous contributions that modern statistics can make to certain kinds of problems in economics and business and can discriminate between the kind of problems that can be tackled in this manner and those which cannot.

It should be realized, however, that statistical methodology has yielded, and is yielding, important results in many other fields of inquiry—notably in physics (molecular behavior, quantum mechanics, etc.), in genetics, in the analysis of agricultural experiments, in psychology and public health, to mention but a few of the more important ones. It forms a part of what is commonly called the scientific method and as such should be part of the training of an educated person. Statistics are used to bolster all kinds of claims in civic and political life and, as Darrell Huff has made entertainingly clear in his "How to Lie with Statistics," often are misused.[1] The ability to recognize and expose such misuse is an important intellectual weapon in a free society.

While statistical methods are based on mathematical laws and are thus objective, statistical findings will always reflect to some degree certain assumptions incorporated with the choice of methods and data that are highly subjective. It is therefore necessary to stress that a statistician is not a detached, impersonal, ivory tower scientist, but rather one who has to know a great deal about the background of the problem upon which he is working, or else form a partnership with one who does.

In conclusion, it may be appropriate to illustrate what statistics can do. The example chosen refers to the phenomenon that a manufacturer's labor costs decline with the number of units manufactured, as workers learn to do the job better and in less time. The relationship is known as a "Learning Function" or a "Progress Function."[2] The following incident, reflecting on the usefulness of this statistical progress function, is reported by Frank J. Andress:

During World War II an executive of a home appliance manufacturing company chanced to cross paths with an executive of a large West Coast aircraft firm. The appliance executive mentioned that it had taken his company two years to determine the exact cost of the electric refrigerator which it manufactured.

The aircraft executive pointed out that in many cases his company had been forced to determine costs on similar items in a matter of a few minutes, and said, "I'll bet you a steak dinner that I can predict the cost of your 100,000th refrigerator within 10 per cent accuracy by using a learning curve based on aircraft production."

The manufacturing executive accepted the bet. The only information he fur-

[1] Darrell Huff, *How to Lie with Statistics* (New York, W. W. Norton & Co., 1954).
[2] Werner Z. Hirsch, "Manufacturing Progress Functions," *Review of Economics and Statistics*, 34:143–155 (May, 1952).

nished was the weight of the refrigerator and the cost of the first unit produced. During the next few minutes he watched while the aircraft executive worked with pencil, ruler, and log-log graph paper.

When he had completed plotting the curve, the aircraft executive stated: "Your 100,000th unit should cost you $162.50."

"Just drop the 50 cents," the appliance executive said. "It was actually $162.00."[3]

[3] Frank J. Andress, "The Learning Curve as a Production Tool," *Harvard Business Review*, 32:87 (January-February, 1954).

II

Getting Meaning Out of
a Mass of Data

The leader, mingling with the vulgar host,
Is in the common mass of matter lost.
ALEXANDER POPE

What does this Table 2.1 mean?

To the untrained mind, it means very little. If you are good at scanning a set of figures, you will be able to pick out, after a number of seconds, the salesman who sold most and the one who sold least, and will get the "range" between the highest and lowest dollar value of sales. Also, you may know that you can get an "average" sales value of some sort by adding all the sales figures and dividing the sum by the number of salesmen.

But would you say that a banker, faced with the problem of whether to grant a loan to one of the salesmen whose last week's sales are listed here, would be able to obtain important background information for his decision from these data—*even though he does not know which of the letters refers to that particular salesman?* As a matter of fact, he can predict with about 63 per cent confidence that his man sold no less than $11,050 worth of cigarettes last week. How this and similar conclusions can be reached on the basis of a set of figures such as this, with some knowledge of simple statistical techniques, is the subject of this chapter.

Now let us acquaint you with the story of which the above data are a part:

Mr. C. C. Camel is regional sales representative of the "Lucie Tastes Better" Tobacco Company—LUTABE for short—makers of fine nationally advertised cigarettes. Mr. Camel, who only recently came to this area, is to attend a conference of all of LUTABE's sales representatives. He wants to be well informed about recent developments in his territory so as to make a good impression on the executives who will be present. Therefore, he has

6

Table 2.1 ALPHABETICAL ORDERING
(Sales of LUTABE cigarettes of 35 salesmen in the first week of October, 1957.)

Name of Salesman	Dollar Cigarette Sales	Name of Salesman	Dollar Cigarette Sales
A	5,900	U	16,600
B	14,500	V	8,000
C	6,700	W	10,400
D	12,500	X	13,700
E	9,200	Y	11,500
F	11,800	Z	13,100
G	13,400	AZ	14,900
H	19,000	BZ	18,500
I	14,000	CZ	3,000
J	8,400	DZ	12,500
K	12,700	EZ	10,600
L	15,900	FZ	10,000
M	23,000	GZ	15,800
N	9,500	HZ	16,800
O	10,900	IZ	9,000
P	12,100		
Q	7,800		
R	12,500		
S	15,500		
T	17,800		

Source: Hypothetical figures.

had his 35 salesmen phone in their last week's sales figures. His secretary had been busy all the previous day writing down the salesmen's weekly sales figures as they came in.

When, after alphabetically arranging the names of the salesmen, she hands Mr. Camel a sheet with 35 names and figures, i.e., Table 2.1, he can't help scratching his ear, mumbling "I can't make head or tail out of these figures. What the heck do they mean?" After some minutes of contemplation he turns to his secretary and says: "You arranged the data alphabetically, but this order does not appear to be very useful. Couldn't you arrange them in order from the lowest to the highest value?"

When she brings in her new table (Table 2.2), Mr. Camel finds it easier to get an idea about the extreme sales figures and, more important, the *range* between them, that is, the difference between the highest and the lowest sales figure. But he is not satisfied yet. He asks himself if it would not be worth while to have another table in which the figures would be grouped according to magnitude, so that he could tell at a glance how many salesmen sold, for example, between $8,000 and $11,000 worth of cigarettes.

He isn't sure how best to do this, for he wants his tables to look profes-

Table 2.2   ARRAY
(Sales of LUTABE cigarettes of 35 salesmen
in the first week of October, 1957.)

Dollar Cigarette Sales	*Dollar Cigarette Sales*
3,000	13,100
5,900	13,400
6,700	13,700
7,800	14,000
8,000	14,500
8,400	14,900
9,000	15,500
9,200	15,800
9,500	15,900
10,000	16,600
10,400	16,800
10,600	17,800
10,900	18,500
11,500	19,000
11,800	23,000
12,100	
12,500	
12,500	
12,500	
12,700	

Source: Table 2.1.

sional, but he is aware that such problems are included in the subject matter commonly referred to as "Statistics."   Fortunately, he has little trouble in obtaining a statistics text.   It turns out to be "Elementary Statistics" by Professor Sigma P. Ekks, and Mr. Camel starts reading what it has to say about arranging data in tabular form.

2.1. FREQUENCY DISTRIBUTIONS

Leafing through the textbook, Mr. Camel finds that his second table (Table 2.2) is what is known as an *array*, i.e., an orderly arrangement of data according to their magnitude from the smallest to the largest value. The array indicates at a glance the extreme values and the range between them.

However, there are other ways to arrange data, and each of them brings out different information.

First, there is the *frequency distribution*.   This is what Mr. Camel had in mind when he felt that the data ought to be *grouped according to magnitude*, so he reads carefully what the learned "Prof. Ekks" has to say:

"A frequency distribution is an orderly arrangement of a series of data classified according to the magnitude of its variate. *Variate* is each of a set of tabulated numbers that can vary from item to item. If, for instance, we were to analyze the annual payroll of the Acme Lumber Mill, our variate would be annual wages, and they will tend to vary from one worker to the next. Variates thus form the statistician's raw material for much of his work. The statistician studies numerical characteristics of items. The numerical value of a given characteristic we call an *observation*. Returning to our earlier example, we might find worker A's wages amounting to \$4,723. This annual wage of \$4,723 of worker A is an observation, and so is that of worker B, etc.

"For any set of data, several different frequency distributions may be set up, all of which may be correct. One may decide on more *classes* or fewer classes, i.e., groups into which variates may be divided, and wider *class intervals* or narrower class intervals. But there are certain rules that must be observed in order to get an appropriate frequency distribution.

"By pointing to some guideposts in the construction of frequency distributions we will help you learn their construction.

"Let us begin with the issues of how many classes should be constructed and how large *class intervals* should be. By a *class interval* we mean the difference between a *lower class limit* and an *upper class limit*. There is no cut and dried rule for deciding on the number of classes. The number of classes should neither be too small nor too large. More specifically we may suggest that they should not usually be fewer than 5, nor more than 20. The more observations we have, the more classes might be needed.

"As a guide to indicate the approximate number of classes called for, we may use Sturges' rule:

$$k = 1 + 3.3 \log N, \tag{2.1}$$

where k is the number of classes,

N is the number of observations, and

log is an ordinary (Briggsian) logarithm to the base of ten."

Since Mr. Camel's series is composed of 35 observations, i.e., $N = 35$, $k = 1 + 3.3 \log 35 = 1 + 3.3(1.5441) = 6$. However, for a number of considerations which will be discussed below, he will eventually decide to classify the 35 items into 7 classes.

So Camel reads on:

"The number of classes selected also depends on such additional considerations as whether a *monomodal* distribution would result. A monomodal distribution, as shown in Chart 2.1, is distinct from a *bimodal* one (Chart 2.2) in that the former has a single peak if plotted as a graph. Many monomodal distributions are shaped like a bell, while a camel's hump shape represents a bimodal distribution. Another consideration that influences

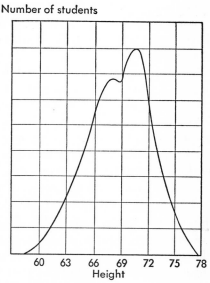

Chart 2.1 MONOMODAL
DISTRIBUTION

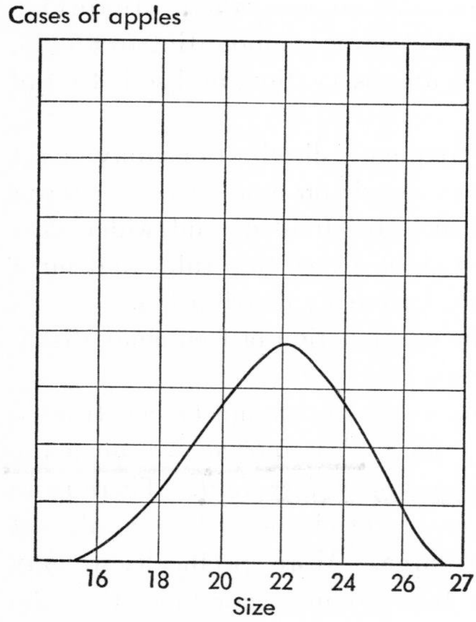

Cases of apples

Size

Source: Hypothetical data.

Chart 2.2 BIMODAL
DISTRIBUTION

Number of students

Height

Source: Hypothetical data.

the number of classes is whether observations cluster around the *class mid-point*, which as the name indicates is the point in the middle of the class.

"*Clustering* of observations at or near the center of the class—the class mid-point—gains in importance since in a frequency distribution the individual values of a given class interval are represented by their class mid-point.   Clearly, a close clustering of observations around the class mid-point enhances both representativeness and usefulness.   Consider the sales of a candy counter where most sales are multiples of 5 cents.   If intervals are 3 to 7 cents, 8 to 12 cents, etc., observations will cluster around the mid-points 5 cents, 10 cents, etc.

"Also the size of the class interval is important in constructing frequency distributions.   There is no reason why the lower limit of the lowest class cannot be below the lowest value of the series; and similarly, why the highest value of the highest class cannot be greater than its highest value.

"There is one further important point to be considered. In constructing frequency distributions classes must be made *exclusive*, so that there can be no argument into which one a particular observation should be placed. Before we show how to select class limits so that they do not overlap, we will digress for a moment to discuss the selection of proper class limits.

"It is fairly common to distinguish between what is often referred to as *continuous* as against *discrete* series. Discrete data are given in terms of indivisible units and are represented by whole numbers, also called integers. As examples you might think of the number of salesmen, successes, failures, houses, books, airplanes, etc. A series in which the values of the variate change by infinitely small amounts, e.g., weight, is a continuous one. Such continuous measures can conceivably be found at any point along a continuous linear scale. Depending on how fine our equipment is, we can measure height and weight in practically infinitely small units. Most measurements, whether of continuous or discrete data, are approximations. They are not accurate in any absolute sense. They lack precision because of the human element in measuring, and, in some cases, the variability of the physical measure. Thus, the only really authentic yardstick for measuring length is made of a special metal and kept by the Bureau of Standards under special conditions under which we practically never use our yardsticks.

"Since many measurements are approximations, taken to the nearest multiple of the unit used, it is often appropriate to substitute an interval for a point. The limits of the interval are 1/2 of a unit on either side of the measurement. We understand that we should take the pinpointed claim of the fisherman that he caught a 5-lb. bass (if we believe him at all!) to mean that he caught one weighing somewhere between 4.5 and 5.5 lb.—an interval. Thus we should begin to look upon measurements as intervals, and not as finite points. The usefulness of this procedure will become clearer once we start to discuss statistical inference.

"Let us return now to our more immediate problem of determining exclusive class intervals. If, for instance, weekly wage information has been collected not in terms of dollars and cents, but just in terms of dollars, a lower class limit of $41 could be interpreted as extending from $40.50 to $41.50. An upper class limit of $60 could similarly be interpreted as extending from $59.50 to $60.50. Consequently an interval identified by the limits $41 and $60 can be interpreted as extending from $40.50 to $60.50. While the interval will be written $41–$60, the *real* limits or *boundaries* of the interval are $40.50 and $60.50. The next interval reads $61–$80. The upper and lower boundaries are $60.50 and $80.50. Since all the data are given in terms of dollars and not fractions thereof, such an interpretation of class intervals dispels doubt as to the class in which a given wage figure is to be placed. A $60 item goes into the first interval; a $59 item goes into the first, too; yet a $61 item goes into the second interval, etc. Since the wage data are not reported in units smaller than a dollar, the issue of where to place an item such as $60.50, for example, does not arise. Thus, the overlapping of the real boundaries—$60.50 is both the upper boundary of the first class and the lower boundary of the second class—eliminates possible gaps between classes and yet keeps them exclusive.

"Thus, if measurements have been taken to the nearest dollar, the boundaries will be plus and minus 1/2 dollar; if the measurements were to the nearest 10 dollars the boundaries would be plus and minus 5 dollars; if to the nearest 100 dollars the boundaries would be plus and minus 50 dollars; and if to the nearest 1,000 dollars the boundaries would be plus and minus 500 dollars, and so on."

Having read to this point, Mr. Camel is ready to construct his own frequency distribution, and comes up with Table 2.3. Since the figures his

Table 2.3 (ABSOLUTE) FREQUENCY DISTRIBUTION
(Sales of LUTABE cigarettes of 35 salesmen in the first week of October, 1957.)

Cigarette Sales per Salesman, in Dollars	Number of Salesmen
2,100– 5,000	1
5,100– 8,000	4
8,100–11,000	8
11,100–14,000	11
14,100–17,000	7
17,100–20,000	3
20,100–23,000	1
Total	35

Source: Table 2.2.

salesmen phoned were in terms of hundreds of dollars, he realizes that they are only approximations. So he writes the upper limit of the first class in his table as $5,000, but knows that its upper boundary is really $5,050, and that the upper boundary of the second class is $8,050. Thus, when he comes to salesman V in his array, whose sales totaled $8,000, there is no doubt in Camel's mind into which class this figure goes: it has to go into the second class. That is how he makes his classes mutually exclusive, as required by the rule in the text.

Camel mulls over the frequency distribution a while longer; then he asks himself: "Why couldn't I just call the highest class '$20,050 and over' instead of limiting it to between $20,100 and $23,000? It might make a better impression to leave the upper limit open to speculation." However, he finds that "Prof. Ekks" says one should avoid *open-end distributions, as* he calls those left open at either the upper or lower end, or both. It seems that open-end distributions do not lend themselves to some of the most important computations that could give one more insight into the nature of the data. What's more, open-end distributions are difficult to portray graphically.

One further point strikes Mr. Camel as he reads on. The textbook recommends that the class intervals should, whenever possible, be so constructed that they are of equal width. *Uniform intervals* are apparently a convenience. Well, he had already, by instinct or by luck, made all his intervals $3,000 wide, so that was correct.

Camel now summarizes the points that are to be considered in the construction of a frequency distribution.

1. The number of classes must be appropriate to the number of items in the series, making possible a monomodal distribution in which the observations in a particular class cluster around its mid-point. The last consideration should also guide the determination of the size of class intervals.

2. There must be no overlapping of classes.

3. Open-end classes should be avoided whenever possible.

4. Uniform class intervals are a convenience and should be aimed at.

Table 2.4   (RELATIVE) FREQUENCY DISTRIBUTION
(Sales of LUTABE cigarettes of 35 salesmen in the first week of October, 1957.)

Cigarette Sales per Salesman, in Dollars	Percentage of ALL Salesmen
2,100– 5,000	3
5,100– 8,000	11
8,100–11,000	23
11,100–14,000	31
14,100–17,000	20
17,100–20,000	9
20,100–23,000	3
Total	100%

Source: Table 2.3.

Finally, Camel draws up a *relative* frequency distribution (Table 2.4) that shows the proportion of salesmen whose sales fell into the same seven intervals. In Table 2.3 the frequencies were in absolute units, i.e., number of salesmen.   The table shows, for instance, that four salesmen sold somewhere between $5,100 and $8,000 worth of cigarettes last week.   Instead of stating the total number of salesmen that fall into a certain sales group, the relative frequency distribution (Table 2.4) tells Camel what percentage of all salesmen sold, for instance, between $5,100 and $8,000 worth.   To convert the absolute into a relative frequency distribution, Camel simply divided the frequency of each class by the total number of frequencies of the series and multiplied that number by 100.

2.2. SIGNIFICANT DIGITS

Mr. Camel's thoughts now return to the remark in the textbook that most measurements are approximations.   He knows, of course, that the data from which he started, those in Table 2.1, are approximations, having been rounded off to the nearest $100.   He has often wondered why it seemed legitimate in some sets of circumstances, but not in others, to round off figures.   Also, in many cases when working with figures some of which were rounded off and some of which were not, he has had to decide how many decimals to carry, and has wished for a rule to guide him.   Just then he happens to come across a discussion by "Prof. Ekks" that throws light on this matter and, realizing that it is of importance for anyone undertaking a statistical project, he proceeds to read it carefully:

"Approximate measurements are common.   Whenever numbers are approximations, some of their digits are *significant* and others insignificant. *A digit is significant if it is known to be correct and not merely designed to indicate the position of other digits.*   Let us illustrate what we mean by this. If Mr. Smith sold his business for $127,984, all six digits of this number are known to him to be correct and, therefore, are significant.   If later, either having forgotten or not caring for the detail, he tells a friend that he got $128,000 for his business, the last three digits are known to Smith not to be correct.   They are approximations and as such are insignificant.   Only the first three digits of 128,000 are significant.

"A few rules may prove helpful:

1. All digits except zeros are significant.   Thus, 73,962 has five significant digits, 94 has two significant digits, 195 has three significant digits, etc.
2. Zeros are significant only under certain circumstances:
    a. If the zeros are preceded and followed by digits other than zero.   For instance, 800,734 has six significant digits.
    b. Zeros are not significant if they are at the extreme left of the number.   Thus,

Reprinted by permission of Newspaper Features Syndicate, Inc.

"We have either sixty-four dollars and twenty-two cents, seventy-one dollars and eighty-five cents or fifty-nine dollars and sixty-three cents in the treasury. It never comes out the same."

0.00000037 has two significant digits, 0.00000937 has three significant digits, etc.

c. If the number has as its last digit a zero that is to the right of the decimal, this zero, and every zero in front of it and preceded by a significant digit, is significant. In 35.490 the zero is significant and there is a total of five significant digits.

d. However, if the number has as its last digit a zero that is to the left of the decimal, this zero may or may not be significant. Whether or not this zero is significant depends on whether it is known to be correct. If we had counted in tens and come up with the sum of 930 the zero is not significant. If we had counted in single units, e.g., 921 + 9 = 930, the zero is significant. Should 930 stand for 929.5 to 930.5 the zero is significant.

"Now let us see how this knowledge of significant digits helps us in adding and subtracting numbers. It is important to realize that *the accuracy of the results of additions and subtractions cannot exceed that of the least accurate component.*   In the following example we will see how this 'weakest link in a chain' rule applies in addition:

$$
\begin{array}{r}
37.9 \\
147.22 \\
49.2967 \\
100.013 \\
\underline{2,307.20} \\
\overline{2,641.6}
\end{array}
$$

"On first look it is apparent that these five measurements are not of equal precision, and that the first number is the least precise.   We do not know what follows the 9 in the first number.   Therefore, carrying the sum to more than one decimal would result in spurious accuracy, and the result will be given in terms of one digit to the right of the decimal.   Adding up the column gives a sum of 2,641.6297.   This figure will be rounded to one digit to the right of the decimal.   Since 297 is smaller than 500 the last three digits will be dropped.   The sum is: 2,641.6.   Had they been larger than 500, e.g., 2,641.6785, the 6 preceding 785 would have been increased to 7; the sum would have been: 2,641.7.   If the last 3 digits had been 500, the preceding digit would have remained unchanged and the last 500 dropped since the 6 that precedes them is an even number.   Thus, a 2,641.6500 is rounded to 2,641.6.   Should the digit preceding the 500 be an odd number, this odd number would be increased by 1.   Thus, a 2,641.7500 is rounded to 2,641.8.

"What about multiplying and dividing?   The general rule is that in *multiplying or dividing data that are approximations the end result can never have more significant digits than had that number with the fewest significant digits entering into the computation.*   4.257 has 4 significant digits.   If we multiply this number by 4.3, which has 2 significant digits, the product will also have 2 significant digits.   The product is 18.

"There is one modification to this rule.   It concerns *constants,* which are the direct opposite of variates, in that they are numbers that do not vary from observation to observation, but instead retain the same value.   When data are multiplied or divided by a constant, the result can have as many significant digits as had the number that was multiplied or divided by the constant.   Thus, 246 pairs of shoes are 246/12, or 20.5, dozen pairs of shoes. Since 246 has 3 significant digits and 12 is a constant, all 3 digits in 20.5 are significant.

"We think it appropriate to sound a note of warning not to confuse accuracy with significant digits as a criterion. The accuracy criterion in the 'weakest link in a chain rule' refers to the position of the digit in relation to the decimal, while starting and ending with the same number of significant digits in the rule that governs multiplications and divisions, refers to our knowledge of a given digit to be correct.

"Now, one final example will be given. Five mail sacks are brought to a mail-order plant to be weighed. Based on the weight of incoming mail and on the assumption that there are approximately 41 orders per pound of mail, the number of orders in the mail is estimated. To expedite matters 5 clerks take one sack each and weigh it. Here are the weights they recorded that need to be summed and then multiplied by 41.

$$50.4$$
$$42$$
$$49.35$$
$$50.0$$
$$47.973$$

"Before we add this column we had better determine the number of significant digits the sum can have. Since there is a 42 that has no significant digit to the right of the decimal, the sum will be an integer—240. Now, our final interest does not rest with this sum, but its multiplication by 41. Since the sum is not the final result we might leave it with as many decimals as possible, multiply it, and only then identify the significant digits. This procedure would, however, be very burdensome and we will, therefore, establish at each step the significant digits, carry one additional digit, and drop the rest before undertaking additional computations. Thus, in spite of the fact that in adding these five numbers only integers are significant, we will carry, whenever possible, 1 digit to the right of the decimal. We add

$$50.4$$
$$42$$
$$49.4$$
$$50.0$$
$$\underline{48.0}$$
$$239.8$$

This sum of 239.8 we multiply by 41, and since 41 has only 2 significant digits the final result is 9,800 orders."

2.3. FREQUENCY DISTRIBUTIONS
AND CONFIDENCE INTERVALS[1]

Having read this discussion of significant digits, Mr. Camel puts down the textbook with the feeling that the information is going to prove useful on many future occasions. He gathers up the tables he has prepared for the sales meeting, puts them in his brief case, and heads for home.

By coincidence, however, soon after dinner he receives a telephone call from a Mr. Paul Mal, a banker, who wants to see him in order to ask his opinion of one of the men in his sales force who has applied to the bank for a loan. Camel explains that he has not been in his job long and does not know his salesmen well, but will be glad to be of whatever help he can.

When Mr. Mal arrives, he explains that the application is an urgent one and he has promised the salesman, Mr. Kent, an answer in the morning. All he wants to find out from Mr. Camel is how Jim Kent has been doing lately as far as his cigarette sales go.

Explaining to Mr. Mal that only this morning he has obtained data on last week's sales from his salesmen, Camel opens his brief case to take out the tables he has brought home. But his embarrassment is great when he finds that he has brought with him only Tables 2.3 and 2.4, the frequency distributions, and had left in his office Table 2.1, which listed each salesman alphabetically. The figure for Jim Kent's last week's sales is in Tables 2.3 and 2.4, too, but has lost its identity.

But Mal says: "Don't worry. Let me see those tables. I know some statistics, which I find very useful in my job, and I can probably get some helpful information from them."

"I see that Table 2.4 is a relative frequency distribution. It says here that about 23, 31, and 20 per cent, respectively, of all your agents sold between \$8,100 and \$11,000, \$11,100 and \$14,000, and \$14,100 and \$17,000 worth of cigarettes. Frequencies of different classes can be added up, you know, so that $23 + 31 + 20 = 74$ per cent of all salesmen sold somewhere between \$8,100 and \$17,000 worth of LUTABE cigarettes. Almost three-fourths of all your agents fall into this category, selling between \$8,100 and \$17,000 worth of cigarettes. This is a most revealing statement."

For instance, the fact that the relative frequency of the fourth class is about 31 (or about 31 per cent of all agents sold between \$11,100 and \$14,000 worth of cigarettes) offers Mal further important information. Since neither Mal nor Camel know whether Kent is a particularly good or a very

[1] The concept of a confidence interval will be developed more rigorously in Chapter VIII.

poor salesman, Mal concludes that there is a 31 per cent likelihood that Kent sold between \$11,100 and \$14,000 worth of cigarettes last week.

"You may say," Mal remarks, "that I can conclude with a 31 per cent confidence that Kent's sales were between \$11,100 and \$14,000. \$11,100 to \$14,000 would be called a 31 per cent confidence interval. Now, a banker likes to be able to place more confidence than that in his opinion. By broadening our confidence interval—that is the interval in which we can place a known confidence—for instance, from between \$11,100 and \$14,000 to between \$8,100 and \$17,000, I could state with a 23 + 31 + 20 or 74 per cent confidence that Kent actually sold between \$8,100 and \$17,000 of cigarettes. I could choose any level of confidence. If I would like to be entirely sure I could take the entire range: that is, a 100 per cent confidence interval. I can be sure then that Kent sold between \$2,100 and \$23,000 worth of cigarettes. You realize, of course, Mr. Camel, that the last conclusion is not very meaningful."

"I see," replies Camel, *"the smaller the interval, that is, the more pinpointed the information, the smaller the confidence we can place in it and vice versa.* But, Mr. Mal, as a banker, should you make decisions on the basis of such flimsy information? I thought loans should be granted on the basis of facts only."

Apparently this question arouses Mr. Mal's temper. "Facts, facts!" he shouts, "that's all I hear all day. How many times do we have black and white facts when we have to make a decision? Most decisions involve the future. Who has facts about the future? If I waited for facts I could never decide either to make a loan or to reject an application. Ninety-nine times out of a hundred, when you make a decision all you have to go on is the kind of information that enables you to have a certain degree of confidence that the outcome will be within a certain range. Should we therefore stop acting? Certainly not, only we should learn some statistics so that we can be more precise about the degree of confidence with which we make our decision. Then, we can really calculate risks instead of just talking about calculated risks all the time."

Mr. Camel is interested, yet he feels it his duty to get his guest back on his subject, so he asks: "Well, I see how you can make a statement about the likelihood of Jim Kent's selling between \$11,100 and \$14,000 worth of cigarettes, but wouldn't you be more interested in a minimum figure? Wouldn't it be more important for you to know that Kent sold last week no less than, say, \$11,050 worth?"

"That's true," says Mal, "and I can learn about that from your tables, too." Looking once more at the relative frequency table (Table 2.4), Mal

sees that 3 per cent of all salesmen sold between $20,100 and $23,000 worth
of cigarettes, or 3 per cent sold at least $20,050 worth of cigarettes.   Nine
per cent sold $17,100 to $20,000 worth; or 3 + 9 or 12 per cent sold at least
$17,050 worth.   Finally 3 + 9 + 20 + 31 or 63 per cent of the salesmen
sold at least $11,050 worth of cigarettes.   From this Mal concludes: "There
is a 63 per cent likelihood that Jim Kent sold at least $11,050 worth of
cigarettes.   Now this statement involves a *cumulative* frequency distribution.   To facilitate such statements as this one, you can construct
cumulative frequency distributions, both *absolute* and *relative* ones.   As you
will easily realize, there are in fact two types of such cumulative frequency
distributions, the 'less than' and the 'more than' (or 'at least') cumulative
frequency distributions."
   "Here, let me set them up for you."   Camel gets him some sheets of
paper and a pencil, and Mr. Mal draws up Table 2.5, explaining that it is an

Table 2.5   (ABSOLUTE) "LESS THAN" CUMULATIVE FREQUENCY DISTRIBUTION

(Sales of LUTABE cigarettes of 35 salesmen in the first week of October, 1957.)

Dollar Cigarette Sales	*Number of Salesmen*
Less than 2,050	0
" " 5,050	1
" " 8,050	5
" " 11,050	13
" " 14,050	24
" " 17,050	31
" " 20,050	34
" " 23,050	35

Source: Table 2.3.

Table 2.6   (ABSOLUTE) "MORE THAN" CUMULATIVE FREQUENCY DISTRIBUTION

(Sales of LUTABE cigarettes of 35 salesmen in the first week of October, 1957.)

Dollar Cigarette Sales	*Number of Salesmen*
More than 2,050	35
" " 5,050	34
" " 8,050	30
" " 11,050	22
" " 14,050	11
" " 17,050	4
" " 20,050	1
" " 23,050	0

Source: Table 2.3.

absolute *"less than" cumulative frequency table*, and Table 2.6, which is an absolute *"more than" cumulative frequency table*. "Either from these or directly from Table 2.4 you can derive the *relative 'less than'* and *relative 'more than' cumulative frequency tables*," adds Mr. Mal and draws up Tables 2.7 and 2.8.

Table 2.7   (RELATIVE) "LESS THAN" CUMULATIVE
FREQUENCY DISTRIBUTION

(Sales of LUTABE cigarettes of 35 salesmen in the first week of October, 1957.)

Dollar Cigarette Sales	Percentage of Salesmen
Less than 2,050	0
" " 5,050	3
" " 8,050	14
" " 11,050	37
" " 14,050	68
" " 17,050	88
" " 20,050	97
" " 23,050	100

Source: Table 2.4.

Table 2.8   (RELATIVE) "MORE THAN" CUMULATIVE
FREQUENCY DISTRIBUTION

(Sales of LUTABE cigarettes of 35 salesmen in the first week of October, 1957.)

Dollar Cigarette Sales	Percentage of Salesmen
More than 2,050	100
" " 5,050	97
" " 8,050	86
" " 11,050	63
" " 14,050	32
" " 17,050	12
" " 20,050	3
" " 23,050	0

Source: Table 2.4.

2.4. CHARTING

After all these explanations, Mr. Camel offers Mal a LUTABE cigarette. While he lights it, Mal goes on talking. "You say now that arranging your data in form of a frequency distribution makes them easier to understand. Well, the other day I sat in on a meeting of research directors of some major industrial companies.

"The research director for a steel firm remarked that top management of his company insists that all findings and recommendations be presented in

tabular form.   At this point the research director for one of the major
chemical companies in the United States spoke up and said that his management has difficulty making sense out of figures and demands that everything
be submitted in graphical form.   This discussion points to the fact that some
people are at greater ease with figures and tables and others with graphs.

Cartoon by George Lichty reproduced by permission of the Chicago Sun-Times
Syndicate.

"These graphs and charts are too confusing! . . . call the treasurer
and let's have a peek in the till . . . "

Often a graphical presentation of data is more dramatic and makes rough
comprehension of data easier."
    "I always feel that graphs are much more impressive," remarks Camel.
"As a matter of fact, I wish I had these data in graphic form for my sales
representatives' meeting tomorrow."
    "Would you like me to help you turn these into graphs?" inquires Mr.
Mal eagerly.   "You don't have to worry about my time—I might learn

some more useful things about Mr. Kent in the process." Mr. Camel, of course, is agreeable, so Mal starts a little lecture:

"There are three major graphical forms in which frequency distributions can be presented: the *histogram, smoothed histogram,* and *polygon.* A *histogram* is constructed by laying out a horizontal scale, representing the variate in its units of measurement, for example, dollar cigarette sales per salesman, and a vertical scale representing the frequency, that is, in this case, number of salesmen. Using the class interval as a base we erect on it bars whose areas correspond to the number of salesmen that fall into the particular interval. Here, I am turning your data into a histogram, using 'real' class limits. Let's call this Chart 2.3.[2]

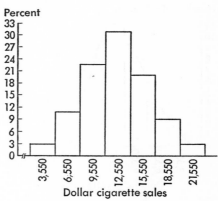

Chart 2.3 (ABSOLUTE) HISTOGRAM	**Chart 2.4** (RELATIVE) HISTOGRAM
(Sales of LUTABE cigarettes of 35 salesmen in the first week of October, 1957.)	(Sales of LUTABE cigarettes of 35 salesmen in the first week of October, 1957.)

Source: Table 2.3.   *Source:* Table 2.4.

"So far I talked about graphical presentations of absolute frequency distributions. Histograms can also represent relative frequency distributions. Here, I am drawing Chart 2.4, which is a relative histogram, based on your Table 2.4.

"In many cases the rugged corners of histograms can be smoothed, so that the periphery becomes curvilinear. We are justified in smoothing a histogram, since its irregularities are not necessarily inherent in data. They are in part due to our particular selection of class intervals and, possibly, to inaccuracies in the measurement of the data. Therefore, so long as the

[2] Mr. Mal forgot to add that as a general rule the horizontal and vertical scales should be divided into regular intervals, all starting from the origin zero. There are occasions when it is more convenient to "break" either or both axes. In Chart 2.3 the horizontal axis is broken, since we are not interested in the area between 0 and 2,050.

total area under the curve is equal to the total area in the rectangles, we are justified in smoothing a histogram. The smoothing is usually done graphically—here, watch me do it, Mr. Camel. This is Chart 2.5. However, it could also be done by means of mathematical formulas. In practice, the smoothing process involves lopping off as much from any one bar as is added to it. The end product of this process is a *smoothed histogram.*

"Another way of portraying a frequency distribution, by means of a curve and not rectangles, is in the form of a *frequency polygon.* This time, instead of constructing bars above class intervals, I am locating points above class mid-points. Their distance from the horizontal line corresponds to the frequency of the particular class. Look at Chart 2.6. The class mid-point

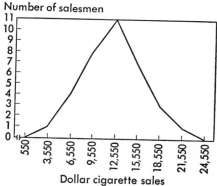

Chart 2.5 SMOOTHED HISTOGRAM

(Sales of LUTABE cigarettes of 35 salesmen in the first week of October, 1957.)

Number of salesmen

Dollar cigarette sales

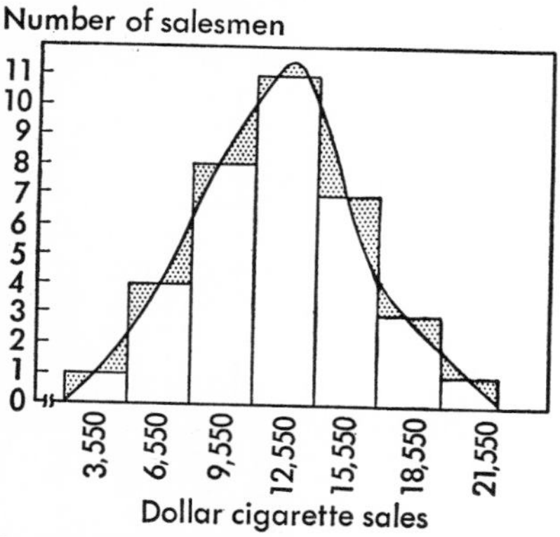

Source: Table 2.3.

Chart 2.6 POLYGON

(Sales of LUTABE cigarettes of 35 salesmen in the first week of October, 1957.)

Number of salesmen

Dollar cigarette sales

Source: Table 2.3.

of the first interval is $\dfrac{2,100 + 5,000}{2}$ or 3,550. A single salesman falls into the first class, so I draw in point *a* 1 unit above \$3,550 on the horizontal axis. The mid-point of the second interval is $\dfrac{5,100 + 8,000}{2}$ or 6,550 and the frequency is 4. So point *b* in chart 2.6 is drawn in 4 units above 6,550. In the same way I draw the other 5 points. I connect these mid-points by a series of straight lines and close the curve at the base by bringing the lines down to the mid-points of the classes at the extremes of the distribution with zero frequencies (at \$550 and \$24,550). Here you have Chart 2.6.

"Clearly histograms and polygons can also represent relative frequency distributions. Portraying relative frequency distributions in the form of a smoothed histogram or polygon can be particularly helpful. You can look upon Charts 2.5 and 2.6 as representing relative frequency distributions. The entire area under the smoothed histogram in Chart 2.5 represents 100 per cent or 1.00. The area above a certain class interval will correspond to the relative size of that class. For instance, the first class, $2,050 to $5,050, represents both about 3 per cent (0.03) of the salesmen and of the area of the smoothed histogram. The area above $5,050 to $8,050 is 11 per cent (or 0.11) of the total, and so on. Similarly, the area above $2,050 to $8,050 is 3 + 11 or 14 per cent of the total area of the smoothed polygon. While there are some differences between the smoothed histogram and the polygon, the area of the latter can be interpreted similarly.

"This reminds me of our cumulative frequency distributions. They, too, can be presented in chart form. They are called *ogives*. The 'more than' and 'less than' absolute ogives are shown in Chart 2.7. These two intersect at the median value of the series." (Mr. Camel does not know yet that a median is a measure of central tendency and divides the series into two equal halves when presented as an array. But he will find out in the next chapter.)

Chart 2.7 ABSOLUTE "MORE THAN" AND "LESS THAN" OGIVES

(Sales of LUTABE cigarettes of 35 salesmen in the first week of October, 1957.)

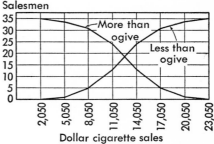

Source: Tables 2.5 and 2.6.

"There is one further type of chart that has intrigued me for a long time. I don't know whether you will have much use for this sort of graphical presentation, but it might nevertheless interest you.

"I am referring to the *Lorenz curve*, which helps appraise and demonstrate the degree of inequality of income of a group of people. The Lorenz curve is most commonly used to show inequality of income in a country and, sometimes, to make comparisons between countries or between different time periods. Instead of addressing myself to an entire country, let me take a hypothetical group of 100 men in one and the same profession. Table 2.9 contains the pertinent information. The first three columns are the same as are found in any frequency distribution table. To form a Lorenz curve I begin by multiplying the class mid-point (Column 3) by the frequency of that class (Column 2) to obtain the total income of the class (Column 4).

"In Column 5 I form the cumulative values of these total incomes and in Column 6 I reduce them to percentage figures by dividing them all by the

Table 2.9 LORENZ CURVE DATA OF 100 INCOME EARNERS

Income	Fre-quency	Mid-point	Income of Group	Cumu-lative Income	% Cu-mulative Income	Cumu-lative Frequency	% Cu-mulative Frequency
1	2	3	4	5	6	7	8
				0	0	0	0
$ 1,001– 2,000	4	1,500	6,000				
				6,000	0.7	4	4
2,001– 3,000	5	2,500	12,500				
				18,500	2	9	9
3,001– 4,000	10	3,500	35,000				
				53,500	7	19	19
4,001– 5,000	20	4,500	90,000				
				143,500	18	39	39
5,001– 7,000	30	6,000	180,000				
				323,500	40	69	69
7,001– 10,000	15	8,500	127,500				
				451,000	55	84	84
10,001– 15,000	8	12,500	100,000				
				551,000	67	92	92
15,001– 30,000	5	22,500	112,500				
				663,500	81	97	97
30,001– 50,000	2	40,000	80,000				
				743,500	91	99	99
50,001–100,000	1	75,000	75,000				
				818,500	100	100	100

Source: Hypothetical data.

total income, the last number in Column 5. These cumulative values are staggered with respect to the original classes, to indicate that they refer to the class boundaries. I then form the cumulative frequencies at each boundary (Column 7); and finally reduce these cumulative frequencies to percentage values by dividing them all by the total frequency, 100 (Column 8). The data in Columns 6 and 8 are the basis for the Lorenz curve, with the percentage cumulative income plotted against the percentage cumulative frequency (Chart 2.8). In addition to connecting these points, I draw a diagonal that goes through the origin of the chart. This diagonal represents the extreme condition of a completely equal income distribution. For instance, it shows a situation where the poorest 20 per cent of the people get 20 per cent of the total income, 30 per cent get 30 per cent of the income, and so on.

  "The area between the line of equal distribution and the curve portraying the actual status of income inequality indicates the extent of the inequality. By and large, the smaller the area between these two lines, the more equal the income distribution, and vice versa.

"But that is not the only use to which the Lorenz curve can be put. If I wish to know what percentage of the total income goes to the lower quarter of the people, I find 25 per cent on the horizontal scale, find the corresponding point on the curve, and carry this over to the vertical scale. Here is the answer: The lower quarter of the people receive 7 per cent of the income received by all 100 people. I could do the same if my Lorenz curve would pertain to the population of the entire United States, or of any other country."

When finally Mr. Camel escorts the banker to the door, both are convinced that they spent a profitable evening. Of course, Mr. Mal has certain other information on which to base his decision concerning a loan to Jim Kent; but we are exploring statistics, and not loan practices.

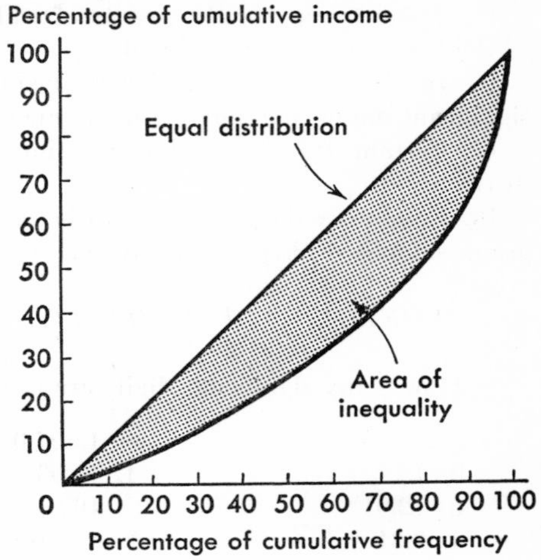

Chart 2.8 LORENZ CURVE

Percentage of cumulative income

Percentage of cumulative frequency

Source: Table 2.9.

WHAT WE HAVE LEARNED:

1. An array is an arrangement of data according to their magnitude.

2. A frequency distribution is an orderly arrangement of a series of data classified according to the magnitude of its variate.

3. A class is a group of variates in a frequency table.

4. A variate is each of a set of tabulated numbers which can vary from item to item.

5. An observation is the numerical value of a given characteristic of an item.

6. The lower class limit is the lowest value of the class and the upper class limit is the highest value of the same class.

7. A class interval is the difference between the lower and upper class boundaries.

8. A monomodal distribution is a distribution with a single peak, while a bimodal distribution is one with two peaks.

9. A class mid-point is the point in the middle of the class, and as such it is often used to represent the values of the class.

10. Open-end distributions are open either at the upper or lower end of a frequency distribution, or both.

11. We set up arrays and frequency distributions, because it facilitates making sense out of a mass of data.

12. Depending on whether the frequencies are expressed in absolute or relative terms we have an absolute or relative frequency distribution.

13. Most measurements must be checked with regard to precision and significant digits.

14. A digit is significant if it is known to be correct and not merely designed to indicate the position of the other digits.

15. The accuracy of the results of addition and subtraction cannot exceed that of the least accurate component.

16. In multiplying or dividing approximations, the end result can never have more significant digits than any of the numbers which entered into the computation.

17. Certain types of confidence intervals can be calculated from frequency distributions.

18. Frequency distributions can be presented graphically in the form of a histogram, smoothed histogram, polygon, ogive, or Lorenz curve, among others.

SEE WHETHER YOU KNOW IT:

→ 1. How many significant digits are in the following figures:

a. 0.003	e. 1,507.0	i. 13.73
b. 12	f. 11.03	j. 1.007
c. 12.01	g. 102.4	k. 120.03
d. 0.31	h. .079160	l. 10,300

2. What is the sum of exercises:

a. 1a + 1b	c. 1c + 1d	e. 1a + 1h.
b. 1b + 1c	d. 1e + 1h	

→ 3. Round the following data to two digits to the right of the decimal:

a. 73.19001	e. 120.87499	i. 3.875
b. 121.31	f. 17.655	j. 4.974999
c. 2.9753	g. 234.700	k. 10.26500
d. 18.005	h. 11.111	l. 79.32500

4. What is the sum of the data in the left column of Exercise 1 divided by (a) 4.1; (b) the approximate measure 4; and (c) the constant 4.2.

5. What is the sum of the data in the middle column of Exercise 1 times (a) 97.76; (b) 90.0; and (c) the constant 9.2.

6. Subtract the sum of the data in the right column of Exercise 1 from that in the left column.

7. The table on p. 29 shows the hours worked by 189 piece-rate workers in the garment industry in the first quarter of the year:

    a. Arrange them in an array. Make whatever useful statements you can think of, based on this array of data.

    b. Construct an absolute frequency distribution and plot it as a frequency polygon, frequency histogram, and smoothed frequency histogram. In case you may wish to know, the logarithm of 189 is 2.27646.

    c. Construct a relative frequency distribution and indicate the likelihood with which you could assert that one of these garment workers, a Mr. Homer

Number	Hours Worked	Number	Hours Worked	Number	Hours Worked	Number	Hours Worked
1	329.75	48	544	95	236	142	399.75
2	388	49	539	96	120	143	412
3	446.25	50	494.25	97	280	144	459
4	446.75	51	515	98	181.25	145	262
5	524.25	52	524.75	99	340	146	162.75
6	305.25	53	378.75	100	340	147	272
7	427.7	54	412	101	480	148	161.75
8	311.3	55	397.5	102	480	149	208
9	476	56	450.25	103	335.75	150	125
10	484	57	336.25	104	391.25	151	125.75
11	465.5	58	376.50	105	88	152	25.5
12	465.5	59	466	106	350.75	153	24.25
13	487.5	60	344	107	351.75	154	48
14	399.5	61	505	108	352.75	155	40
15	472	62	516	109	375.5	156	444
16	481	63	367.25	110	361.75	157	363.25
17	459.5	64	342.25	111	378.5	158	428.75
18	462.3	65	471	112	401	159	453
19	196.5	66	394.75	113	273.25	160	70.75
20	465.92	67	222.25	114	279	161	437.25
21	460	68	302.5	115	280	162	481
22	492	69	430	116	357	163	309
23	492	70	540.25	117	345.75	164	305
24	330	71	540.25	118	432	165	407.25
25	330	72	294.75	119	419.5	166	546
26	428	73	445.75	120	427.75	167	410.75
27	428	74	620.25	121	444	168	353.75
28	387.75	75	307.75	122	427.25	169	409.75
29	381	76	273.75	123	381.25	170	467.25
30	492	77	273.75	124	368	171	378
31	389.25	78	454.75	125	419	172	379.5
32	492	79	460.5	126	461	173	400.5
33	364.25	80	449	127	462.5	174	327.75
34	260	81	502.5	128	353	175	537.5
35	384	82	502.5	129	351	176	490.25
36	328	83	484.5	130	428	177	423
37	424	84	482	131	429.5	178	424
38	424	85	482	132	428	179	424.25
39	120	86	476	133	420	180	370.5
40	343	87	509.5	134	120	181	316
41	327	88	408	135	213.5	182	150.5
42	332	89	408	136	435.25	183	473.5
43	274.5	90	447.75	137	428	184	480
44	393.5	91	435.5	138	398.5	185	493.75
45	546.5	92	483.5	139	383	186	379.5
46	470.25	93	483.5	140	282	187	498.25
47	357	94	399	141	448	188	186.75
						189	346.75

Town, had worked in the first quarter of the year somewhere between 300 and 500 hours.

    d. Construct "more than" and "less than" relative frequency distributions and from them read off the likelihood that Mr. Homer Town worked at least about 520 hours in the first quarter of the year.

8. a. Draw a frequency histogram and polygon of the following weekly wage data:

Weekly Wage	Frequency	Relative	Class midpoint
$25.01–30.00	3	1.6	27.5 ~~27.5.0~~
$30.01–35.00	19	10.2	32.5
$35.01–40.00	22	11.8	37.5
$40.01–45.00	34	18.4	42.5
$45.01–50.00	42	22.7	47.5
$50.01–55.00	30	16.2	52.5
$55.01–60.00	23	—12.4	57.5
$60.01–65.00	8	4.3	62.5
$65.01–70.00	4	2.1	67.5
		99.7	

    b. What is the likelihood that one particular worker, Hal Miller, will earn somewhere between $40.01 and $60.00 a week?

    c. What is the likelihood that he earns between $25 and $70 a week?

    d. What is the likelihood that he earns $30.005 or less a week?

    e. What is the likelihood that he earns at least $65.005, $55.005 a week?

    f. What percentage of the workers earn less than $60.005 a week?

  9. Draw an ogive of the data given in 8a.

  10. Draw a Lorenz curve of the following data:

Property Value per Owner	Number of Owners
$001– $500	15
$501– $1,000	11
$1,001– $2,000	5
$2,001– $5,000	4
$5,001–$10,000	3
$10,001–$20,000	1
$20,001–$50,000	2

  11. With the help of the Lorenz curve of Exercise 10 find:

    a. The fraction of the total property owned by the upper 20 per cent of the owners.

    b. The fraction of the total property owned by the lower one fourth of the owners.

    c. The fraction of the owners who own half of the total property.

  12. The following table contains the grades given to 57 students who took the introductory course in Economics in the last semester:

100	68	64	83	79	65
67	82	85	77	78	75
87	80	80	74	71	58
94	73	82	85	90	69
76	83	99	88	76	68

75	82	68	72	72	61
77	70	86	84	59	63
64	53	90	93	80	
67	79	77	83	71	
89	93	60	80	80	

a. Construct an absolute frequency table.
b. Construct a relative frequency table.
c. Construct a relative "more than" frequency table.
d. Construct an absolute histogram and smooth it.
e. Construct a polygon.
f. Construct a "less than" ogive.

III

"On the Average"

The average U.S. soldier weighs 155 lbs., is 5 feet 8½ inches tall, wears a size 38 uniform, marches in a size 9-D shoe, measures 14½ inches around the neck, has

a 32 sleeve length,
a 36.3 inch chest,
a 30.6 inch waist,
and a hip measurement of 36.36 inches.

ANTHROPOMETRIC SURVEY,
UNITED STATES ARMY.

Mr. Camel soon discovers that interesting as charts, arrays, and frequency distributions may be, they nevertheless fail to convey concisely how his series of data compares with other series of data. Would it not be convenient if he could point to the sales of one specific salesman as being representative, or an *average*, of those of his entire sales force?

Searching in "Prof. Ekks'" textbook, Mr. Camel finds that there are various types of averages or, as statisticians also sometimes call them, "measures of central tendency" or "most typical values." Furthermore, he finds that the word "average," derived from the latin word "havaria," has a most interesting history. In former times, when the sea posed much more serious hazards to ships than it does today, ships in danger of sinking used to throw portions of their cargo overboard. Soon it became a custom to prorate the value of lost goods among all merchants who had cargo on the ship so as to compensate those whose goods had been lost. The sea damage to cargo in transit became known as *havaria*. This term later was used to denote the amount of compensation each merchant was called upon to pay. "Average," which finds its root in "havaria," is thus associated with the

32

early phases of risk spreading, i.e., insurance. In addition to the *arithmetic mean*, which is the one most commonly used, there are the *median, mode, geometric mean,* and *harmonic mean,* to mention the more common ones.

In order to learn which is the most useful type of average for his purpose, Camel reads "Prof. Ekks'" chapter on "Measures of Central Tendency," which begins as follows:

3.1. STATISTICAL SHORTHAND

"Statistical work often covers many types of numerical data. In Table 3.1 we have a set of data comprised of 7 observations. It pertains to the number of hours worked in the first week of 1953 by 7 workers in a store.

Table 3.1 HOURS WORKED BY 7 WORKERS
IN THE FIRST WEEK OF 1953

Worker's Number	Hours Worked, x
1	50
2	30
3	40
4	25
5	45
6	10
7	45
Total	245

Source: Hypothetical data.

"For the sake of simplicity we shall represent the variate of this problem, number of hours worked, by the symbol x. Often x, y, or z is used to denote variates. It is convenient to use a subscript to denote x, e.g., i, so that x_i will stand for the number of hours worked during the first week of 1953 by the ith worker. Since the store has 7 workers, i can be any of the numbers 1, 2, 3, 4, 5, 6, or 7. The statistician is fond of saying in such a case, i runs from 1 to 7. If we were to ask how many hours did Worker 5 work in the first week of 1953, we could put it more briefly: what is x_5?—assuming that we defined x as the number of hours worked by a worker in the first week of 1953. Examining Table 3.1, we find that $x_5 = 45$. Without sacrificing precision, a symbol such as x and a subscript such as i are a kind of statistical shorthand and very useful."

Mr. Camel stops reading for a moment, and applies the symbols to his own problem. Defining x as last week's sales, he writes $x_{10} = \$8,400.$ and

knows that this means that Salesman J (Number 10 in Table 2.1) sold
$8,400 of cigarettes last week.   Camel continues in "Prof. Ekks'" chapter:

"The first step in finding the arithmetic mean is to total all the variates;
the second step is to divide this sum by the number of variates included.
In our work hour example, the first step means that we add the number of
hours worked in the first week of 1953 by the first worker to that of the
second worker, to that of the third worker, etc.   All this can be written in
our statistical shorthand as:

$$x_1 + x_2 + x_3 + \cdots + x_7. \tag{3.1}$$

To simplify this formula, we will introduce one further notation that again is
convenient statistical shorthand.   If we write a capital Greek sigma, Σ, it
will mean "the summation of . . . ."   Equation 3.1 can be written:
$\sum_{i=1}^{7} x_i$, which can be read as: the summation of x_i where i runs from 1 to 7.

To calculate $\sum_{i=1}^{7} x_i$ we add up the total hours of Table 3.1.

"This procedure can be generalized.   Instead of specifying the precise
number of observations of the variate, we can simply use N, where N can be
any number.   We would thus write $\sum_{i=1}^{N} x_i$, meaning the summation of x_i,
where i runs from 1 to N.

"By this same method we can handle every variate that lends itself to a
process of summation.   Here are a few examples:

$$\sum_{i=1}^{5} x_i^2 = x_1^2 + x_2^2 + x_3^2 + x_4^2 + x_5^2.$$

$$\sum_{i=1}^{N} z_i^3 = z_1^3 + z_2^3 + z_3^3 + \cdots + z_N^3.$$

$$\sum_{i=1}^{4} x_i f_i = x_1 f_1 + x_2 f_2 + x_3 f_3 + x_4 f_4."$$

Again Mr. Camel interrupts his reading to apply the symbols to his own
case:

$$\sum_{i=1}^{35} x_i = x_1 + x_2 + x_3 + \cdots + x_{35}.$$

Back to the textbook:

"Let us examine some applications of summations. We have the number of hours the 7 workers worked in the first week of 1953: $\sum_{i=1}^{7} x_i$. We might also have the number of hours the same 7 workers worked during the remainder of January, 1953. If we denote the number of hours worked per worker in the last three weeks of January, 1953, by y_i, the total number of hours worked by the same 7 workers in the last three weeks is $\sum_{i=1}^{7} y_i$. Instead of falling back on the original data, number of hours worked by each worker in the two periods, we can simply total the two summations and know how many hours these 7 workers worked in January, 1953.

"Thus,

$$\sum_{i=1}^{N} (x_i + y_i) = \sum_{i=1}^{N} x_i + \sum_{i=1}^{N} y_i, \tag{3.2}$$

or, in brief,

$$\Sigma(x + y) = \Sigma x + \Sigma y.$$

In case data for three periods are to be added, the very same rule holds:

$$\Sigma(x + y + z) = \Sigma x + \Sigma y + \Sigma z.$$

For the case of differences, instead of sums, the rule is

$$\Sigma(x - y - z) = \Sigma x - \Sigma y - \Sigma z.$$

If we would like to state this relationship as a rule, we could say: *The summation of the sum (or difference) of two or more variates is equal to the sum (or difference) of their separate summations.*"

Mr. Camel interrupts his reading for a moment and, sitting back in his chair, he tries to apply this rule to sales data from three different territories. After some contemplation he comes up with the idea that all the rule means is that there are two ways in which to get the sum of subtotals. He writes down some assumed sales data of five salesmen in three sales territories. Sales in his territory he denotes with x, those in his friend Smith's territory y, and those in Blake's territory z. In case there are but five salesmen in each of the territories, there will be 5 x_i's, 5 y_i's, and 5 z_i's. Camel puts some corresponding imaginary numbers into a table (Table 3.2). He readily sees that he could add the x_i's, y_i's, and z_i's horizontally (full arrow). He adds

x_1 to y_1 to z_1, or in his case $7,500 + 6,000 + 18,000$, which equals $31,500$. He does the same for the second, third, fourth, and fifth lines and finally adds

the $x_i + y_i + z_i$, where i runs from 1 to 5.   In short he gets $\sum\limits_{i=1}^{5} (x_i + y_i + z_i)$,

which equals $155,500$.

Table 3.2   ILLUSTRATION OF SUMMATION RULE

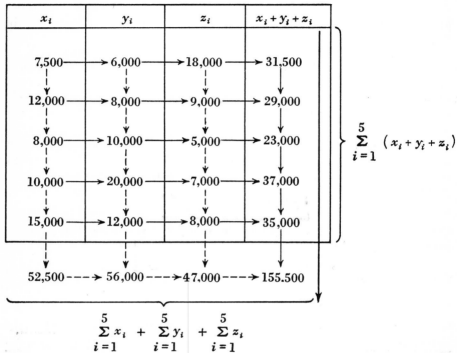

Source: Hypothetical data.

Then he tries the other method and first sums the x_i's, then the y_i's, and finally the z_i's (broken arrow).   Having found these subsums, he adds them

and gets $\sum\limits_{i=1}^{5} x_i + \sum\limits_{i=1}^{5} y_i + \sum\limits_{i=1}^{5} z_i$, which turns out $155,500$, the same sum

that was obtained by the first method.

He returns to his reading:

"We had seen before that not all data in a series are necessarily variates, that is, not all data vary in value from observation to observation.   Some are constants and do not vary.   If we have to multiply a series of observations by a constant and then sum, we can save ourselves much work by simply multiplying the sum of all observations by the constant, instead of first multiplying each observation by the constant. This rule makes sense, since nobody would think of multiplying the number of hours worked by each worker by 60 in order to get the total figure in terms of minutes. Instead, we take the sum in Table 3.1, 245 hours, and multiply it by 60. The rule is that *the summation of a constant (let us say,* k) *times a variate is* ✳ *equal to the constant times the summation of the variate.* This rule can be expressed symbolically as:

$$\sum_{i=1}^{N} kx_i = k \sum_{i=1}^{N} x_i,$$ (3.3)

or in brief,[1]

$$\Sigma kx = k\Sigma x.$$

"The constant k can be an integer or a fraction. The rule about the summation of products of variates and constants is a worksaver, in that it reduces N multiplications or divisions plus one addition to one multiplication or division plus one addition.

"A further rule is that *the summation of a constant* k, *from 1 to* N, *equals the product of* k *and* N. This is the simple, well-known fact that one multiplication takes the place of N additions. Symbolically it can be written as:[2]

$$\Sigma k = Nk.$$ (3.4)

3.2. ARITHMETIC MEAN

"The rules developed in the preceding paragraphs will prove helpful in the understanding of many statistical concepts. We will immediately apply them to define and calculate the arithmetic mean. The arithmetic mean of

---

[1] The validity of this rule can be shown in the following way:

$$\sum_{i=1}^{N} kx_i = kx_1 + kx_2 + kx_3 + \cdots + kx_N$$
$$= k(x_1 + x_2 + x_3 + \cdots + x_N)$$
$$= k \sum_{i=1}^{N} x_i.$$

[2] The Validity of this rule can be shown in the following way:

$$\sum_{i=1}^{N} k = k + k + k + \cdots + k = Nk.$$

a set of numbers $x_1, x_2, x_3, \ldots, x_N$ is the sum of the x_i's divided by N. If μ, (the Greek m, which is pronounced mu) denotes the arithmetic mean of x, we can express the arithmetic mean symbolically (assuming from now on, unless stated to the contrary, that the variate runs from 1 to N) as:

✳ UNGROUPED

$$\mu = \frac{\Sigma x}{N} = \frac{1}{N} \sum x. \tag{3.5}$$

"The arithmetic mean of the working hours of 7 workers in the store in the first week of 1953 is $\dfrac{50 + 30 + \cdots + 45}{7} = 35$ hours."

Mr. Camel puts the book aside and writes down the formula $\mu = \dfrac{\Sigma x}{N}$. In his case, $\mu = \dfrac{\Sigma x}{35}$ which, as he realizes, means just what he knew already: to get the mean, he must add all the weekly sales values and divide by the number of salesmen, i.e., 35. He reads on:

"The preceding discussion involved the calculation of an arithmetic mean from raw data, i.e., data that are ungrouped. A slight modification in the calculation is called for if we are dealing with data already grouped into a frequency distribution. We will then use the class mid-point to represent the data in the class. This shows the importance of selecting class intervals with a mid-point such that the data cluster around it. If the distribution is approximately symmetrical about its central peak there will be a clustering of observations toward the center of the distribution. Consequently, mid-points in classes below the center are likely to be below their true arithmetic means. The opposite will hold for classes above the center. However, as long as the distribution is symmetrical or close to it these errors will cancel out. From this we can conclude that if the distribution is asymmetrical, i.e., if there are many more observations in the higher or lower values, these errors will not cancel and we are well advised to go back to the ungrouped data or the array and calculate the mean from them.

"If data have been arranged into a frequency distribution of k classes, the arithmetic mean can be obtained by adding the products of the mid-points and frequencies of each and every class and dividing this sum by the total number of observations. The arithmetic mean from grouped data hence is:

✳ GROUPED DATA

$$\mu = \frac{\sum\limits^{k} xf}{N} \tag{3.6}$$

where x stands for the midpoints of a class, f the number of observations in the class, k is the number of classes, while N is the total number of observations."

Mr. Camel starts to apply what he has learned to his own problem (see Table 3.3). First, class mid-point and class frequency are multiplied ($x_1f_1 = 3,550 \times 1 = 3,550$; $x_2f_2 = 6,550 \times 4 = 26,200$; etc.). After summing these products—they amount to 430,250—he divides them by 35, the number of his salesmen. The mean turns out to be $12,290.

Table 3.3 ARITHMETIC MEAN FROM GROUPED
DATA BY THE LONG METHOD

Class Mid-point x	*Fre-quency* f	xf
1	2	3
3,550	1	3,550
6,550	4	26,200
9,550	8	76,400
12,550	11	138,050
15,550	7	108,850
18,550	3	55,650
21,550	1	21,550
Total		430,250

$$\sum_{}^{k} xf = 430,250$$

$$N = 35$$

$$\mu = \frac{\sum_{}^{k} xf}{N} = \frac{430,250}{35} = 12,290$$

Source: Table 2.3.

Notations: N = number of observations.
μ = arithmetic mean
x = class midpoint
f = class frequency

Camel remembers that before, when calculating the mean from the original data sheet (Table 2.1), he found it to be $12,500. He checks his arithmetic, but cannot find any mistake. Leafing through "Ekks'" text, he comes across the statement: "Means calculated from frequency distributions and the original data will tend to differ. The difference will depend on how symmetrical the distribution is and how closely observations cluster around the class mid-points."

"This explains it," Mr. Camel tells himself. "My distribution probably is not fully symmetrical; nor do the observations cluster very closely around the class mid-points. It is best, therefore, to fall back on the original data.

"Apparently whenever either the distribution is not symmetrical or observations do not closely cluster around the class mid-points it is best to use the original data.

"Anyway, it is still cumbersome to calculate means from grouped data. I don't like to multiply large class mid-points with large frequencies. I wonder if there isn't a short-cut method by which arithmetic means can be calculated from grouped data?"

Again "Prof. Ekks" provides the answer. After a brief search, Camel discovers that there is indeed a short method. This involves the use of a

Chart 3.1 ABSOLUTE HISTOGRAM WITH x AND
u SCALES

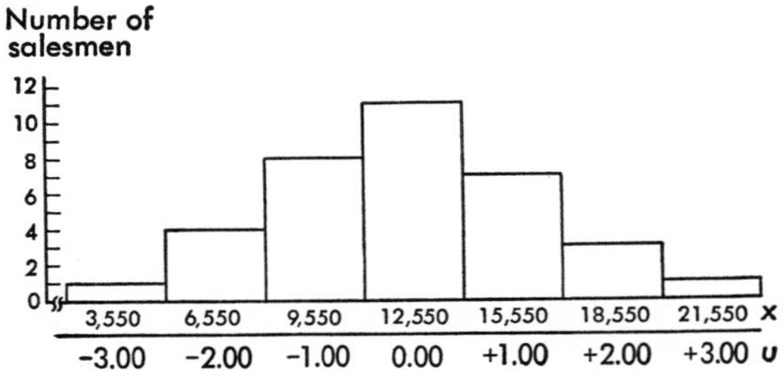

Number of salesmen

Source: Table 2.3.

histogram such as his Chart 2.3, but with a change of scale on the horizontal axis. Following the book's instructions, he replaces the value 12,550 by 0, 15,550 by +1, 18,550 by +2, etc., and comes up with Chart 3.1. However, he can't help asking himself whether this drastic change in scale is legitimate, and again finds an answer in the text.

"You will ask what right we have to change the scale. The scale doesn't matter. You know that you can measure length both by inches and by centimeters, and some rulers carry both scales. Perhaps an even better example is the measurement of temperature on a Fahrenheit or Centigrade scale. To convert centigrade into Fahrenheit you use the formula: $F = \frac{9}{5}C + 32$. The short-cut method for finding the arithmetic mean from grouped data does about the same. You subtract from each mid-point a constant; let it be called x_o."

This appears logical to Mr. Camel, so he proceeds to work out the short-cut method for finding the arithmetic mean from group data. The mid-point of the middle class—in a locational sense, of course—is designated as x_o and in his case the middle class is the fourth class, whose midpoint is 12,550. To get the new values for x (x') we subtract 12,550 from each x and record the results in the x' column. This has been done in Column 3 of Table 3.4.

Table 3.4 ARITHMETIC MEAN FROM GROUPED DATA BY THE SHORT METHOD

Class Mid-point x	Fre-quency f	$x - x_o = x'$	$\dfrac{x'}{c} = u$	uf
1	2	3	4	5
3,550	1	−9,000	−3.00	−3.00
6,550	4	−6,000	−2.00	−8.00
9,550	8	−3,000	−1.00	−8.00
12,550	11	0	0.00	0.00
15,550	7	+3,000	+1.00	+7.00
18,550	3	+6,000	+2.00	+6.00
21,550	1	+9,000	+3.00	+3.00
Total				−3.00

$$\sum_{}^{k} uf = -3$$

$$\mu = \frac{c \sum_{}^{k} uf}{N} + x_o = \frac{(3,000)(-3.00)}{35} + 12,550 = 12,290$$

Source: Table 2.3.

Notations: μ = arithmetic mean
c = class interval
x = class midpoint
f = class frequency
$u = \dfrac{x - x_o}{c}$
x_o = mid-point of middle class
N = number of observations

Looking now at this column, Camel readily sees that all the data have 3,000, the class interval (c) in common. So why not divide each x' by the class interval 3,000? That is what he has done now in Column 4, where

$$u = \frac{x - x_o}{c} = \frac{x'}{c}.$$

Dividing −9,000 by 3,000 leaves him with a −3.00, in place of −6,000 he has −2.00, etc. In the final column he places the products of each uf; since the u's are so small he can even do these multiplications in his head.   But now he must consult the book again.

"You remember the long formula for finding the arithmetic mean from grouped data: $\dfrac{\sum\limits^{k} xf}{N}$.   Now, $\dfrac{\sum\limits^{k} uf}{N}$ will, of course be much smaller than $\dfrac{\sum\limits^{k} xf}{N}$, simply because each and every u is so much smaller than x.   Specifically, the u's are smaller than the x's, since we subtracted from each one the value of the class mid-point of the middle class (x_o) and divided each by the class interval (c).   It is common sense then, in order to undo what we had done to simplify the computations, we must first add x_o and get $\dfrac{\sum\limits^{k} uf}{N} + x_o$ and then multiply each u by c and get $\dfrac{\sum\limits^{k} cuf}{N} + x_o$.   Instead of multiplying each u by the constant c, we will take advantage of Rule 3.3, which states that the summation of a constant times a variate is equal to the constant times the summation of the variate.   Therefore, we can put the c outside the summation and have the short-cut formula for finding the arithmetic mean from grouped data:

$$\mu = \frac{c \sum\limits^{k} uf}{N} + x_o."$$

(3.7)

Using his data, Camel finds that $\mu = \dfrac{(3,000)(-3.00)}{35} + 12,550$ or $12,290$. Thus, both methods for grouped data gave identical results.

And now Mr. Camel is ready to see what the textbook has to say about the uses of the arithmetic mean and the other averages.

"The arithmetic mean is perhaps the most widely used average.   There are, however, circumstances under which the arithmetic mean either cannot be found or will not be appropriate.

"Clearly, if we are given an open-end frequency distribution we will be unable to find the arithmetic mean.   We will not know the mid-point of the class that is open at one end.   Open-end distributions thus make it impossible to find the arithmetic mean.

"When the frequency distribution is badly skewed, the arithmetic mean will not be an appropriate measure of central tendency. By its very nature the arithmetic mean is affected by the value of every item, including the extreme values. Consequently a badly skewed distribution will produce an arithmetic mean that in no useful sense is typical or representative of the data.

"We would not like to leave the discussion of the arithmetic mean without briefly indicating what is perhaps its most important aspect. As we will soon see, the arithmetic mean together with a measure of dispersion, called the standard deviation, constitute the basic tools for making inferences, a subject of great interest throughout this book.

3.3. WEIGHTED MEAN

"Sometimes in place of a simple arithmetic mean of the type discussed above we need a *weighted mean.* For instance, we might wish to know the average charge for a hospital room in Chicago in 1957. It would be wrong to find the charges of all the hospitals in the city, add them, and divide by the number of hospitals. This would give a hospital with 100 beds the same weight as a hospital with 800 beds.

"Insofar as the community is concerned, more people will pay the rates that prevail in the large hospitals than those of the small ones. To find a more meaningful mean, we weight the charges of the different hospitals by the number of patient-days per annum, or some other measure reflecting the relative importance of each hospital. If we denote weight by w and otherwise use the same notations as before, the weighted mean can be found by using the following formula

$$\mu = \frac{\Sigma wx}{N}. \tag{3.8}$$

WEIGHTED MEAN

3.4. MEDIAN AND MODE

"Besides the arithmetic mean there are such averages as the *median, mode, geometric mean,* and *harmonic mean.*[3] Of major importance are the first two and they will, therefore, be elaborated on.

"The *median* is a positional measure of central tendency; it divides the series into two equal halves when presented as an array. Consequently there are as many observations above it as below it. Half of the observa-

[3] For a discussion of averages other than mean, median, mode, see such textbooks as William A. Neiswanger, *Elementary Statistical Methods* (rev. ed.) (New York, The Macmillan Company, 1956), or Frederick E. Croxton and Dudley J. Cowden, *Applied General Statistics* (2d ed.) (New York, Prentice-Hall, Inc., 1955).

tions are above and half below the median.   When the distribution is symmetrical, mean and median (as well as mode) all coincide; but when the distribution is *skewed*, i.e. departs from symmetry, this no longer is true. Certain distributions are characteristically skewed.   For example, the distribution of income in virtually all countries is skewed to the right—also called positively skewed—for, as we all know, there are many more people with low incomes then with high incomes.   In Chart 3.2 we have portrayed both a symmetrical and a positively skewed distribution.   When the distribution is skewed to the right the median lies to the left of the mean. When the distribution is skewed to the left, and there are more observations in the higher values, the median lies to the right of the mean.

Chart 3.2   SYMMETRICAL AND SKEWED DISTRIBUTIONS

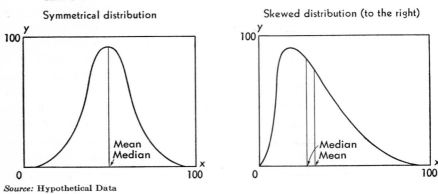

Source: Hypothetical Data

"Whenever the distribution is skewed we must decide which average is the most appropriate under the circumstances.   Consider the case of the young man who, before buying his home in suburban Parkview, was told by a real estate salesman that the average income in Parkview had been found by an official survey to be around $20,000.   After buying the house and living in it for a short time, he begins to wonder whether he really moved into such a high-class neighborhood.   Some of the people that live near him impress him as not yet having made the $20,000-a-year bracket.   Then, one day, the weekly neighborhood news-letter cites the most recent Census data, according to which the average income of Parkviewers was found to be a mere $5,000.   The fact of the matter is that both figures can be correct. The first was most likely an arithmetic mean, which is influenced by the positive skewness of all income distributions.   There are likely to be in Parkview, as everywhere else, many persons with small incomes and a very few with very large incomes.   Two or three families with an income of around $100,000 a year can greatly increase the arithmetic mean, although many of the people earn less than $5,000. The Census figure is a median and because of the inherent skewness of the income distribution, it is in this instance more appropriate and meaningful than the arithmetic mean.

"The median is readily found by arranging the data in the form of an array and finding the observation that has just as many observations above

Reprinted from Collier's by permission, copyright 1953, The Crowell-Collier Publishing Company.

"Average annual income here's about $12,000. There's fifty of us clears $2,000 and one fellow makes half a million"

it as below it. If the number of observations in the series is odd, e.g., 47 or 69, we can find the proper observation in the array by using the formula

$$\frac{N+1}{2}. \tag{3.9}$$

"It is important to realize that Formula 3.9 is not the median. Instead, it tells us how many of the observations of the array we have to count until we reach the measurement that is the median value.

"If the number of observations in the series is an even number, there will be no one value that divides them into two equal parts. In such a case, the median is the arithmetic mean of the two middle values, and the median value may not coincide with an actual value in the series."

At this point Camel stops and reaches for his pencil. He begins to figure what the median sale of his salesmen was. Thirty-five salesmen is an odd number of salesmen. The value that divided 35 into two equal parts is $\frac{N+1}{2}$ or $\frac{35+1}{2}$ or 18. Turning to the array (Table 2.2) he finds the 18th number to be \$12,500. Thus \$12,500 is the median sale. While this is very simple, he wonders what he would do if instead of 35 he had only 32 salesmen (the three with the highest sales were eliminated). In that case $\frac{N+1}{2}$ would be equal to $\frac{32+1}{2}$ or 16.5. Therefore, he would look up the 16th and 17th values in the array and calculate their mean. The 16th sales figure is \$12,100 and the 17th is \$12,500. The median would be

$$\frac{12,100 + 12,500}{2} \quad \text{or \$12,300.}$$

Returning to "Prof. Ekks'" textbook, Camel reads about *modes:*

"The mode is that value of a series which appears more frequently than any other. Of all the values in the series the mode is most likely to occur. We use the mode in preference to the other averages if we like to point to the most typical or modal value of the series. Unlike mean and median, the mode of a monomodal distribution always coincides with an actual value in the series.

"Take the problem of managing the basement operation of a department store. Basement merchandise must be inexpensive; that is what customers look for when they go there. One way to make low prices possible is to have a large turnover per square foot of floor space. In order to meet this criterion, basement operations usually carry modal size merchandise. A large assortment of sizes is carried by the upstairs departments. The basement, in order to get the largest possible turnover, carries sizes that fit the largest possible number of people. The volume operations of dime stores and grocery chains, to mention just a few, are also pitched to the modal customer.

"Or let us look at the following story from *Fortune:* Pan American Airways took a look at the customers who had booked advance reservations on its round trip European tourist services (fare: \$486 to London and back), and found a heavy influx of skilled workers, foremen, and salesmen. It said that their typical passenger was a $5,000-a-year man who was going up in a plane for the first time. Apparently in their analysis Pan American World Airways used a mode. Had they chosen to represent the average passenger in terms of a mean figure, both income and number of previous flights would probably be higher, for both tend to have positively skewed distributions."[4]

Mr. Camel closes his book and turns to his array of salesmen (Table 2.2) to find their modal sales. He finds that almost all observations occur but once; the exception is $12,500, which occurs three times and, therefore, is the modal sales value. If he were to cite the typical sales of his salesmen in the period under consideration, the mode would best fit the purpose. He wonders, though, whether it was a mode as a measure of the typical that the author of a recent cartoon had in mind. In this cartoon a real estate agent shows a young couple a new home and says: "It's designed for the average family . . . a commodious, fully enclosed 2-car garage with a handy small house attached for convenient living."

WHAT HAVE WE LEARNED:

1. Some statistical shorthand and three rules of manipulation and how to use them:
   a. The summation of a sum (or difference) of two or more variates is equal to the sum (or difference) of their separate summations: $\Sigma(x + y + z) = \Sigma x + \Sigma y + \Sigma z$.
   b. The summation of a constant, k, times a variate is equal to the constant times the summation of the variate: $\Sigma kx = k\Sigma x$.
   c. The summation of a constant, k, from 1 to N, equals the product of k and N, $\Sigma k = Nk$.

2. Definition of an arithmetic mean and methods of calculating it:
   a. The arithmetic mean is the sum of all observations in the series divided by the number of observations.
   b. Formula for ungrouped data: $\mu = \dfrac{\Sigma x}{N}$.
   c. Formula for long method for grouped data: $\mu = \dfrac{\sum\limits^{k} xf}{N}$.
   d. Formula for short method for grouped data: $\mu = \dfrac{c\sum\limits^{k} uf}{N} + x_o$.

3. Definition and method for calculating a median, where the median is a positional measure of central tendency dividing the series when arranged as an array into two equal halves.

4. Definition and method of calculating a mode, where the mode is the value of a series which appears most frequently.

[4] *Fortune*, June, 1952, p. 82.

5. Differences between arithmetic mean, median, and mode and the circumstances under which these three averages are used.

TRY YOUR HAND AT THE FOLLOWING PROBLEMS:

→ 1.

a. $\sum_{i=1}^{6} x_i =$

e. $\sum_{i=1}^{N} (x_i - y_i + z_i) =$

b. $\sum_{i=1}^{3} \frac{z_i}{c} =$

f. $\sum_{i=1}^{N} (cx_i + y_i + z_i) =$

c. $\sum_{i=1}^{4} cy_i =$

g. $\sum_{i=1}^{N} (x_i - \mu)^2 =$

d. $\sum_{i=1}^{2} (cy_i - \mu)^2 =$

h. $\sum_{i=1}^{N} x_i^2{}_m$

→ 2. The M. C. department store delivered in the first 6 months of the year 130,000, 162,950, 107,000, 200,000, 179,871 and 131,376 packages, respectively, to the homes of its customers.

    a. Use an arithmetic mean to find the average monthly delivery during this period.

    b. What is the median monthly delivery figure?

    c. What is the modal monthly delivery figure?

3a. Using the data of Table 3.1, find the median number of hours worked by the 7 workers in the first week of 1953.

    b. Find the mode.

    c. Find the arithmetic mean and compare the mean, median, and modal values.

4. Give three examples from the world of business of the appropriate use of an arithmetic mean, a median, and a mode, respectively.

5. A customer parking garage of a downtown store finds that the number of cars that seek parking facilities varies greatly from day to day over the week. Last year the store had 20 attendants in the garage on Mondays, 10 on Tuesdays, 15 on Wednesdays, 10 on Thursdays, 5 on Fridays, and 30 on Saturdays.

    a. Find the mean number of attendants for the week.

    b. Find the median number of attendants for the week.

    c. Find the modal number of attendants for the week.

6. "Nearly all the distribution curves on human sex behavior are strongly skewed to the right. The means are quite regularly higher than the location of the body of the population would lead one to expect. A few high rating individuals apparently raise the mean, giving a distorted picture using the arithmetic mean."[5] What average would be most appropriate under the circumstances? Why?

[5] Alfred Kinsey, W. B. Pomeroy, and C. E. Martin, *Sexual Behavior of the Human Male* (Philadelphia, W. B. Saunders Co., 1948).

IV

Dispersion

There is another kind of little figure . . . . It is the one that tells the range of things or their deviation from the average that is given . . . . Place little faith in an average . . . when those important figures are missing. Otherwise you are as blind as a man choosing a camp site from a report of mean temperature alone. You might take 61 degrees as a comfortable annual mean, giving you a choice in California between such areas as the inland desert and San Nicolas Island. . . . But you can freeze or roast if you ignore the [little figure]. For San Nicolas it is 47 to 87 degrees but for the desert it is 15 to 104.[1]

DARRELL HUFF

So far, so good. Mr. Camel knows now what mean, median, and mode are, and that for his data these three measures of central tendency coincide. He understands that since all three coincide his sales force is well balanced in that it has neither an unusually large proportion of excellent salesmen nor an undue proportion of poor ones.

But one thing is puzzling Mr. Camel. He begins doodling, like this:

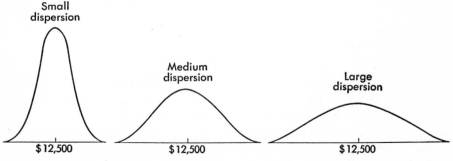

He is beginning to be aware of the fact that an average alone—be it a

[1] Darrell Huff, *How to Lie with Statistics* (New York: W. W. Norton & Co., Inc., 1954.)

mean, median, or mode—does not mean very much.   If he knew only that the mean sales of last week were $12,500, he still would not know *how typical or how meaningful* that $12,500 sales figure was.   Did most of the salesmen come close to that figure, or did most of them *deviate* from it by far, that is, sell way above or way below $12,500 worth?   He remembers that one of the men had sales of only $3,000, while his best man's sales amounted to $23,000.   This difference between the highest and the lowest sales figure, he remembers, is known as the *range.   This range measures the dispersion* of the data, specifically it measures the dispersion between the two extreme values of the data.   The larger the range the farther some data *deviate* from the mean.   Looking back at his doodles, his eyes come to rest on the one at the right.   In his mind he places a 3,000 at the extreme left of this doodle and a 23,000 at the extreme right, and concludes that his sales data appear to have a large dispersion.   But he immediately realizes that the range is not too useful a measure of dispersion in that it says nothing about the observations in between the two extremes.   Are there many of them near the mean and if so how many?

As he looks up from his doodles, his mind strays to a discussion he had with his wife a few days before.   Claiming that their 18-month old son should be checked by a doctor because he is not walking yet, Mrs. Camel had quoted Dr. Benjamin Spock's widely read book, *Baby and Child Care,* to the effect that the average child learns to walk at the age of 15 months. "Bobby isn't walking at 18 months, so he must be retarded," she cried. Mr. Camel had reassured her that if 15 months is the average age of learning to walk, there must be about as many children who learn to walk later as there are children who walk earlier.   But he had left vaguely uneasy when making this explanation because, as he now realizes, he wished he had some idea how many children deviate from the average either way, and by how much. That is exactly what he feels should be known about the average sales data, too.

As he notes that the next chapter of "Prof. Ekks'" textbook is entitled "Measures of Dispersion," Mr. Camel reads on:

"If I were to ask each of my students to guess my weight and then would plot these guesses in the form of a smoothed histogram, it would look something like Chart 4.1, provided that the number of students who participated in this guessing game was large.   About the same general distribution would be found if we were to measure with the aid of a steel measuring tape the height of all male students in our university or the weight of a few thousand cartons of large Grade A eggs.

"Many phenomena exhibit about the same type of distribution. This distribution rises to a single central peak, i.e., is monomodal; as one moves out from the central peak in either direction the distribution tapers off regularly; and, furthermore, this distribution is symmetrical about its central peak.

"We call a distribution with these three general characteristics a *normal distribution*, which is so common in everyday life that mathematicians have devised a mathematical formula that closely describes the normal distributions that we encounter in innumerable phenomena.[2] The (mathematical) normal distribution or normal curve is monomodal, symmetrical about its peak, and its tails extend indefinitely in both directions, that is, although the curve comes closer and closer to the horizontal axis it never touches it.

Chart 4.1 NORMAL DISTRIBUTION

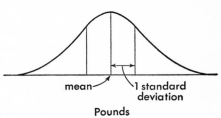

"Since a normal distribution is symmetrical about its central peak, the value of this peak is the mean value of the distribution. Only to the extent that the distribution is not fully symmetrical will there be a discrepancy between the mean and peak values.

"With the frequency distribution of so many phenomena normal in shape much attention has been given to finding a measure of dispersion that fits this situation. If we were to mark an interval from the mean that extends a given distance to the right of it, we could refer to this distance as to a *deviation*. The deviation (from the mean) would be smaller or larger depending on the distance. Within this interval there would lie a given area under the normal curve. Since the normal curve is symmetrical about its mean the same area lies above a deviation of equal size regardless of whether it is to the right or left of the mean. All this is readily seen in Chart 4.1.

4.1. CALCULATING A STANDARD DEVIATION

"Since all normal distributions are of the same shape, would it not be helpful if we could devise a measure that would relate deviation to the relative area under the normal curve above it? *The standard deviation* is just

[2] The equation of the normal distribution curve can be written as:

$$y = \frac{1}{\sigma \sqrt{2\pi}} e^{\frac{-(x-\mu)^2}{2\sigma^2}}.$$

such a measure. It is an average deviation, the average being a somewhat complex mean. If, after finding the arithmetic mean, we calculate the deviations of all the individual observations from this mean, square these deviations, find the mean of these squares, and then extract the square root, we have the standard deviation.

"Let us see how this works. As an example we can take the following 5 observations, and assume they are normally distributed: 2, 2, 1, 3, and 2. In order to find the standard deviation of these 5 observations, we will first find their mean value. It is 10/5 or 2. We next compute the 5 deviations from the mean (Column 2 in Table 4.1). In the following step we square

Table 4.1   CALCULATING THE STANDARD DEVIATION

x	$(x - \mu)$	$(x - \mu)^2$
1	*2*	*3*
2	0	0
2	0	0
1	−1	1
3	1	1
2	0	0
	Total	2

Source: Hypothetical data.

$$\sigma = \sqrt{\frac{\Sigma(x - \mu)^2}{N}} = \sqrt{\frac{2}{5}} = 0.6$$

the deviations in Column 2, add these squares, and divide their sum by 5. The mean of the squared deviations is 0.4, with 0.6 being its square root and thus the standard deviation of this series of data.

"To state this method formally, the standard deviation is the square root of the mean of the squared deviations from the arithmetic mean. We will connote the standard deviation as σ (read: sigma) and, using our statistical shorthand, we can reduce this lengthy verbal definition to

$$\sigma = \sqrt{\frac{\Sigma(x - \mu)^2}{N}}, \qquad (4.1)$$

where, as before, x = the variate

μ = the mean of the variate

N = the number of observations.

If we denote $(x - \mu)$ as d (standing for deviation), we are able to write

$$\sigma = \sqrt{\frac{\Sigma d^2}{N}}. \tag{4.2}$$

"If we leave off the radical sign, i.e., square the standard deviation, we get what is called the *variance*."[3]

Looking up from his book, Mr. Camel decides to find the standard deviation for the sales of his salesmen. He does so in Table 4.2, where, knowing that the mean is 12,500, he sets out to find the 35 deviations (Column 3), which he then squares (Column 4) and totals. Taking the square root, he comes up with a standard deviation of 4,050.

Searching for simpler ways to find the standard deviation, he finds another formula in "Prof. Ekks'" textbook. According to this formula the standard deviation of x is the square root of the difference between the mean of the squared x's and the square of the mean of the x's.

In short:

$$\sigma = \sqrt{\frac{\Sigma x^2}{N} - \left(\frac{\Sigma x}{N}\right)^2} \tag{4.3}$$

or,[4]

$$\sigma = \sqrt{\frac{\Sigma x^2}{N} - (\mu_x)^2}.$$

Applying this formula to his data, Mr. Camel first squares each of his 35 sales observations, totals the squares, and then divides them by N. This gives him the first term of the formula. Squaring the mean, he has the

---

[3] The variance $\sigma^2 = \dfrac{\Sigma(x - \mu)^2}{N} = \dfrac{\Sigma d^2}{N}$.

[4] Making use of some of the manipulation rules of the preceding chapter, it is readily seen that the two equations for finding the standard deviation are mathematically equal to each other. Neglecting the radicals,

$$\frac{\Sigma(x - \mu)^2}{N} = \frac{\Sigma x^2}{N} - (\mu_x)^2$$

$$= \frac{1}{N} \sum (x^2 - 2x\mu_x + \mu_x{}^2)$$

$$= \frac{1}{N} \sum x^2 - \frac{2}{N} \mu_x \sum x + \frac{1}{N} N\mu_x{}^2$$

$$= \frac{\Sigma x^2}{N} - 2\mu_x{}^2 + \mu_x{}^2$$

$$= \frac{\Sigma x^2}{N} - (\mu_x)^2.$$

Table 4.2 STANDARD DEVIATION FROM UNGROUPED DATA
(Sales of LUTABE cigarettes by 35 salesmen in the first week of October, 1957.)

Number	x	$x - \mu$	$(x - \mu)^2$
1	2	3	4
A	5,900	−6,600	43,600,000
B	14,500	2,000	4,000,000
C	6,700	−5,800	33,600,000
D	12,500	0	0
E	9,200	−3,300	10,900,000
F	11,800	− 700	490,000
G	13,400	900	810,000
H	19,000	6,500	42,200,000
I	14,000	1,500	2,250,000
J	8,400	−4,100	16,800,000
K	12,700	200	40,000
L	15,900	3,400	11,600,000
M	23,000	10,500	110,200,000
N	9,500	−3,000	9,000,000
O	10,900	−1,600	2,560,000
P	12,100	− 400	160,000
Q	7,800	−4,700	22,100,000
R	12,500	0	0
S	15,500	3,000	9,000,000
T	17,800	5,300	28,100,000
U	16,600	4,100	16,800,000
V	8,000	−4,500	20,200,000
W	10,400	−2,100	4,410,000
X	13,700	1,200	1,440,000
Y	11,500	−1,000	1,000,000
Z	13,100	600	360,000
AZ	14,900	2,400	5,760,000
BZ	18,500	6,000	36,000,000
CZ	3,000	−9,500	90,200,000
DZ	12,500	0	0
EZ	10,600	−1,900	3,610,000
FZ	10,000	−2,500	6,250,000
GZ	15,800	3,300	10,900,000
HZ	16,800	4,300	18,500,000
IZ	9,000	−3,500	12,200,000
Total			575,040,000

Source: Table 2.1.

$$\sigma = \sqrt{\frac{1}{N} \sum_{i=1}^{N} (x_i - \mu)^2}$$

$$= \sqrt{\frac{1}{35} (575,040,000)}$$

$$= \sqrt{16,429,000} = 4,050.$$

second term, which he subtracts from the first before he finally extracts the square root.

In this manner he finds

$$\sigma = \sqrt{\frac{6,040,000,000}{35} - 156,000,000} = 4,050.$$

Mr. Camel now asks: "What about calculating the standard deviation from a frequency distribution?" The textbook has the following formula:

GROUPED
DATA

$$\sqrt{\frac{\sum\limits_{}^{k} x^2 f}{N} - \left(\frac{\sum\limits_{}^{k} xf}{N}\right)^2} \qquad (4.4)$$

where x denotes the class mid-point and f the class frequency. Table 4.3 summarizes these calculations with $\sigma = \$3,950$. The difference in σ,

Table 4.3 STANDARD DEVIATION FROM GROUPED DATA BY THE LONG METHOD

Class Mid-point x	Frequency f	xf	x^2	$x^2 f$
3,550	1	3,550	12,600,000	12,600,000
6,550	4	26,200	42,900,000	171,600,000
9,550	8	76,400	91,200,000	729,600,000
12,550	11	138,050	157,500,000	1,732,500,000
15,550	7	108,850	241,800,000	1,692,600,000
18,550	3	55,650	344,100,000	1,032,300,000
21,550	1	21,550	464,400,000	464,400,000
Total	35	430,250		5,835,600,000

Source: Table 2.3.

$$\begin{aligned}
\sigma &= \sqrt{\frac{\sum\limits_{}^{k} x^2 f}{N} - \left(\frac{\sum\limits_{}^{k} xf}{N}\right)^2} \\
&= \sqrt{166,730,000 - (12,293)^2} \\
&= \sqrt{166,730,000 - 151,120,000} \\
&= \sqrt{15,610,000} \\
&= 3,950.
\end{aligned}$$

whether calculated from the grouped or ungrouped data, as in the case of the arithmetic mean, is due to the fact that the distribution is not completely symmetrical and to the insufficient clustering of observations around mid-points.

Mr. Camel then comes across a short-cut method for finding the standard deviation. Like the short-cut method for finding the arithmetic mean, this method, too, simplifies the computations by changing the scale. The formula is

$$\sigma = c \sqrt{\frac{\sum\limits_{}^{k} u^2 f}{N} - \left(\frac{\sum\limits_{}^{k} uf}{N}\right)^2}.$$ (4.5)

The application of this formula to the sales data is shown in Table 4.4.

Table 4.4 STANDARD DEVIATION FROM GROUPED DATA BY THE SHORT METHOD

Class Mid-point x	Frequency f	u	uf	$u^2 f$
1	*2*	*3*	*4*	*5*
3,550	1	−3.00	−3.00	9.00
6,550	4	−2.00	−8.00	16.0
9,550	8	−1.00	−8.00	8.00
12,550	11	0.00	0.00	0.00
15,550	7	+1.00	+7.00	7.00
18,550	3	+2.00	+6.00	12.0
21,550	1	+3.00	+3.00	9.00
Total			−3.00	61.0

Source: Table 2.3.

$$\sigma = c \sqrt{\frac{\sum\limits_{}^{k} u^2 f}{N} - \left(\frac{\sum uf}{N}\right)^2}$$

$$= 3,000 \sqrt{\frac{61.0}{35} - \left(\frac{(-3.00)}{(35)}\right)^2}$$

$$= 3,000 \sqrt{1.743 - 0.007}$$

$$= 3,000 \sqrt{1.736}$$

$$= 3,950.$$

4.2. STANDARD DEVIATION IN RELATION TO AREA UNDER THE NORMAL CURVE

Mr. Camel soon realizes that areas under normal curves have been analyzed in terms of standard deviations about the mean. The one standard deviation or one-sigma range, i.e., the area under the normal curve that extends from the mean-minus-one standard deviation to the mean-plus-one standard deviation, includes roughly 68 per cent or about two thirds of the area under the normal curve. The area under the normal curve within the interval

Chart 4.2 STANDARD DEVIATION IN RELATION TO NORMAL CURVE

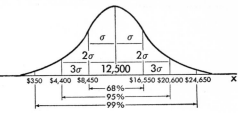

Source: Table 2.3.

of the mean plus and minus 2 standard deviations (two-sigma range) includes about 95 per cent; and that within the interval of the mean plus and minus 3 standard deviations (the three-sigma range) about 99 per cent of the area under the normal curve.

Remembering that the mean of his 35 data was $12,500 and the standard deviation $4,050, Camel draws Chart 4.2. The one-sigma range extends from $8,450 to $16,550; the two-sigma range extends from $4,400 to $20,600; and the three-sigma range extends from $350 to $24,650. Now it becomes clear that the larger the sigma of a given distribution, the flatter the normal curve (see doodle at right on page 49), and vice versa.

4.3. CHECKING FOR NORMALCY

Camel examines his sales data (Table 2.1) in the light of these conclusions. He finds that the sales of 25, or 71 per cent, of the 35 salesmen fell into the one-sigma range; the sales of 33 salesmen, or 92 per cent, fell into the two-sigma range; all 35 sales fell into the three-sigma range. These results are consistent with what we would expect from normally distributed data and the slight discrepancies could be due to the small sample. However, there is also a chance that the distribution is not entirely normal.

Camel turns to "Prof. Ekks'" textbook to see whether there is a simple method that helps to check distributions for normalcy. Here is what he finds:

"While it is difficult to decide whether data closely approximate a normal distribution, it is relatively easy to determine whether data fall along a straight line. Normally distributed data fall along a straight line if arranged as a relative 'less than' cumulative frequency and plotted on normal curve graph paper. Thus, to test data for normalcy, we construct a relative 'less than' cumulative frequency distribution as we have done in Table 2.7. On the normal curve graph paper we plot the variate along the horizontal axis and the cumulative frequency along the vertical axis."

Camel accordingly plots his sales data arranged as a relative "less than"

Chart 4.3   TESTING THE NORMALITY OF A DISTRIBU-
TION WITH THE HELP OF NORMAL CURVE
GRAPH PAPER
(Sales of LUTABE cigarettes of 35 salesmen in the first week of
October, 1957.)

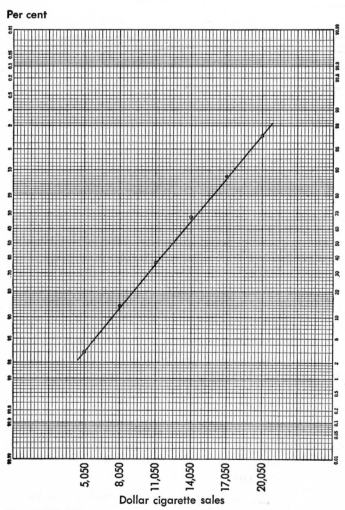

Per cent

Dollar cigarette sales

Source: Table 2.7.

cumulative frequency distribution on this paper. He finds that they fall closely along a straight line, which gives Camel confidence in the conclusions he had reached in the preceding paragraph.

4.4. NOT ALL DISTRIBUTIONS ARE NORMAL

Mr. Camel fully realizes that there are economic phenomena that are not normally distributed. Some may resemble a *J-shaped* or *reverse J-shaped curve*, such as Chart 4.4. For instance, a chart of the demand deposits, income, or wealth of the people of the United States will show up as a reverse *J*-shaped curve. The majority of the people hold reasonably small demand deposits, have relatively low incomes, and own relatively small assets. At the same time there are relatively few very rich people.

Some economic series conform to a *U-shaped curve*. If we make a frequency distribution of the nations of the world using as the criterion their state of economic development, we will find a bunching at the two extremes. Most countries are either highly developed or are underdeveloped. Few fall into the middle. The same holds for a frequency distribution of unemployed persons classified by age groups. The unemployed, if we mean those who do not work, are the very young and the very old. Chart 4.5 shows the way they group. In a few cases we find a *rectangular or uniform frequency distribution* where all the class frequencies are of about uniform magnitude (See Chart 4.6).

Chart 4.4 (REVERSE) *J*-SHAPED DISTRIBUTION

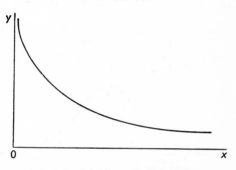

Chart 4.5 *U*-SHAPED DISTRIBUTION

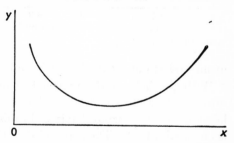

Chart 4.6 RECTANGULAR DISTRIBUTION

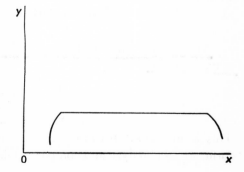

4.5. STANDARD DEVIATIONS AND CONFIDENCE INTERVALS

Mr. Camel looks back at Chart 4.2. Suddenly it strikes him that the banker, Mr. Mal, might not have needed the frequency distribution to make up his mind about Jim Kent's application. Had he had only the mean and the standard deviation of the weekly sales figures last night, Mr. Mal could have asserted that there is a 68 per cent likelihood that Jim Kent sold between $8,450 and $16,550 worth of cigarettes last week. Actually, that is reasonably close to the statement Mal had made from the data in the frequency distribution, namely that there was a 74 per cent likelihood that Kent had sold last week between $8,100 and $17,000 worth of cigarettes.

Chart 4.7 NORMAL CURVE WITH AC-TUAL AND *z* SCALES

(Sales of LUTABE cigarettes by 35 salesmen in the first week of October 1957.)

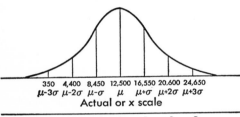

| 350 | 4,400 | 8,450 | 12,500 | 16,550 | 20,600 | 24,650 |
| μ-3σ | μ-2σ | μ-σ | μ | μ+σ | μ+2σ | μ+3σ |

Actual or x scale

| -3 | -2 | -1 | 0 | +1 | +2 | +3 |

z scale (in standard deviation units)

Source: Chart 4.2.

Camel could also have told Mal that there is a 95 per cent likelihood that Kent sold between $4,400 and $20,600 worth of cigarettes, or a 99 per cent likelihood that Kent sold between $350 and $24,650.

But of course Mr. Mal had been interested most of all to know that Kent sold above a certain minimum. How could mean and standard deviation have helped in this context?

With the help of the textbook, Camel converts his normal distribution into what may be called a standard form. All it involves is a change in the labeling of the horizontal axis; *x*, in this case weekly cigarette sales in dollars, is changed into *z*. The zero point of the *z* scale is at the mean value, μ, and its unit of length is the distance from μ to $\mu + \sigma$, as in Chart 4.7. Thus Camel sees that all distributions in standard form have in common a zero mean and a unit standard deviation. The textbook continues:

"Any normal curve can be presented in standard form by means of the transformation:

$$z = \frac{x - \mu}{\sigma}.$$

(4.6)

This is important because once we translate distributions into standard form, we can analyze and compare each by referring to a normal curve with a mean of 0 and a standard deviation of 1 for which areas have been measured. We are interested in the proportion of observations that fall within a certain class interval. Is not this proportion equivalent to the relative size of the area under the normal curve within the interval in question?

Chart 4.8 NORMAL CURVE AREA

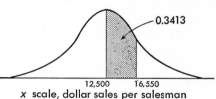

x scale, dollar sales per salesman

"If we could find, then, the relative area under the normal curve within the class interval, we would have the proportion of observations in that class interval. With this objective in mind, areas under the normal curve in standard form have been analyzed and are reproduced in Table I of the Appendix. In this table, the area corresponding to a certain class interval expressed on the *z* scale is the proportion of the area under the normal curve extending from 0 to that *z* value."

Camel tries this technique on his data, choosing an area to the right of the mean. He asks himself: "What proportion of all salesmen sold between $12,500 and $16,550 worth of cigarettes?" He starts by converting the values which are given in *x*, in this case dollar units, into *z* units, using the formula $z = \dfrac{x - \mu}{\sigma}$, *z* for *x* = 12,500, which he calls z_2, equals $\dfrac{12,500 - 12,500}{4,050}$ = 0. He might have known this since he set up the *z* scale so that the mean equals zero. $z_1 = \dfrac{16,550 - 12,500}{4,050} = 1.00$. Turning to Table I of the Appendix (which has been reproduced on p. 397), he finds in the column

Chart 4.9 NORMAL CURVE AREA

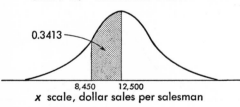

x scale, dollar sales per salesman

for a *z* value of 1.00 a normal curve area of 0.3413, and for a *z* of 0 an area of 0.00. Subtracting from 0.3413 this 0.00 he is left with 0.3413. This means that 34.13 per cent of the salesmen sold between $12,500 and $16,550 worth of cigarettes, if the distribution were perfectly normal (Chart 4.8).

When the lower boundary of the class interval he chooses is smaller than the mean, he gets negative *z* values (Chart 4.9). In Table I of the Appendix no areas for negative *z* values are given. Since the normal curve is symmetrical, and thus the left half of the curve equals the right half, negative and positive *z* values will, except for the sign, be alike. Thus, when he asks for the proportion of salesmen selling between \$8,450 and \$12,500 he looks for the shaded area to the left of the mean in Chart 4.9. z_1 is -1 and z_2 is equal to 0. He then looks up the area under the normal curve for $z = -1$ and $z = 0$. The difference between the two areas is 0.3413, which means that 34.13 per cent of the salesmen also sold between \$8,450 and \$12,500 worth of cigarettes.

If Camel were asking for the proportion of the salesmen selling between \$8,450 and \$16,550, i.e., $\mu \pm \sigma$, he would add the two area figures: $0.3413 + 0.3413 = 0.6826$ (Chart 4.10). Or, about 68 per cent of all salesmen sold between these two figures. He realizes that, according to his former terminology, he is talking about the one-sigma range. Similarly, he could find proportions for any other interval. Looking at Chart 4.10,

Chart 4.10 NORMAL CURVE AREA

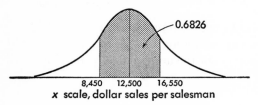

x scale, dollar sales per salesman

he sees a certain area to the right of the shaded one. How large is it? Well, he knows that the normal distribution is symmetrical around the mean. Half (or 0.5000) of the area is to the left and half (or 0.5000) to the right of the mean. If the entire area to the right of the mean is 0.5000 and the shaded area was found to cover 0.3413, is not then the little area in the right tail $0.5000 - 0.3413$ or 0.1587? Or, since z_1 on the x scale means sales of \$16,550, he can conclude that 15.87 per cent of the salesmen sold \$16,550 or more. The same can be done for the area of the left tail: 15.87 per cent of the salesmen sold \$8,450 or less (Chart 4.10).

One further question arises in Camel's mind. What about finding an area that is not centered at the mean? He works out such a case in Chart 4.11. What proportion of the salesmen sold between \$15,000 and \$20,000? He can find that proportion by referring to Chart 4.11. If he could ascertain what percentage of the area is within the interval \$12,500 to \$20,000 and subtract from it

Chart 4.11 NORMAL CURVE AREA

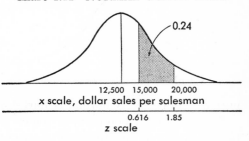

the percentage within the interval \$12,500 to \$15,000, he would have the answer. This is how to find the first area:

$$z_2 = \frac{20,000 - 12,500}{4,050} = +1.85,$$

or an area of 0.47 of the total.

$$z_1 = \frac{15,000 - 12,500}{4,050} = +0.616 \text{ or } 0.23$$

of the total. Subtracting 0.23 from 0.47, we find that 0.24 of the total area is in the $15,000 to $20,000 interval. In conclusion, 24 per cent of all salesmen sold between $15,000 and $20,000 of cigarettes.

Now Mr. Camel's mind returns to banker Mal's problem. The banker had wanted to know how likely salesman Kent was to have had at least a certain minimum sales volume. As a rough idea, Camel assumes that if Mal could conclude that Kent had sales last week of no less than $10,000 he would constitute a good credit risk. "Knowing mean and standard deviation of the sales of 35 salesmen—remember, one of them is Kent— could Mal have calculated the likelihood of Kent's having had sales of no less than $10,000?" Camel tries to work out a way to do this in relation to normal curve areas. He draws Chart 4.12. He would like to find the area of the shaded part. It constitutes the proportion of salesmen selling for no less than

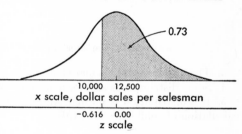

Chart 4.12 NORMAL CURVE AREA

0.73

10,000 12,500
x scale, dollar sales per salesman

−0.616 0.00
z scale

$10,000 (or for at least $10,000). The shaded area encompasses the entire right half of the curve, whose area, as we know, is 0.5000. The remaining part of the shaded area lies in the left half of the curve and needs to be calculated. $z_1 = \dfrac{10,000 - 12,500}{4,050}$ or -0.616. For a z value of 0.616, the area under the normal curve is about 0.23. Adding 0.23 of the left half to 0.5000 of the right half, we get 0.73. In other words, about 73 per cent of all salesmen had sales of at least $10,000. Or, and this would be of even greater importance to banker Mal, there is a 73 per cent likelihood that Kent last week sold not less than $10,000 worth of cigarettes.

Camel realizes that such a likelihood can be figured for any minimum or maximum amount of sales that he might select. The method would always be the same. He would draw a normal curve, standardize the data in z units, and find the corresponding area under the normal curve. Thus, he could have concluded with a 24 per cent confidence that Kent sold between $15,000 and $20,000 of cigarettes, or with a 68 per cent confidence that he sold between $8,450 and $16,550 of cigarettes, and so on.

Actually, knowing only mean and standard deviation, Mal can reach as useful conclusions as when he knew the entire frequency distribution.

WE HAVE LEARNED:

1. Before the representativeness of a mean can be assessed, the standard deviation of the data needs to be known.

2. A standard deviation is the square root of the mean of the squared deviations taken from the arithmetic mean.

   a. The formula for the long method for ungrouped data is $\sqrt{\dfrac{\Sigma(x-\mu)^2}{N}}$

   b. The formula for the short method for ungrouped data is $\sqrt{\dfrac{\Sigma x^2}{N} - \left(\dfrac{\Sigma x}{N}\right)^2}$

   c. The formula for the long method for grouped data is $\sqrt{\dfrac{\sum\limits^{k} x^2 f}{N} - \left(\dfrac{\sum\limits^{k} xf}{N}\right)^2}$

   d. The formula for the short method for grouped data is $c\sqrt{\dfrac{\Sigma u^2 f}{N} - \left(\dfrac{\Sigma uf}{N}\right)^2}$

3. The variance is the squared standard deviation.

4. Some distributions are normal, others J-shaped, U-shaped, or rectangular.

5. If a distribution is normal, knowing mean and standard deviation allows the calculation of confidence intervals.

TRY TO SOLVE THE FOLLOWING PROBLEMS:

1. Twelve grocery stores in a town sell a pound of 93 score butter for 59, 61, 63, 61, 62, 58, 67, 63, 62, 64, 60, and 65 cents respectively. Use the long method to find the standard deviation.

2. a. Use the frequency distribution of weekly wages given in Exercise 8 of Chapter II for the purpose of applying the short method to find the variance.

   b. What is the likelihood that one particular worker, Hal Miller, will earn somewhere between $40 and $60 a week, assuming a normal distribution of wages?

   c. What is the likelihood that he earns between $25 and $70 per week?

   d. What is the likelihood that he earns $30 or less a week?

   e. What is the likelihood that he earns at least $65 a week?

   f. What percentage of the workers earn less than $60 a week?

   g. Compare the results with those you got at the end of Chapter II and explain the reasons for any discrepancies.

3. Use the long method to find the standard deviation of the data in Table 3.1 in Chapter III.

FORTRAN STATEMENT

IDENTIFICATION

CONTINUATION

C FOR COMMENT

STATEMENT NUMBER

STANDARD FORM 888157

GLOBE 127

4. a. In the last quarter of 1953 a group of 189 garment workers worked an average of 400 hours with a standard deviation of 50 hours. With what degree of confidence can you assert that Homer Town, one of the 189 garment workers, worked in the last quarter of 1953 somewhere between 300 and 500 hours, assuming a normal distribution of working hours?

   b. At least 520 hours?

   c. Compare the results with those you got at the end of Chapter II, explaining reasons for discrepancies.

5. On the assumption that the 10,000 male students of a certain college have a mean height of 68 inches and a standard deviation of 2.0 inches and assuming a normal distribution of height:

   a. What is the likelihood that the basketball coach will find any students who are 6 feet 2 inches tall or taller?

   b. How many students 6 feet 1 inch tall or taller is he likely to find?

   c. What percentage of the male student body will have to bend their heads trying to walk through the historic 6-foot archway built way back when people supposedly were shorter than they are today?

   d. What is the maximum number of students who might compete to escort the newly selected football queen, who is but 5 feet 5 inches tall and wants an escort who is at least 2 inches taller than she is?

6. Three hundred customers in a department store were timed as to how long they had to wait before a "Will Call" window. It was found that on the average they waited 120 seconds, with a standard deviation of 30 seconds. The waiting period is normally distributed around the mean.

   a. What is the probability that any one of these 300 customers waited for 4 minutes or longer?

   b. What is the likelihood that any one of the customers waited for 1 minute or less?

   c. How many customers are likely to have had to wait for 2 minutes or more?

V

Superstition, Hunch, and the
Laws of Chance

All business proceeds on beliefs, or judgments of probabilities, and not on certainties.

CHARLES W. ELLIOT

5.1. MAKE UP YOUR MIND; YOU ARE TAKING CHANCES

The future is unknown to us. Yet every day we are forced to make decisions involving future and, therefore, uncertain events. When we are faced with the problem of taking a raincoat or trusting the skies, of buying a car now or waiting another year, of supporting one candidate or another in an election, we are forced to base our decision in part on guesswork. Everyone is thus taking chances. The chances taken are likely to be especially big in the world of business; virtually all decisions involve uncertain future conditions and events. Businessmen who are successful in their enterprises are often said to have "good business judgment," implying that their guesses prove correct more often than those of others. It is true that the more simple laws that govern what is called "chance" are common sense, and this probably accounts for the fact that most of us manage somewhat successfully to make daily decisions about an unknown future. Yet the continued existence of astrologers, fortunetellers, and the like attests to the fact that many decisions are so complex that they leave people bewildered and clutching at those beliefs in supernatural influences that we call superstitions.

The laws of chance, embodied in what is often called probability theory, are in the words of the eminent French mathematician Emile Borel, "of interest . . . not only to card and dice players, who were its godfathers, but also to all men of action, heads of industries or heads of armies, whose success depends on decisions, which in turn depend on two sorts of factors, the one known or calculable, the other uncertain and problematical . . . "[1]

It should not surprise us, however, that the first impetus to the study of the laws of chance came from gamblers. Always eager to develop a "system," and probably disappointed by the waywardness of Goddess Fortuna or by their other superstitious beliefs, some of them began in the seventeenth century to take their gambling problems to eminent mathematicians. In such a fashion Galileo, Pascal, Fermat, and others were persuaded to apply their genius to problems of chance, which opened up the way to the development of probability theory. Pascal's important contribution to this science stemmed from some work on gambling problems that his gambler friend de Méré asked him to solve. Other pioneering work in this field was done by a man who was a gambler himself, the Italian Cardano. He was also an astrologer, murderer, thief, and scientist, with a fantastic career. His name is still connected with the solution of a famous algebraic problem that he had stolen; and yet he was an outstanding mathematician in his own right. His contributions to astrology were less outstanding. When his forecast of his own death proved wrong, he committed suicide.[2]

By the late eighteenth century, the study of the laws of chance no longer needed the helping hand of gamblers. A number of scholars had addressed themselves to the field of probability and early in the nineteenth century the famous Frenchman Laplace and the German Gauss carried our knowledge of the subject many important steps forward.

The downfall of the feudal system in Europe and the expansion of national economies inspired such men as De Moivre, Nicholas and Daniel Bernoulli, Euler, and D'Alembert to develop probability theory further and apply it for the first time to the financial, public health, military, and political fields. In more recent years R. A. Fisher, father and son Pearson, and J. Neyman developed a sampling theory based on the laws of probability. Today a comprehensive theory of probability exists. Use of probability theory in the fields of business and economics has been relatively slow, particularly if we compare these fields with physics, astronomy, and genetics. But in recent years much progress has been made.

Let us now take a look at some of the problems where knowledge of the laws of chance can help in making better decisions.

[1] H. D. Levinson, *The Science of Chance* (New York, Rinehart and Company, 1950), p. 10.
[2] O. Ore, *Cardano, The Gambling Scholar* (Princeton, Princeton University Press, 1953).

5.2. "NOT A CHANCE IN THE WORLD"

Bennett Cerf recently related the following little anecdote:

In a village barber shop, the shears snipped merrily away and the barber's dog lay close beside his master's chair, his eyes riveted on the customer in the chair. Said customer—a city slicker named Todman—remarked, "That dog of yours seems mighty fond of watching you cut hair." "T'ain't that," chuckled the barber. "He knows the chances are 'bout two to one that 'fore I've finished, I'll snip off a bit of your ear."

Odds, probabilities, and chances enter not only the village barber's conversation. We find them in the thinking and talking of almost everybody. We hear businessmen sum up their opinion of a business venture by giving it "not a chance in the world." We may overhear a conversation that gives the competition "a fifty-fifty chance," or "an even chance." Or we may listen in on a conversation between a foreman and a plant superintendent about replacing equipment, with the foreman stating that there is "an excellent chance" that the production goal set for the month will be met. By this he may mean that the chances are better than fifty-fifty that production will be according to schedule.

Goethe described the plight of all of us when he remarked that, "There is nothing more frightful than ignorance in action." Reasoning in terms of odds, chances, or probabilities is one weapon by which we attempt to reduce this ignorance. We measure probability with a scale marked zero at one end and unity at the other. Probability may then be looked upon as the rating we give to the possibility of an occurrence. The top end of the scale is marked 1.0 and represents certainty. Here we place events about whose occurrence we are absolutely sure. According to the old adage, only death and taxes fall into this category. If we denote the probability of event A occurring by $p(A)$, under certainty $p(A) = 1.0$.

On the lower end of the scale we have $p(A) = 0.0$, which means that the occurrence of a given event is completely improbable. The probability that Al's Corner Grocery in Bakersfield, Arkansas (300 inhabitants) should sell groceries to 100,000 housewives on a busy Friday afternoon is nil. There is neither enough room in Al's store for that many housewives, nor are there enough housewives in and near Bakersfield, Arkansas. Most of us would say: "There isn't a chance in the world" that Al will serve that many housewives; in brief $p(A) = 0.0$.

Obviously, most probabilities fall in between the two extremes. A buyer for a retail store may purchase a certain line of dresses if he considers their profitable sale most probable, i.e., if he believes p to be greater than 0.50. To this day most estimates of probabilities made about business are qualitative.

One of the foremost challenges facing business today is to quantify probabilities of economic phenomena. How this can be done will be discussed and illustrated a little later. Some such probabilities that we will soon calculate are marked on our probability scale:

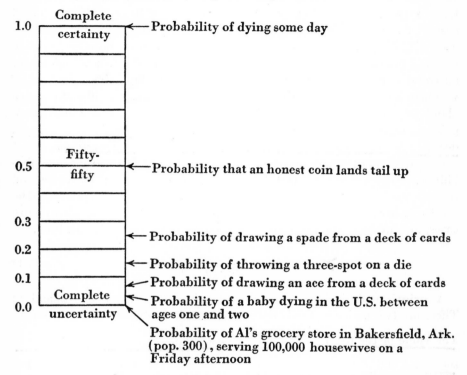

Thus, for example, when tossing an honest dime into the air, the probability of its landing tails up is 0.50; or the probability of throwing a three-spot on an honest die is 1/6 or 0.17; the probability of drawing a spade from a full deck of cards is 0.25; and that of drawing an ace is 1/13 or 0.08. The probability of a baby's dying in the U.S. between the ages of one and two is 0.00414.

5.3. WHAT ARE THE CHANCES?

So far we have been talking about probability without specifically defining it. To facilitate the measurement of probability we offer below what may be called an operational definition.

Definition of probability.   The definition most commonly accepted at present pertains to relative frequency, with which we are already thoroughly acquainted.   We will define the *probability of an event as the number* x *of success cases divided by the total number* n *of all cases (that is, success cases* x *plus failure cases* f*), provided that all cases are equally likely of occurrence.*[3] Empirical determination of probability involves, thus, the long-run relative frequency in which there are numerous repetitions (see " . . . all cases . . . ").   What does that mean?   If we flip an honest coin we expect a relative frequency of tails of 0.50.   We do not expect, however, that 10 flips will produce all the time exactly 5 heads and 5 tails.   We cannot expect an equal number of heads and tails every time we flip coins.   Instead, if we make a large number of throws, i.e., in the long run, we will end up with about as many heads as tails.   But as Lord Keynes, the famous British political economist, is reported to have said, "In the long run we are all dead."   Many probability ratings are not based on very long runs.

Our definition presents us with a working method for measuring probabilities.   We enumerate the total number of all mutually exclusive and equally likely success and failure cases or, depending on the problem, the total number of trials; divide the success cases by the success plus failure cases, and we have the probability of the particular event *A*.   In brief,

$$p(A) = \frac{x}{(x+f)} = \frac{x}{n}. \tag{5.1}$$

A priori probability.   How do we gain knowledge about x and f? There are two major methods that can be used, depending on the problem. The value of the ratio $\frac{x}{(x+f)}$ may be ascertainable by the very nature of the event, and can thus be determined on a priori grounds.   These are the a priori probabilities.   They are common in gambling problems, but are less applicable to business and economics.   Let us illustrate a case of a priori probability and the reasoning about it.   What are the chances of throwing a three-spot on a die?   If we throw a die, six sides, all different, can appear face up.   Since a die is symmetrical (we are talking about an honest die), all six different outcomes are equally likely.   There are 6 possible cases and, therefore, the probability of getting a success, i.e., throwing a three-spot, is 1/6.   In this case the answer is ascertainable without much effort.   A priori probabilities are common to problems involving throwing coins, drawing

---

[3] The logical difficulty with this definition is its circular reasoning.   In order to know whether cases are "equally likely" we need to know their probability of occurrence, the objective of our definition.

cards, waiting for street lights to change, movements on a mechanical assembly line, to mention but a few examples.

Empirical probability. In most everyday problems the ratio $\dfrac{x}{(x+f)}$ is not self-evident and not ascertainable. Instead, it must be *empirically estimated*. We could also have estimated the probability of throwing a three-spot empirically. We could have thrown the die many times and recorded the outcomes. Dividing the empirically found number of successes—in this case throws of three-spots—by the total number of throws, we could estimate the *empirical probability* of throwing a three-spot. The empirical probability of an event is the fraction of cases in which the event has occurred in the past. Would we anticipate exactly 20 three-spots every time we make 120 throws? Most certainly not. Such an outcome would indeed be a coincidence. We are likely to have somewhat more or less than 20 throws of three-spots, although 20 is the most probable result.

There is a major difference between a priori and empirical probabilities. An a priori probability can always be expressed as a precise number while an empirical one is an estimate and, therefore, only an approximation. Most statistical probabilities of interest to business and economics are based on empirical probabilities, and we are well advised to preface them with an "approximately." Although usually empirical probabilities are based upon numerous experiences, sometimes we have but a single experience. We obviously can never include all possible experiences and certainly not the one about which anticipatory decisions are made. There would be little use for empirical probabilities as a basis for statistical estimates unless we could expect at least a few comparable experiences. Specifically, we hope that the past experience on which the probability is based will prove similar to the anticipated one, and vice versa. Common sense, experience, and thorough analysis must help us determine the closeness of the similarity and the reliability of the numerical probability.

Let us take an example from the life insurance field. We all are aware of the principle underlying insurance, namely, that numerous individuals make small periodic contributions commensurate with the probability of losses, and, in case of contingency, they or their beneficiaries are paid relatively large sums. The insurance company determines the magnitude of the periodic payments, or premiums, primarily by estimating the probability of losses, or of deaths in the case of life insurance.

There is no a priori method of determining such a probability. Instead, mortality tables based on actual experience have been constructed to give us empirical probabilities. Today most insurance companies rely on the Commissioners' 1941 Standard Ordinary Mortality Table.   CSO, as it is usually called, was compiled from the experience of American companies in the period 1930 to 1940, which begins with a group of 1,000,000 people at one year of age.   The group obviously decreases annually by the number of its members who died during that period.   Thus, of the 1,000,000 members 5,770 died between the ages of one and two, 4,116 others before they got to be three, 3,347 others before they got to be four, and so on.   If we divide the number dying in a particular year by the number of group members surviving at the year's beginning, e.g., at the age of two: $\frac{4,116}{994,230}$ = about 0.00414, we get the probability of death at that particular age (see Table 5.1).   Those who are just 18 and are interested in knowing their chances of celebrating their 19th birthday can do so by referring to Table 5.1.   The probability of not living to blow out 19 candles is very slight, i.e., about 0.00230.

Based on this concept, insurance companies calculate their risk and the corresponding premium.   To offer a one-year term insurance for the 18th year of life, a company would multiply the probability of death of the policy holder, which we found to be 0.00230 for the 18th year of life, by the protection, let us say in this case $10,000.   Thus the premium[4] would amount to 0.00230 × $10,000 or $23.

Expectations.   We will call this premium of $23 for a one-year term insurance a *fair* premium, just as a $1 bet in a game in which 1,000 people participate with one of them sure to win $1,000 is a *fair* bet.   *A bet is fair if it equals the probability of winning times the total stakes or potential gain.*   With the probability of winning in the last example equal to 0.001 and the stakes $1,000, the fair bet was 0.001 × $1,000 or $1.00.

In a sense a fair bet is the expectation of a given potential gain to materialize; and a fair premium is the expectation of a given potential contingency to occur.   Both have been expressed in dollars.   Thus, for instance, one chance in a thousand of winning $1,000 has an expectation of gain valued at $1.   We should have little trouble in realizing the relationship between

---

[4] $23 is a raw figure to which a loading charge to cover the company's administrative expenses must be added and, if the premium is prepaid, the company's receipt of interest on the prepaid account deducted.   The reader rightly will say that since the probability of death increases with age the premium would increase annually at a time when he himself is paying his company continuously the same amount.   His observation is correct and the reason is that he does not own a one-year term insurance policy, which is not generally available, but most likely a 10- or 20-year term, limited term, ordinary life, or endowment insurance, which in practically all cases have premiums that are equalized over time. Their calculation is based on the same principle, i.e., the loss probability over the total period of insurance is estimated from CSO tables, adjustments are made for loading charge and interest, and the cost is averaged over the period of payment.

Table 5.1 MORTALITY TABLE

Age	Probability of Death at a Given Age	Age	Probability of Death at a Given Age	Age	Probability of Death at a Given Age
0	0.02258	33	0.00412	66	0.04296
1	0.00577	34	0.00435	67	0.04656
2	0.00414	35	0.00459	68	0.05046
3	0.00338	36	0.00486	69	0.05470
4	0.00299	37	0.00515	70	0.05930
5	0.00276	38	0.00546	71	0.06427
6	0.00261	39	0.00581	72	0.06966
7	0.00247	40	0.00618	73	0.07550
8	0.00231	41	0.00659	74	0.08181
9	0.00212	42	0.00703	75	0.08864
10	0.00197	43	0.00751	76	0.09602
11	0.00191	44	0.00804	77	0.10399
12	0.00192	45	0.00861	78	0.11259
13	0.00198	46	0.00923	79	0.12186
14	0.00207	47	0.00991	80	0.13185
15	0.00215	48	0.01064	81	0.14260
16	0.00219	49	0.01145	82	0.15416
17	0.00225	50	0.01232	83	0.16657
18	0.00230	51	0.01327	84	0.17988
19	0.00237	52	0.01430	85	0.19413
20	0.00243	53	0.01543	86	0.20937
21	0.00251	54	0.01665	87	0.22563
22	0.00259	55	0.01798	88	0.24300
23	0.00268	56	0.01943	89	0.26144
24	0.00277	57	0.02100	90	0.28099
25	0.00288	58	0.02271	91	0.30173
26	0.00299	59	0.02457	92	0.32364
27	0.00311	60	0.02659	93	0.34666
28	0.00325	61	0.02878	94	0.37100
29	0.00340	62	0.03118	95	0.39621
30	0.00356	63	0.03376	96	0.44719
31	0.00373	64	0.03658	97	0.54826
32	0.00392	65	0.03964	98	0.72467

Source: Adjusted from the *Commissioners' 1941 Standard Ordinary Mortality Table.*

probability and expectation. In general we can say that the expectation E of a given venture is the probability p that it will succeed times the gain g that will result if it does succeed. In short,

$$E(A) = p(A) \times g(A). \tag{5.2}$$

While businessmen often think and speak in terms of expectations, expected profits, or expected losses, they do not always realize that what they may subconsciously be doing is evaluating and then multiplying probabilities and stakes. Knowing what goes into the calculation of an expectation, they can often refine and improve their estimates. To obtain good estimates of expected profits from alternative ventures, it is best to seek the advice of well-qualified persons regarding the probability of profits from alternative ventures, as well as the magnitude of the potential profit. In this way we would go behind the concept of expectation and, instead of trying to quantify it directly, start by quantifying its two components, probability and stake.

Some examples. Empirical probabilities are sometimes calculated in connection with baseball earned-run and batting averages, controlling the quality of spare parts and merchandise, auditing, radio and television Hooper Ratings, credit risks, to mention but a few. For example, a batting average of 0.333 means that in the season under way the player hit safely once in every three official times at bat. If we can assume that his performance so far can be looked upon as indicative of his batting success for the rest of the season, this figure would be very useful. However, it is questionable whether this assumption will always be valid. We should not make the mistake of claiming that after two hitless trips to the plate the player is sure to hit on the next appearance. We would have neglected the long run nature of probability ratings.

According to our definition, for $p(A)$ to be equal to $\dfrac{x}{(x+f)}$, all $(x+f)$ cases must be equally likely. In throwing dice this means that the die is honest, a fall on each of its six sides is equally likely, and the value of one toss has no effect on the next toss. With empirical probabilities this proviso requires that all cases included have an equal chance to turn out successfully or unsuccessfully. Knowledge of the situation must be relied upon to reveal whether equal likelihood prevailed.

Some persons, among them famous scholars, have gone to considerable trouble in estimating probabilities of various happenings. A number are fallacious. In "Peter Simple," Captain Marryat tells of the sailor who supposedly knew all about probability theory. When his ship engaged the enemy he searched for the first hole made in the side of the ship by an enemy cannon ball and put his head into it, reasoning that, according to "a calculation made by Professor Innman, the odds were 32,647 and some decimals to boot, that another ball would not come in at the same hole."

The midshipman apparently got only a first taste of the laws of chance and obviously had trouble digesting them. His reasoning is similar to that on which the *maturity of chance* theory in gambling is based. According to this theory one should favor bets on outcomes that in the past have turned up less frequently than others. However, the fact remains that after 15 throws of a coin which were all heads, the odds of throwing a tail are still 1:1. Why consider only the last 15 throws? If more previous throws had been taken into account, there may have been many more tails than heads. It is true that before we start flipping coins the odds are enormously against getting 15 heads in a row. But once we made the first flip, the next is judged on its own; its chances of being a head or a tail are fifty-fifty.

Similar reasoning could have helped our midshipman. Before the naval engagement got under way, the chances that two cannon balls would land on the same spot were very slim indeed. However, after the first hit, the chances of a second shot hitting a particular spot are independent of where the first shot landed.

Remember the surgeon who discussed a difficult and hazardous operation with the patient's mother? "Why," said the surgeon, "Jimmy's chances couldn't be better. It is known that 1 out of 10 of these operations is a success, and luckily for Jimmy, my last 9 operations have proved fatal."

5.4. SOME LAWS OF CHANCE

Having learned to count the spokes of the wheel of fortune, what about adding, substracting, and multiplying them?

We will learn four laws of chance:

1. How to subtract probabilities of mutually exclusive events. (Two events are mutually exclusive if they cannot happen at one and the same time.)
2. How to add probabilities of mutually exclusive events.
3. How to multiply probabilities of independent events.
4. How to multiply probabilities of dependent events. (Two events are dependent upon each other if the outcome of the first has a distinct effect upon the probability of the second event occurring.)

The subtraction law. We often hear people say, "there is a fifty-fifty chance." For instance, there is a fifty-fifty chance that Army wins the kickoff toss from Navy. Yet there is also a fifty-fifty chance that it will not win, but lose. What we did in the second sentence was to subtract the probability of a win or success from 1.0, the probability of a certain event. Army cannot win or lose at one and the same time; neither can Navy. Therefore, these two events are mutually exclusive. The probability of

Army winning the kickoff toss is 0.50, that of not winning the kickoff toss is 1.0 − 0.50 or 0.50.

In general for mutually exclusive events, the probability of failure of event A, $q(A)$, is equal to one minus the probability of success of event A, $p(A)$. In brief,

SUBTRACTION
LAW

$$q(A) = 1.0 - p(A). \tag{5.3}$$

Here are some additional examples.

If an automatic elevator stops 10 seconds at a particular floor and takes 40 seconds to come back, the probability of finding the elevator waiting is 1/5 or 0.20. The probability of not making the elevator but having to wait for it is 1.0 − 0.20 = 0.80. (Minor deviations from these figures will result from the fact that we may not be able to squeeze into the elevator as soon as it arrives and just before it departs.) Or, let's look at this example. The probability of any member of Congress having had formal law training is estimated at about 0.60. Consequently,[5] the probability of Representatives and Senators having a background other than law is 0.40.

The addition law. The *addition law* can be illustrated by the wise oracle, "you will either get a head and win or get a tail and lose." Since getting head or getting tail are the only possible outcomes when we flip a coin, and these two outcomes are mutually exclusive, we can be certain that for getting heads or tails $p = 1.0$, and that the oracle is correct. The probability of either getting a head or a tail is 0.50 + 0.50 or 1.0. We can call the probability of getting a head $p(A)$ and that of getting a tail $p(B)$, and denote the probability of getting either one $p(A$ or $B)$. We can now generalize and state that, provided A and B are mutually exclusive events:

ADDITION
LAW

$$p(A \text{ or } B) = p(A) + p(B). \tag{5.4}$$

Thus, the probability of one of two mutually exclusive events occurring is the sum of their two probabilities. For instance, the probability of throwing either a two- or a six-spot is 1/6 + 1/6 = 2/6 = 1/3. This addition law can also be applied to more than two probabilities. We can state that the probability of one or another of several mutually exclusive events occurring is the sum of the probability of occurrence of each of the different events. We can illustrate this last statement in terms of the following example. Let us suppose that a certain store is very anxious to have as many customers as possible pass by and see a certain display once they are in the store. There are five ways by which customers can walk through

[5] J. H. Ferguson and D. E. McHenry, *American Federal Government* (New York, McGraw-Hill, 1950), p. 260.

the store. The probabilities of a customer's using these different ways are 1/3, 1/6, 1/4, 1/8, and 1/8, respectively. There is but one spot in the store that will be passed by customers taking the first three ways. We can calculate the probability of people passing the display at that spot by adding 1/3, 1/6, and 1/4, which is 4/12, 2/12, 3/12 = 9/12 = 3/4 = 0.75, which means that there is a probability of about 0.75 that a customer will pass the display. We can state it differently and say that on the average 75 out of every 100 customers are likely to pass the display. The method can be used to select the best spot for displays, to adapt the counter arrangement to customer traffic, or to locate plain-clothes men who watch for shoplifters, to mention but a few of the applications.

The multiplication law of independent events. We consider events to be *independent* of each other if the outcome of the first has *no* effect upon the probability that the second will occur. Two events are dependent if the outcome of the first *has* an effect upon the probability of the second. If, for example, we draw two cards from a full deck and ask for the probability that both are hearts, it is important to know whether the drawing was a replacement drawing, i.e., whether the card drawn first was replaced before the second card was drawn. If the first card was replaced, the second drawing could not be affected regardless of what card was drawn first (assuming proper reshuffling). If it was replaced, then the probability that the second card will be a heart is 1/4, regardless of whether the first card was a heart or some other card. The two events in a replacement drawing are *independent*. If, on the other hand, the first card was not replaced, then the probability of the second card being a heart is either 12/51 or 13/51, depending on whether the first card was or was not a heart. The two events in a drawing without replacement are *dependent*.

In order to find the probability that two events occur jointly, we count the ways in which the joint or composite event can succeed and the ways in which it can fail. Event A (success *or* failure) can happen in any of $x_A + f_A$ ways, and following any of these event B can happen in any of $x_B + f_B$ ways. The total number of ways in which the pair of events can take place is $(x_A + f_A) \times (x_B + f_B)$. Likewise, event A can succeed in any of x_A ways, and following any of these event B can succeed in any of x_B ways. There are $x_A \times x_B$ ways in which the two events can occur jointly. The probability that events A and B, or $p(A$ and $B)$, will occur jointly, provided they are independent, is

$$\frac{x_A x_B}{(x_A + f_A)(x_B + f_B)} = \frac{x_A}{(x_A + f_A)} \times \frac{x_B}{(x_B + f_B)} = p(A) \times p(B). \quad \text{❋}$$

MULT. LAW

The probability that two (or more) independent events will take place jointly is the product of the separate probabilities of the events.

In short, in case events are independent,

$$p(A \text{ and } B) = p(A) \times p(B). \tag{5.5}$$

Let us apply the multiplication law.

William Schwenk Gilbert said in his song "When I First Put This Uniform On":

> It's one to a million
> That any civilian
> My figure and form'll surpass.[6]

This might appear to be an unmitigated boast, and yet odds of $1:1,000,000$ may not be exaggerated after all. Let us illustrate this point by considering the problem of a large manufacturing concern looking for a new manager. We can show the board of directors why they were so far unsuccessful in finding the right man. The members of the board had done a conscientious job in detailing all qualifications the new manager must have. He was to have at least ten years of successful managerial experience in the industry, be 6 feet, 4 inches or more in height, be willing to live in the small community in New Mexico in which the plant is located, and be somewhat conservative. The salary was left open. Well, let us assume that the probability of finding a man with ten or more years of successful managerial experience in that industry is about 0.0001, that of finding a man 6 feet 4 inches or taller is also 0.0001, that of finding a man willing to live in a small community in New Mexico is 0.4, and, finally, that of finding a man who can be classified as somewhat conservative is 0.25.

Let us say that we are justified in assuming that these four characteristics are independent of one another. Now let us ask ourselves what is the probability of finding a person endowed with all these attributes. To answer this query we simply multiply all these numerical probabilities. In our example: $0.0001 \times 0.0001 \times 0.4 \times 0.25$, which tells us that a man endowed with all the attributes required by the board is so unique as to be one in a billion. One of every billion people will have the required set of attributes. We can be pretty sure that the board cannot find such a man, regardless of salary. The board had better revise its requirements.

By the multiplication law you are now also able to prove what I am sure you knew all the time, namely, that your girl friend is one in a billion, if not in a trillion. For if you multiply the probabilities of finding in one person

[6] William Schwenk Gilbert, *Patience*, Act I.

all the many features that make her so dear to you, you will end with just about that number. Thus, this law helps to establish the uniqueness of each one of us. Everyone is unique, and we should not forget this fact in an age in which uniformity is so widely worshiped.

There is another way of explaining the multiplication law of independent events. Let us assume that n_1 persons in a population of size N have char-

Chart 5.1 GRAPHICAL PORTRAYAL OF PREVALENCE OF THREE CHARACTERISTICS IN A POPULATION

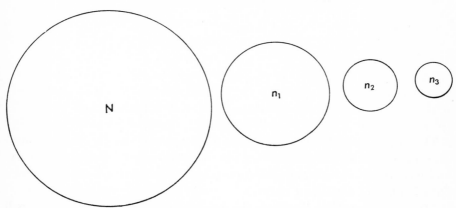

acteristic 1; n_2 in the same population have characteristic 2; and n_3 in the same population have characteristic 3. In Chart 5.1 we have assigned arbitrary numbers to N, n_1, n_2, and n_3. If we place circles n_1, n_2, and n_3 into circle N, without permitting any overlapping of the three smaller circles, the relative area of N that these three smaller circles occupy is indicative of the probability of a person with either of the three characteristics being selected. Thus, Chart 5.2 illustrates the addition law. On the other hand, if we ask what is the probability of a person with all three characteristics being selected, the answer would be the relative size of the area of N occupied by the overlapping of

Chart 5.2 GRAPHICAL PORTRAYAL OF ADDITION LAW

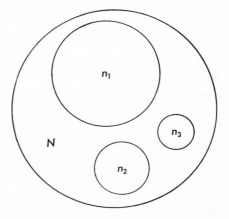

all three of the smaller circles, the shaded area in Chart **5.3**. **Thus,** Chart 5.3 portrays the multiplication law of independent events.

Chart 5.3   GRAPHICAL PORTRAYAL OF MUL-
TIPLICATION LAW OF INDEPENDENT
EVENTS

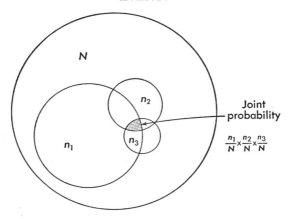

The multiplication law of dependent events.   So far we have been concerned with the multiplication law of independent events.   Actually, however, there are two multiplication laws, the other one being the multiplication law of dependent events.

After one event has occurred, the probability that a second event will take place, dependent upon or conditioned by the first one, is called a *conditional probability.*   For example, let us draw two cards from a full deck of cards without replacing the first in drawing the second, and ask ourselves what is the probability that the second card is a heart.

There are 13 hearts in a full deck of cards, so that the probability of the first card's being a heart is 13/52 or 1/4.   The probability of the second card's being also a heart depends upon or is conditioned by the suit of the first card.   If the first card was a heart, the probability that the second card drawn jointly is a heart is 12/51; otherwise it is 13/51.   Either one is a conditional probability.

We can derive the multiplication law of dependent events in about the same way as we derived the corresponding law for independent events.   The total number of ways in which events A *and* B can occur is $(x_A + f_A)$ times $(x_B + f_B)$.   Event A can succeed in x_A ways, and following any of these there will be x_B ways in which event B can succeed.   There are, therefore, $x_A \times x_B$ ways in which both events will succeed.   Since the two events are dependent on each other and B follows A, x_B is the number of ways in which B succeeds after A has already occurred.   Thus, the probability that two dependent events will occur jointly is equal to the probability that the first will occur times the conditional probability that the second will occur, the latter being computed on the assumption that event A has already occurred, and hence being denoted as $p_A(B)$.

In short, in case events are dependent upon one another,

$$p(A \text{ and } B) = p(A) \times p_A(B). \qquad \text{※} \qquad (5.6)$$

Dependent events can have two kinds of relation to each other: These are complementarity and substitutability. Whether a conditional probability is smaller or larger than an unconditional one depends on the nature of the relationship between the events. Complementarity leads to an increase and substitutability to a decrease.

Let us examine some practical implications of these concepts. Most retailers know that the purchase of one item often induces that of certain others. With this interrelation in mind, they train salesmen, and group their products, sales counters, and departments. For instance, most men's shoestores also carry socks and most paint stores sell brushes and the like. The stores have taken cognizance of the complementarity of these lines. Let us say that the probability of a store's customers buying shoes and only shoes is about 0.20, and that the equivalent figure for socks is about 0.15.

The conditional probability of customers buying socks once they have bought shoes is higher, e.g., about 0.30. All three probabilities called for empirical determination. The probability of customers buying both shoes and socks is about $0.20 \times 0.30 = 0.06$. Loss leaders featured by many stores are based on this principle. The store selects a product, making sure that it is in wide demand and, at the same time, one that is likely to be supplemented by the purchase of numerous other products, i.e., engender a high conditional probability of sale in other products. If the store makes the right choice, the probability of people buying the product as leader is high, so is the conditional probability of additional sales, and sales will be up.

The highest value a conditional probability can assume is 1.0. Take the field of real estate. The probability of the average American buying a house on May 3, 1960 is very low, perhaps 0.00001. The probability that he will buy a lot is even smaller. Yet, the probability that those who buy a house will also buy a lot—namely, the one on which the house stands—is, with minor exceptions, 1.0. The same holds true for the purchase of a new car and tires. Both are package deals and in both cases, the conditional probability being 1.0, the probability of the two events taking place is equal to that of the leading event. If the probability of a house purchase is 0.00001 and the conditional probability of the lot purchase is 1.0, the joint probability is 0.00001.

What about substitutability? Butter and oleomargarine are substitutes for each other. As a family buys more oleomargarine, it will usually buy less butter. If the probability of buying butter is about 0.30, the corresponding conditional probability is much smaller, that is, the probability of buying butter as well as oleomargarine is much smaller. While the dairy industry should have known that, it took steps that improved the competitive position of oleomargarine by raising the price of butter at a time when oleomargarine was becoming less expensive and more generally accepted by the public. As a result, per capita butter consumption declined for many years, until in 1954 the government's price support for butter was lowered. Thus, knowledge of conditional probabilities and their use can help in many business decisions.

What if the conditional probability is zero? We may recall having seen some large billboards the railroads have been sponsoring along the main highways of the country. On them a well-dressed traveler is seen relaxing in a cool and clean railroad compartment, and in large letters they say, "Next time try the train." Why next time and not this time? Well, the railroads recognized the fact that going by car and taking the train are substitutes for each other to the extent that the one excludes the other. For the driver reading the railroad advertisement, the conditional probability of taking the train at that moment is zero.

Probabilities versus odds. Let us turn briefly to another issue. Sometimes chances are stated in probabilities (varying between 0.0 and 1.0), and in other instances they are given in odds, as by the village barber. There is no difficulty in converting one into the other. If we take seriously the barber's remark that the odds are about 2 to 1 he will snip off a bit of his customer's ear, what does it mean? We may say that in the long run two out of every three customers who unsuspectingly climb into his barber chair will have bits of their ears snipped off, i.e., $p = 2/3$. How did we convert odds into probabilities? Odds of 2 to 1, i.e., 2 successes to 1 failure, can also be written as 2:1. This can be converted into a probability of 2/3 since $p = \dfrac{x}{(x + f)} = \dfrac{2}{2 + 1} = 2/3$. Likewise, a probability of 4/5 is the same as odds of 4:1.

5.5. MULTIPLE CHOICE

In order to calculate a priori probabilities it is necessary first to learn how many possible alternative outcomes there are to an event. For instance, let us assume that in a TV contest there are 4 different chips in a bowl, marked A, B, C, and D. The contestant is blindfolded and is to draw first one chip, replace it in the bowl, and then make a second drawing. The contest rules stipulate that in order to win the contestant must get chip A on the first draw and D on the second. Drawing D on the first and A on the second will not win the prize.

If we are to figure out the probability of winning in such a contest, we have to establish first how many different choices of 2 items out of a group of 4 different items are possible. Since the chip drawn is replaced each time and can thus appear twice, and since the order in which the outcome appears is important, the following multiple choices are possible:

$$
\begin{array}{cccc|}
AA & AB & AC & AD \\[4pt]
BA & BB & BC & BD \\[4pt]
CA & CB & CC & CD \\[4pt]
DA & DB & DC & DD \\ \hline
\end{array}
\;4
$$

$$4$$

We can count 16 different multiple choices. The probability of winning is 1/16.

In this example, four different outcomes are possible in each individual drawing: A, B, C, and D. We thus can choose from 4 different items, picking 2 items at a time, with the second item only being picked after the first one has been replaced.

The number of different multiple choices of 4 items taken 2 at a time, duplication being permissible, i.e., AA, BB, etc. being possible, is 4^2 or 16. As a general rule we can state that the number of different multiple choices of n items taken x at a time, duplication being possible, is n^x.

In brief,

$$\boxed{nMx = n^x,} \tag{5.7}$$

where M denotes the number of different multiple choices, n is the number of items from which we are making our selection, and x is the number of different items in each arrangement involving replacement drawing.

In general it can be said that *multiple choices are arrangements of items where order is important*, i.e., $AB \neq BA$, *and duplication of components admissible*, i.e., we can have such arrangements as AA and BB. ($\neq$ means "is not equal to.")

Let us consider some more examples of multiple choices.

If we had 10 chips in the bowl and made 2 drawings, nMx would be $10M2$ or 10^2, which is 100. nMx rapidly assumes large values.   If, for instance, we have 100 chips and replacing each we draw 4 chips, nMx will equal 100^4, or 100,000,000.

Or, let us consider the problem of the company that carries handkerchiefs, each with 3 initials.   Peter Simple Smith would have the initials PSS. The company is considering stocking handkerchiefs with all possible initials. How many different sets of initials would it need?   Here nMx is $26M3 = 26^3 = 17,576$.   That is more than the company probably bargained for, and it would most likely give up the idea of a complete stock.

From knowing nMx, the number of multiple choices, it is but a short step to estimate the probability of any particular choice or outcome.   In the equation $p(A) = \dfrac{x}{(x+f)}$, $(x+f)$ is nMx and x is the number of particular choices under consideration.   For instance, the probability of drawing one particular combination, i.e., 2 particular coins in a given order out of a bowl of 4 coins (with the first coin having been replaced) is $1/16$.   Likewise, the probability of drawing 1 particular combination of 2 coins in a given order from a bowl of 10 coins is $1/100$.   The probability of drawing 2 particular coins from a bowl of 10 coins, with order making a difference, is the probability of drawing 1 selection of a given order, $1/100$, plus the probability of drawing 1 selection of the other order, i.e., $1/100 + 1/100$ or $1/50$.

5.6. ARRANGEMENTS OR PERMUTATIONS

Frequently we are interested in the total number of different ways in which items can be arranged so that the order of components is important, yet no two arrangements are alike.   Arrangements of this sort, i.e., where *the order of the components is important but duplication of components is inadmissible*, are called *permutations*.

Let us illustrate the nature of permutations by considering the problem of the office manager who wants to give call letters to his files.   He decides to use letters A, B, C, D, E, F, G, taking 2 letters at a time; but he stipulates —and this is very important—that under no circumstances may an arrangement contain the same 2 letters.   Under these conditions then AA or BB is inadmissible, while AB would be filed under A, and BA under B, thus constituting two arrangements.   By using but 7 letters, 2 at a time, how many files can he codify?

The following permutations are possible:

AB	AC	AD	AE	AF	AG
BA	BC	BD	BE	BF	BG
CA	CB	CD	CE	CF	CG
DA	DB	DC	DE	DF	DG
EA	EB	EC	ED	EF	EG
FA	FB	FC	FD	FE	FG
GA	GB	GC	GD	GE	GF

7

6

They total 7×6 or 42 permutations. A filing system of 42 files can be instituted. Since order is a factor, AB will not be the same as BA. AB would come under A and come first; BA would be filed under B. To make sure we agree that AB is different from BA, we might think of trying to dial PA 7000 on the telephone instead of AP 7000.

As the number of files exceeds 42, the letters H, I, J, etc., can be added. Were the manager to borrow all 26 letters of the alphabet, still using 2 different letters at a time, 26×25 or 650 permutations and, therefore, 650 different files, would become possible.

Now let us take a shoe company that has decided to codify its merchandise by using the alphabet. We will be surprised to see how many articles can be codified by using 3 *different* letters of the alphabet. But we might decide that calculating the number of permutations of 26 letters, taking 3 different ones at a time, is too involved to be done by the tabular method used so far. The following rule will always help find the number of permutations:
The number of permutations of n *items taken* x *at a time, all different, is*
$n(n - 1) \cdots$ *to x terms or factors.* n *factorial*

In brief,

$$n \text{ Perm } x = n(n - 1) \cdots (n - x + 1), \tag{5.8}$$

where Perm denotes the number of permutations, and the other notations are the same as before.[7]

---

[7] To explain this rule further, let us return to the question of how many 3-letter words can be formed if no letter is used more than once in any word.

Here is the answer:

Let us apply the formula to our problem of codifying merchandise by taking 3 different letters at a time. The number of permutations of 26 letters taken 3 at a time, i.e.,

$$26 \text{ Perm } 3 = (26)(26 - 1)(26 - 3 + 1)$$
$$= (26)(25)(24)$$
$$= 15,600.$$

The number of permutations of 4 items taken in groups of 4 is similarly 4 Perm 4 or (4)(3)(2)(1), which is 24; and that of 5 items in groups of 5 is 5 Perm 5 or (5)(4)(3)(2)(1), which is 120. Products of the kind (4)(3)(2)(1), (5)(4)(3)(2)(1), and any others that run down to one are encountered often enough that a special name has been coined for them, and they have been given a special notation. (4)(3)(2)(1) is called 4 *factorial* or, in short, 4!; and, similarly, (5)(4)(3)(2)(1) is called 5 factorial, or 5!.

To help us get used to factorials, the following products and quotients are presented. If the results are not obvious, we can easily understand them by expanding the factorials.

For instance:

$$(4!)5 = 5! = 120$$

$$\frac{(3!)}{3} = 2! = 2$$

$$\frac{(7!)}{(6!)} = 7$$

$$\frac{(7!)}{(5!)} = 7 \times 6 = 42$$

$$\frac{(6!)}{(6)(5)} = 4! = 24$$

$26(26 - 1)(26 - 2)$, which is also equal to
$26(26 - 1)[26 - (3 - 1)]$ or $26(26 - 1)(26 - 3 + 1)$.

Since in this example $n = 26$ and $x = 3$, a more general form of writing this expression is:

$$n(n - 1)(n - x + 1).$$

If more than 3 different letters are used at a time, i.e., if x is greater than 3, additional terms have to be added. They would appear between $(n - 1)$ and $(n - x + 1)$. For example, if $x = 5$, we have,

$$26(26 - 1)(26 - 2)(26 - 3)(26 - 4) = 26(26 - 1)(26 - 2)(26 - 3)(26 - 5 + 1).$$

A more general form then would be:

$$n(n - 1) \cdots (n - x + 1).$$

$$\frac{(5!)}{(3!)} = 5 \times 4 = 20.$$

[handwritten: $n(n-1)(n-2)\cdots$]

Also, $(n - 1)! = \dfrac{n!}{n}$, and if $n = 1$, *[handwritten: $(n-n+1)($]*

$$(1 - 1)! = \frac{1!}{1}, \text{ which is } 0! = 1.$$

It is important to remember that 0! is equal to 1. *[handwritten: ✳ WHY IS THAT]*

Now that we know about factorials we should have little trouble to see that

$$n \text{ Perm } x = n(n - 1) \cdots (n - x + 1) = \frac{n!}{(n - x)!}. \qquad (5.9)$$

To illustrate this formula, consider the case of Mr. and Mrs. Carlos, who had been greatly surprised to win first and second prize, respectively, in the drawings of a lottery. Without telling her husband, Mrs. Carlos had bought a ticket, and so had Mr. Carlos. A total of 100,000 tickets had been sold. 100,000 × 99,999 or 9,999,900,000 different arrangements were possible, and 9,999,900,000 different pairs of tickets could have been formed. Once we know the total number of different permutations possible, we divide the number of the particular permutation, i.e., those we are interested in, by n Perm x, the total number of possible permutations. Thus, there had been a 1/9,999,900,000 probability of Mr. and Mrs. Carlos having winning tickets, with Mr. Carlos cashing the first prize.

5.7. COMBINATIONS

In *permutations*, the order of the grouped items is important; in *combinations*, the order does not matter. *Combinations are arrangements of items where order is unimportant and duplication of components is inadmissible.* *[handwritten: ✳]*

Consider the five directors of the Bee-Bo Bubble Gum Company who are to select two of their group to represent them in Washington. In how many ways can the two emissaries be chosen? This is a problem of combinations, since we do not care whether Mr. B. B. Gum will be elected first and then Mr. G. G. Bubble, or vice versa.

If, however, the delegation were to have a chairman and a vice-chairman, order would have to be considered and our problem would be one of permutations. Specifically, there are 5 Perm 2 or 20 ways in which the five directors could choose a chairman and a vice-chairman. Let us see what these ways are. If we call the directors A, B, C, D, and E, the following groupings are possible:

AB	AC	AD	AE	
BA	BC	BD	BE	
CA	CB	CD	CE	5
DA	DB	DC	DE	
EA	EB	EC	ED	

4

Selecting *A* first (that is, chairman) and *B* second (that is, vice-chairman) is distinctly different from selecting *B* first and *A* second. If a chairman and a vice-chairman are to be elected, *AB* and *BA* are two different arrangements.

However, this is not the problem facing the board of directors of the Bee-Bo Bubble Gum Company. They merely wish to elect two men who will have equal standing in the delegation. Thus, their order of election does not matter. *AB* equals *BA*; they are one combination and, by definition, order plays no role. Similarly, $AC = CA$, $AD = DA$, $AE = EA$, $BC = CB$, $BD = DB$, $BE = EB$, $CD = DC$, $CE = EC$, and $DE = ED$. A table of permutations thus contains duplicates insofar as combinations are concerned. Not only can we be sure that the number of combinations will be smaller than the corresponding number of permutations, but in our case we know that there will be exactly half as many. As a matter of fact, there will always be $x!$ times as many permutations as corresponding combinations. In our case the combinations will be:

AB	AC	AD	AE
BC	BD	BE	
CD	CE		
DE			

In general, *it can be stated that the number of combinations of* n *items taken* x *at a time, regardless of order, is equal to the number of permutations divided*

by x!; *or* $\dfrac{n(n-1) \cdots \text{to x factors}}{x!}$.

In brief, using the same notations as before and with C to denote the number of combinations,

$$nCx = \frac{n(n-1) \cdots (n-x+1)}{x!}, \tag{5.10}$$

$$\frac{n(n-1) \cdots (n-x+1)}{x!} \text{ is also equal to } \frac{n!}{x!(n-x)!}, \tag{5.11}$$

which is a common form of writing combinations, although the first form has computational advantages.[8]

The probability that Mr. Bubble and Mr. Gum will be elected to go to Washington, assuming the election is on the basis of drawing lots, can now be readily calculated. We divide this particular combination, x, by the total number of different combinations, $(x + f)$. In this case $(x + f) =$ $5C2$, which is equal to $\dfrac{5!}{2!(5-2)!}$, or 10 different ways in which the two-man delegation can be selected. Thus, if the selection is made by flipping coins or any other random device, Mrs. B. B. Gum and Mrs. G. G. Bubble will have a 10 per cent chance of having their husbands selected to go to Washington.

5.8. MULTIPLE CHOICE VERSUS PERMUTATION VERSUS COMBINATION

The following little scheme may serve to illustrate the interrelationships between *multiplicity of choice*, *permutations*, and *combinations*.

AA	AB	AC	
BA	BB	BC	**Multiplicity of choice**
CA	CB	CC	

AA	AB	AC	
BA	BB	BC	**Permutations**
CA	CB	CC	

AA	AB	AC	
BA	BB	BC	**Combinations**
CA	CB	CC	

[8] To show the equality of $\dfrac{n!}{x!(n-x)!}$ and $\dfrac{n(n-1) \cdots (n-x+1)}{x!}$, take the example where $n = 26$ and $x = 5$. Then

There are fewer permutations than corresponding multiple choices of, in this instance, three letters in groups of two, and still fewer combinations. This is so because in permutations we have introduced the limitation that equal items cannot be taken together and thus AA, BB, and CC are ruled out. This means also that when all choices are independent, i.e., one does not affect the other, we are dealing with a multiple choice problem. In both permutations and multiple choice, order is important. However, in combinations order is not important, so that $AB = BA$, $AC = CA$, and $BC = CB$. As in the case of permutations, equal items cannot be taken together. Therefore, there are always fewer combinations than permutations. Or look at it this way: Combinations may be thought of as products of numbers, as, for instance, 3×9 is equal to 9×3; while permutations may be thought of as numbers formed by digits, as, for instance, 39, which is not equal to 93.

WE LEARNED ABOUT:

1. The universality of uncertainty.

2. Reasoning in terms of probabilities is the weapon by which we attempt to cope with uncertainty.

3. The probability of an event A is the number x of successful cases divided by the total number $(x + f)$ of successful and failure cases, provided that all x plus f cases are equally likely of occurrence; in short, $p(A) = \dfrac{x}{(x + f)}$.

4. We can measure probability along a probability scale, extending from 0.0, complete uncertainty, to 1.0, full certainty.

5. We distinguish between an a priori probability, one that is ascertainable because of the nature of the event, and an empirical probability, namely, the fraction of cases in which the event has occurred in the past.

6. By an expectation or mathematical expectation E of a venture we mean the probability p that it will succeed times the gain g which will result if it does succeed; in short, $E = p \times g$.

7. The probability of failure of event A, $q(A)$, is equal to one minus the probability of success of event A, $p(A)$, on the assumption that the two events are mutually exclusive; in short, $q(A) = 1.0 - p(A)$.

8. The probability of one of two mutually exclusive events occurring is the sum of their two probabilities; in short, $p(A \text{ or } B) = p(A) + p(B)$.

$$\frac{n!}{x![n-x]!} = \frac{(26)(25)(24)(23)(22)(21)(20)(19) \cdots (3)(2)(1)}{[(5)(4)(3)(2)(1)][(21)(20)(19) \cdots (3)(2)(1)]}.$$

$(21)(20)(19) \cdots (3)(2)(1) = 21!$ is both in the numerator and denominator and thus they cancel. We are left with $\dfrac{(26)(25)(24)(23)(22)}{(5)(4)(3)(2)(1)}$, which can also be written

$$\frac{n(n-1)(n-x+1)}{x!}.$$

9. The probability that two independent events will take place jointly is the product of the separate probabilities, in short, if A and B are independent, $p(A \text{ and } B) = p(A) \times p(B)$.

10. The probability that two dependent events will occur jointly is equal to the probability that the first will occur times the conditional probability that the second will occur; in short, if A and B are dependent events, $p(A \text{ and } B) = p(A) \times p_A(B)$.

11. After one event has occurred the probability that a second event depending upon or conditioned by the first one will take place is called a conditional probability.

12. Multiple choices are arrangements of items where order is important and duplication of components admissible. The number of different multiple choices of n items taken x at a time, duplication being possible, is n^x.

13. Permutations are arrangements of items where order is important but duplication of components inadmissible. The number of permutations of n items taken x at a time, all different, is $\dfrac{n!}{(n-x)!}$.

14. Combinations are arrangements of items where order is unimportant and duplication of components inadmissible. The number of combinations of n items taken in groups of x different items regardless of order is equal to $\dfrac{n!}{x!(n-x)!}$.

SEE WHETHER YOU CAN COUNT THE SPOKES OF THE WHEEL OF FORTUNE:

1. In throwing a die, what is the probability of getting three four-spots in three successive throws?

2. On the southwestern corner of the campus is a street light. For 60 seconds westbound and eastbound traffic going straight and turning right has the right of way; then for 30 seconds westbound and eastbound traffic turning left has the right of way; thereafter northbound and southbound traffic going straight and turning right moves for 60 seconds; and finally northbound and southbound traffic can turn left for 30 seconds.

   a. If you want to know your chances, as a driver, of not having to wait at the intersection, what type of probability would you calculate, *empirical* or *a priori?*
   b. What is the probability that you would have to wait on being westbound and wanting to go straight?
   c. What are the chances that, going east, you would not have to wait before you could make a left turn?

3. Using the *Commissioners' 1941 Standard Ordinary Mortality Table*, what are the chances that a seventy-year-old man having been elected to high office will outlive his first year in office? What about a ninety-year-old man?

4. Preceding the 1953 World Series the odds were 7:5 that the Yankees would beat the Dodgers. What were the chances given the Dodgers to win?

5. You win in a game of craps by throwing two dice whose sum of turned-up spots is 7 or 11   What are your chances of winning the game on the first throw?

6. You live at the start of a bus line. A bus departs every five minutes. What is the probability that you will not wait more than one minute before the bus takes off?

7. A store uses a drawing to give away three turkeys. No single customer can win more than once. One hundred customers participate in the drawing. What are a customer's chances of winning?

8. On Washington's birthday, merchants in the District of Columbia hold "50-cent sales." An appliance store advertised new television sets for 50 cents. The advertisement stated that there would be two such sets for sale at this low price and that they would be sold in the following manner: From all customers who were in the store at 11:00 A.M. and had made a purchase, a lady and a gentleman would be chosen at random. Eighty men and 80 women were in the store at 11:00 A.M. and all had made their purchases.

    a. What was the probability that Mrs. Barbara Hall, who had just finished buying her toaster, would be able to purchase a 50-cent television set?

    b. What was the probability of Mr. and Mrs. Hall each winning a set?

    c. What was the probability of either Mr. Hall or Mrs. Hall winning a set?

9. If instead of the states, the federal government were to license all the 58 million cars in the United States, would license plate identifications constructed from 4 digit numbers and all possible pairs of letters in the alphabet either before or behind the 4 digits give each and every car a unique identification?

10. a. $6! =$ d. $7! =$ g. $\dfrac{n!}{(n-1)!} =$

    b. $\dfrac{720}{120} =$ e. $\dfrac{22!}{20!} =$ h. $\dfrac{n!}{n} =$

    c. $\dfrac{99!}{98!} =$ f. $\dfrac{33!}{(33)(32)} =$ i. $\dfrac{1!}{1} =$

                                                    j. $0! =$

11. There are 20 workers in a plant. One of them is to be chosen to work the night shift and a second to work on Sunday. Dice are to be used to make the selection. What are the chances of Jim and Norman, who work in this plant, to be selected, Jim to work the night shift and Norman to work on Sunday?

VI

Inference

By a small sample we may judge of the whole piece.
MIGUEL DE CERVANTES

6.1. SAMPLE VERSUS POPULATION

Mr. C. E. Wilson, president of LUTABE Tobacco Company, in his speech opening the meeting of LUTABE's regional sales representatives, registers concern about the company's future sales. He is worried about recent news stories that claim, without foundation he feels, that cigarette smoking may produce certain ill effects. The company's scientists are thoroughly convinced that this is not true. He calls on the meeting to discuss the problem, to appraise the effect of this news on the public, and to make some recommendations.

After a few sales representatives have offered some general remarks, Mr. Camel takes the floor. "Gentlemen," Mr. Camel announces, "before coming to this meeting I canvassed sales in my territory. If the news stories had any effect on our sales, it should have been felt during the most recent two weeks. My salesmen sold on the average more cigarettes in either of the last two weeks than in any one of the previous weeks of the last two months."

More cheerful, Mr. Viceroy, the Company's general sales manager, thanks Camel for his interesting and encouraging news and asks whether anyone else brought similar data. No, nobody has anything to contribute.

"Well, we are certainly glad to know that in your territory, Mr. Camel, sales have not fallen off. But what about the rest of the country? Would it not be best to get some information about the other parts of the United

States, too? The only trouble is that to contact all our 9,900 salesmen will not be an easy task. Also, we should really have this information before our conferences are over, so that this meeting can use it to draw up recommendations." After some contemplation he concludes, "It might be best to call in our research staff and see whether they have a suggestion."

Yes, Research has a plan. It would indeed be too expensive and time-consuming to canvas all 9,900 salesmen as to their sales. Neither can the sponsors of a radio or television program afford to ask everybody, let us say, above the age of three, whether he or she likes the Jack Benny show. Such a complete canvas is virtually impossible in most instances. A complete enumeration would cover in the statistician's language a *population*, also sometimes called a universe.

Let us see how we can define a *population*. We already know from Chapter II that an observation is the numerical value of a given characteristic of an item. If we had a table showing the sales of each of the 9,900 LUTABE salesmen in a particular week, we would have 9,900 observations. This would be a complete collection of all observations of this particular characteristic and, therefore, would be a population. In general, we can state that a population is the collection of all observations of some characteristic. As long as Mr. Camel was interested only in the sales in his territory his 35 salesmen constituted the population, a population of 35 observations. Mr. Viceroy is interested in sales throughout the country, i.e., the sales of LUTABE's 9,900 salesmen. In this case these 9,900 observations constitute the population. In the one case we were speaking about a population of 35 salesmen's sales; in the other about a population of 9,900 salesmen's sales.

In everyday life the term "population" refers to a collection of human beings. But statistical populations need not be human; as a matter of fact, they often are not.

Since collecting all observations, i.e., canvassing all 9,900 salesmen as to their sales, is impractical, Research suggests instead that a *sample* be taken. A sample is a part or subset of observations taken from the population; and *sampling* is the procedure by which information is obtained from only a part of the population. The individual observation included in the sample is a *sample unit* or *su*. Research is convinced that by getting information from a carefully selected and properly designed sample, the meeting of sales representatives could have important information before its adjournment.

We may not fully realize how many of man's activities constitute sampling. Let us watch Charles Lamm measuring the width of his window. He needs some new cornices and wants to know what length they should be.

He measures the window and finds it 6 feet 3 inches wide. He writes down the measurement. The next thing that happens is that his spouse, with typical wifely trust, comes in "to make sure" that he has gotten the right figures down. She measures the window in the same way Charles had done and finds it to the 6 feet and 3½ inches wide. Seeing his baffled look, she graciously measures a second time and is surprised to find the window 6 feet and 2½ inches wide this time. If they had continued to take measurements they would have come up with still other figures.

The discrepancies between measurements result from the weaknesses and imperfection of the human eye, and the measuring process. In fact, we are best off to consider each particular measurement as a sample observation taken from a population. The size of the population in this case is the number of measurements (not necessarily different measurements) that we can take of the window width. Obviously it is an infinitely large number. Thus each measurement of the width of the window is a sample observation from an infinitely large population. Such a population is called an *infinite population,* and is distinct from a *finite population,* which contains a fixed number of observations.

These measurements tend to have an interesting characteristic, though. If we were to take a large number of measurements, they would approximate a normal distribution. Its mean would be the best estimate we could get of the mean of the population. To get the best estimate of our window's width we would be well advised to take a number of measurements and settle on their average. Since practically all measurements are sample observations and thus estimates, we should never overstate their definiteness and precision. Instead, we are best off to state them in terms of intervals.

In some cases, sampling is the only possible method, and in others, sampling is the best method. As we have seen, some populations are of infinite size and there is no way to canvass an infinite population. Also, there is *destructive sampling*, which is best illustrated by the process of testing the quality of candies in a box. If the test or method of measurement destroys the item, we cannot test the entire population. This holds, for example, in measurements of tensile strength or breaking point, durability, and performance.

For other cases, sampling can be the better method because canvassing the entire population proves too expensive and time-consuming. Also, sampling permits more attention to details, employment of better trained interviewers, more complete supervision, and more adequate questionnaires.

Leonard Engel some time ago headed an article in Harper's Magazine "Caution: Medical Statistics at Work." In it he states:

The National Office of Vital Statistics' death tables are based on the causes of death listed on death certificates. In the case of an individual struck by an automobile, there is seldom doubt as to the cause of death. Certification of accidental death can be accepted even from the Kansas coroner who reports all deaths not due to accidents as due to "coronary" disease (spelled seventeen different ways in the death certificates he has filed so far).[1]

Sample information can hardly be inferior to the results of this complete enumeration.

That sample results can even be superior to a complete enumeration is a rather surprising fact. Not many people realize that the Bureau of the Census evaluates the quality of Census information and even sometimes adjusts Census data on the basis of sample information. Both the 1940 and 1950 Censuses were followed up by a carefully designed and painstakingly carried out Post-Enumeration Sample Survey. The position of the Bureau of the Census is well summarized in the following statement made by A. R. Eckler who is associated with this program: "I believe that a Post-Enumeration (Sample) Survey carried out on a basis insuring high quality operation is one of the more powerful devices thus far applied in measuring the quality of the Census."[2]

6.2. PARAMETER VERSUS STATISTIC

We will now introduce some concepts and notations to help us distinguish between a descriptive measure of a population distribution, also called a *parameter*, and a descriptive measure pertaining to a sample, called a *statistic*. A sample measure, or statistic, such as the mean weekly cigarette sales of a carefully selected and properly designed sample of salesmen, helps *estimate* or *infer* the value of the corresponding parameter, mean weekly cigarette sales of all salesmen. The standard deviation is another descriptive measure, and before long we will learn about others.

Parameters describe the large number of observations that make up the population. We do not know the parameter—if we did, sampling would be unnecessary; its value "is Greek to us." It appears appropriate, therefore, from here on to connote parameters by using the letters of the Greek alphabet. Statistics will be denoted by the small letters of the Latin alphabet. μ (read: mu) is, then, the population mean, while m (or $\bar{x}$) is the sample mean. σ (read: sigma) is the population standard deviation, while

---

[1] Leonard Engel, "Caution: Medical Statistics at Work," *Harper's Magazine*, 209:79 (January, 1953).

[2] A. R. Eckler, "Extent and Character of Errors in the 1950 Census," *The American Statistician*, 7:15 (December, 1953).

s is the sample standard deviation. π (read: pi) will refer to the population percentage or proportion and *p* to the sample percentage or proportion. The notations that will be used can be summarized in the following fashion:

Descriptive Measure	Notation for (Population) Parameter	Notation for (Sample) Statistic
Mean	μ (read: mu)	m or $\bar{x}$
Standard deviation	σ (read: sigma)	s
Per cent or proportion	π (read: pi)	p
Correlation coefficient	ρ (read: rho)	r
Regression coefficient	B (read: beta)	b

Thus, for example, the average number of cigarettes smoked by the American adult per day is a parameter. It is a population mean, μ, and we do not know its magnitude. However, we can make inferences about this parameter, by interviewing a carefully selected and properly designed sample of adults about their smoking habits. From these sample data we can compute the number of cigarettes smoked by the average adult interviewed, and on the basis of this statistic, the sample mean, m, we can infer the magnitude of the parameter μ.

6.3. SELECTING *su*'s

By and large there are two ways of picking sample units or *su*'s. One way is to select *su*'s arbitrarily, as a result of which we come up with a so-called *judgment sample*. The shortcomings of judgment samples are well expressed in Euripides' indictment: "My inclination gets the better of my judgment."[3] No two men are likely to agree on the representativeness of a judgment sample. Thus, its results do not lend themselves to scientific inferences.

Instead of making an arbitrary selection, we are usually better off to rely on a *statistically random* selection of *su*'s. By so doing, we come up with a *probability sample* in the sense that all members of the population have preassigned and known probabilities of being selected for the sample. For this reason a probability sample possesses the great advantage of lending itself to a convenient appraisal of the nature and precision of the estimated value and to making decisions on a risk known and agreed upon in advance. These topics will be developed later.

[3] *Medea*, line 1078.

Table 6.1 TABLE OF RANDOM DIGITS

	1	2	3	4	5	6	7	8	9	10	11	12	13	14
1	10480	15011	01536	02011	81647	91646	69179	14194	62590	36207	20969	99570	91291	90700
2	22368	46573	25595	85393	30995	89198	27982	53402	93965	34095	52666	19174	39615	99505
3	24130	48360	22527	97265	76393	64809	15179	24830	49340	32081	30680	19655	63348	58629
4	42167	93093	06243	61680	07856	16376	39440	53537	71341	57004	00849	74917	97758	16379
5	37570	39975	81837	16656	06121	91782	60468	81305	49684	60672	14110	06927	01263	54613
6	77921	06907	11008	42751	27756	53498	18602	70659	90655	15053	21916	81825	44394	42880
7	99562	72905	56420	69994	98872	31016	71194	18738	44013	48840	63213	21069	10634	12952
8	96301	91977	05463	07972	18876	20922	94595	56869	69014	60045	18425	84903	42508	32307
9	89579	14342	63661	10281	17453	18103	57740	84378	25331	12566	58678	44947	05585	56941
10	85475	36857	53342	53988	53060	59533	38867	62300	08158	17983	16439	11458	18593	64952
11	28918	69578	88231	33276	70997	79936	56865	05859	90106	31595	01547	85590	91610	78188
12	63553	40961	48235	03427	49626	69445	18663	72695	52180	20847	12234	90511	33703	90322
13	09429	93969	52636	92737	88974	33488	36320	17617	30015	08272	84115	27156	30613	74952
14	10365	61129	87529	85689	48237	52267	67689	93394	01511	26358	85104	20285	29975	89868
15	07119	97336	71048	08178	77233	13916	47564	81056	97735	85977	29372	74461	28551	90707
16	51085	12765	51821	51259	77452	16308	60756	92144	49442	53900	70960	63990	75601	40719
17	02368	21382	52404	60268	89368	19885	55322	44819	01188	65255	64835	44919	05944	55157
18	01011	54092	33362	94904	31273	04146	18594	29852	71585	85030	51132	01915	92747	64951
19	52162	53916	46369	58586	23216	14513	83149	98736	23495	64350	94738	17752	35156	35749
20	07056	97628	33787	09998	42698	06691	76988	13602	51851	46104	88916	19509	25625	58104
21	48663	91245	85828	14346	09172	30168	90229	04734	59193	22178	30421	61666	99904	32812
22	54164	58492	22421	74103	47070	25306	76468	26384	58151	06646	21524	15227	96909	44592
23	32639	32363	05597	24200	13363	38005	94342	28728	35806	06912	17012	64161	18296	22851
24	29334	27001	87637	87308	58731	00256	45834	15398	46557	41135	10367	07684	36188	18510
25	02488	33062	28834	07351	19731	92420	60952	61280	50001	67658	32586	86679	50720	94953
26	81525	72295	04839	96423	24878	82651	66566	14778	76797	14780	13300	87074	79666	95725
27	29676	20591	68086	26432	46901	20849	89768	81536	86645	12659	92259	57102	80428	25280
28	00742	57392	39064	66432	84673	40027	32832	61362	98947	96067	64760	64584	96096	98253
29	05366	04213	25669	26422	44407	44048	37937	63904	45766	66134	75470	66520	34693	90449
30	91921	26418	64117	94305	26766	25940	39972	22209	71500	64568	91402	42416	07844	69618
31	00582	04711	87917	77341	42206	35126	74087	99547	81817	42607	43808	76655	62028	76630
32	00725	69884	62797	56170	86324	88072	76222	36086	84637	93161	76038	65855	77919	88006
33	69011	65795	95876	55293	18988	27354	26575	08625	40801	59920	29841	80150	12777	48501
34	25976	57948	29888	88604	67917	48708	18912	82271	65424	69774	33611	54262	85963	03547
35	09763	83473	73577	12908	30883	18317	28290	35797	05998	41688	34952	37888	38917	88050
36	91567	42595	27958	30134	04024	86385	29880	99730	55536	84855	29080	09250	79656	73211
37	17955	56349	90999	49127	20044	59931	06115	20542	18059	02008	73708	83517	36103	42791
38	46503	18584	18845	49618	02304	51038	20655	58727	28168	15475	56942	53389	20562	87338
39	92157	89634	94824	78171	84610	82834	09922	25417	44137	48413	25555	21246	35509	20468
40	14577	62765	35605	81263	39667	47358	56873	56307	61607	49518	89656	20103	77490	18062
41	98427	07523	33362	64270	01638	92477	66969	98420	04880	45585	46565	04102	46880	45709
42	34914	63976	88720	82765	34476	17032	87589	40836	32427	70002	70663	88863	77775	69348
43	70060	28277	39475	46473	23219	53416	94970	25832	69975	94884	19661	72828	00102	66794
44	53976	54914	06990	67245	68350	82948	11398	42878	80287	88267	47363	46634	06541	97809
45	76072	29515	40980	07391	58745	25774	22987	80059	39911	96189	41151	14222	60697	59583
46	90725	52210	83974	29992	65831	38857	50490	83765	55657	14361	31720	57375	56228	41546
47	64364	67412	33339	31926	14883	24413	59744	92351	97473	89236	35931	04110	23726	51900
48	08962	00358	31662	25388	61642	34072	81249	35648	56891	69352	48373	45578	78547	81788
49	95012	68379	93526	70765	10592	04542	76463	54328	02349	17247	28865	14777	62730	92277
50	15664	10493	20492	38391	91132	21999	59516	81652	27195	48223	46751	22923	32261	85653

Source: Interstate Commerce Commission, *Table of 105.000 Random Decimal Digits* (Washington, D C. May, 1949), p. 1.

A random selection of *su's* is readily accomplished with the aid of a *table of random numbers*. Table 6.1 is part of one such table. In a table of random numbers the digits 0,1,2, . . . , 9 are so arranged that each one has an equal chance of appearing in a particular position. We may think of this table as having been constructed by some such process as drawing numbers out of a large bowl or throwing a die over and over. While in practice a much more complicated process is used to derive the order in which the digits appear in a table of random numbers, a similar chance factor is present. All digits appear with equal frequency.

There are a number of tables of random numbers. Perhaps the two leading ones are the Interstate Commerce Commission's *Table of 105,000 Random Decimal Digits*, published in 1949, and *A Million Random Digits with 100,000 Normal Deviates*, prepared by the Rand Corporation.[4] In Table 6.1 we have reproduced the first page of the Interstate Commerce Commission table, the digits being arranged in groups of five.

Let us see how the research department of LUTABE could use this table to select a sample of 300 salesmen from a numbered list of 9,900 salesmen. Such a numbered list of observations is called a *frame* and helps identify the observations that have been selected for inclusion in the sample, i.e., the sample units.

The research department could select any of the 30 pages of the table of random numbers and begin at any point on that page. Thereafter it could mark off 300 successive four-digit sequences, and pick as the sample units the names of the salesmen whose number corresponds to each of the four-digit numbers. (We need four-digit numbers since the population size, 9,900, is composed of four digits. Were we to work with three-digit numbers, salesmen corresponding to numbers that are larger than 1,000 would have no chance of being included in the sample. If we work with a five-digit number, we will draw too many numbers for which we have no corresponding salesmen in the population).

For instance, let us assume that the research department begins with page 1 (our Table 6.1) and chooses for its starting point the 2, which is found in Column 1 and Row 27, as the first of the four digits to make up the number. Reading horizontally and then vertically, its sample will consist of the names corresponding to numbers 2967, 74, 536, 9192, 58, etc. The 39th number happens to be 9973, for which we do not have an opposite name, since our population consists of only 9,900 observations. We

---

[4] Interstate Commerce Commission, *Table of 105,000 Random Decimal Digits* (Washington, D. C., May 1949, Statement No. 4914) and *A Million Random Digits with 100,000 Normal Deviates* (Glencoe, Illinois, The Free Press, 1956).

therefore ignore that number and move to the next one. In this fashion 300 numbers are picked and their opposite names constitute the sample.

Instead of reading the numbers horizontally, we could read them vertically, diagonally, or in any other consistent manner. Whatever be the detailed method, we must identify each unit of the population with the help of a number and select the sample unit on the basis of digit sequences drawn from a table of random numbers.

There are times when we desire to make a random selection of *su*'s and we either do not have readily available a table of random numbers or its use is too laborious. Under such circumstances we can apply a *systematic* process to draw our sample units. For instance, if we know that 99,000 observations constitute our population and we need a sample of 300, we can *systematically* select every 99,000/300 or 330th observation. To start with we pick a number between 1 and 330, e.g., 158, and the name in the frame corresponding to that number is our first *su*. The second *su* is the name opposite the 488th number, and the third *su* is the name opposite the 818th number, etc.

In 1953 Carmine G. DeSapio, boss of Tammany Hall, sampled registered Democrats in the City of New York to ascertain their views on whether Wagner or Impelliteri should be the party's candidate for mayor. A systematic sample selection was relied upon. Every tenth registered Democrat was selected, starting at some number between 1 and 10, let us say 7, and adding thereafter 10 each time to find the next one. What was the outcome? The voters' preference, as revealed by the survey, caused DeSapio to support the candidacy of Wagner. When the election resulted in a Wagner landslide, DeSapio's power position at Tammany Hall was finally established. He even got a bouquet from the Republican *New York Herald Tribune*, which conceded that for once Tammany Hall had done something useful and commendable.[5]

Systematic sample selection has one main limitation. It is not appropriate if the characteristic sampled is subjected to periodic changes of fixed duration. If, for example, sales vary by the day of the week, a systematic sample selection that picks every 28th day would tend to be biased, since it would pick the same weekday every four weeks.

6.4. SAMPLE DESIGN: A BIRD'S-EYE VIEW

While we have acquainted ourselves with the nature of a probability sample and also considered ways of obtaining one, the fact remains that

[5] R. L. Heilbronner, "Carmine G. DeSapio," *Harper's Magazine*, 210:23–33 (July, 1954).

there are numerous types of probability samples. These types vary, depending upon the *sample design* employed. For instance, in designing a sample we may randomly select *su*'s from the population as a whole, or we may first subdivide the population into special segments or *strata* and randomly select *su*'s from each stratum. In the first case we would have relied upon a *simple* or *unrestricted random sample design*, while in the second a *stratified* or *restricted random sample design* would have been employed. Another sample design or group of sample designs relies upon geographical areas or *clusters* as elements of its frame. A cluster is a group of units of some population that usually can be readily identified in terms of its location, e.g., census tract or a city block. If we have no frame of the individual population members, we can often obtain a frame of clusters and draw probability samples of clusters and, sometimes as a second stage, draw probability samples of elements in the clusters. Depending upon the circumstances, a *simple* or *unrestricted random cluster* or a *stratified* or *restricted random cluster sample design* is used.

Historically, the *unrestricted random sample* design was the first developed by statisticians. It is used to this day and is a very appropriate method whenever a frame of population members is available and the population is reasonably homogeneous in relation to the characteristic under consideration. For example, if the research department of LUTABE is in possession of an appropriate frame and knows that the sales of its salesmen are about the same all over the country it could make a random selection of 300 salesmen from its population as a whole, i.e., its frame of 9,900 salesmen. The selection could be made with the help of a table of random numbers or a systematic process.

Restricted or *stratified random sample designs* are used when it is known that different segments or strata exist in the population. We stratify the population, i.e., divide it into strata so that each stratum is more or less homogeneous, and make a random selection of *su*'s from each stratum. Finally, we combine the *su*'s from the different strata to form one total sample.

We may better understand such a sample design if we return to the problem facing the research department of LUTABE and assume that part of the sales force represents only LUTABE while another part handles the accounts of two or three companies manufacturing an allied line. Sales are no doubt affected by whether the salesman represents only one firm or has a divided loyalty. The research department would be well advised to split its sales force into two segments or strata, take separate samples of each, get mean sales for each group, and weight each mean according to the relative importance of the stratum in the population to get a weighted mean sale. The result is likely to be more accurate than unrestricted random sampling, since the researcher is assured of representation of the two types of salesmen in the sample. Once the sample is properly stratified, this type of sample design, by requiring randomness only within strata, tends to reduce the potential errors involved in random selection. The stratification process need not be limited to one characteristic but, depending on the circumstances, we can stratify on the basis of a number of characteristics. [6]

Cluster area sample designs, though of recent origin, have proved to be a most important device. For instance, at the end of World War II, war-ravaged Greece needed to know the size of its population and, in preparation for a general election, the number of its eligible voters. It was decided to get this information from sample data. A cluster area sample design was used. The same was done in Bengal to estimate the jute crop. The United States Departments of Agriculture, Labor, and Commerce today heavily rely on cluster area sample designs in estimating unemployment and income, as well as the size of the United States population.

When we make use of a cluster area sample design we do exactly what the name implies, namely sample areas of clusters with each cluster containing a group of units, often called *listing units*, which can be households, dwelling units, males, etc. Whenever we do not have a complete list of the *members* of the population, we can fall back on a list of the *areas* occupied by members of the population and select a number of these areas at random. The areas may be census tracts or city blocks, or any other geographical area that is clearly defined. After an area has been randomly selected all the listing units, i.e., the entire cluster, may be included in the sample. Alternatively, and usually more efficiently, we could subsample the cluster and interview only the listing units in the subsample. The subsample can be selected with the help of Sanborn maps, which have been produced for most city blocks in the larger cities of the United States by the Sanborn Map

---

[6] There are two main methods of stratification: proportional and disproportional. If the standard deviations in the different strata are about the same, i.e., the distributions in the strata have about equal dispersions, the number of su's selected from each stratum should be in proportion to its relative size in the population. Thus, should the standard deviation of sales by exclusive sales representatives be about the same as that by non-exclusive ones and 80 per cent of the 9,900 salesmen fall into the first group and 20 in the second, we would also select 80 per cent of the su's from the first and 20 per cent from the second group. If, however, the standard deviations are not equal, disproportionate stratification would produce more accurate estimates, with the size of the sample strata both reflecting the relative size of the strata in the population and their standard deviations.

Company, New York (primarily for fire insurance purposes). The Sanborn map shows all the buildings in a given block. On the basis of this map we can divide the sample block into a number of compact segments of buildings promising to have about the same number of listing units and select at random one of these segments to be interviewed in its entirety. Alternatively, we can accomplish about the same objective without a Sanborn map. We can visit the sample block and make a list of all listing units, starting at, say, the northeast corner of the block, and going around the block. We can then number the units and draw a random sample of the desired size.[7]

6.5. ERRORS OF SAMPLING VARIATION

We now return to LUTABE's research department, which needs a sample of sales data for the two weeks preceding and the two weeks following the cancer announcement. The mean sample sales can then be calculated for each of the two periods. Given these two sample means (statistics), the company can decide with a predetermined risk of being wrong whether the mean sale of all LUTABE salesmen differed *significantly* in the two periods. Furthermore, the mean sales figures for the LUTABE sales force in the two periods can be estimated.

Before embarking on the sampling assignment, Research must turn to Mr. Viceroy for advice. "How confident do you need to be that there is or isn't a difference in the average sale per LUTABE salesman in the two periods?" asks the director of research. "Dead sure, if possible," retorts Viceroy. "Sorry, we can't offer you certainty," says the research director, and before Viceroy can ask his famous "Why not?" he goes on to explain. We can conceive of the explanation proceeding in the following fashion.

Let us illustrate our problem by using a full deck of cards. We will disregard the fact that some of the cards are clubs, others spades, hearts, and diamonds, and observe only their numerical values. The numerical values of the cards, i.e., the observations, run from 2 to 10; Jack, Queen, King, and Ace will be assigned values of 11, 12, 13, and 14, respectively. Our population is, thus, composed of 52 observations.

Since in this case all the values of the observations are known, we can readily calculate the population mean, i.e., the parameter, to be 8.0. But

---

[7] All too often public opinion pollsters have been using a modification of cluster area sampling that can produce extremely inaccurate results. The method is often referred to as *quota sampling*. Quota sampling derives its name from the fact that the number of *su*'s, i.e., quota, from each cluster, often a city, is set in advance for each interviewer. It is then up to the interviewer to select his quota as he pleases, opening the way for *biases* that may cause the sample results to deviate from the true situation.

now let us forget this knowledge for a moment and draw two samples of size 10 each. Each sample is thus composed of 10 *su*'s (sample units). How do we sample cards? Well, we shuffle the cards and draw one. Let us say it is a 4. We replace this card, shuffle, draw again, and again until we have drawn 10 cards. If this has been done carefully, these ten cards will constitute a *random sample* of 10 cards. By replacing the card, and carefully shuffling, before making the next drawing, we gave each card more or less of an equal chance of being drawn in any one drawing.[8] As was stated earlier, the great advantage of a probability sample is that it lends itself to a convenient appraisal of the nature and precision of the estimated value and to making decisions of a known risk.

Let us say that one of our samples produced a mean value of 9.0 and the other of 6.0. Since we know in this case that both samples came from the same population whose mean is 8.0, we can be sure that the difference between the two sample means can be attributed to the sampling process, i.e., the difference reflects *sampling variation* and not an actual difference between the means of the two populations.

For instance, let us assume that the 52 cards constitute our population of the weekly sales of the 9,900 LUTABE salesmen and such a number as a 6 on a card represents a weekly sale of cigarettes amounting to $6,000 by a given salesman. Drawing the first sample of 10 cards is then equivalent to sampling 10 salesmen as to their sales in the period preceding the news item unfavorable to smoking; and drawing the second sample of 10 cards represents a sampling of 10 salesmen as to their sales in the period following the announcement. Finding mean values of 9.0 and 6.0, respectively, would mean that the salesmen sampled in the period preceding the news announcement sold on the average $9,000 per week and those sampled after the announcement sold on the average $6,000. Since the sample mean of the second period is smaller than that of the first, can we be sure also that the average sale of all 9,900 LUTABE salesmen has decreased from the first to the second period? Our answer is obviously "No," since the parameter (represented in our example by the average value in the deck of cards) is known not to have changed. We used the very same deck of cards and in each drawing the mean value of all cards, the parameter, was 8.0, or $8,000 in terms of sales.

We know the answer from the start. But in practice we do not know whether our population has changed. As a matter of fact, whether the population has changed is usually the main subject of inquiry. When we

---

[8] In survey work this method is not precise enough, and random number tables are used instead.

find in sampling work differences between two statistics, we do not know whether these differences are due to sampling variations or reflect changes in parameters, or both. We thus need a method that helps us make a decision whether a difference between two statistics could have been brought about purely by sample variation, and, thus, is *insignificant*, or whether it more probably reflects actual differences between the parameters, and thus is a *significant* difference. To develop a method that efficiently separates between significant and insignificant differences is the main objective of Chapters XI and XII.

About the same underlying reasoning and principles that will be produced to build the decision-maker will also be used to make inferences from statistics about parameters. This topic is usually discussed under the heading of "estimation of confidence intervals," and will be taken up in Chapters IX and X.

6.6. BIAS

While a sample that is carefully designed and properly selected allows the drawing of inferences with a known and calculable risk, the management of LUTABE should be aware that any *bias* that may creep into the sample data may make the results *inaccurate*, useless, or worse, misleading. We must, therefore, turn our attention now to the dangers of bias for which we must constantly be on guard.

Who has not heard of the fiasco of the *Literary Digest?* In 1936, after polling about 10 million Americans on their preferences between Roosevelt and Landon, the magazine predicted: "Alf by a landslide." When the voters overwhelmingly reelected Franklin D. Roosevelt, the *Digest* was forced to eat more crow than it could readily digest, and so it folded. In making the poll, a sampling method was used that was believed to yield accurate results, while in reality the method contained a source of bias that caused the results to differ from the true situation.

While there are many sources of bias, we have tried to categorize them into ten main groups. The bias that caused the *Literary Digest* poll to be inaccurate can be said to have in part come about by an *unrepresentative list of respondents*. The millions of Americans who were polled, and the overwhelming majority of whom showed a preference for Landon, had been selected from telephone directories, lists of automobile registrations, and the *Digest*'s list of subscribers. In short, these lists overrepresented the more prosperous people who apparently were favorably disposed to the Republican candidate, and thus led to inaccuracy.

If the interviewee learns *who is sponsoring the survey*, conscious as well as subconscious prejudices for or against the sponsor are likely to bias his answers. For instance, if the United States Steel Company were to sponsor a survey of its labor force asking them whether they thought that nationwide unions constituted a threat to the American way of life, we would know the answer of organized labor in advance. Union members would resent the question, in the belief that the company was making the survey to use the results against organized labor. Even those who had no clear-cut position on the matter before, would be likely to answer in the negative once they realized who sponsored the question.

Another possible source of bias is the *questionnaire* itself. The researcher who asks a question similar to "Did you stop beating your wife?" can never hope to obtain meaningful results. Thus, when one of the foremost financial newspapers in the United States polled 169 corporations, shortly after the outbreak of the Korean war in 1950, on whether they had engaged in price gouging and hoarding of raw material, more than two thirds answered in the negative; and all the reader can do is wonder why one third would incriminate themselves. In general, great care must be taken not to include leading questions.

Even if the question is well phrased, the *interviewer* may cause the interviewee to give biased replies. In World War II about 500 Negroes in Southern cities were interviewed, partly by white interviewers and partly by Negro interviewers. When asked, "Do you think it is more important to concentrate on beating the Axis, or to make democracy work better at home?" white interviewers received the answer, "Beat the Axis" 62 per cent of the time, while Negro interviewers received this answer only 39 per cent of the time. The racial background of the interviewer seems to have biased the results. A desire not to appear disloyal in the eyes of somebody outside one's own community may have been the source of the distortion.

Robert Bendiner, hearing about an opinion poll designed to learn about the "ideal" number of children per family, commented:[9]

Asked on a lonely summer day, with the kids away at camp, a mother may fondly answer three or four, or even more. But put the question to her late on a winter afternoon, with the same blessings tearing up the floorboards, and the answer may be not only different but unprintable.

Between a lonely summer afternoon and a dreary winter day the *disposition of the interviewee* has greatly *changed*.

[9] Robert Bendiner, "National Q & A Game—The Polls," *The New York Times Magazine*, August 23, 1953, p. 39.

The passage of time can give rise to further bias. Retail sales change by the season, urban automobile traffic changes by the day and by the hour. Thus, care must be exercised to avoid selecting an *unrepresentative survey time*. The very same street corner that finds traffic badly bottled up around 5 P.M. is often virtually deserted two hours later. Depending upon

Reprinted by permission of NEA Service, Inc.

"What we want from the advertising department, Hodgins, is an impartial survey showing that 99 per cent of American women are crazy about our product!"

the objective and the time chosen for the survey, the results can be badly biased and inaccurate.

An especially difficult problem is introduced in connection with the *handling of late reports*. Most surveys insist on a clearly defined cutoff date. Returns not in by that day will be ignored. By so doing it is hoped to prevent changes in the population from biasing the results. While this is desirable, the researcher may leave out reports without which the sample is unrepresentative. For instance, if the personal interview method is used to learn about people's line of work, it will take many visits to the home of a traveling salesman before he can be contacted. Similar selectivity can prevail in late returns of mail surveys. In commercial survey work a desire to finish early tends to make for an early cutoff date.

This problem of *nonresponse* is most serious when a mail questionnaire is used. Some time ago it was reported that the average Yaleman of Class '24 makes $25,000 a year. This is a pretty high figure and there are many reasons for its being so high. By and large, those who feel that their Alma Mater has no reason to be proud of their success, even if they have kept Yale authorities informed of their addresses, are likely to throw such questionnaires into the wastebasket. This nonresponse makes for an upward bias, since those who do not reply are more likely to fall into a category with low incomes.

The *statistical method* itself can produce a bias. Most methods are based on given assumptions, as we will see later, and when they are not met the results are likely to be biased.

The battle against biases is not an easy one. Perhaps the bias that is most devastating in its effects and yet most difficult to eliminate finds its origin in the *researcher's predilections* and *partiality*. "What we want from the advertising department, Hodges, is an impartial survey showing that 99 per cent of American women are crazy about our product," coming from the boss, is not likely to produce accurate results.

In summary, whenever we make inferences we must carefully guard against biases. If we have succeeded in keeping our data bias-free, we can control errors that come about because of sample variation.

WHAT WE HAVE LEARNED:

1. A population is a complete collection of all observations of a given characteristic.

2. A sample is a subset of observations taken from the population.

3. Sampling is the procedure by which information is obtained about part of the population.

4. A sample unit or *su* is an elementary unit that has been included in the sample.

5. An infinite population is one that is composed of an infinitely large number of observations; while a finite population contains a fixed number of observations.

6. A parameter is a descriptive measure, such as mean or standard deviation, pertaining to the population; while a statistic is a descriptive measure pertaining to the sample.

7. With the help of sampling we can infer the value of a parameter.

8. Sampling can at times be more reliable in its results than a complete enumeration.

9. The selection of a sample is random, when every observation has an equal chance of being drawn into the sample.

10. If we select sample units at random we come up with a probability sample.

11. A random selection of sample units can be accomplished with the help of a table of random numbers, or through a systematic process by which we select every *n*th observation for inclusion in the sample.

12. Among the most important types of probability samples are the simple or unrestricted random sample design, the stratified or restricted random sample design, and the various cluster area sample designs.

13. Differences between two statistics are insignificant if they can be attributed to sampling variation; otherwise they are significant.

14. A bias comes about when a sampling method is used that is believed to yield accurate results while in fact the statistics obtained differ systematically from the parameter, i.e., are consistently either too high or too low.

15. A bias can come about because of:
   a. Unrepresentative respondents
   b. Prejudices toward survey sponsor
   c. Questionnaire design
   d. Interviewer
   e. Changing disposition of respondent
   f. Unrepresentative survey time
   g. Handling of late reports
   h. Nonresponse
   i. Statistical method
   j. Researcher's predilections.

CHECK WHAT YOU KNOW ABOUT INFERENCE:

1. If we were interested in measuring the per capita income of the 170 million Americans, what would constitute our population?

2. Give three examples of finite populations.

3. Give three examples of infinite populations.

4. Enumerate a number of important reasons that can make sample information superior to information obtained by canvassing the entire population.

5. Let us assume that we flipped 8 dimes and two of them landed tail up. When we made a second throw of these 8 dimes, we found 50 per cent of them landed tail up.
   a. Did we fulfill the conditions of random sampling? Why?
   b. Explain the difference between the two results and interpret its meaning.
   c. In general, what reasons for differences between the results of two throws can you point to, and how do they relate to the results of our example?

6. Could we take the statistics pertaining to the 35 salesmen in Mr. Camel's sales territory and generalize from them about all 9,900 LUTABE salesmen? Explain in detail why such an inference is or is not possible.

7. Show the various steps through which you would go in drawing a random sample of size 10 from a population of 90,000 observations, and present an appropriate list of 10 random numbers taken from the random numbers given on p. 98.

8. Explain how you would draw a systematic sample of size 10 from a population of size 90,000.

9. Analyze some surveys that were taken recently and point to at least three biases that may have entered into the results. Place these biases into the ten categories given in this chapter and indicate ways that could have helped eliminate them.

10. An "indignant husband" recently advised wives not to let their husbands put them on a payroll in return for the housework they do. Agreeing that there have been many letters to newspapers, urging husbands to pay their wives a salary, he claimed that these letters had been written by husbands. To support his contention that these letters were a male plot, he revealed that he made an informal poll on this topic. No wife he had talked to really wanted to be paid a salary for performing her household chores; but many husbands thought it a great idea. Analyze this poll, categorizing its sampling method and biases.

11. Indicate three types of sample design and give one example of each.

VII

Sampling Distribution of Means

Whenever a large sample of chaotic elements are taken in hand and mar-shalled in the order of their magnitude, an unsuspected and most beautiful form of regularity proves to have been latent all along.

SIR FRANCIS GALTON

7.1. A PARLOR GAME

Jim Green thought that he had devised a new family game and had decided to try it out on his friends. When the Smiths, the Millers, and the Neelys had arrived, Jim explained the game. "Here are 20 coins, play money, of course, all alike except that different numbers are printed on them indicating their penny value. All twenty coins do not necessarily have different values. You, Beth, are going to select a few of them and without looking put them into this dark bowl. Then one of us is going to draw a coin, write down the figure on it, put the coin back, draw a second coin, record its value and replace it. Then, he said, "we will all guess what the average value of the coins in the bowl is, or we may say the value per coin. At the end we will take out the coins in the bowl to find the true value per coin of those Beth put in, and the one whose guess is closest wins."

Jim draws a coin. It is a 4. He puts it back into the bowl and draws another coin, a 1. Jim guesses that the value per coin in the bowl is 5 cents. Beth suggests a 4, her husband Elmer thinks 2 is a good guess, the Millers suggest a 3 and a 1, Lucy Green thinks it is a 5. But Amos Neely, smiling proudly, announces to the crowd that tonight he is going to beat them all. He has a "system." "Two and a half pennies, that is my guess."

After everybody had his guess, Jim suggests that Beth might draw two new coins out of the bowl. She first draws a 1 and after having replaced the

111

coin she draws a **3**. Everybody offers a further guess. Amos, using his "system," picks 2. And so the game goes on. Finally, Jim suggests that they may have had enough and might wish to check who is the winner.

They find that there had been four coins in the bowl, 1.0, 2.0, 3.0, and 4.0. "Therefore," says Lucy, who is fast with figures, "the value per coin is 10/4 or 2.5 pennies." After all eight of them completed their figuring, they find that there seems to be something to Amos's "system." *In toto* his guesses had been better than those of the rest, far better. The average of all his guesses is off by only 0.3.

Amos, in good humor, now offers his "system" for sale. Well, he confesses that according to his system the best possible guess of the value per coin in the bowl is the average value of the two coins drawn. Why? Let us see.

7.2. SAMPLE MEAN VIS-À-VIS POPULATION MEAN

Consider what was in the bowl: a 1.0, a 2.0, a 3.0, and a 4.0. As they had calculated it, the mean value of the coins in the bowl, i.e., the population of coins in the bowl, is 10/4 or 2.5 pennies. From this population of 4 coins, a sample of two coins is drawn at random. We remember from Chapter VI that in selecting *su*'s—in this case coins—at random, we give each coin in the bowl an equal chance of being selected. Therefore, after drawing one coin and registering its value, we replace it before we draw another coin. We must replace the coin before making a new drawing, because otherwise it would not be given a chance to be picked the next time.

Under those conditions we have $N^n = 4^2 = 4 \times 4$ or 16 multiple choices in selecting random samples of size 2 from a population of 4.[1] Amos could have drawn 16 different sets of samples of two coins. He could have calculated the mean of each set and used it as an estimate of the average value of the population of coins in the bowl. All the (16) possible means that Amos could have come up with are shown in Table 7.1. The mean value of these means is

$$\frac{1.0+1.5+2.0+2.5+1.5+2.0+2.5+3.0+2.0+2.5+3.0+3.5+2.5+3.0+3.5+4.0}{16}$$

$$= \frac{40.0}{16} = 2.5 \text{ pennies.}$$

Thus, both the mean of the population of coins and the mean of the means

[1] In Chapter V the formula n^x was shown to be useful in finding the total number of multiple choices. In the case of a random sample, n of Formula 5.7 is the population size (usually connoted by us by N) and x is the sample size (usually connoted by us by n). Formula 5.7 can be rewritten as N^n.

Table 7.1   VALUES OF SAMPLE MEANS

Coin Value in Cents	1.0	2.0	3.0	4.0
1.0	1.0	1.5	2.0	2.5
2.0	1.5	2.0	2.5	3.0
3.0	2.0	2.5	3.0	3.5
4.0	2.5	3.0	3.5	4.0

of all possible random samples of two is 2.5 pennies, i.e., $\mu = \bar{m}$.   However, *Amos or anybody else usually would not draw all the possible random samples, before estimating the parameter.   Instead, he would draw a single sample, compute the sample mean, and try to infer from it the value of the parameter.*

Since the population mean is equal to the mean of the sample means, by using the arithmetic mean of the two randomly drawn coins as an estimate of the mean coin value in the bowl, Amos' estimate will be right on the average.   On the average, therefore, the sample mean equals the mean of the population of coins in the bowl, i.e., $m \doteq \mu$, where $\doteq$ denotes "on the average (or approximately) equal to."   The probability of different sample means occurring is given in Table 7.2, with the data of Table 7.1 arranged as a relative frequency distribution.

Is this statement true just because we have a population of size four and

Table 7.2   DISTRIBUTION OF SAMPLE MEANS OF SAMPLES OF 2 COINS DRAWN FROM A POPULATION OF 4 COINS WITH VALUES OF 1¢, 2¢, 3¢, AND 4¢, RESPECTIVELY

Value per Coin in Sample (Sample Means in Cents)	Number of Sample Means	Probability of Sample Mean Occurring
1.0	1	0.062
1.5	2	0.125
2.0	3	0.187
2.5	4	0.250
3.0	3	0.187
3.5	2	0.125
4.0	1	0.062
Total	16	1.00

Source: Table 7.1.

a sample of size two? By no means. Should we decide to draw 3 coins from a population of size 4, we can select at random $N^n = 4^3 = 4 \times 4 \times 4$ or 64 different samples.

From Table 7.3 we learn that the mean values of the 64 sets of samples of three randomly drawn coins add up to 160. (This value is readily found by adding up the products of the individual coin values and the number of samples, i.e., the products of the first two columns of Table 7.3.) When we

Table 7.3 DISTRIBUTION OF SAMPLE MEANS OF SAMPLES OF 3 COINS DRAWN FROM A POPULATION OF 4 COINS WITH VALUES OF 1¢, 2¢, 3¢ AND 4¢, RESPECTIVELY

Value per Coin in Sample (Sample Means in Cents)	Number of Sample Means	Probability of Sample Mean Occurring
1.00	1	0.016
1.33	3	0.047
1.67	6	0.094
2.00	10	0.156
2.33	12	0.187
2.67	12	0.187
3.00	10	0.156
3.33	6	0.094
3.67	3	0.047
4.00	1	0.016
Total	64	1.00

divide these 160 pennies by 64, the number of samples, we have 2.5 as the mean value of the means of the three randomly drawn coins. In a similar fashion, we find that the mean value of 256 different samples of size 4 that can be drawn from a population of size 4 is 640/256 or also 2.5 pennies. For our own satisfaction we may try our hand at taking different populations, of size 3 and 5, and we will come up with the same results.

Amos' "system" is based on a famous law, if we may call it such. We have not proved it; such is not our purpose. But in our examples we have illustrated that *the mean of all the different sample means is the same as and, therefore, is the mean of the population of the individual values from which the samples are taken*.

Therefore, the arithmetic mean of the sample offers an *unbiased* estimate of the population mean. An estimate is *unbiased* if the average of the sample estimates comes nearer and nearer to the true population value as the number of samples (all of the same size) is increased indefinitely. As a matter of fact, estimates based on the arithmetic mean of the sample have a second important property. They are *efficient* in that they result in minimum sampling variation, i.e., a lower standard error than any other estimate of the population mean. Because of all these characteristics, there seems to be good reason to use the sample mean to infer the population mean. That is exactly what Amos has done.

Amos' system, however, does not end here. It lends itself to valuable extensions. By using the sample means to estimate the population mean, Amos can make some calculations about the quality of his guess: how likely is his guess to be off and by how much?

First let us use hindsight to evaluate the quality of Amos' guesses based on his "system." In the bowl were 4 coins: a 1.0, a 2.0, a 3.0, and a 4.0. Looking again at Table 7.2 we find that the sample means vary from 1.0 to 4.0. The probability of Amos' system producing a 1.0 is very slim; specifically it is 1/16 (or 0.062). The same holds true for 4.0. We can say that the probability of Amos' system producing either a 1.0 or a 4.0 is 1/16 + 1/16 or 1/8 (or 0.125). And similarly, the probability of getting a 1.5, 2.0, 2.5, 3.0, or 3.5, all of which are at most off the true mean by 1.0, is 1.0 − 1/8 or 7/8 (or 0.875). Consequently, by (randomly) drawing two coins from a bowl (population) of 4 coins, there is a 0.875 probability that by averaging the values of the two coins, i.e., sample observations, our estimate will differ from the true mean by 1.0 penny or less. Similarly, there is a 0.187 + 0.250 + 0.187 or 0.625 probability that such an estimate will be off the true mean by more than 0.5 of a penny. In the case of the sample of 4.0 and 1.0, there is a 0.625 probability that an interval of 2.5 ± 0.5 pennies (± means: plus or minus), that is, an interval extending from 2.0 to 3.0 pennies will contain the true mean.

Or, if we draw at random *three* coins from the bowl, there is according to Table 7.3 a 0.156 + 0.187 + 0.187 + 0.156 or 0.686 probability of Amos' method producing an estimate that will miss the true value by 0.5 of a penny or less. Drawing *four* coins, the probability of such an outcome according to Table 7.4 is 0.121 + 0.156 + 0.172 + 0.156 + 0.121 or 0.726.

Let us examine our results for a moment. When we took a random sample of two coins, we found that there was a 0.625 probability of our estimate differing from the true coin mean by 0.5 of a penny or less. With three coins this probability is 0.686, and for four coins it becomes 0.726. The probability of making an estimate of the same quality appears to increase as the number of coins drawn from the bowl, i.e., the size of the sample, increases. We will have to say more about this important phenomenon below.

It is easy to find probabilities of erring. We might wish to use, for instance, a probability of 0.95. Within what range would we expect the estimate to fall 95 per cent of the time? Or, we may ask, what is the 95 per cent confidence interval? If 95 per cent of the means are supposed to fall inside the range, 100 − 95 per cent, or 5 per cent, will fall outside it. Five per cent of the 256 different sample means of samples of size 4, are, let us say roughly, about 10. The 10 means farthest removed from the true mean are one at 1.0, four at 1.25, four at 3.75, and one at 4.0. This leaves us with a 95 per cent confidence interval extending from about 1.5 to 3.5 (The reader can benefit from calculating other confidence intervals).

Table 7.4 DISTRIBUTION OF SAMPLE MEANS OF SAMPLES OF 4 COINS DRAWN FROM A POPULATION OF 4 COINS WITH VALUES OF 1¢, 2¢, 3¢ AND 4¢, RESPECTIVELY

Value per Coin in Sample (Sample Means in Cents)	Number of Sample Means	Probability of Sample Mean Occurring
1.00	1	0.004
1.25	4	0.016
1.50	10	0.039
1.75	20	0.078
2.00	31	0.121
2.25	40	0.156
2.50	44	0.172
2.75	40	0.156
3.00	31	0.121
3.25	20	0.078
3.50	10	0.039
3.75	4	0.016
4.00	1	0.004
Total	256	1.00

While we might like the idea of calculating the quality of guesses based on Amos' system, we are likely, after some reflection, to wonder: "All this is very well, but didn't we assume in our calculations that we knew how many coins there were in the bowl and even the value of each and every one of them? Clearly Amos, who did not have this information, could not calculate the quality of his guesses." However, it is possible to calculate the quality of an estimate even though we do not know the size of the population and the characteristics of each and every one of its members. This is, indeed, one of the great achievements of modern statistics. Let us consider this in terms of Jim Green's parlor game.

7.3. NORMAL DISTRIBUTION OF SAMPLE MEANS

The population of 4 coins constitutes a *rectangular* (probability) distribution, since the different coin values appear in uniform frequency (see Chart 7.1). Yet, if we plot the probability distribution of the 16 sample means

Chart 7.1 PROBABILITY DISTRIBUTION OF POPULATION OF 4 COINS WITH VALUES OF 1¢, 2¢, 3¢, AND 4¢, RESPECTIVELY

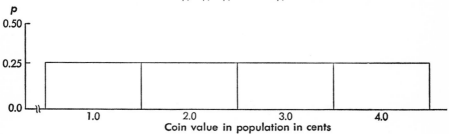

that come about by taking random samples of sets of two coins (and we have done this in Chart 7.2), we obtain a distribution that is reasonably normal. Charts 7.3 and 7.4 portray probability distributions of 64 and 256 sample means, with samples of size 3 and 4, respectively, which become even more normal. We could select populations of various other shapes and plot

Chart 7.2 PROBABILITY DISTRIBUTION OF SAMPLE MEANS OF SAMPLES OF 2 COINS DRAWN FROM A POPULATION OF 4 COINS WITH VALUES OF 1¢, 2¢, 3¢, AND 4¢, RESPECTIVELY

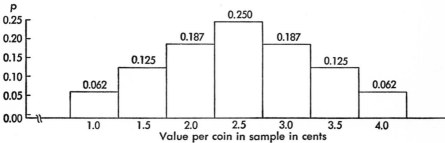

Source: Table 7.2.

the distributions of means, often also referred to as *sampling distributions.* Unless the population is very badly skewed the sampling distribution will approach normality. This phenomenon has been observed and analyzed by mathematicians. It is expressed in a famous law, which states that *means of random samples taken from a population—whether normal or not— approach a normal distribution around their mean (which we showed to be the*

Chart 7.3 PROBABILITY DISTRIBUTION OF SAMPLE MEANS OF SAMPLES
OF 3 COINS DRAWN FROM A POPULATION OF 4 COINS WITH
VALUES OF 1¢, 2¢, 3¢ AND 4¢, RESPECTIVELY

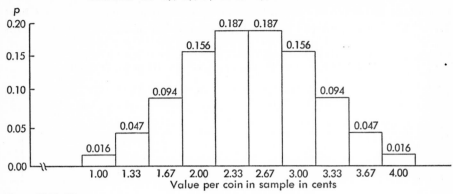

Source: Table 7.3.

same as the true mean) particularly as the size of the sample increases. Since
to prove this law is outside the scope of our efforts, we have only illustrated
it. Shooting craps furnishes another good example. A rectangular distribution of a population leads to a reasonably normal distribution of 36
sample means.

Chart 7.4 PROBABILITY DISTRIBUTION OF SAMPLE MEANS OF SAMPLES
OF 4 COINS DRAWN FROM A POPULATION OF 4 COINS WITH
VALUES OF 1¢, 2¢, 3¢, AND 4¢, RESPECTIVELY

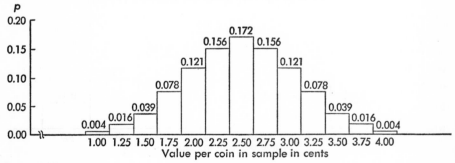

Source: Table 7.4.

We know that as the size of the sample increases, most distributions of
sample means—whether they do or do not come from a normally distributed
population—are normally distributed around the population mean. This
is particularly true if the sample is large, i.e., has 30 or more sample units.
In such a case we can use the sample means and the standard deviation of
the sampling distribution to make probability statements based on areas

under the normal curve.[2] Knowing the standard deviation of the sampling distribution of means, often also referred to as *standard error of the mean*, we can state that the one-sigma range will contain about two thirds of all sample means. Or, and this is more important, the probability that a sample mean will differ from the true mean by more than one standard error (of the mean) is $1.00 - 0.68$ or 0.32. Similarly, the probability that a sample mean will differ from the true mean by more than two standard errors is $1.00 - 0.95$ or 0.05. We might say, that we expect an error that is larger than 2 standard errors only about 5 per cent of the time. Using his "system," Amos would expect his guess to differ by more than 2 standard errors of the mean only about 5 per cent of the time.

7.4. STANDARD ERROR OF THE MEAN

This should remind Amos that he actually does not know the standard error of the mean. Fortunately we can obtain a good estimate of its magnitude, based on relations between the standard error of the mean, i.e., standard deviation of the sampling distribution of means, the standard deviation of the population, and the standard deviation of the sample mean.

Before we examine these relations, it might be worthwhile to remind ourselves of the different types of distributions that are under consideration. They are three in number. First, we have the *population distribution*. Chart 7.1 portrays the population distribution of our case. The values along the horizontal axis are x's, e.g., coin value in the population, the mean value is the population mean, μ, and the standard deviation is that of the population, σ.

The second type of distribution is the *sample distribution*. Our samples are of size 2, 3, and 4, and are too small to constitute distributions that can readily be drawn. In case we had larger samples, we could plot these sample values along the horizontal axis. The mean value of this second distribution is the sample mean, m, and the standard deviation is that of the sample, s.

Finally, there is a third type of distribution, i.e., the distribution of sample means or the *sampling distribution* of means. (Later we will meet sampling distributions of percentages, etc.) Charts 7.2, 7.3, and 7.4 are examples of sampling distributions of means. They portray the distribution of the means of the various samples. Along the horizontal axis the sample mean values are plotted, e.g., value per coin in sample. The mean value of this

[2] The only difference between this problem and those we dealt with before is that this time our observations are means and the mean really is the mean of means. Insofar as areas under the normal curve are concerned, this difference is of no consequence.

distribution is the mean of the sample means, $\bar{m}$, and the standard deviation is the standard deviation of the sample means or the standard error of the mean, $\sigma_{\bar{x}}$.

We are now ready to examine the relations between the standard deviation of the population, the standard deviation of the sample, and the standard deviation of the sampling distribution. For this purpose, let us return to Jim Green's parlor game and calculate the standard deviation or, in order to avoid working with square roots, the variance of the population of coins: $\sigma^2 = \dfrac{\Sigma(x - \mu)^2}{N}$. In Jim's case, this is equal to[3]

$$\frac{(1.0 - 2.5)^2 + (2.0 - 2.5)^2 + (3.0 - 2.5)^2 + (4.0 - 2.5)^2}{4} = 1.25.$$

Let us also calculate the variance of the sample means, i.e., the square of the standard error of the mean. This variance is equal to the summation of the squares of the differences between the individual sample means and the mean of the sample means, divided by the number of samples. To distinguish between the size of the population of samples or sample means on the one hand and the size of the population of individual observations on the other, we will denote the first by L and the latter, as usual, by N.

In brief, $\sigma_{\bar{x}}^2 = \dfrac{\Sigma(m - \bar{m})^2}{L}$.

In our case,

$$\sigma_{\bar{x}}^2 = \frac{(1.0-2.5)^2 + 2(1.5-2.5)^2 + 3(2.0-2.5)^2 + 4(2.5-2.5)^2 + 3(3.0-2.5)^2 + 2(3.5-2.5)^2 + (4.0-2.5)}{16}$$

$$= 0.625.$$

$\sigma_{\bar{x}}^2$ is more readily calculated by using the formula:

$$\sigma_{\bar{x}}^2 = \frac{\Sigma m^2}{L} - \left(\frac{\Sigma m}{L}\right)^2 = 6.875 - 6.250, \text{ or } 0.625.$$

Let's compare σ^2 with $\sigma_{\bar{x}}^2$:

$\dfrac{\sigma^2}{\sigma_{\bar{x}}^2} = \dfrac{1.25}{0.625} = 2.00$, which is the size of the sample; two coins had been randomly drawn. That the ratio between population variance and variance of sample means equals the size of the sample is no coincidence. If we make the calculation for the three-coin case, and we encourage the reader to do so, the ratio $\dfrac{\sigma^2}{\sigma_{\bar{x}}^2}$ is $\dfrac{1.25}{0.416}$ or 3.00; and in the case of 4 coins the ratio $\dfrac{\sigma^2}{\sigma_{\bar{x}}^2}$ is $\dfrac{1.25}{0.3125}$ or 4.00. All this helps us to illustrate a very important relationship, which

[3] σ^2 actually is more easily calculated from: $\dfrac{\Sigma x^2}{N} - \left(\dfrac{\Sigma x}{N}\right)^2$.

mathematicians have rigorously proved, namely that $\frac{\sigma^2}{\sigma_{\bar{x}}^2} = n$, the sample

size.   Conversely,

$$\sigma_{\bar{x}}^2 = \frac{\sigma^2}{n} \text{ and } \sigma_{\bar{x}} = \frac{\sigma}{\sqrt{n}}.$$

The standard error of the mean ($\sigma_{\bar{x}}$) equals the standard deviation of the popula-
tion (σ) divided by the square root of the sample size ($\sqrt{n}$).

Thus, because of the relationship $\sigma_{\bar{x}} = \frac{\sigma}{\sqrt{n}}$, the standard error of the mean
is for all practical purposes always smaller than the standard deviation of
the population.   This amounts to saying that the distribution of sample
means is more compact than that of the population, i.e., relatively more
observations are close to the mean.   This is entirely logical since by averaging sample observations extreme values of the population tend to offset one
another so that the average will be closer to the true mean than these
extreme values.

It is common sense that the more compact the sampling distribution, i.e.,
the smaller $\sigma_{\bar{x}}$, the more precise the estimate.   Since $\sigma_{\bar{x}} = \frac{\sigma}{\sqrt{n}}$ we immediately realize that the larger the sample the smaller $\sigma_{\bar{x}}$ and the more precise
the estimate.   We saw that $\sigma_{\bar{x}}$ for a sample of size 2 is $\sqrt{0.625}$, while that
for a sample of size 3 is $\sqrt{0.416}$ and that for a sample of size 4 is $\sqrt{0.313}$.
Thus, in order to improve the precision of estimates we can always increase
the sample size.   Yet because of the nature of the relation between $\sigma_{\bar{x}}$ and n,
we do not double the precision of the estimate by doubling the sample size.
Instead, to double the precision the sample must be increased four times.
For instance, if $\sigma_{\bar{x}} = 2$, $\sigma = 6$, and $n = 9$, to double the precision of the
estimate, i.e., reduce $\sigma_{\bar{x}}$ by 2, we must quadruple the sample: for $\sigma_{\bar{x}}$ to equal
1 while $\sigma = 6$, n must be 36, i.e., $1 = \frac{6}{\sqrt{36}} = \frac{6}{6}$.

Well, have we made much progress towards devising a method of finding
the standard error of the mean if the population is unknown?   On the surface we have little to show for our efforts.   We knew all the time that
$\sigma_{\bar{x}}^2 = \frac{\Sigma(m - \bar{m})^2}{L}$ and yet could not apply this formula, since obviously the

population mean is unknown.   Using $\sigma_{\bar{x}} = \frac{\sigma}{\sqrt{n}}$ assumes that we know the

population variance.   Yet, if we do not know the population mean we
usually are not likely to know its variance either.   Fortunately, however,
there exists a very useful relation between the population variance and a

sample variance which *enables us to use the variance of a single sample to replace the population variance in the equation* $\sigma_{\bar{x}} = \dfrac{\sigma}{\sqrt{n}}$. To do this we must first learn more about the relationship between sample and population variance.

Again using Jim's parlor game, we will calculate the variance of each of the 16 sample means. The formula for the variance of sample data can be derived from formula 4.1 on page 52. It will read

$$s^2 = \frac{\Sigma(x - m)^2}{n}. \tag{7.1}$$

In this example, in which the sample is small, we do well to adjust for the downward bias of the squared deviations, by dividing by $n - 1$ instead of n. Thus, the variance of the sample mean 1.0, which results from drawing a 1.0 twice is $\dfrac{(1.0 - 1.0)^2 + (1.0 - 1.0)^2}{2.0 - 1.0}$ or 0.0. Similarly, the variance of the sample mean of 1.5 is $\dfrac{(2.0 - 1.5)^2 + (1.0 - 1.5)^2}{2.0 - 1.0}$ or 0.5. Such calculations have been made for all 16 sample means and they are summarized in Table 7.5. Averaging all 16 sample variances, we find that the sample means have an average sample variance of 20/16 or 1.25.

Table 7.5   VARIANCE OF SAMPLE MEANS

Coin Value in Cents	1.0	2.0	3.0	4.0
1.0	0.0	0.5	2.0	4.5
2.0	0.5	0.0	0.5	2.0
3.0	2.0	0.5	0.0	0.5
4.0	4.5	2.0	0.5	0.0

Are we surprised to find the average sample variance and the population variance exactly alike? This is no coincidence.[4] On the contrary, it is a fixed relation, and permits us to claim that *on the average the sample variance is equal to the variance of the population.*

Thus, to find the standard error of the mean we will, since we do not know the standard deviation of the population, substitute for it the standard deviation of the sample. Therefore, *the standard error of the mean is approxi-*

---

[4] You can become more confident of the stability of this relation by making similar calculations for sample size 3 and 4 as well as populations of other sizes.

mately equal to the standard deviation of the sample (s) *divided by the square root of the sample size.* In brief:

$$\sigma_{\bar{x}} \doteq \frac{s}{\sqrt{n-1}} \cdot \sigma_{\bar{x}} \doteq \frac{s}{\sqrt{n}}.$$

7.5. CONFIDENCE INTERVALS

For illustrative purposes we took a very small sample of only two sample units. In sampling work we take much larger samples, frequently of hundreds and thousands of *su*'s. However, since the number of random samples, i.e., multiple choices, of large size taken from large populations is huge and virtually unmanageable, we preferred to use for illustrative purposes an *N* of 4 and an *n* of 2, which already meant working with 16 samples of 2 *su*'s each.

The usefulness of the concepts developed in this chapter is that with the help of the sample mean and the approximation $\dfrac{s}{\sqrt{n-1}}$ of the standard error of the mean we can make *confidence interval estimates of population means.* While the details of obtaining confidence interval estimates from sample data will be developed in the next chapter, it might be helpful to put such an accomplishment into proper perspective. We may do so by keeping the efforts of banker Mal and sales representative Camel in mind. Initially, confidence interval estimates were calculated with the help of entire relative frequency distributions (Chapter II). Lacking such detailed information, Mr. Camel was later able to calculate confidence intervals based on a knowledge of the population mean and population standard deviation (Chapter IV). Finally, with the help of the concepts developed in this chapter it becomes possible—and the following chapter will elaborate on this contention—to calculate confidence intervals which with a known probability will contain the population mean, merely with the help of the mean and standard deviation of the sample that we take.

WHAT WE LEARNED

1. A sample mean is on the average equal to the population mean.
2. Sample means of large samples, regardless of the form of the population distribution, are about normally distributed around their mean and the population mean.
3. The probability that a sample mean will differ from the true mean by more than one standard error (of the mean) is about 0.32, by more than two standard errors about 0.05, and so on.

4. The standard error of the mean $(\sigma_{\bar{x}})$ equals the standard deviation of the population divided by the square root of the sample size $\left(\dfrac{\sigma}{\sqrt{n}}\right)$.

5. On the average the sample variance (s^2) is equal to the variance of the population (σ^2).

6. The standard error of the mean $(\sigma_{\bar{x}})$ is approximately equal to the standard deviation of the sample divided by the square root of the sample size (and, if the sample is small, the sample size minus 1).

In brief, for large samples $\sigma_{\bar{x}} \doteq \dfrac{s}{\sqrt{n}}$,

for small samples $\sigma_{\bar{x}} \doteq \dfrac{s}{\sqrt{n-1}}$

NOW SEE WHAT YOU CAN DO WITH THE FOLLOWING PROBLEMS:

1. Does tripling the precision of an estimate mean the same as reducing the standard error of the mean three times?

2. Does tripling the size of a sample increase its precision threefold?

3. Does the precision of an estimate depend on the size of the sample or the sample size relative to the size of the population?

4. Increasing the size of the sample from 49 to 1,225 sampling units has what effect on the standard error of the mean?

5. If you considered the 35 observations of Table 2.1 in Chapter II, p 7, a random sample, what would be the approximate standard error of the mean?

6. Relate the following three distributions to one another: distribution of sample data, distribution of population data, and distribution of sample means, emphasizing the units along the horizontal scale, the means and standard deviations, and the shape and compactness of the three distributions.

7. We know that $\sigma_{\bar{x}}$ equals $\sqrt{\dfrac{\Sigma(m-\bar{m})^2}{L}}$ and also is equal to $\dfrac{\sigma}{\sqrt{n}}$. Show why or why not either formula is useful for finding the value of the standard error of the mean after we have made a sample survey.

8. A sample survey in which 3,000 union members were interviewed revealed that their average annual contribution for educational and political purposes amounted to \$25 with a standard deviation of \$15. Based solely on this information, would you be able to say whether or not the population and/or the sampling distribution of contributions are approximately normally distributed around their mean, and why?

9. Explain why (a) the population mean can be closely approximated by a sample mean, (b) sampling distributions of large samples are approximately normal, and (c) the standard error of the mean is approximately equal to $\dfrac{s}{\sqrt{n}}$, illustrating your contention with the help of throws of two dice.

10. Is a sampling distribution or a population distribution more compact? Why?

VIII

Estimating Means and Totals

A woman's guess is more accurate than a man's certainty.
RUDYARD KIPLING

8.1. CONFIDENCE INTERVAL ESTIMATE OF MEAN

One September night in 1953 some 6,500 volunteer workers rang doorbells in greater St. Louis, Missouri, soliciting contributions for financing an educational community television station. The next day $100,000 rolled into the campaign headquarters in old shoeboxes, shopping bags, envelopes, and similar receptacles. Except for the total amount, little else was known about the campaign. Was this campaign a success? And what lessons might other cities learn from the pioneering experiment? (St. Louis was the first city in the U.S. to attempt the financing of educational television by a door-to-door campaign.)

It was felt that these questions deserved an answer, but how could one get any idea of the conduct of the campaign when the volunteer workers had kept no records?

A statistical Sherlock Holmes was hired to retrace the steps of the campaign workers and "reconstruct what happened on the night of September 24th." Specifically, he was asked to answer the following questions: (1) What was the average contribution? (2) What proportion of people who were approached did contribute?

Making contact with all the 6,500 volunteers and recording their recollections as to how many persons each interviewed, how many contributions they received, etc. (even if they still remembered these details) was out of the question. It would be too expensive and too time-consuming—and the longer it took, the less the volunteers would remember about the campaign.

125

The only way these answers could be obtained was by an estimate based on a probability sample. This, as the reader will realize by now, makes a definite answer impossible, but enables us to state with a known, and often predetermined, confidence that the answer, e.g., the true mean, is contained in an interval of a known width. We will refer to the level of confidence of the estimate as its reliability and to the width of the confidence interval of the estimate as its definiteness. Thus we can say that probability samples make possible estimates of known, and often predetermined, reliability and definiteness.

Let us start with the first question. "What was the average contribution?" The statistical Sherlock Holmes knew how much money had been collected by the 6,500 volunteers. If he could assert with a known confidence about how many contributions the average volunteer had received, multiplying this average by the number of volunteers would give an estimate of the number of contributors. By dividing the $100,000 contributed by this estimate he could estimate the average contribution. We will now watch the statistical detective at work.

His first step was to pick a random sample (with the aid of a table of random numbers) of volunteer workers. The sample size he chose was 100. These 100 campaign workers were asked to fill out a questionnaire containing such questions as "How many people did you contact?" "How many people contributed?" etc.

When he analyzed the answers to these questionnaires, he found that the average volunteer in the sample had received 9.6 contributions with a standard deviation of 6.0. How could he estimate the average number of contributions obtained by all 6,500 campaign workers, i.e., the population mean, from this sample mean?

The practical problem of making such estimates is to find two values, a lower and an upper one, which form an interval having a known and calculable probability of containing the true value. The procedure is very simple. We add and subtract from the sample mean a value reflecting both the required level of confidence and the standard error of the mean, i.e.,

$z\dfrac{s}{\sqrt{n}}.$ (Those who do not care to know the reason for this procedure can proceed directly to formula 8.1. The others may wish to follow the ensuing reasoning.)

In Chapter VII it was shown that, in general, sample means are about normally distributed around the mean of the population. If we know the population mean and the standard error of the mean, it is easy to find two points within which, for instance, 68 per cent of the sample means are expected to fall. We called this interval the one-sigma range, and we can be 68 per cent confident that the mean of a given sample, e.g., the sample we have taken, falls within this interval extending from $\mu - 1.0\sigma_{\bar{x}}$ to $\mu +$ $1.0\sigma_{\bar{x}}$. This is not the only interval that will contain 68 per cent of the sample means. For instance, we could place all 68 per cent of the area in the upper tail of the normal curve, or in the lower tail, etc. Because of the curvature of the normal curve, placing $100 - 68$ or 32 per cent of the area in such a way that equal halves are in the two tails of the normal curve will produce the narrowest interval containing 68 per cent of the total area of the normal curve. Since we are interested in the narrowest possible interval, we will in the future usually place half of the area of nonconfidence, i.e., the total area under the normal curve minus the area of confidence, into each of the two tails.

However, we do not know the population mean. As a matter of fact, our objective is to find an interval in which we can place a given confidence, 68 per cent in this case, that it will contain the population mean. But, having taken a sample, we know the sample mean and the sample standard deviation, and with their help we can approximate the standard error of the mean. Our sample mean has, for instance, a 68 per cent probability of falling in the one-sigma range extending from $\mu - 1.0\sigma_{\bar{x}}$ to $\mu + 1.0\sigma_{\bar{x}}$. There is a 68 per cent probability that our specific sample mean m lies in that interval and, therefore, is no further from the true mean μ than one standard error of the mean either way. By adding one standard error to the value of the sample mean we will have created an interval that has a 34 per cent probability of containing the true mean. While this interval is particularly likely to contain the true mean in case it is larger than our sample mean m, there is a second interval that is particularly likely to contain the true mean in case it is smaller than m. This second interval, which also has 34 per cent probability of containing μ, is obtained by subtracting one standard error from the value of the sample mean. Since the probability of the first interval containing μ is 0.34 and the probability

Chart 8.1   68 PER CENT CONFIDENCE INTERVAL OF μ

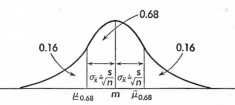

of the second containing μ is also 0.34, the probability that either the first or the second interval contains μ is, by the addition law of probability, $0.34 + 0.34$ or 0.68 (see Chart 8.1).

The first case helps us define the upper 68 per cent confidence limit, which will be connoted $\bar{\mu}_{.68}$, and which is approximated by $m + 1.0 \dfrac{s}{\sqrt{n-1}}$. Large samples, i.e., 30 or more su's, do not need to be adjusted by subtracting 1 from n; therefore, for large samples $\bar{\mu}_{.68} \doteq m + 1.0 \dfrac{s}{\sqrt{n}}$. Likewise, we can find the lower 68 per cent confidence limit, which is connoted by $\underline{\mu}_{.68}$, and which is approximated, in case the sample is large, by $m - 1.0 \dfrac{s}{\sqrt{n}}$. The notation for the 68 per cent confidence is $\underline{\bar{\mu}}_{.68}$. It is approximately equal to $m \pm 1.0 \dfrac{s}{\sqrt{n}}$.

In this way, the statistical detective calculated the lower 68 per cent confidence limit of the average number of contributions per volunteer $\underline{\mu}_{.68}$ to be about $m - 1.0 \dfrac{s}{\sqrt{n}}$ or $9.6 - 1.0 \dfrac{6.0}{\sqrt{100}}$ or 9.0 contributions. The upper 68 per cent confidence limit he found to be $9.6 + 1.0 \dfrac{6.0}{\sqrt{100}}$, or 10.2 contributions.

Our detective is not accustomed to playing so low a percentage. Using a confidence level other than 68 per cent, he would multiply the approximation of the standard error $\dfrac{s}{\sqrt{n}}$ by a factor other than 1.0.

In general confidence limit and interval formulas, z is substituted for 1.0. Depending on the confidence level required, the proper z value is obtained from Table I in the Appendix. One of the more common levels of confidence is the 95 per cent level, the z value for which (for large samples) is 1.96; for a 90 per cent confidence level z is 1.64; for a 99 per cent level of confidence z is 2.58, to mention a few of the more commonly used ones.

In general, for large samples:
the lower confidence limit of the population mean is

$$\underline{\mu} = m - z\sigma_{\bar{x}} \doteq m - z \frac{s}{\sqrt{n}}; \tag{8.1}$$

the upper confidence limit is

$$\bar{\mu} = m + z\sigma_{\bar{x}} \doteq m + z \frac{s}{\sqrt{n}}; \tag{8.2}$$

and the confidence interval is

$$\underline{\bar{\mu}} = m \pm z\sigma_{\bar{x}} \doteq m \pm z \frac{s}{\sqrt{n}}. \tag{8.3}$$

In many studies in business and economics the **95 per cent confidence** level is thought most appropriate. The statistical Sherlock Holmes finds the 95 per cent confidence interval of the average number of contributions per volunteer to extend from $9.6 - 1.96 \dfrac{6.0}{\sqrt{100}}$ or 8.4 to $9.6 + 1.96 \dfrac{6.0}{\sqrt{100}}$ or 10.8.

In Chart 8.2 we have plotted the 68 per cent confidence interval obtained by our detective. The width of the interval, delineated by the **lower and**

Chart 8.2   68 PER CENT CONFIDENCE AND RELIABILITY

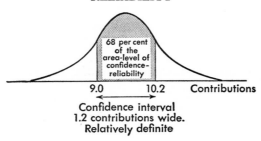

upper confidence limits, i.e., 9.0 and 10.2 contributions, respectively, **is the** definiteness of the estimate. The area under the normal curve **within this** interval (shaded in the chart), expressed as a percentage of the **total area** under the normal curve, is the level of confidence or reliability associated with the estimate. In Chart 8.3, the 95 per cent confidence **interval is**

Chart 8.3   95 PER CENT CONFIDENCE AND RELIABILITY

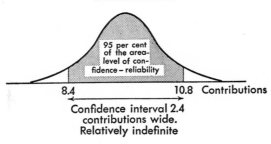

portrayed. Here the width and the relative area are larger, i.e., **the estimate** is less definite, yet more reliable.

Some additional examples appear in order. Let us take the **problem of** the department store that would like to estimate the gross shortage per sale due to clerical errors. A random sample of 2,000 sales checks was carefully checked and found to understate the average sale by 4.00 cents with a standard deviation of 1.0 cent. We would like to be 96 per cent confident in our estimate of the average clerical error.

In answering this question, we may start by asking which formula to apply. Since we seek a confidence interval estimate of a mean and our sample is large, we use Formula 8.3, i.e.,

$$\underline{\mu} \doteq m \pm z \frac{s}{\sqrt{n}}.$$

The department store knows that in its case,

$$m = 4.00,$$
$$s = 1.0, \text{ and}$$
$$n = 2,000.$$

Substituting this information into Formula 8.3, we have

$$\underline{\mu} \doteq 4.00 \pm 2.05 \frac{1.0}{\sqrt{2,000}} = 4.00 \pm 2.05 \frac{1.0}{44.7} = 4.00 \pm 0.046.$$

We can thus assert with a 96 per cent confidence that in this department store the true shortage per sale lies within the interval 3.95 cents to 4.05 cents.

8.2. PLANNING THE SIZE OF THE SAMPLE

Why did the statistical detective sample 100 volunteers? why no more than 100? and why no less than 100? In some respects we had placed the cart before the horse, for before we start sampling we should decide how large a sample should be covered in the survey. There is, however, a good reason for proceeding in the order that we have selected. Once we know the formula for finding confidence interval estimates, it is but a short step to determining the proper sample size.

How then could our Sherlock determine what size sample he should draw? Chronologically, he would sit down to consider what reliability and definiteness he would like his estimate to have. Decisions upon the proper level of reliability and definiteness are highly subjective. Such decisions will reflect the gravity of inappropriate actions that could come about in case an erroneous estimate is used as the basis for action. An error in the estimate of the number of contributions obtained per volunteer for the financing of educational television will not have very serious repercussions—they are likely to be much less serious than those caused by an erroneous estimate concerning the magnitude of the gross shortage per department store sale, particularly if the store institutes remedial means more costly than the errors it is trying to correct. Clearly, therefore, a more definite and reliable estimate is needed by the department store executive than by those persons concerned with learning something about the door-to-door campaign.

How reliable and definite an estimate should be is a highly subjective decision. It requires, among other things, estimating the expense of enlarging the survey, and balancing this expense against the cost of taking unwarranted actions because of an estimate giving an incorrect picture of the facts.

Once the decision concerning appropriate levels of reliability and definiteness has been reached, this information, together with information about the order of magnitude of the standard deviation of the sample to be drawn, will make it possible to estimate the size of the sample.

Let us see why and how. We remember the formula (Formula 8.2) of the upper confidence limit of a mean to be:

$$\bar{\mu} \doteq m + z \frac{s}{\sqrt{n}}.$$

Knowing m, s, z, and n, we found $\bar{\mu}$, the upper confidence limit. But as in any single equation having but one unknown, there is no reason why we could not solve equation 8.2 for an unknown other than $\bar{\mu}$, for instance, n, the sample size. In that case we could solve for n directly by using Formula 8.2, or we might prefer to reorganize the equation so that n stands by itself on the left side. In that case the equation assumes the following form,[1]

$$n \doteq \frac{z^2 s^2}{(\bar{\mu} - m)^2}. \tag{8.4}$$

In Equation 8.4, z^2 reflects the required level of reliability, $(\bar{\mu} - m)^2$ the required definiteness and s the standard deviation. It might take a second look to realize that $(\bar{\mu} - m)$ represents half the width of the acceptable confidence interval, just as $(m - \mu)$ is the other half of the confidence interval; the two taken together make up the entire interval.

While z and $(\bar{\mu} - m)$ have been subjectively arrived at, some knowledge about s still remains to be gained. However, before sampling is undertaken we clearly do not know what the sample standard deviation is. How can

---

[1] $\bar{\mu} \doteq m + z \dfrac{s}{\sqrt{n}}$ can also be written as $\bar{\mu} - m \doteq z \dfrac{s}{\sqrt{n}}.$ Squaring both sides we have, $(\bar{\mu} - m)^2 = \dfrac{z^2 s^2}{n}$, or $n \doteq \dfrac{z^2 s^2}{(\bar{\mu} - m)^2}.$

we learn about its order of magnitude? Usually, there will be one of the following two ways open to us. We know that even if the mean value changes over time the standard deviation pertaining to a given phenomenon tends to remain fairly stable. For this reason we can often make use of standard deviations derived from previous studies. If no previous studies have been made and there is no other prior information available, we can take a small sample in advance and calculate its standard deviation. Usually we like to pretest our questionnaire anyhow, and in conjunction with this test we can get information about the order of magnitude of the sample standard deviation. Since our knowledge about the sample standard deviation is merely an estimate, we are well advised to overestimate it and thus play safe by taking a sample that is somewhat larger than perhaps is necessary. The other sequel is, that with s being only roughly estimated, there is no point in insisting on excessive precision in solving Equation 8.4 for n. While in our first computation we will use a z of 1.96 for a 95 per cent reliability, in the future a value of 2.0 will be sufficiently precise when we solve Equation 8.4.

Let us return to the detective and assume that he, in co-operation with his employers, had agreed upon a 95 per cent confidence level and a confidence interval width of 2.0. Say that he estimated the standard deviation at 6.2 contributions.

Now we are ready to find n, which is approximated by $\dfrac{z^2 s^2}{(\bar{\mu} - m)^2}$.

$$z = 2.0,$$
$$s = 6.2, \text{ and}$$
$$(\bar{\mu} - m) = 1.0.$$

Therefore, $n \doteq \dfrac{2.0^2 \times 6.2^2}{1.0^2}$ or 150. He needs a sample of 150 campaign workers to answer his questionnaire. However, he is afraid that interviewing about 150 persons will take too long and, in the meantime, memories are likely to fade. He is willing to accept a wider confidence interval of 2.5 contributions. Recalculating n he finds that he needs about $\dfrac{2.0^2 \times 6.2^2}{1.25^2}$ or a sample comprising 98 volunteers. To play safe, he decides on a sample of size 100. This, then, is the reason why the sample size in the previous section was 100. This sample produced a 95 per cent confidence interval about 2.4 contributions wide. A sample standard deviation somewhat smaller than anticipated is responsible for a slightly more precise estimate than had been deemed necessary.

8.3. HOW RELIABLE IS THE ESTIMATE?

Since we know that

$$\underline{\mu} \doteq m - z \frac{s}{\sqrt{n}},$$

it takes little effort to show that

$$z \doteq \frac{(m - \underline{\mu})}{s/\sqrt{n}}. \qquad (8.5)$$

On the basis of Formula 8.5 we can calculate the reliability of given estimates. Take the case of the railroad that had 900 of its freight cars selected at random and sampled as to the average number of days the cars were in transit during July. The sample revealed that the company's freight cars had been in transit during July an average of 21 to 22 days, the standard deviation being 10 days. To find the reliability of this estimate, the company can make the following computation:

$$z \doteq \frac{(m - \underline{\mu})}{s/\sqrt{n}} = \frac{0.5}{10/\sqrt{900}} = 1.5.$$

With the help of Table I in the Appendix it can be found that a z value of 1.5 corresponds to an 87 per cent confidence level.

8.4. CONFIDENCE INTERVAL ESTIMATE OF TOTAL

The statistical detective has reached the stage where he is 95 per cent confident that the interval extending from 8.4 to 10.8 contributions per volunteer will contain the true value of the mean. Now his mind moves in a different direction. There were exactly 6,500 volunteer workers known to have participated in the campaign. Multiplying this number by the lower and upper limits of the 95 per cent confidence interval of contributions per volunteer will give him the 95 per cent confidence interval of the total number of contributions made to the campaign.

Since the confidence interval of the mean is already known, we simply multiply the lower and upper limits, respectively, by the total number of volunteers N. In this case, the lower 95 per cent confidence limit will be approximately $8.4 \times 6,500$ or 54,000 contributions, and the upper limit $10.8 \times 6,500$ or 70,000 contributions. If we denote the lower confidence limit of a total or aggregate by $\underline{\theta}$ (pronounced *theta*), the upper one by $\bar{\theta}$, and the confidence interval of a total or aggregate by $\bar{\bar{\theta}}$, we can state that, if the sample is large:

$$\underline{\theta} \doteq \underline{\mu} \times N; \tag{8.6}$$

$$\bar{\theta} \doteq \bar{\mu} \times N; \text{ and} \tag{8.7}$$

$$\underline{\theta} \doteq \underline{\mu} \times N. \tag{8.8}$$

However, in many instances we do not know the confidence interval of the mean and do not care to compute it. Instead, we wish to compute directly the confidence interval of the total or aggregate. The appropriate formula for large samples is:

$$\underline{\theta} \doteq T - z \frac{Ns}{\sqrt{n}}; \tag{8.9}$$

$$\bar{\theta} \doteq T + z \frac{Ns}{\sqrt{n}} \tag{8.10}$$

$$\underline{\theta} \doteq T \pm z \frac{Ns}{\sqrt{n}}, \tag{8.11}$$

where $T = mN$.

As is clearly evident, these formulas are derived by multiplying the corresponding forms of 8.1, 8.2, and 8.3 by N.

Holmes' methodical mind has already calculated that at a 95 per cent level of confidence $\underline{\theta} \doteq (9.6 \times 6,500) - 1.96 \dfrac{(6,500 \times 6.0)}{\sqrt{100}} = 54,000$ and $\bar{\theta} \doteq (9.6 \times 6,500) + 1.96 \dfrac{(6,500 \times 6.0)}{\sqrt{100}} = 70,000.$

The total number of contributors can be estimated as between about 54,000 and 70,000. Actually the detective does not stop here. Remembering that total campaign contributions amounted to $100,000, by dividing the lower and upper limit into $100,000 he finds the 95 per cent confidence interval of the magnitude of the average contribution. He concludes with a 95 per cent confidence that the $1.40 to $1.80 interval will contain the true contribution of the average contributor.

Confidence intervals of population totals are important in connection with work on a state's or country's total income. Let us assume that of the 12,200,000 people who lived in California in 1953, 1,000 were sampled and found to have an average per capita income of $2,040 with a standard deviation of $1,500. What was the 95 per cent confidence interval of the total income of the population of California in 1953?

The 95 per cent confidence interval will be approximated by $T \pm z \dfrac{Ns}{\sqrt{n}}$;

it extends from about $23.8 to $26.0 billion. Were the data correct, we could be 95 per cent confident that the true 1953 annual income of the people of the Golden State would be contained in the $23.8–$26.0 billion interval.

8.5. SMALL SAMPLES

Sometimes we work with samples of fewer than 30 *su*'s. How can confidence intervals be estimated for such small samples? In the preceding chapter we stated that means of random samples taken from a population, whether normal or not, approach a normal distribution around their mean (which we showed to be the same as the true mean), *particularly as the size of the sample increases*. Now we can be more precise about the sample size problem. When the sample size is smaller than 30, we encounter some serious problems in relation to the approximation involved in using the sample standard deviation. W. S. Gosset, who published under the pen name of Student, showed that another theoretical distribution, called after him the *Student-t distribution*, becomes applicable under such circumstances. The sampling distribution of means of small samples taken from a normally distributed population is approximated by the Student-*t* distribution, i.e., the distribution of the statistic

$$t = \frac{m - \mu}{s} \sqrt{n - 1}. \tag{8.12}$$

The *t* distribution is symmetrical but flatter than the normal distribution and approaches the normal curve as the sample size increases (See **Table II** in the Appendix and Chart 8.4).

The areas under a *t* distribution curve have been calculated and are shown in Table II in the Appendix. Since the *t* distribution is symmetrical, we need tabulate its areas only for one half of the curve. As in the case of the normal distribution, only the positive values are tabulated.

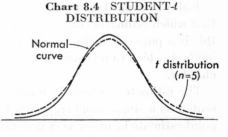

Chart 8.4 STUDENT-*t* DISTRIBUTION

Normal curve

t distribution (*n*=5)

Even this is quite an undertaking, however, since *t* assumes different values, depending on *n*. Usually we are interested in 99, 98, 95, and 90 per cent levels of confidence. We therefore are in particular need of *t* values above or below which we can expect to find 0.5, 1.0, 2.5, and 5.0 per cent of the area under the curve. Let us denote the value of *t* above (or below) which we find the highest (or the lowest) one half of 1 per cent of the area under the curve as $t_{.005}$. Similarly, $t_{.05}$ will be the value above or below which 5 per cent of area under the curve lies.

There is another point that must be mentioned in connection with small samples. We always get a better estimate of the standard deviation of the sampling distribution when we divide the sample standard deviation by $\sqrt{n-1}$ instead of by $\sqrt{n}$. For small samples the confidence interval of the population mean is:

$$\underline{\mu} \doteq m \pm t \frac{s}{\sqrt{n-1}}. \tag{8.13}$$

Here is an example:

If the statistical detective had sampled only 26 volunteers instead of 100, what would be the 95 per cent confidence interval of contributions per average volunteer?

With

$$n = 26,$$
$$m = 9.6,$$
$$s = 6.0, \text{ and}$$
$$t_{.025} \text{ (for } n = 26) = 2.06.$$
$$\underline{\mu} \doteq m \pm t_{.025} \frac{s}{\sqrt{n-1}} = 9.6 \pm 2.06 \frac{6.0}{5}.$$

We could assert, therefore, with 95 per cent confidence that (based on a sample of 26 volunteer workers) the average volunteer collected between about 7 and 12 contributions.

8.6. POINT ESTIMATES

Today the most generally accepted statistical method of estimation is that which estimates confidence intervals. We gave numerous reasons why this is a powerful method. However, we would like to mention one other method, which to no small extent is based on laws explored in the preceding chapter.

The estimate we have in mind is a *point estimate*, i.e., an estimate presented as a single number, which fulfills some important conditions. If a point estimate is, under very general conditions, both unbiased and efficient, we have *a useful estimate*.

When is an estimate unbiased and under what conditions is it efficient? We recall that an estimate is *unbiased* if the average of the sample estimates comes nearer and nearer to the true population value as the number of samples (all of the same size) is increased indefinitely. In the preceding chapter it had been shown in an example, and we had stated that it could be proved to be generally true, that the arithmetic mean, m, meets this condition.

In general it can be said that an estimate is *efficient* if it produces estimates that fluctuate as little as possible from sample to sample, i.e., have the smallest possible sampling variation measured in terms of standard deviations.

We usually prefer confidence interval estimates to point estimates. Point estimates are unlikely to be precisely equal to the parameter, and they do not indicate the margin of error to which they are subject. Confidence interval estimates make possible estimates of a known or predetermined reliability and definiteness, and in this characteristic lies their merit.

YOU LEARNED

1. The first step in designing a sample for estimating a confidence interval is to decide on an appropriate level of confidence, i.e., reliability of the results, and width of the confidence interval, i.e., definiteness of the results. Agreement on appropriate criteria of reliability and definiteness is purely subjective and reflects the relative importance of the issues, and availability of time and resources.

2. The appropriate sample size can be calculated once reliability and definiteness of results are agreed upon and a rough estimate of the magnitude of the standard deviation is available.

3. The reliability of a confidence interval estimate of a mean based on a large sample can be calculated from: $z \doteq \dfrac{(m - \mu)}{s/\sqrt{n}}$.

4. If the sample is small, i.e., if n is smaller than 30, we use in order to get a confidence interval estimate of a mean a t value in place of a z value and approximate the standard error of the mean by $\dfrac{s}{\sqrt{n-1}}$. The confidence interval of a population mean based on a small sample is: $\bar{\mu} \doteq m \pm t\,\dfrac{s}{\sqrt{n-1}}$.

5. The confidence interval of a population mean based on a large sample is: $\bar{\mu} \doteq m \pm z\,\dfrac{s}{\sqrt{n}}$.

6. The confidence interval of a population total or aggregate based on a large sample is: $\bar{\theta} \doteq Nm \pm z\,\dfrac{(Ns)}{\sqrt{n}}$.

7. In planning a survey to estimate population means, the proper sample size can be computed from: $n \doteq \dfrac{z^2 \times s^2}{(\bar{\mu} - m)^2}$.

SEE HOW WELL YOU CAN MAKE THE FOLLOWING ESTIMATES:

1. In January, 1954, a sample survey of 1,713 Negroes was made in St. Louis. The question asked was the number of years of formal schooling the interviewee had had. (For instance, a person with 8 years in grammar school and 3 years in high school would be considered to have a total of 11 years of formal schooling). It was found that the average Negro in the sample had 8.20 years of formal schooling with a standard deviation of 2.10 years.

   a. What statement can you make with 99 per cent confidence regarding the average schooling of Negroes in St. Louis?

   b. With St. Louis in 1954 having a population of 171,000 Negroes, what statement can you make with 99 per cent confidence concerning the total number of years the Negro population of St. Louis had spent in school prior to 1954?

2. OPS Airlines has a fleet of 13 DC3's. Last year 28 of its flights were checked as to the number of passengers carried on arrival in St. Paul. These 28 flights, which constitute a representative sample of all OPS flights coming into St. Paul, had an average of 17 passengers with a standard deviation of 5.0 passengers. If you are willing to assume a 5 per cent risk of being wrong in the long run, what statement can you make about the average number of passengers per OPS Airlines' flights coming into St. Paul last year?

3. A research organization has been assigned the job of estimating, with the help of a sample survey, the indebtedness of the average family in the United States. After careful consideration it has been decided to insist on an estimate having a 97 per cent level of confidence, which will be off the true value by no more than $150 either way. How large a sample is called for?

4. A sample survey covering 1,000 families revealed that the average home in the community had 4.2 rooms, with a standard deviation of 1.0 rooms.

   a. How confident can you be that the average home in the community has somewhere between 4.0 and 4.4 rooms?

   b. If the community has 124,000 homes, what statement can you make with 94 per cent confidence regarding the total number of rooms in the community?

5. A trade organization representing druggists has decided to learn more about the average annual drug bill of New Yorkers. It would like to pinpoint the estimate and not permit it to be off by more than $5.00 either way, and it insists on placing 95 per cent confidence in the estimate. Make any additional assumptions you need, and determine the required sample size.

6. A representative sample of 3,000 persons was taken and interviewees asked about their annual medical bill in 1956. The mean bill turned out to be $65.00 with a standard deviation of $15.00. What can you say with 90 per cent confidence about the total medical bill of all 165.0 million Americans?

7. Twenty-seven families were interviewed as to their monthly rent. They were found to pay an average of $42 monthly rent, with a standard deviation of $6.50. Make a 98 per cent confidence interval estimate.

8. A sample of 1,600 sample units revealed that the number of inhabitants per dwelling has a standard deviation of 0.25 inhabitants. With what confidence can we assert that the sample mean does not deviate by more than 0.15, either way, from the true number of inhabitants per dwelling?

9. Six hundred twenty-one Boston families were sampled as to their last year's income. The sample produced a mean of $2,900, with a standard deviation of $850. With a risk of being wrong two times in a hundred, estimate last year's total income of the 900,000 families in Boston.

10. Discuss the difference between a confidence interval estimate and a maximum-likelihood estimate.

11. A recent sample survey of 1,960 families revealed that their average amount of installment debt was $420.0 with a standard deviation of $100.0. What can you say with 92 per cent confidence about the installment debt of the average family in the United States?

12. The 1955 Survey of Consumer Finances found that the mean 1954 income of the 2,805 families surveyed was $4,900. Assuming the standard deviation was $1,100, how confident can we be that the mean 1954 income of all families in the United States was somewhere between $4,850 and $4,950?

IX

Binomial Distribution—Success or Failure, How Likely Are They?

And I believe that the Binomial Theorem and a Bach Fugue are, in the long run, more important than all the battles of history.

JAMES HILTON

9.1. PROBABILITY OF FINDING DEFECTIVES

Leaders of the business community have realized for some time the desirability of impressing the younger generation with the wonders and might of American industry. Many companies open their doors to visiting school classes, making available to them the best of their talents in order to explain to these youngsters the achievements of which the company is especially proud. The other day, the president of the Hobby-Bobby Toy Company personally conducted a tour of students. When they came to a machine that makes rubber balls, he decided to use the balls as an example of the high degree of standardization and quality reliability of toy manufacturing. An engineer by training, he remembered that the rubber ball machine was most reliable, producing on the average no more than 2 per cent defective balls. With this in mind, he proceeded to pick five rubber balls that were just coming off the machine, and in the presence of the visitors, had them checked as to their defects. The test was very simple: the ball was submerged in water and squeezed so that any hole in it would be revealed by air bubbles coming to the surface. Most unfortunately, two of the five balls were duds and produced bubbles. One might think that this revelation would embarrass the proud host, but it did not. He led the group to the company auditorium and started to lecture.

Well, young men and women, you must think that I am either running a fourth-rate establishment that produces many defective rubber balls, or that you caught me bragging, or both. Mind you, I am not going to try to explain away the fact that you found two out of five rubber balls defective. I would like, however, to explain to you in some detail how an inspection result such as we obtained can come about, what it means to us, and what we intend to do about it. Let me say first—and I know this will startle you—that we are not going to do a thing about it. I knew when I had you inspect five balls that there was a slim chance that you would find one defective ball and an even slimmer chance that you would find two of them faulty. As a matter of fact, we know that in about four out of 1,000 cases we are likely to find two out of five balls defective. We know this from the *binomial distribution* that helps us estimate the probability of one set of alternatives.

I had instructed the foreman to set up the machine and maintain it so that we will get on the average no more than 2 per cent rejects. It would be too expensive to make sure that there would be no more than 1 or 1/2 per cent rejects. Rubber balls are permitted to have a hole once in a while. No human lives are endangered, you understand.

I knew that there was about four one-thousandths of a chance that you would find two of the five balls defective. Our customers receive on the average a 98 per cent perfect product, although it sometimes happens that one particular customer has a smaller percentage, while another has a completely defect-free shipment. They trust us that their shipments over the years will even out to a 98 per cent perfect product. In order to assure ourselves of this outcome, we have a quality control unit. Every day we take a predetermined number of samples at fixed intervals and test them. This test is based on the *binomial distribution* that helps us estimate the probability of one set of alternatives, which in our case is good versus defective balls. Here is the chart (Chart 9.1) that goes with the rubber ball machine that we inspected. In the 11 tests preceding the one we made

Chart 9.1 CONTROL CHART
(Defective balls in sample lots of 5 balls each.)

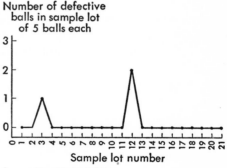

Number of defective balls in sample lot of 5 balls each

Sample lot number

Source: Hypothetical data.

together, in ten cases no rejects were found and in one case, a single ball was faulty. The assistant foreman tells me just now that, since this group made its reading, another two tests have been made, and neither produced a single defective ball. By the way, there was, of course, a chance that our finding two defective balls was not entirely due to chance but that something may have gone wrong with the machine or the raw rubber fed into it. However, the last two readings make this most unlikely and we will not investigate this possibility unless we get more rejects than we should during the next few hours.

Binomial formula. The executive's calculations, much of his quality control, and his confidence in the uniformity of his product are based on the binomial distribution, which is associated with the name of Jacob Bernoulli (1654–1705). Let us look into this useful mathematical device. We are assuming that 2 per cent of the rubber balls are defective, i.e., the probability of getting a defective ball is 0.02. By drawing 5 balls at random, 5, 4, 3, 2, 1, or none can be defective. Since our selection involves a total of 5 items, there are $5 + 1$ or 6 possible outcomes or events. Here is the general rule: Whenever we can select n different items, there will be $n + 1$ different possible outcomes or events.

What is the probability of these events? On the assumption that in the long run 2 per cent of all balls are defective, the probability that all 5 balls drawn in succession will be defective is $(0.02)^5$. Let us take another possibility, namely 4 defective balls and one perfect ball. The probability of drawing 4 defective balls is $(0.02)^4$ and that of drawing one perfect ball is (0.98). But we must take into account that ball Number 1 might be all right and the others duds, or Number 1 might be a dud, Number 2 perfect and the rest duds, etc. In other words, there are $5C4$ or 5 combinations in which 4 defective balls and 1 perfect ball may be combined. If we multiply these three values, i.e., $(0.02)^4 \times (0.98) \times 5$, we have the answer: there is a 0.000000784 probability that 4 of the 5 balls sampled will be defective.   (In the first case, i.e., where all the balls are defective, and in the sixth case, i.e., where all the balls are perfect, there is only one possible combination; and thus the values $(0.02)^5$ and $(0.98)^5$, respectively, remain unchanged).

We could go on and do this for all the possible events. In fact, we have made all the calculations in Table 9.1. Column 5 gives the probability of each of the six possible events.

We may also look at the problem from this viewpoint: If we select 5 balls and each one is either defective or perfect, i.e., falls in one of two categories (hence the name "binomial," which means "two names"), we know that we must get either 0, 1, 2, 3, 4, or 5 defective balls. Consequently, the probability of getting either 0, 1, 2, 3, 4, or 5 defective balls will be 1.0. From Chapter V, we know that by the addition law of probability the probability of K mutually exclusive events occurring is $p(A) + p(B) + \cdots + p(K) = 1.0$. Thus, in our case of 5 balls and, therefore, 6 different events, $p(A) + p(B) + p(C) + p(D) + p(E) + p(F) = 1.0$. Event A means finding 0 defectives, event B, 1 defective, etc.

Does this mean that $p(A)$ equals $1/6$? Not by any means. The probabilities of the six possible events are not all equal. If, for example, the true proportion of defectives in the large group or population of balls from which we select 5 balls is 0.80, i.e., of all balls produced 80 per cent are defective, it seems reasonable that the probability of getting 4 defectives out of our sample of 5 is greater than that of getting 1 defective. It now becomes clear that the probabilities of the 6 possible results will not only be unequal but that they will differ, depending on the proportion of defectives in the population from which the 5 are chosen. Regardless of their individual magnitudes, however, they will add up to 1.0.

Table 9.1 PROBABILITIES OF 0 TO 5 REJECTS OF A TOTAL OF FIVE BALLS TESTED AND THEIR RESPECTIVE EXPECTED FREQUENCY
(Assuming that $p = 0.02$)

Number of Defectives	Probability of Successive: Defectives	Non-defectives	Number of Combinations	Probability of Events with Indicated Number of Defectives	Expected Frequency*
1	*2*	*3*	*4*	*5*	*6*
5	$(0.02)^5$		1	$(0.02)^5 \quad = 0.0000000032$	0.0000024
4	$(0.02)^4$	(0.98)	5	$5(0.02)^4(0.98) = 0.000000784$	0.059
3	$(0.02)^3$	$(0.98)^2$	10	$10(0.02)^3(0.98)^2 = 0.0000768$	0.57
2	$(0.02)^2$	$(0.98)^3$	10	$10(0.02)^2(0.98)^3 = 0.003764$	2.80
1	(0.02)	$(0.98)^4$	5	$5(0.02)(0.98)^4 = 0.0922$	69
0		$(0.98)^5$	1	$(0.98)^5 = \quad 0.9039$	677.9
	Total			1.00	750

* The expected frequency of an event is the product of the probability of the event (associated with a given number of defectives) and the total number of cases.

The problem is to allocate this total probability of 1.0 among the 6 possible alternative sample results. We can do this by considering the total probability of 1.0 to be $(0.02 + 0.98)^5$, which is $(1.0)^5$ or 1.0. The six values in Column 5 of Table 9.1 are equivalent to the six terms obtained by expanding the binomial expression of $(0.02 + 0.98)^5$, and add up to 1.0. These 6 parts of the total of 1.0 are equal to the probabilities we are looking for.

In our case p is 0.02 and q is 0.98. We can therefore write this binomial in a more general form, namely $(p + q)^5$, which is equal to 1.0.[1]

The expansion of $(p + q)^5$ is

$$p^5 + 5p^4q + 10p^3q^2 + 10p^2q^3 + 5pq^4 + q^5.$$

[1] Expressions of the type $(p + q)^n$ on first glance may appear unfamiliar; but you will remember $(a + b)^2$, which is equal to $a^2 + 2ab + b^2$ and is perhaps the simplest binomial we know.

The numerical coefficients, often also called binomial coefficients, are:

1   5   10   10   5   1

which can be expressed as combinations, i.e.,[2]

$5C5$ $5C4$ $5C3$ $5C2$ $5C1$ $5C0.$

They can be looked upon as the expansion of $5Cx$.

Having left out of the expansion of $(p + q)^5$ all the numerical coefficients, we are left with

p^5 p^4q p^3q^2 p^2q^3 pq^4 $q^5.$

They can be looked upon as the expansion of $p^x \times q^{5-x}$.

$(p + q)^5$ can therefore be written as $\displaystyle\sum_{x=0}^{5} 5Cx(p^x)(q^{5-x}) = 1.0$; and since in

our case p is 0.02, we have $\displaystyle\sum_{x=0}^{5} 5Cx(0.02^x)(0.98^{5-x}) = 1.0$.   If we should be

---

[2] Pascal devised about 300 years ago a triangle, called "Pascal's Triangle," from which one can read off very neatly the binomial coefficients that go with different n's.   Here is Pascal's Triangle.   You will notice that after the first two, any binomial coefficient in this triangle is the sum of the two just above it.

PASCAL'S TRIANGLE

Number in the Sample-n	Binomial Coefficients									
1					1		1			
2				1		2		1		
3			1		3		3		1	
4		1		4		6		4		1
5	1		5		10		10		5		1
6	1		6		15		20		15		6		1
7	1		7		21		35		35		21		7		1
8	1		8		28		56		70		56		28		8		1
9	1		9		36		84		126		126		84		36		9		1

asked about the probability that all five randomly selected balls will be defective, we put a 5 in place of the x and get $5C5(0.02^5)(0.98^0)$, which is equal to $1(0.02^5)1$ or 0.0000000032. This answer coincides with that in the first row of Column five in Table 9.1. Similarly, we can find the probability of having picked 4, 3, 2, 1, or no defective balls. In Chart 9.2 these results are plotted as a histogram representing a so-called binomial distribution. Specifically, it is the binomial distribution for $p = 0.02$ and $n = 5$, with x varying between 0 and 5. For

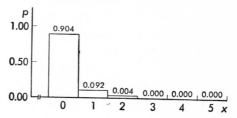

Chart 9.2 BINOMIAL DISTRIBUTION FOR $p = 0.02$ AND $n = 5$

each value of x there is a corresponding bar on the binomial chart.

The general formula for the binomial distribution is:

$$nCx(p^x)(q^{n-x}) \text{ or } \frac{n!}{x!(n-x)!}(p^x)(q^{n-x}).$$ (9.1)

Frequently we are not satisfied to know the probability of successive events. Let us take our rubber ball example. If we draw, let us say, a sample of 5 balls 750 times, we need to know how many times we can expect to find 5, 4, 3, 2, 1, or no defective balls. This kind of question can be answered by multiplying the binomial distribution by, let us say M, the total number of trials (in our case 750). The resulting number is the *expected frequency* of outcomes (see Column 6 in Table 9.1).[3]

Some examples. Let us see what the binomial distribution can do for the student who, while not adverse to good grades, likes extracurricular activities as well. One day the instructor informs the class that next week there will be an examination. Eight multiple choice questions, each permitting four alternatives, will be given. In order to get a grade of C, five of the eight questions must be answered correctly. What are the chances of getting a C in the examination, if the student is guided solely by random guessing?

$$n = 8, x = 5, p = 0.25.$$

Therefore,

$$\frac{n!}{x!(n-x)!}(p^x)(q^{n-x}) = \frac{8!}{5!(3)!}(0.25^5)(0.75^3) = 56(0.00097)(0.422) = 0.02;$$

[3] The formula for the expected frequency is therefore:

$$nCx(M)(p^x)(q^{n-x}) \text{ or } \frac{n!M}{x!(n-x)!}(p^x)(q^{n-x}).$$

or our student has but a 0.02 probability of answering correctly five of the eight questions, should he choose to gamble.

Finally, let us see what the binomial distribution can do for the farmer who wishes to increase his dairy herd. Farmer Jones has 20 cows, all two to three years old. While he considers buying some more cows in order to increase his herd rapidly, it occurs to him that he might rely on the offspring of his own cows. During the next four months alone, ten of them will calve. Obviously only heifers will increase his herd. He thinks that if eight of his expected ten calves were to be heifers, he would not need to buy cows at this time. He wonders what his chances are to get eight heifers. (We exclude the possibility of twins or triplets as well as cases of death; or we might say that these cases are assumed to cancel each other.)

$$n = 10, \ x = 8, \ p = 0.50.$$

Therefore,

$$\frac{n!}{x!(n-x)!} \ (p^x)(q^{n-x}) = \frac{10!}{8!(2)!} \ (0.50^8)(0.50^2) = 45(0.50^{10}) = 45(0.00097)$$
$$= 0.044;$$

or there is about a 0.044 probability that eight out of farmer Jones's next ten calves will be heifers.[4]

Shape of binomial distribution. Looking at the shape of the binomial distribution in Table 9.1., we see that it is skewed. There are also binomial distributions that are symmetrical. The rule is (and it is an important one) that *as p gets closer and closer to being equal to q, i.e., as p approaches 0.50, and as n increases, the binomial distribution becomes more and more symmetrical and more normal; or to put it differently, the binomial distribution is closely approximated by the normal distribution if np or nq are 5 or more.*

[4] Farmer Jones is probably not particular about getting exactly 8 heifers; he wouldn't mind at all having more than 8. The probability of getting at least 8 heifers is slightly greater than that of getting exactly 8 heifers. To calculate the probability of getting at least 8 heifers, we would have to calculate the probability of getting 9 and 10 heifers in addition to the probability of getting 8. The chances of getting 9 heifers out of 10 calves is smaller than that of getting 8 out of 10, and getting 10 out of 10 is even more unlikely. Let us calculate these latter two probabilities.

$$\frac{10!}{9!(1)!} \ (0.50^9)(0.50^1) = 10(0.50^{10}) = 0.0097.$$

$$\frac{10!}{10!(0)!} \ (0.50^{10})(0.50^0) = 1(0.50^{10}) = 0.00097.$$

Adding these three probabilities, i.e., 0.0436 + 0.0097 + 0.00097, we can conclude that there is a 0.054 probability that Farmer Jones will get at least 8 heifers from his 10 cows who are to calve within the next 4 months. He is well advised to go out and buy some cows.

In Chart 9.3, we see a binomial distribution with p equal to q. Although n is small (it is 6), this distribution is symmetrical and approximately normal. The opposite holds true, too. Very lopsided success/failure ratios, particularly for small samples, will be badly skewed. Our rubber ball example exhibits a strong skewness (see Chart 9.2). Chart 9.4 portrays an in-between case.

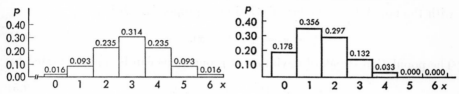

Chart 9.3 BINOMIAL DISTRIBUTION FOR $p = 0.50$ AND $n = 6$ **Chart 9.4** BINOMIAL DISTRIBUTION FOR $p = 0.25$ AND $n = 6$

9.2. THE BINOMIAL SAMPLING DISTRIBUTION OF PERCENTAGES

Our interest in the binomial distribution is justified by the fact that it well describes the *sampling distribution of proportions, percentages, and probabilities*.[5]

Rubber balls, as so many products, have the dichotomous characteristic of either being defective or nondefective. The entirety of rubber balls produced by the Hobby-Bobby Toy Company constitutes a *binomial population*, since all observations are classified as having or lacking a certain characteristic. From this binomial population random samples, all of size n, can be drawn, and their statistics will form a sampling distribution of proportions. Sampling distributions of proportions can have a variety of shapes. However, if the sample is large and the success cases are about equal to the failure cases, or $n\pi$ is about $n(1 - \pi)$, as approximated by np and nq, this sampling distribution can be closely approximated by the normal distribution.

What about the mean and standard deviation of the sampling distribution of proportions? The mean of the sampling distribution as well as of the binomial population is[6]

$$\mu = \pi, \tag{9.2}$$

[5] From now on what is stated about proportions will also hold for percentages and probabilities.

[6] Proportions can be thought of as special cases of the mean. They can be calculated with the help of Formula 3.5 that $\mu = \dfrac{\Sigma x}{N}$, and have the same properties as the mean. If we define a variate x as a ball that can be defective or nondefective, and give a defective

and can be approximated by

$$\mu \doteq p. \tag{9.3}$$

Like the standard error of the mean, the standard error of proportions is the standard deviation of the population divided by the square root of the sample size.

$$\sigma_p = \frac{\sigma}{\sqrt{n}},$$

with the population standard deviation of proportions being[7]

$$\sigma = \sqrt{\pi(1 - \pi)}. \tag{9.4}$$

The population standard deviation of proportions can be approximated by

$$\sigma \doteq \sqrt{p(1 - p)} = \sqrt{pq}. \tag{9.5}$$

Thus, the standard error of proportions is

$$\sigma_p = \frac{\sqrt{\pi(1 - \pi)}}{\sqrt{n}} = \sqrt{\frac{\pi(1 - \pi)}{n}}, \tag{9.6}$$

and can be approximated by

$$\sigma_p \doteq \frac{\sqrt{pq}}{\sqrt{n}} = \sqrt{\frac{pq}{n}}. \tag{9.7}$$

---

ball the value 1 and a nondefective ball that of 0, Σx is the number of defectives among all N balls. $\frac{\Sigma x}{N}$ is both μ and the proportion of defective balls in the population, π.

[7] We can readily verify Formula 9.4. For instance, in the case of the Hobby-Bobby Toy Company, with $\pi = 0.02$,

$$\sigma = \sqrt{\pi(1 - \pi)} = \sqrt{0.02(1 - 0.02)} = \sqrt{0.02(0.98)}.$$

We know from Formula 4.3 on page 53 that $\sigma = \sqrt{\frac{\Sigma x^2}{N} - \left(\frac{\Sigma x}{N}\right)^2}$. The smallest group of observations that can have exactly 2 per cent 1's is one of 100, with 2 1's and 98 0's; $\Sigma x = 2$. Since x is always 1 or 0, and since $1^2 = 1$ and $0^2 = 0$, $\Sigma x^2 = 2$. Thus,

$$\sigma = \sqrt{\frac{\Sigma x^2}{N} - \left(\frac{\Sigma x}{N}\right)^2} = \sqrt{\frac{2}{100} - \left(\frac{2}{100}\right)^2}$$

$$= \sqrt{\frac{2}{100}\left(1 - \frac{2}{100}\right)}$$

$$= \sqrt{\frac{2}{100}\left(\frac{98}{100}\right)}$$

$$= \sqrt{0.02(0.98)}.$$

9.3. THE NO-BI (NORMAL-BINOMIAL DISTRIBUTION) KINSHIP

We have stated that under certain conditions the binomial distribution can be approximated by the normal distribution. To demonstrate the closeness of this relationship, we will apply normal curve methods as well as binomial methods to one and the same problem. We will analyze the following hypothetical case: One Willy Lyman Miller has the reputation that about half of the customers he waits on make a purchase. One day Sam Greene, the sales manager, without Miller's knowledge, makes a bet that next Saturday 11 of Miller's first 19 customers will make a purchase. At night, when he tells his son about the bet, Junior remarks after some contemplation, "Dad, you placed a poor bet; you really don't have much of a chance."

How come? How poor are Greene's chances? Let us first use the binomial method. Since $n = 19$, $x = 11$ and $p = 0.50$,

$$\frac{n!}{x!(n-x)!} (p^x)(q^{n-x}) = \frac{19!}{11!8!} (0.50^{11})(0.50^8)$$
$$= 75,582(0.00049)(0.0039)$$
$$= 75,582(0.000001911)$$
$$= 0.1444.$$

This is rather an involved calculation.[8] Why don't we use the normal curve method? Before we try our hand at this, we must point to one major difference between the normal and the binomial distribution, one which prevails even where their shapes closely approximate each other. Binomial distributions are essentially discrete distributions. We encounter only whole (or integral) numbers of successes or failures; not so normal distributions, which are continuous. To be able to use the normal instead of the binomial distribution, we use a trick. We spread the discrete variate over a continuous scale. In our example we will spread 11 from 10.5 to 11.5. Next we calculate the area under the normal curve above the 10.5 to 11.5 interval. The method for accomplishing this is well known to us from Chapter IV. First we calculate the z value for 10.5 (z_1) and then the z value for 11.5 (z_2). These z values are then interpreted in terms of areas under the normal curve and finally one is subtracted from the other.

---

[8] It is true that with the help of binomial-probability paper the computational work could be reduced. For a description of how to use such paper see Wilfred J. Dixon and Frank J. Massey, Jr., *Introduction to Statistical Analysis* (New York, McGraw-Hill Book Company, Inc., 1951), pp. 196–99.

Since our data are sample and not population data, z instead of being equal to $\dfrac{x - \mu}{\sigma}$ will be equal to $\dfrac{x - m}{s}$. In this case,

m is the mean of success cases in the sample, and
s is the standard deviation of success cases in the sample.

Both m and s are expressed in absolute numbers, while mean and standard deviation of the binomial population were stated in relative numbers, i.e., proportions.

We stated earlier that mean and standard deviation of the binomial population are approximately equal to the statistics p and $\sqrt{pq}$, respectively. By multiplying p by n and $\sqrt{pq}$ by $\sqrt{n}$ we convert the relative values to absolute ones, giving us[9]

$$m = np \text{ and } s = \sqrt{npq}.$$

Thus,
$$m = np = 19 \times 0.50 = 9.5, \text{ and}$$
$$s = \sqrt{npq} = \sqrt{9.5 \times 0.50} = 2.18.$$

Then,
$$z_1 = \frac{10.5 - 9.5}{2.18} = \frac{1.0}{2.18} = 0.46, \quad \text{and}$$
$$z_2 = \frac{11.5 - 9.5}{2.18} = \frac{2.0}{2.18} = 0.92.$$

The area under the normal curve for $z_2 = 0.92$ is 0.3212 and that for $z_1 = 0.46$ is 0.1772. As shown in Chart 9.5, we are interested in the shaded area between 10.5 and 11.5 customers.

Chart 9.5   FINDING AREAS UNDER NORMAL CURVE

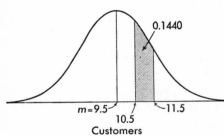

The difference between them is 0.1440, which is also the probability that Willy Miller will succeed in selling to 11 of his next 19 customers and that Manager Greene will win his bet. Junior was right, and he could have obtained his result by using either the normal distribution or binomial distribution method. As we see, the difference in the results, 0.1444 and 0.1440, is practically nil.

Even in this relatively simple problem—remember that instead of dealing with 19!, 0.50^{11}, and 0.50^8, we might perhaps be confronted with something

[9] In reality we multiply the variance $s = pq$ by n, which gives us npq, and obtain the standard deviation by the square root.

like $200!$, 0.45^{191}, and 0.55^9—the convenience of the normal distribution method can be appreciated.

Cumulative probabilities. Often we are interested in knowing not the probability of selling to 11 of the next 19 customers, i.e., a specific probability, but instead, what the chance is to sell to at least 11 of 19 customers, i.e., a cumulative probability. This actually is a much more common type of problem. The binomial distribution method would require solving the same binomial equation 9 times. We would have to calculate the probability of Miller's selling to 11, 12, 13, 14, 15, 16, 17, 18, and 19 of his next 19 customers, and then add these probability figures.

If we use the normal curve method we have no more work than when we calculated the probability of Miller's selling to a specific number of customers. As a matter of fact, it involves less work. Here is what we do: Since z_2 is at the very right end of the normal curve, we know that its value is 0.5000. We are left with calculating z_1 and subtracting its corresponding area under the normal curve from 0.5000. As before, z_1 is 0.46 and its corresponding area under the normal curve is 0.1772. $(0.5000 - 0.1772) = 0.3228$, which also is the probability that Willy Miller will sell a bottle of hair tonic, a cement mixer, or whatever it is he may be selling to at least 11 of his next 19 customers.

WHAT WAS LEARNED:

1. A binomial population is one in which all observations are classified as having or lacking a certain characteristic.

2. A binomial distribution is a probability distribution expressing the probability of one set of dichotomous alternatives, e.g., success or failure.

3. The formula of the binomial distribution is

$$nCx(p^x)(q^{n-x}) \text{ or } \frac{n!}{x!(n-x)!}(p^x)(q^{n-x}).$$

4. With the help of the binomial formula we can calculate the probability of getting x successes in n trials given n, x, and p.

5. The magnitudes of p and n uniquely determine a particular binomial distribution.

6. The binomial distribution is closely approximated by the normal distribution, particularly if n is large and $p = q$, or when np and nq are both 5 or more. Since the use of normal curve area tables is much simpler than computations based on the binomial distribution, this kinship is of great importance.

7. The sampling distribution of proportions can be well described by the binomial distribution, with the true mean $\mu = \pi$ and the true standard deviation $\sigma = \sqrt{\dfrac{\pi(1 - \pi)}{n}}$, which can be approximated by $\mu \doteq p$ and $\sigma \doteq \sqrt{\dfrac{pq}{n}}$.

8. The fact that the sampling distribution of proportions can be closely approximated by the normal distribution, in case $n\pi$ and $n(1 - \pi)$ are both 5 or more, is very important, since it greatly facilitates the estimation of confidence intervals for proportions.

DRAW ON BERNOULLI'S WORK AND ANSWER THE FOLLOWING QUESTIONS:

1. If 30 per cent of attacking aircraft are expected to be shot down before reaching their target, what is the likelihood that all 5 attacking planes will reach their target?

2. If air defense had been perfected to such an extent that 70 per cent of the attacking aircraft would probably be downed before being able to hit their target, in what percentage of the time can we expect to have downed all 5 enemy planes before they can attack?

3. Bankers are becoming increasingly interested in seeing that their clients apply good business practices in their operations. One morning the executive vice-president of a bank enters the department store of a client to check its sales personnel. While 80 per cent of the store's sales force is topnotch, the other 20 per cent are substandard. The executive vice-president observes eight salesmen while they are waiting on customers. What are the chances that he will find four of them substandard?

4. Jim, Bill, and Dick Smith are all partners in the law firm of Smith, Smith, and Smith. While they are supposed to be in their office at 9 o'clock in the morning, the Smiths have the reputation of not getting to the office on time 6 out of 10 mornings. One morning, Mr. Frank P. Mogul, one of the Smiths' most important clients, enters the offices of the law firm at 9 o'clock sharp. Mr. Mogul is known for his respect for punctuality. His coming is unannounced and he finds none of the three Smiths in their office. Enraged, he severs his business connections with Smith, Smith, and Smith. When the Smiths hear about his reasons for this, they are upset and an argument ensues, in which Jim asks Dick, "With each of us late 60 per cent of the time, what are the chances of a client meeting all three of us on time in the morning?" What is the answer to this loaded question?

5. When five dice are thrown simultaneously, calculate the probabilities of 0, 1, 2, 3, 4, and 5 of the throws being six-spots. Plot this binomial distribution in the form of a histogram.

6. Continental Can Works, Inc., manufactures metal containers on the West Coast. All containers pass through a machine that inspects the outside shape and contour and automatically rejects substandard containers. This part is a 100 per cent inspection. For all the other characteristics a sample test is used. If operation is set up in such a manner that on the average 6 per cent of all containers are nonuniform in glass thickness, and at fixed intervals samples of 7 containers are taken, what is the probability that there will be no more than one reject in an inspection batch?

7. Using the data of Exercise 6, construct a histogram of the various possible numbers of rejects in an inspection batch.

8. Using Pascal's Triangle, compute the expected frequency of getting 3, 2, 1, or 0 tails, if three honest coins are tossed each time and if the total number of your tosses is 25.

9. The Whiteflour Bread Company sends its trucks to stores to deliver fresh bread and pick up stale loaves.   In the past 5 per cent of its weekly deliveries have been returned stale.   This daily figure has been stable for a long time.   Based on this information, design a problem that can be solved by means of the binomial distribution, and solve it.

10. The makers of Sleek-Lick hair tonic had for years been sponsoring a radio show that they thought was listened to by about 5 per cent of the population.   A newly hired assistant to the president of the company suggested that the company check whether such a percentage of the population really tunes in on the program. A carefully designed sample of 150 persons revealed that only 5 persons were listening to the Sleek-Lick program.   On the assumption that 5 per cent of the population tune in on the program, how likely is it that in a sample of 150 listeners at least 5 are found listening to the show?

X

Estimating Percentages

According to a 1947 United States Department of Agriculture survey of 2,203 males 16 years or older: 98 per cent of all American males own socks![1]

10.1. CONFIDENCE INTERVAL ESTIMATE OF PERCENTAGE

Often we are interested in estimating population characteristics other than the mean or total. Estimates of population percentages, proportions, or probabilities are very commonly called for. For instance, the second question the statistical detective whom we met in Chapter VIII had been asked to answer was: "How many of the people who were called upon to contribute to the campaign for educational television did, in fact, do so?" We know the response obtained from our sample of 100 volunteer workers: 82 per cent of the families visited made contributions. To take this sample percentage and use it to generalize about the percentage that holds for the entire population is our immediate task.

Population percentages can be inferred from sample percentages. Such inferences are possible because of the properties of the distribution of sample percentages developed in the preceding chapter. We recall that the distribution of sample percentages is binomial with its mean

$$\mu \doteq p,$$

Formula 9.3, and its standard deviation,

$$\sigma_p \doteq \sqrt{\frac{pq}{n}}.$$

---

[1] U.S. Department of Agriculture, *Men's Preferences Among Selected Clothing Items* (Washington, D.C., 1949), p. 7.

Formula 9.7. It was also pointed out that the binomial distribution of sample percentages can often be approximated by a normal distribution, particularly when the sample is large and the success cases are about equal to the failure cases. Hence, the formula for confidence intervals of percentages is:

$$\bar{\pi} = p \pm z\sigma_p \doteq p \pm z\sqrt{\frac{pq}{n}}. \tag{10.1}$$

Let us apply this formula to the problem of estimating people's responsiveness to the plea for educational television funds.

The random sample of 100 volunteer workers showed that 82 per cent of the families called on made a contribution. What is the 95 per cent confidence interval?

With $n = 100$, $p = 0.82$, and $z = 1.96$,

$$\bar{\pi} \doteq p \pm z\sqrt{\frac{pq}{n}} = 0.82 \pm 1.96\sqrt{\frac{(0.82)(0.18)}{100}} = 0.82 \pm 0.07.$$

The 95 per cent confidence interval extends from about 0.75 to 0.89. The statistical detective can assert with 95 per cent confidence that the interval 0.75 to 0.89 contains the true percentage of those interviewed who made a contribution toward the financing of educational television.

These computations assume that the sampling distribution is normal, an assumption not entirely met by our example. Tables have been developed, and one of them has been reproduced in Table III of the Appendix, which take into consideration the possible skewness of the sampling distribution of percentages.

To illustrate the use of this table, let us find the 95 per cent confidence interval of the true percentage of housewives in the United States who use instant coffee, based on a sample of 1,000 housewives of whom 30 per cent were using it. The rows of the table indicate the sample percentage and the columns the sample size. Thus we look for the row that corresponds to a p of 0.30 and the column for sample size 1,000, i.e., the last column. We find that the 95 per cent interval extends from 27 to 33 per cent, and could assert with a 95 per cent confidence that the 27 to 33 per cent interval contains the true percentage of housewives in the United States using instant coffee.

If the statistical detective had used Table III in the Appendix he would have concluded that the 95 per cent confidence interval extends from 0.73 to 0.89. There is a slight difference between the two results, which by and large can be explained in terms of a slightly skewed sampling distribution.

Let us consider one further example. When the television industry began to wonder whether it was getting overcommercialized, a sample survey was made. A random sample (100 advertising executives, television executives, agency account men, and advertising managers) was asked "Is TV over-commercialized?" 59.5 per cent of those interviewed replied "Yes." Using Formula 10.1, the 95 per cent confidence interval is approximated by:

$$\underline{\bar{\pi}} \doteq p \pm z \sqrt{\frac{pq}{n}} = 0.595 \pm 1.96 \sqrt{\frac{(0.595)(0.405)}{100}}$$
$$= 0.595 \pm 0.096.$$

The 95 per cent confidence interval extends from about 0.499 to 0.691, or from 50 to 69 per cent, and about the same conclusions are reached when Table III in the Appendix is used.

10.2. HOW LARGE A SAMPLE IS NEEDED?

In planning a sample survey the all-important first step is to determine the appropriate sample size. In some cases, Table III in the Appendix can be used to find the appropriate sample size for 95 per cent confidence interval estimates. Given the desired width of the confidence interval and some idea about the parameter, we can turn to the table, search for this interval, and then read off the column heading the corresponding n.

The following example can illustrate the procedure: While a survey in 1955 revealed that 39 per cent of those interviewed considered themselves Republicans, prior to the 1956 Presidential elections a new survey was to be made. It was decided to find a 95 per cent confidence interval, 6 per cent wide. Using 39 per cent as bench mark for an interval 6 per cent wide, we would look for the column in which the 36-42 per cent interval lies. We find this interval in the last column with $n = 1,000$.

Even in the absence of tables we can make rough estimates of the needed sample size by using Formula 10.1 or a modification thereof. To plan confidence interval estimates of means we used Formula 8.4, that $n \doteq \frac{z^2 s^2}{(\bar{\mu} - m)^2}$; and to get rough estimates of the sample size needed to estimate percentages we can use the formula

$$n \doteq \frac{z^2 pq}{(\bar{\pi} - p)^2}. \tag{10.2}$$

Once we have decided on the required reliability (z) and the definiteness ($\bar{\pi} - p$) of the estimate, and have some idea about the magnitude of the percentage to be expected (p), we can get a rough estimate of the corresponding sample size.

To apply Formula 10.2, consider the problem of the manufacturer of summer suits, who would like to broaden the acceptance of light-weight woolen suits. He wants to estimate the percentage of men who have or once had a light-weight all-wool suit for summer. He requires 90 per cent confidence in the results and insists that the width of the confidence interval not exceed 2.0. Before computing the required sample size, he tests his questionnaire and finds that of those interviewed, 13 per cent had a woolen summer suit at one time or another. On the basis of the subjective decision to use a z of 1.64 and ($\bar{\pi} - p$) of 0.01 and assuming that the 13 per cent figure is an acceptable first approximation of the parameter, he computes

$$n \doteq \frac{z^2 pq}{(\bar{\pi} - p)^2} = \frac{1.64^2 (0.13)(0.87)}{0.01^2} = 3,000.$$

What if the clothing manufacturer has no idea whatever about how large π might be and has no time to conduct a pretest?

If we examine Table III in the Appendix we see, for instance, that for a sample of size 100, the width of the 95 per cent confidence interval is 4 per cent if p is 0.00. As p assumes larger values, the width of the interval increases and is largest for a p of 0.50, when it is 20 per cent. The same holds true for other sample sizes. Thus, not knowing p, we could assume it to be 0.50 and compute n with the help of Formula 10.2, obtaining an interval of *at least* the width required. Unless the parameter is really 0.50, the sample size so calculated will always be larger than actually needed.

With p assumed to be 0.50, Formula 10.2 can be simplified.

$$n \doteq \frac{z^2 (0.50)(0.50)}{(\bar{\pi} - p)^2} = \frac{z^2 (0.25)}{(\bar{\pi} - p)^2} = \frac{z^2 (\frac{1}{4})}{(\bar{\pi} - p)^2} = \frac{z^2}{4(\bar{\pi} - p)^2}. \quad (10.3)$$

To illustrate the application of Formula 10.3, let us assume that labor leaders in 1954 polled their members as to whether they favored merging the American Federation of Labor with the Congress of Industrial Organizations. In order to be *at least* 90 per cent confident that the results would be off by no more than 2.0 either way, a sample is needed of the approximate size of

$$\frac{z^2}{4(\bar{\pi} - p)^2} = \frac{1.64^2}{4(0.02)^2} \doteq 1,700.$$

The ideas and techniques developed in this chapter, as well as in Chapter VIII, can help replace hunches, guesses, and "guestimates" by interval estimates in which a predetermined confidence can be placed. However, there is another problem area, often overlapping the one discussed so far, which is of no less interest.   The executive in private industry and government has as his main function the making of decisions.   In the next two chapters we will develop some powerful tools that can help in making decisions and in assessing the risks that accompany them.

SEE WHAT WE HAVE LEARNED:

1. There is much similarity between the estimation of confidence intervals of means and of percentages.   Both are based on the same principles.

2. For large samples with π about 0.50, or more generally with $n\pi$ and also $n(1 - \pi)$ more than 5, the sampling distribution of percentages is approximated by a normal distribution, whose mean can be approximated by p and standard error by $\sqrt{\dfrac{pq}{n}}$.

3. There are tables available, as for instance Table III in the Appendix, from which confidence intervals of percentages can be read off.

4. After agreeing on the appropriate reliability and definiteness of the required estimate, the sample size called for can be roughly calculated by using the formula: $n \doteq \dfrac{z^2 pq}{(\bar{\pi} - p)^2}$, if we have some idea of the value of p.

5. If we have no idea of the magnitude of p, we can compute the sample size roughly by using the formula: $n \doteq \dfrac{z^2}{4(\bar{\pi} - p)^2}$, which will give us a sample of at least sufficient size.

6. The confidence interval of a population percentage can be roughly estimated from a large sample by using the formula: $\bar{\pi} \doteq p \pm z \sqrt{\dfrac{pq}{n}}$, if $n\pi$ and $n(1 - \pi)$ is more than 5.

NOW SEE WHETHER YOU CAN SOLVE THE FOLLOWING PROBLEMS:

1. The Institutional Furniture Company, builders of fine furniture for the office and college classroom, has received numerous requests for classroom chairs with writing facilities for left-handed students.   Before the company is willing to build such chairs it would like to know something about the percentage of left-handed students in colleges and universities.   Having designed a questionnaire and pretested it on a random sample of 114 students, the company finds 19 of them to be left-handed.
   a. If the company would like to learn about the percentage of left-handed students in the United States and have a 95 per cent confidence that the results are not off by more than 1.0 per cent either way, how large a sample is called for?
   b. Having taken a sample of the necessary size and finding that 17 per cent of the students sampled are left-handed, what inferences could the Institutional Furniture Company draw?
2. The Political Action Committee of a large union, in planning its program,

would like to know how its members feel on whether unions should have more say about the government.

    a. How large a sample would they need if they insisted on 95 per cent confidence in the results and are willing to be off by no more than 3.0 per cent either way?

    b. If another union had found p to be 55 per cent, how large a sample would be needed by the Political Action Committee?

    3. Having surveyed a representative sample of 1,000 farmers on their attitude toward wheat acreage allotments, and having received a favorable reply from 615 of them, with what degree of confidence can you assert that of the more than a million wheat farmers in the U.S., 59 to 64 per cent will favor allotments?

    4. A recent nationwide sample of 4,010 families revealed that 41 per cent use instant coffee and 59 per cent regular coffee. What is the 99 per cent confidence interval of those using instant and those using regular coffee?

    5. In November, 1955, a sample of adults in Britain and in the United States was asked to identify Columbus, Shakespeare, Napoleon, Beethoven, Karl Marx, Aristotle, Raphael, Leo Tolstoy, Freud, and Rubens. The results were as follows:

Name	p *in the U.S.*	*95% Confidence Interval*	p *in Britain*	*95% Confidence Interval*
Columbus	0.90		0.88	
Shakespeare	0.78		0.94	
Napoleon	0.73		0.82	
Beethoven	0.62		0.85	
Karl Marx	0.39		0.53	
Aristotle	0.33		0 42	
Raphael	0.30		0.41	
Leo Tolstoy	0.24		0.41	
Freud	0.22		0.23	
Rubens	0.15		0.42	

Assuming that each sample had been of size 1,000, fill in the 95 per cent confidence intervals.

    6. A survey of 500 men, asked why they prefer cotton pajamas, produced the following results:

Reasons Why Owner Prefers a Cotton Pajama	*Sample Percentage*	*95 Per Cent Confidence Interval*
Is comfortable to wear	55	
Is durable and wears well	15	
Has nice appearance	3	
Has good laundering characteristics	17	
Price is good value for the money	6	
Is only kind ever worn	13	

Find the 95 per cent confidence intervals.

7. The 1955 Survey of Consumer Finances revealed the following information concerning the percentage distribution of consumer income:

Income Fifth	Percentage Money Income before Taxes	95 Per Cent Confidence Interval
Highest fifth	44	
Second	24	
Third	17	
Fourth	11	
Lowest fifth	4	
	100 %	

Source: *Federal Reserve Bulletin*, June 1955, p. 617.

On the assumption that the survey covered 2,800 families, find the 95 per cent confidence interval and summarize your findings so that they are readily understood by persons having no formal training in statistics.

XI

Decisions about Means

Once to every man and nation comes the moment to decide.
J. R. LOWELL

11.1. THE MAKING OF DECISIONS

One of the most important prerequisites for any able business executive, actual or aspiring, is the ability to make judicious decisions. But this ability is also essential for the statesman, the politician, the juror, the soldier, and so on—in fact, for every one of us in our private lives.

Calculated risk. When making difficult decisions, the phrase that "we take a *calculated risk*" is frequently used. For example, when in 1955 the House Democratic leader in Congress backed President Eisenhower's request for a Congressional resolution committing the United States to defend Formosa, he stated that "our country is taking a calculated risk in this new and sudden policy." We are told, too, that General Bradley had maintained in December, 1944, but a thin line in the Ardennes as a calculated risk in order to concentrate troops in more vital places. Miss Tallulah Bankhead relates in her charming autobiography that when John Emery asked her to marry him, she consulted a friend who advised her: "You've always wanted to try everything. . . . This will round out your experience. . . . It's a calculated risk."[1]

Obviously, in none of these cases was the risk actually calculated and in fact no one claims that it could have been. However, there are certain kinds of decisions that lend themselves to statistical techniques and to ways of making the risk of wrong choice assessable and agreed upon in advance.

[1] Tallulah Bankhead, *Tallulah* (New York, Dell Publishing Company, Inc., 1953), p. 256.

The risk in decision-making generally originates from the fact that the decision must be based on incomplete information and is made without knowledge about the future. Most decisions involve four possibilities. These may be illustrated by referring to the problem facing young Barbara, who has just had a proposal of marriage from Bob. She is flattered, happy, and yet unsure. "Should I marry Bob?" she keeps asking herself. Somehow she must reach a decision. One way of doing this is reading the tea leaves or, even better, picking the petals off a red rose to find out whether the last petal goes with "I will" or with "I won't." There really should be better ways of deciding this question. If she thought clearly, Barbara could reason that she faces four possibilities. If she declines Bob's proposal she may be making the mistake of her life, in that she rejects the man she should have married. Her decision would then have been unwise. If, instead, she accepts Bob's proposal she may be marrying one who will prove to be the wrong man for her. This is another mistake.

On the other hand, if Barbara agrees to marry Bob it may also turn out to have been a good decision. Or else, in refusing him she may be rejecting a man who is wrong for her. In her choice between accepting and rejecting the proposal, Barbara must thus consider two possible unhappy outcomes and two happy ones. These are the four possibilities or situations that face Barbara. How can she make the right decision? Would it not be wonderful if she could know the probabilities of making a wrong choice?

Of course, marriage is not based on a cold probability calculation. Nevertheless, it could be helpful if Barbara had clearly in mind the four situations that she cannot escape. As a matter of fact, her father might appreciate such level-headedness. He himself may use some kind of a probability calculus. For instance, suppose Barbara's suitor is seventy-two years old. "Such marriages usually do not last long," he might say. Men of seventy-two are unlikely to live very much longer. He could even turn to a Mortality Table and cite empirical probabilities concerning the duration of such a marriage.

For Barbara it may be unimportant how long her marriage to Bob will last; or she may not be dismayed by the prospect of a happy yet short-lived marriage. This depends on what appears desirable and valuable to Barbara. This argument involves value judgments that generally enter into decisions, but we are concerned here only with the probability estimates that form the basis for the scientific part of decision-making.

Courts, loyalty boards, generals, business executives, in short everyone who makes decisions can be helped by keeping in mind these four possibilities as a frame of reference. They would do well to think in terms of the likelihood of errors of omission and commission, their repercussions and implications, as well as carefully established decision criteria. Even if the problem does not lend itself to quantification, much help can be derived by an awareness of the two possible types of errors.

In business and economics many problems calling for a decision can be quantified and this enables us to use statistical methods for making decisions.

Null and alternative hypothesis. A relatively simple type of problem in statistical decision-making involves a choice between accepting or rejecting a hypothesis about a mean value. In a way, this kind of a choice resembles the problem of accepting or rejecting a suitor, except that the risks can be readily quantified, as will be shown in the following example to which much of the discussion of this chapter will refer.

The LUTABE tobacco company has learned on good authority, and assumes as correct, that in the year preceding announcements linking smoking with certain ill effects (Period 1) the adult American smoked an average of 8.0 cigarettes per day. To decide whether smoking habits have changed since this announcement was made, the company samples men and women from all over the United States. The question to be decided on the basis of the sample data is whether now (in Period 2) the average number of cigarettes smoked per person per day is different from that of Period 1.[2]

The first step in readying ourselves for a statistical decision is to set up a *null hypothesis* and a corresponding *alternative hypothesis.* It is common practice to start with the hypothesis that there is no difference, i.e., in our cigarette example, that smoking habits before and after the announcement of ill effects were the same. A hypothesis of no or *null* difference is commonly called a null hypothesis, or, in short H_o. More generally, a null hypothesis is enunciated with the intention of seeing whether in the light of sample data it cannot be rejected. Often the null hypothesis is established as one that we expect will have to be rejected.

If smoking habits have changed, a number of different things could have happened to smoking. In a general way, there is the alternative that smoking habits have changed, and in a more specific way, people may be smoking more than before, or people may be smoking less than before. These are *alternative hypotheses* or, in short, H_a's. By and large, the alternative hypothesis says the opposite of the null hypothesis. Only one alternative hypothesis can be tested at a time against the null hypothesis.

Returning to LUTABE's problem, we will assume that 100 persons were surveyed and found to smoke an average of 7.0 cigarettes. Now LUTABE must decide whether the difference between 7.0 and 8.0 is significant. What

[2] From here on "adults" and "people" will be used interchangeably.

constitutes a significant difference? It means that the difference is unlikely to be caused by sample variation and that there is, instead, a reasonably high probability that it reflects differences in the characteristic of the population. This point is best illustrated by once more referring back to a full deck of cards. We used the deck of cards earlier to show that although the mean value of the cards in the deck was 8.0, 10 randomly drawn cards may produce once a mean of 9.0 and once a mean of 6.0. These results we attributed to sampling variation. Let us now draw at random 100 cards. We may discover that the mean of these 100 cards is 7.0. In this case the difference between the sample mean of 7.0 and the population mean of 8.0 is entirely due to sample variation and not to a difference between the first population and the population from which the sample mean is taken, for they are one and the same. It would be a grave error to conclude that there is a significant difference between 7.0 and 8.0. Thus in LUTABE's case: unless and until the difference is found significant, the smaller sample mean should not induce management to take any action under the assumption that smoking has decreased.

How, then, can we know whether such a difference, or as a matter of fact, any difference is significant?

In decision-making we can find ourselves in four different situations:

   I. A correct null hypothesis is rejected
  II. An incorrect null hypothesis is accepted
 III. A correct null hypothesis is accepted
  IV. An incorrect null hypothesis is rejected.

It is common practice to refer to Situation I as involving an *error of Type I*, which is often equivalent to committing a *"sin of commission."* The probability of committing an error of Type I is called α (pronounced alpha). In statistical quality control the probability of committing an error of Type I is often referred to as *producer's risk*. (One may think of it as the risk the producer takes of deciding, for instance, that a batch of suspenders is not up to standard and scrapping it, when there is really no difference between the percentage of defectives in the sample batch and the standard.)

Situation II involves an *error of Type II*, and often means committing a *"sin of omission."* β (pronounced beta) is the probability that an error of Type II be committed, which is also referred to as *consumer's risk*. (One may think of it as the risk the consumer and user of suspenders incurs when a batch of suspenders is passed as up to standard although in reality it has an excessively high percentage of defectives.)

The other two situations are much to our liking. Situation III, i.e., the acceptance of a correct null hypothesis, and Situation IV, i.e., the rejection of an incorrect null hypothesis, make for good decisions. The probability that an incorrect null hypothesis is rejected is called the *power of the test.*

Let us see what all this amounts to in relation to the decision whether or not smoking habits have changed. We are assuming that the management of LUTABE is convinced from studying all the evidence obtainable that the reports of certain ill effects attributed to smoking are not based on facts. Its problem is, thus, only to find out if the adverse publicity has had an effect on smokers. The null hypothesis is that no change has occurred in smoking habits. Incorrectly rejecting this null hypothesis, and committing an error of Type I, is to conclude that smoking habits have changed when they really have not changed. As a result, management might undertake an expensive research and public relations program with the money going to waste. What is more important, if a publicity campaign is started it might make many smokers aware of the claims of dangers who did not previously know about the announcement of ill effects from smoking. Their smoking habits might be adversely affected by the publicity campaign. On the other hand, you never know: a recent cartoon in the *Wall Street*

WALL STREET JOURNAL

Reprinted by permission of the Wall Street Journal.

"I'm a NEW smoker. I never knew how good it was until all this publicity came up."

Journal depicted a board of directors meeting with but one of the directors smoking. When asked, he replied, "I'm a NEW smoker. I never knew how good it was until all this publicity came up." This unlikely possibility aside, there are many undesirable results that may go with an error of Type I and that must be clear in the mind of management. They are the implications of a sin of commission, i.e., taking action when action is not warranted.

What about the implications of committing an error of Type II, i.e., of incorrectly accepting the null hypothesis that smoking habits have not changed? The executives might conclude that there is no significant difference between the sample mean and 8.0 while in reality the Period 2 population mean has slipped considerably. They would then sit back and do nothing at a time when vigorous action is badly needed. As a result, the company is likely to lose business and incur substantial financial losses. A sin of omission would have been committed.

Decision criteria. Since in any decision we face these four situations, including the two ever-lurking risks of error, we need a *decision criterion*. When the research director asks management, "What calculated risk is the company willing to take in deciding what happened to sales?" he is trying to establish what risks of committing an error of Type I and of Type II are considered tolerable.

In answering the question, management is fully aware that the best decision would come about in case that the probability of incorrectly rejecting the null hypothesis were nil and, at the same time, the probability of correctly rejecting the null hypothesis were 1.0, i.e., certainty. Minimizing α so as to reduce it to nil and maximizing the power of the test so as to bring it up to 1.0 would produce a decision that could not be improved upon. It would be the ideal decision, but it also calls for ideal conditions. An α of 0.0 and power of the test of 1.0 require a sample that includes each and every member of the population. It does away with sampling. When we base our decision on a sample, we can never have certainty.

A compromise is called for. In making a compromise it is important to set up workable principles of a good decision: they can simply be stated as minimizing α and maximizing the power of the test in a relative sense. The general principle can also be stated in a slightly different way. The power of the test is the probability of rejecting the null hypothesis in case H_o is wrong; β is the probability of accepting H_o in case H_o is wrong. Consequently β is 1-(power of the test). Thus, we can also say that the objective is to set both α and β at relative minimums.

The selection of acceptable α's and β's must be guided by the desirability of a given outcome and the probability of its occurrence. For instance, management can visualize at least two major outcomes, i.e., in the light of its decision and corresponding action or inaction, cigarette consumption continues to decline or the decline is stopped. How serious it is to commit an error of Type I will then depend on the probable cost to LUTABE of taking corrective measures that were not needed, because sales had not, in fact, decreased. The cost associated with an error of Type II, e.g., of erroneously concluding that sales have remained unchanged, is more difficult to calculate. It is an error of omission. Omitting or delaying remedial action can have far-reaching consequences. Sales may continue to fall, because no action was taken to combat the decline. While the error of Type I can be calculated in dollars and cents, that of Type II does not lend itself easily to such calculation. It is more the missing of an opportunity. The economist calls it an *opportunity cost*, which he fancies to discuss, but AMEN ! has remained reluctant to compute.

Thus, the setting of decision criteria, i.e., deciding what risks of committing the two types of errors are acceptable (or, in other words, deciding upon an appropriate α and β) is largely subjective. When the desirability or undesirability of possible outcomes is evaluated, factors other than money often enter the deliberations. Peace of mind, satisfaction, desire for power, as examples, cannot be easily expressed in terms of dollars.

A good decision calls for finding a region of rejection (R) which permits the making of the decision with a known probability of committing an error of Type I, α, while it minimizes the calculable probability of committing an error of Type II, β, or (and it amounts to the same thing), maximizes the power of the test. Once we have chosen a method that minimizes β (or maximizes the power of the test) we can calculate how large a β and power of the test we have.

The usual method is to stipulate first an appropriate α. Let us say that we agreed on an α of 0.05, that is, we are willing to carry a risk of one in twenty times, in the long run, of rejecting H_o when it is the correct hypothesis. We will then employ a method that will maximize the power of the test, i.e., give the largest possible power for the given α and sample size. Since this maximum is only a relative one, we will often need to know its magnitude; and for this purpose we will have to calculate the power of the test.

The three cases. It is clear that LUTABE's problem can be approached from three points of view:

A. Do people smoke exactly the same number of cigarettes as they did before, or do they not smoke the same number as before?

    B. Do people now smoke more than in Period 1?
    C. Do people now smoke less than in Period 1?

In all three cases the null hypothesis is the same: that people in Period 2 smoke on the average the same number of cigarettes per day as they did in Period 1, i.e., 8.0 cigarettes. However, the three cases call for different alternative hypotheses.

In Case A, the alternative hypothesis is that people do not smoke the same number as they did before. We will call this the "not the same" case. In Case B, the alternative hypothesis is that more than 8.0 cigarettes are smoked on the average per day in Period 2. This is the "more than" case. In Case C, the alternative hypothesis is that less than 8.0 cigarettes are smoked on the average per day in Period 2. This is the "less than" case.

At any one time, the null hypothesis can be considered in conjunction with only one appropriate alternative hypothesis, leaving us with three distinct sets of hypotheses and cases.

11.2. CASE A: SMOKING "NOT THE SAME" AS BEFORE

To begin with, let us take the "not the same" or A case, and develop a decision-maker for it. While we recognize the risks of committing errors of Type I and Type II, *we will begin by controlling only α, the risk of wrongly rejecting the null hypothesis.*

LUTABE has learned on good authority that prior to the unfavorable news announcement people smoked on the average 8.0 cigarettes per day. In the following period a probability sample of 100 adults was found smoking on the average 7.0 cigarettes, with a standard deviation of 4.0. LUTABE is wondering whether a difference of 1.0 cigarettes is significant. Sampling variation could have produced this difference. This sampling variation is reflected in the way the sample means are distributed around their mean. Since the assumed mean in this case is 8.0 and the approximated standard error of the mean is $\dfrac{4.0}{\sqrt{100}}$ or 0.40, we can readily construct the sampling distribution, as has been done in Chart 11.1.

From this distribution we can estimate the probability of a difference of 1.0 cigarettes being due to sampling variation. We can construct intervals in a fashion parallel to the confidence interval estimates of population means made in Chapter VIII. First, let us construct a 95 per cent confidence interval, which will extend from 8.0 − 1.96 (0.40) to 8.0 + 1.96 (0.40), i.e., from 7.2 to 8.8 cigarettes per day. We can assert with 95 per cent confidence

that a difference of 1.0 cigarettes is in excess of what can be attributed to sampling variation. Actually our confidence can be better than 95 per cent. Likewise, the probability of our finding a difference of 1.0 cigarettes is smaller than 5 per cent.

Chart 11.1 SAMPLING DISTRIBU-
TION

These conclusions are readily visualized by looking at Chart 11.1, where the same mean value that is 1.0 smaller than μ, i.e., of 7.0, lies outside the 95 per cent confidence interval. The same holds for the mean value of 9.0.

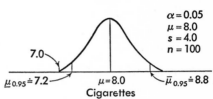

Significance versus confidence. While it is possible to talk about differences in terms of confidence levels, it is much more common to consider differences as being significant or insignificant. This is made possible by the relation that exists between the *level of confidence* and the *level of significance* of a difference, for instance, the difference between a sample and a true or assumed mean. The level of significance is 1.00 minus the level of confidence. Thus, a level of confidence of 0.95 corresponds to a (1.00 − 0.95) or 0.05 level of significance.

When we concluded with a 95 per cent confidence that, under the circumstances, a difference of 1.0 cigarettes is in excess of what can be attributed to sampling variation, we could have stated that a difference of 1.0 is significant at a 0.05 level of significance. If we have 95 per cent confidence that the difference of 1.0 cigarettes is not due to sample variation, there is also a probability of one in twenty that chance variation is the cause, and there is an 0.05 probability that we may be incorrectly rejecting the null hypothesis. A difference that is significant on the basis of a 0.05 level of significance is also significant at an α of 0.05, which is the same thing.

Controlling α in terms of mean values. We can use these ideas and, after choosing an appropriate α and setting up null and alternative hypotheses, calculate the crucial values that will tell us whether to accept or reject the null hypothesis. In our example, we found the 95 per cent confidence interval to extend from 7.2 to 8.8 cigarettes. If our sample mean lies between 7.2 and 8.8 it falls into the region of acceptance; thus we accept the null hypothesis and assert that, on the basis of an α of 0.05, there is no significant difference between the sample mean and assumed mean. Should our sample mean be smaller than 7.2 or larger than 8.8 cigarettes, it would fall into the region of rejection and we would reject the null hypothesis. It will be important to state at what α value the significance test is made. For we can readily visualize that for one α a given difference is significant while for another α the same difference is not significant. Let us examine this issue in relation to LUTABE's problem. We already found the region of acceptance for α of 0.05 to extend from 7.2 to 8.8. Now let us compute the region of acceptance for an α of 0.15: since the z value for an α of 0.15 is 1.44, the 85 per cent confidence interval extends from $8.0 - 1.44 \dfrac{4.0}{\sqrt{100}}$ or

7.4, to $8.0 + 1.44 \dfrac{4.0}{\sqrt{100}}$ or 8.6. Should we draw a sample and find the mean value to be 7.3 cigarettes, this mean value would fall into the first but not into the second region of acceptance. Thus, a difference of 0.7 cigarettes from an assumed mean of 8.0 cigarettes is not significant at an α of 0.05, but is significant at an α of 0.15 (compare Panels *A* and *B* of Chart 11.2).

In general, this method of decision-making comprises three steps:

1. Selecting an appropriate α and enunciating null and alternative hypotheses.
2. Establishing criteria for rejecting or accepting the null hypothesis—finding regions of rejection (R) and acceptance (A).
3. Determining whether the sample mean falls into the region of rejection or acceptance, and reaching the decision.

Chart 11.2 RELATIONSHIP BETWEEN REGIONS OF REJECTION AND ACCEPTANCE AND α AND β

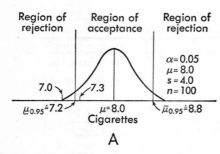

A

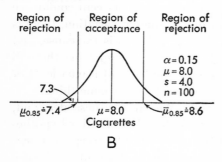

B

Here are the three steps that we would take in LUTABE's case:

1. After careful consideration of the implications of committing an error of Type I, we have decided to work with an α of 0.05, whose corresponding z value is 1.96. Since we assume that in Period 1 on the average 8.0 cigarettes were smoked, the null hypothesis is that in Period 2, regardless of the magnitude of the sample mean found in that period, people still smoke an average of 8.0 cigarettes per day. Similarly, the alternative hypothesis is that in Period 2 people do not smoke an average of 8.0 cigarettes per day.

In brief:

$$H_o: \mu = 8.0, \quad \text{or} \quad \mu - 8.0 = 0.$$
$$H_A: \mu \neq 8.0.$$

2. The lower line of demarcation is at about $\mu - z\dfrac{s}{\sqrt{n}} = 8.0 - 1.96\dfrac{4.0}{\sqrt{100}}$

or 7.2 cigarettes, while the upper line of demarcation is at $\mu + z\dfrac{s}{\sqrt{n}} =$

$8.0 + 1.96\dfrac{4.0}{\sqrt{100}}$ or 8.8 cigarettes (see Chart 11.2A).

The criteria can also be stated in the following way:

Reject H_o, if the sample mean is smaller than ($<$) 7.2 or larger than ($>$) 8.8 cigarettes.

Accept H_o, if the sample mean falls between the two values of 7.2 and 8.8 cigarettes.

3. Since the sample mean is 7.0 cigarettes, and thus is smaller than the crucial value of 7.2, we are forced to reject the null hypothesis. We conclude that, on the basis of an α of 0.05, there is a significant difference in the number of cigarettes smoked by the average adult per day prior to and after the news announcement. Perhaps, after all, some smokers may not have heeded the advice of Ian MacLead, British Minister of Health, who in July, 1954, turned down a request in the House of Commons for a government report on smoking and health. According to a U. P. dispatch the Minister used the opportunity to " . . . recommend to the questioner that if he is a heavy smoker and concerned with what he reads about the connection between cancer of the lung and smoking, that he give up reading."

How significant is a difference? The method for finding the significance of a difference runs somewhat parallel to the method developed in Chapter VIII for determining the degree of confidence that can be placed in a given interval containing the true mean. Turning once more to Chart 11.2, we will ask the question: What percentage of the area under the normal curve lies to the left of 7.0 cigarettes? We need to find the z value of the area above the interval 7.0 to 8.0 and subtract it from half the area under the normal curve, i.e., 0.5000.

In Chapter IV, Formula 4.6 was presented to help find the z value of population distributions: $z = \dfrac{x - \mu}{\sigma}$. Since we are now dealing with sampling distributions, we need to adjust Formula 4.6 to reflect the fact that we are computing the z value of a sampling distribution and not a population distribution. While in Formula 4.6 we are interested in the difference between a given observation x and the population mean, μ, here we are interested in the difference between a given sample mean m and an assumed (or population) mean μ. In the first case the relevant standard deviation was that of the population while in the present case it is the standard error of the mean that concerns us.

Thus, for sampling distributions (of large samples),

$$z = \frac{m - \mu}{\sigma_{\hat{x}}} \doteq \frac{m - \mu}{s/\sqrt{n}}. \tag{11.1}$$

Applying this formula to LUTABE's problem,

$$z \doteq \frac{7.0 - 8.0}{4.0/\sqrt{100}} = \frac{-1.0}{0.40} = -2.5.$$

Turning to Table I in the Appendix, we find that a z value of -2.5 is associated with 0.4938 of the area in the lower half of the normal curve. To the left of 7.0 cigarettes lies only $0.5000 - 0.4938$ or 0.0062 of the lower half area of the normal curve. The probability of finding a sample mean of 7.0 cigarettes at a time when the population mean is 8.0 cigarettes is, therefore, 0.0062 or slightly more than one half of one per cent.

Having disposed of one question, we come to the second, and perhaps more important one. The sampling distribution around $\mu = 8.0$ has mean values falling both below and above it. When in the "not the same" case we ask how significant a given difference is, we are not only concerned with the lower half of the sampling distribution, i.e., we do not care only about negative differences. In the "not the same" case a difference of 1.0 cigarettes means that the average number of cigarettes smoked by a sample of people can be as small as 7.0 and as high as 9.0. Thus, in order to compute the significance of a given difference, when the null hypothesis states that people smoke the same number of cigarettes as before (H_o: $\mu = 8.0$), we must add up the relative areas under the normal curve to the left of 7.0 and to the right of 9.0 cigarettes. The z values for an m of 7.0 and of 9.0 must be calculated. The first is -2.5 and the second $+2.5$. With the help of the z table we can find the corresponding relative areas under the normal curve, i.e., in both cases 0.4938. Subtracting these two values each from 0.5000, i.e., half the area under the normal curve, and adding the residuals, we find the level of significance or α of this difference of 1.0 cigarettes. The conclusion is that under the given circumstances a 1.0 cigarette difference is significant even at an α of 0.0124, i.e., slightly more than one per cent.

Controlling α in terms of z values. Earlier in this chapter a method was presented that made possible the rejection or acceptance of a null hypothesis on the basis of a predetermined α. By this method we computed the crucial values of the variate to delineate the regions of rejection and acceptance and checked into which region the sample mean would fall. In our attempts to measure the significance of a difference, it became clear that instead of delineating the regions of rejection and acceptance in terms of the values of the variate, e.g., number of cigarettes, we could accomplish the same in terms of z values, corresponding to the predetermined α. We would then calculate the z value of the sample data and see whether this value falls into the region of rejection or acceptance.

The first method may be initially easier to follow, but the second is more readily applied to tests of other differences, as will be seen in later chapters.

The making of decisions on the basis of a comparison of z values can be formalized in the following four steps:

see p. 170

1. Selecting an appropriate α and enunciating null and alternative hypotheses.
2. Establishing criteria for rejecting or accepting the null hypothesis (finding regions of rejection and acceptance in terms of values of z).
3. Computing the z value of the sample data.
4. Determining whether the z value of the sample data falls into the region of rejection or acceptance, and reaching the decision.

Before we apply this method, we will make one change in our assumptions. Let us assume that the sample mean was not 7.0 but turned out to be 7.4 cigarettes per day. The assumed mean remains 8.0, $n = 100$, and $s = 4.0$. Applying an α of 0.05, here are the four steps:

1. $H_o: \mu = 8.0$.

   $H_A: \mu \neq 8.0$.

2. Reject H_o, if the z value of the sample data[3] < -1.96 or $> +1.96$. Accept H_o, if the z value of the sample data falls between -1.96 and $+1.96$ (see Chart 11.3).

3. $z \doteq \dfrac{m - \mu}{s/\sqrt{n}} = \dfrac{7.4 - 8.0}{4.0/\sqrt{100}} = -1.5$.

4. Since z turns out to be -1.5 and thus falls into the region of acceptance, we will accept the null hypothesis on the basis of an α of 0.05.

[3] Delineating the regions of rejection and acceptance means stating the z values of their limits consistent with the agreed upon α. We can construct a normal curve around $\mu = 8.0$, which on the z scale is 0.0, and place half of the value into each of the two tails. With α equal to 0.05, 0.025 or 2.5 per cent of the total area under the normal curve will be placed in each tail. The z value for the remaining 0.4750 of the area of the lower and upper half, respectively, according to Table I in the Appendix, is -1.96 and $+1.96$, respectively. Thus, we mark off two lines of demarcation at -1.96 and $+1.96$, as has been done in Chart 11.3.

Performance and power functions. However, in reaching the decision to accept the null hypothesis, LUTABE lays itself open to the possibility of committing an error of Type II, a possibility that we have intentionally neglected so far, and that is one of the four situations we face when making a decision, the danger of accepting an incorrect null hypothesis.

The probability of committing errors of Type I and Type II must ultimately be considered jointly. In our last example, LUTABE was forced to accept the null hypothesis on the basis of an α of 0.05 and in so doing it exposed itself to the dangers of accepting an incorrect null hypothesis. It

Chart 11.3   REGIONS OF REJECTION AND
ACCEPTANCE

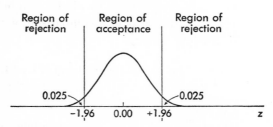

may be committing a sin of omission. To understand this danger, we may assume for a moment that smoking in Period 2 has really decreased considerably, say to 6.0 cigarettes per day. If the parameter in Period 2 were 6.0, what would be the chances of a sample mean derived from this Period 2 population falling into our area of acceptance? Or, in other words, what proportion of samples from a population with a mean of 6.0 will fall into the area of acceptance? That is what β represents; thus, to find β, we must know the α in order to set the areas of acceptance and rejection and we must know the parameter in Period 2 or make assumptions about it. (We do not need to know the sample mean in Period 2.)

Let us see how we can calculate β for a parameter with the hypothetical value of 6.0 cigarettes and α being 0.05, as before. We begin by reminding ourselves that the sample mean values delineating the regions of rejection and acceptance for our null hypothesis are 7.2 and 8.8 cigarettes, respectively, that $\mu = 8.0$, $n = 100$, and $s = 4.0$ (see top of Chart 11.4). Next we calculate β on the supposition that in Period 2, contrary to the null hypothesis that people still smoke on the average 8.0 cigarettes per day, actually only 6.0 cigarettes per day are being smoked. How likely are we under these circumstances to accept the null hypothesis, and in so doing subject ourselves to committing an error of Type II? This question can be rephrased in the following fashion: what is the probability that a sample mean from a sampling distribution around $\mu = 6.0$ with a standard error of about 0.40 falls into the region of acceptance extending from 7.2 to 8.8 cigarettes? Only if a sample mean falls within these limits is there a danger of an error

Chart 11.4 β's AND POWERS OF THE TEST
("Not the same" or A Case.)

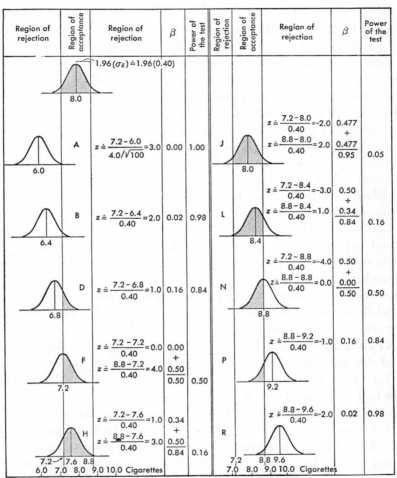

of Type II, i.e., a danger that we may accept a wrong hypothesis. As Panel *A* of Chart 11.4 shows, this probability is virtually zero.

How did we find out that β was virtually zero? We computed the *z* value of the normal sampling distribution bounded by the interval between the sample mean $m = 7.2$, delineating the lower line of demarcation of the region of acceptance, and $\mu = 6.0$, the hypothetical mean of the sampling distribution, converted the z value into the corresponding relative area under the normal curve, and subtracted this value from 0.50.

To find the z value we made use of Formula 11.1, i.e.,

$$z \doteq \frac{m - \mu}{s/\sqrt{n}} = \frac{7.2 - 6.0}{4.0/\sqrt{100}} = +3.0.$$

Referring to Table I in the Appendix, we found that an area of about 0.50 corresponds to a z value of 3.0, leaving $0.50 - 0.50$, or virtually nothing to the right of the lower line of demarcation, i.e., inside the region of acceptance. Thus, $\beta = 0.00$, and we can conclude that if people in Period 2 really smoke 6.0 cigarettes per day, the probability of our accepting the null hypothesis that people smoke an average of 8.0 cigarettes per day is virtually nil. The power of the test, i.e., the probability of our rejecting the null hypothesis that people smoke an average of 8.0 cigarettes per day when this hypothesis is not correct, is $1.00 - \beta$. Therefore, in this case the power of the test is $1.00 - 0.00$ or 1.00.

In Chart 11.4, panels have been drawn and β's and powers computed, on the assumption that in Period 2 people smoke in fact an average of 6.0, 6.4, 6.8, 7.2, 7.6, 8.0, 8.4, 8.8, 9.2, and 9.6 cigarettes per day, when we are testing the null hypothesis that $\mu = 8.0$. We have discussed in some detail the computation of Panel A in Chart 11.4. Panels B and D are fully explained by Panel A.

However, let us pause for a moment and look at Panel F, where we assume that while our null hypothesis is $\mu = 8.0$, μ in fact is 7.2. How likely are we under these circumstances to accept our null hypothesis? Looking at Panel F, it is apparent that in this case the true mean would fall on the lower line of demarcation. The lower half of the sampling distribution around $\mu = 7.2$ would fall into the lower region of rejection. What about the upper half of this sampling distribution? We know that much of it will lie in the region of acceptance, although by mere inspection we do not know whether or not part of its upper tail reaches into the upper region of rejection. Accordingly, we compute the z value for the area standing above the interval $m - \mu$, i.e., $8.8 - 7.2$. This turns out to be 4.0, meaning that virtually the entire upper half of the sampling distribution lies in the region of acceptance. That is why, in case μ in fact is 7.2, β is 0.50 and so is the power of the test.

Next, let us consider the case that assumes μ to be 7.6. Panel H indicates that parts of both the upper and the lower halves of the sampling distribution around 7.6 lie in the region of acceptance. We therefore must compute the z's for the area above $7.2 - 7.6$ and $8.8 - 7.6$, find the corresponding area values and add them together. We find that about 34 per cent of the lower half and all the upper 50 per cent fall into the region of acceptance and we conclude that $\beta = 0.34 + 0.50$ or 0.84; the power of the test is 0.16.

Whenever the hypothetical μ falls into the region of acceptance, we must calculate the two z values and sum the corresponding areas to find β. The reader may be wondering about the case in which the hypothetical true mean and the true mean of the null hypothesis coincide, e.g., both are 8.0 cigarettes. Panel J portrays this case, in which we can find β without any computations. In this case the sampling distribution used to find the region of acceptance coincides with that needed to compute β. The first one was so constructed that, consistent with the α of 0.05, the region of acceptance covered 95 per cent of the area under the curve, and 5 per cent of the area fell into the two regions of rejection. Thus, $\beta = 0.95$ and the power of the test is 0.05.

Finally, we may compare Panels H and L. In one case the hypothetical μ is 7.6 and in the other 8.4 cigarettes. But in both cases $\beta = 0.84$. The same holds if we compare Panels D and P, with the hypothetical μ's being 6.8 and 9.2 cigarettes and β in both cases amounting to 0.16. Whether we assume the true mean to be 6.8 or 9.2 cigarettes, the probability of committing an error of Type II is the same, i.e., 0.16. This finding is no coincidence. In fact, in the "not the same" case the performance and power functions are symmetrical. Whether the hypothetical μ is larger or smaller (by a fixed magnitude) than the μ in the null hypothesis, the β value (and likewise the power) will be the same. Thus, in the "not the same" case it suffices to find the β's (and powers of the test) for either values below or above that of the parameter in the null hypothesis.

In Table 11.1 we present values of β and the power of the test consistent with various alternative values of the parameter and in Charts 11.5 and 11.6 we have plotted these data in the form of a *performance* and *power function*, respectively. The curve in Chart 11.5 is a *performance function, also sometimes called an operating characteristic function, in that it relates the* probability of accepting an incorrect null hypothesis to various alternative values of the parameter. Our performance function is built on the assumption that $\alpha = 0.05$, $n = 100$, and $\sigma_{\bar{x}} \doteq 0.40$.

The inverse of the performance function is the *power function* that relates the probability of rejecting an incorrect null hypothesis to various alternative values of the parameter. The power function can be drawn either by using the information about the power of the test given in Chart 11.4 or by simply inverting the performance function. Like the performance function, the power function will differ depending on the α, n, and $\sigma_{\bar{x}}$.

At this point it may be of interest to the reader to relate the α's and β's. Looking at Table 11.1 and remembering that we were using an α of 0.05 throughout, it becomes clear that $\alpha + \beta$ is not always equal to 1.00. On the contrary, it usually is not equal to 1.00, except when the values of the hypothetical parameter and the parameter in the null hypothesis coincide.

Table 11.1 PERFORMANCE AND POWER TABLE
"Not the same" or A Case.

Number	Hypothetical Value of Parameter (μ)	β	Power of Test
A	6.0	0.00	1.00
B	6.4	0.02	0.98
C	6.6	0.07	0.93
D	6.8	0.16	0.84
E	7.0	0.31	0.69
F	7.2	0.50	0.50
G	7.4	0.69	0.31
H	7.6	0.84	0.16
I	7.8	0.93	0.07
J	8.0	0.95	0.05
K	8.2	0.93	0.07
L	8.4	0.84	0.16
M	8.6	0.69	0.31
N	8.8	0.50	0.50
O	9.0	0.31	0.69
P	9.2	0.16	0.84
Q	9.4	0.07	0.93
R	9.6	0.02	0.98
S	10.0	0.00	1.00

Source: Chart 11.4.

At that point $\alpha = 0.05$ and $\beta = 0.95$. More will be said about the relation between α and β later. Only one more point will be made at this time. We said that the power function of the "not the same" case is symmetrical around the μ value of the null hypothesis. However, at that value the power of the test $= \alpha$. Thus, α determines the general height of the power function. The greater α, the higher the power function, and vice versa.

Let us inquire briefly into the general meaning of what we have done so far in relation to β. We may take the case in which LUTABE had sampled a representative sample of 100 smokers and found that they smoke an average of 7.4 cigarettes per day. LUTABE tests the null hypothesis that people in the United States smoke an average of 8.0 cigarettes per day. Consistent with an α of 0.05 (and $\sigma_{\bar{x}} \doteq 0.40$), LUTABE is forced to accept this null hypothesis, and in so doing it is exposed to the possibility of accepting an incorrect null hypothesis. It wonders how large the probability of an error of Type II is, fully aware that its conclusion depends on the value of the parameter, i.e., the actual average number of cigarettes smoked per day. The company could also reason in terms of the power of the test.

While we have computed the performance and power functions over a wide range, we did so primarily to show the general shape of these functions. Most companies have a pretty good idea of the range within which the

Chart 11.5 PERFORMANCE FUNCTION
("Not the same" or A Case.)

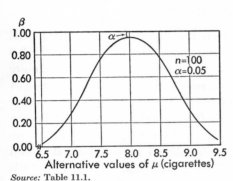

Source: Table 11.1.

Chart 11.6 POWER FUNCTION
("Not the same" or A Case.)

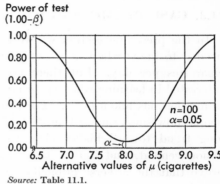

Source: Table 11.1.

parameter is likely to fall. For instance, LUTABE on the basis of its experience and knowledge of the situation may be reasonably sure that people smoke an average of somewhere between 7.4 and 8.2 cigarettes per day. In this case it would compute the power of the test and β merely for this range. It would conclude that β may be as low as 0.69 and as high as 0.95 (and the power of the test as low as 0.05 and as high as 0.31). In general, the power is rather low and this is the result of so small a sample. The larger the sample, the more powerful, in general, the test becomes. This leads to an important question, namely, why in the first place did LUTABE take a sample of 100 *su*'s? As in our discussion of confidence interval estimation, we will later develop a method that will help select a sample size consistent with our requirements of the test.

One last point appears in order. On perusing Table 11.1, it becomes clear that the power of the test is smallest and β largest at, and close to, the value of the parameter in the null hypothesis. On first look that may not make sense. On second thought it will, particularly if we follow the following reasoning: Clearly it is more difficult to detect a very small difference than a large one. For instance, it is harder to detect a difference between 8.00 and 8.05 than one between 8.00 and 8.65. Yet, we are not so alarmed about missing the first difference as we are about the second. If we were to decide that smoking habits have not changed although 8.05 instead of 8.00 cigarettes are smoked on the average, the implications of this decision would usually involve minor dangers. Not so if we reached the same conclusion— that people smoke on the average 8.00 cigarettes per day—while in fact they smoke 8.65 cigarettes. In the latter case, the acceptance of the incorrect null hypothesis is often wrought with many serious consequences. In short, we must consider both the magnitude of β and the magnitude of the difference as a measure of the implications of committing an error of Type II.

11.3. CASE B: SMOKING "MORE THAN" BEFORE

In the preceding section we worked on the supposition that LUTABE needed to know whether or not people smoke on the average exactly 8.0 cigarettes per day. But there are many instances when we are more interested in learning whether an increase or perhaps a decrease of one sort or another has taken place. For instance, LUTABE may wonder whether people now smoke more than they did before. Perhaps there had been a long trend toward higher cigarette consumption previous to the news announcement, and if that trend could be shown to continue, it would prove that the adverse publicity was having no effect. Thus, LUTABE would enunciate the alternative hypothesis that in Period 2 people smoke more than before, with the null hypothesis stating that in Period 2 people smoke the same as before.

A formalized test for Case B, controlling α. If we were to make the test by comparing mean values we would take the following three steps, after agreeing, let us say, on an α of 0.05:

1. H_o: $\mu = 8.0$.
   H_B: $\mu > 8.0$.

2. In Case A, the regions of rejection at the upper and lower tails of the normal curve were of equal size. The "more than" alternative hypothesis calls for placing the entire region of rejection into the upper tail. Why? If we are testing the alternative hypothesis that people smoke more than 8.0 cigarettes a day, and our sample mean is much smaller than 8.0, common sense indicates that we should not accept this alternative hypothesis; nor should we reject H_o. We should accept only the alternative hypothesis that people smoke more than 8.0 cigarettes a day and reject H_o if the people sampled smoke many more than 8.0 cigarettes a day. It is logical that as the sample mean increases, e.g., is 9.0, 10.0, etc., we should be more

inclined to reject the null hypothesis that people smoke the same as before, and accept the alternative hypothesis that people smoke more than before. Thus, our reasoning is consistent with placing the entire region of rejection into the upper tail, as is done in Chart 11.7. In terms of the cigarette example it will become clear that this is the only correct approach. In a

Chart 11.7 β's AND POWERS OF THE TEST
("More than" or B Case.)

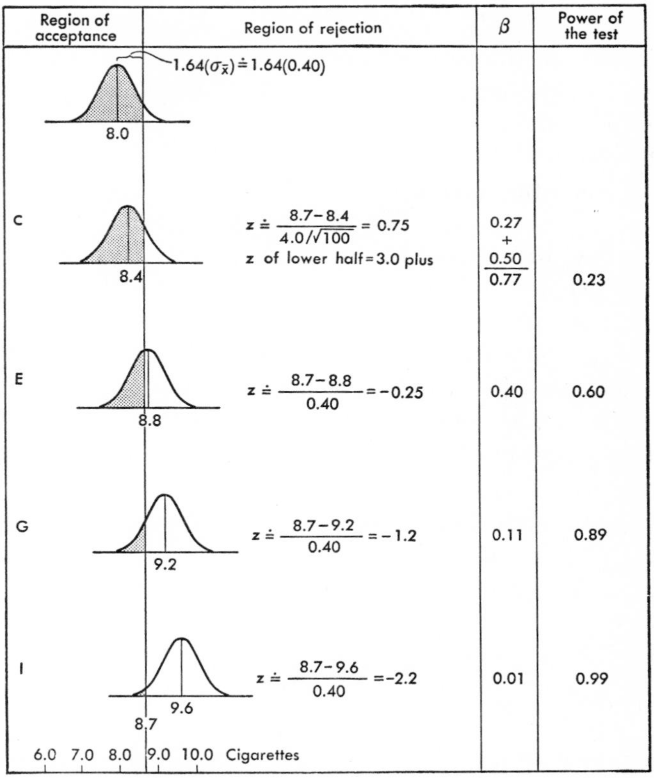

Region of acceptance	Region of rejection	β	Power of the test
$1.64(\sigma_{\bar{x}}) \doteq 1.64(0.40)$			
C 8.4	$z \doteq \dfrac{8.7-8.4}{4.0/\sqrt{100}} = 0.75$ z of lower half = 3.0 plus	0.27 + 0.50 ——— 0.77	0.23
E 8.8	$z \doteq \dfrac{8.7-8.8}{0.40} = -0.25$	0.40	0.60
G 9.2	$z \doteq \dfrac{8.7-9.2}{0.40} = -1.2$	0.11	0.89
I 9.6 8.7	$z \doteq \dfrac{8.7-9.6}{0.40} = -2.2$	0.01	0.99
6.0 7.0 8.0 9.0 10.0 Cigarettes			

sense, in the "more than" case we neglect the lower half of the sampling distribution around $\mu = 8.0$ and ask the question whether as high a value as, for instance, $8.0 + 1.0$, could have been brought about as a result of sampling variation consistent with the agreed-upon α.

We find the mean value that separates the region of acceptance from the region of rejection by using the formula $\mu + z \dfrac{s}{\sqrt{n}}$. For an α of 0.05 the z value will correspond to 45 per cent of the area under the normal curve.

We find it by looking up in Table I of the Appendix the value of z for an area of 0.4500, which turns out to be 1.64. Thus, in our case the line of demarcation is at a mean value of 8.0 + 1.64 (0.40) or 8.7 cigarettes. The corresponding regions of acceptance and rejection for Case B are presented at the top of Chart 11.7.

The criteria can be stated also as follows:

> Reject H_o, if the sample mean > 8.7.
> Accept H_o, if the sample mean < 8.7.

3. If the mean of the sample turned out to be 7.4, we would be forced to accept the null hypothesis and conclude that, on the basis of an α of 0.05, people smoke on the average no more than 8.0 cigarettes, i.e., there is no significant difference.

We could reach the same conclusion by relying on a test that compares z values.

Performance and power functions in Case B.   Thinking it entirely possible that people smoke more than before, LUTABE would not like to make the mistake of accepting the null hypothesis at a time when such a decision is unwarranted. By accepting the null hypothesis, the company would conclude that in Period 2 people smoke fewer, or, at most, just as many cigarettes as they did in Period 1. If this hypothesis is incorrect the company might be led to take unwarranted action. How likely is LUTABE to accept the wrong hypothesis in Case B?

We must go through about the same thinking process and steps as we did in Case A. We start by delineating the area of acceptance, which will be different, in spite of α being also 0.05. In Case B all 5 per cent are placed in the upper tail, while in Case A 2.5 per cent were placed in each tail. With an α of 0.05, we will reject the null hypothesis in Case B, if those included in the sample smoke $\mu + z \dfrac{s}{\sqrt{n}}$ or 8.7 cigarettes . Panel A of Chart 11.7 presents the regions of acceptance and rejection.

To find the performance curve and power function, we again set up different hypotheses about the true number of cigarettes smoked in Period 2. What general shape do we expect the performance curve in Case B to have?

The null hypothesis that people do not smoke more than before, i.e., smoke the same as before, is unlikely to be accepted in case people actually smoke as many as 9.0 or perhaps even 10.0 cigarettes a day. Thus as μ becomes 9.0, 10.0, or 11.0 the chances of accepting H_o in general, and therefore of incorrectly accepting it, decrease, and vice versa. β decreases as μ

assumes larger and larger values; the performance function in Case B slopes downward. The opposite holds true for the power function.

Chart 11.7 presents the β's and powers for various hypothetical values of the parameter. For instance, Panel *C* demonstrates the probability of incorrectly accepting the null hypothesis that $\mu = 8.0$, in case people actually smoke an average of 8.4 cigarettes per day. $\beta = 0.77$ and the power of the test is 0.23.

The β's and powers for alternative hypothetical values of μ are plotted in Charts 11.8 and 11.9.

11.4. CASE C: SMOKING "LESS THAN" BEFORE

LUTABE really may not care whether people smoke exactly 8.0 cigarettes per day. Neither does its management think it likely that in view of the unfavorable news reports people smoke more cigarettes than they did before. If anything, management under the circumstances must be concerned mainly about the possibility that people smoke less than in the past.

A formalized test for Case C, controlling α. We will begin by considering the problem of establishing the null and alternative hypothesis. The alternative hypothesis for the "less than" case is that the mean number

Chart 11.8 PERFORMANCE FUNCTION
("More than" or B Case.)

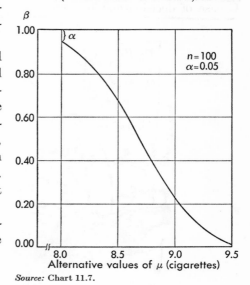

Source: Chart 11.7.

Chart 11.9 POWER FUNCTION
("More than" or B Case.)

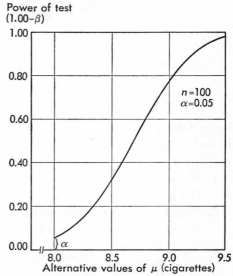

Source: Chart 11.7.

of cigarettes smoked in Period 2 is smaller than that in Period 1; specifically: less than 8.0 cigarettes are smoked in Period 2. This is the *"less than"* or C case of decision-making, where we place the region of rejection in the

Cartoon by George Lichty reproduced by permission of the Chicago Sun-Times Syndicate.

"Surveys that show how many people quit smoking the past year mean nothing, gentlemen! . . . I suspect each person was counted EVERY time he quit . . . "

lower tail of the curve. The alternative hypothesis will read: people in Period 2 smoke less than 8.0 cigarettes per day.

Using a test that compares z values and an α of 0.05:

1. $H_o: \mu = 8.0$.

   $H_C: \mu < 8.0$.

2. Reject H_o, if the z value of the sample is < -1.64.

   Accept H_o, if the z value of the sample is > -1.64.

3. $z \doteq \dfrac{7.4 - 8.0}{0.40} = -1.5$.

4. Since the z value of the sample is larger than -1.64, we are forced to

accept the null hypothesis and infer that, at an α of 0.05, smoking has not decreased significantly.[4]

Performance and power functions in Case C. A sample mean of 7.4 calls for acceptance of the null hypothesis and exposes the company to

Chart 11.10 β's AND POWERS OF THE TEST
("Less than" or C Case.)

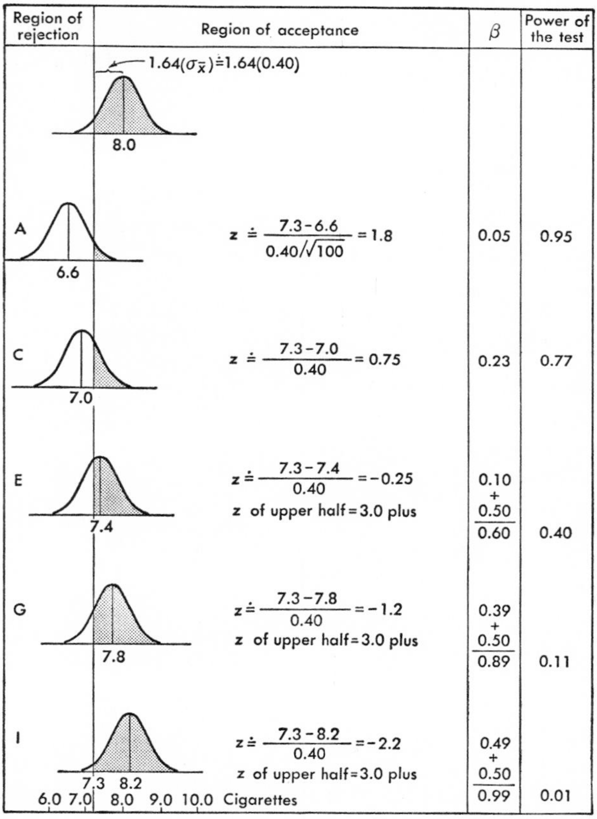

Region of rejection	Region of acceptance	β	Power of the test
	$1.64(\sigma_{\bar{x}}) \doteq 1.64(0.40)$ **8.0**		
A 6.6	$z \doteq \dfrac{7.3-6.6}{0.40/\sqrt{100}} = 1.8$	0.05	0.95
C 7.0	$z \doteq \dfrac{7.3-7.0}{0.40} = 0.75$	0.23	0.77
E 7.4	$z \doteq \dfrac{7.3-7.4}{0.40} = -0.25$ z of upper half = 3.0 plus	0.10 + 0.50 0.60	0.40
G 7.8	$z \doteq \dfrac{7.3-7.8}{0.40} = -1.2$ z of upper half = 3.0 plus	0.39 + 0.50 0.89	0.11
I 7.3 8.2 6.0 7.0 8.0 9.0 10.0 Cigarettes	$z \doteq \dfrac{7.3-8.2}{0.40} = -2.2$ z of upper half = 3.0 plus	0.49 + 0.50 0.99	0.01

the dangers of committing an error of Type II. LUTABE might wish to know the probability of committing this type of error. As before, we would start by finding the number of cigarettes that separates the region of acceptance from the region of rejection. Under the circumstances and on the basis of an α of 0.05, this value is about $\mu - z\dfrac{s}{\sqrt{n}} = 8.0 - 1.64\,(0.40)$ or 7.3

---

[4] We will leave it to the reader to make the test that compares the values of the sample means.

Chart 11.11 PERFORMANCE FUNC-
TION
("Less than" or C Case.)

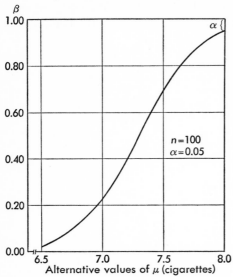

Source: Chart 11.10.

Chart 11.12 POWER FUNCTION
("Less than" or C Case.)

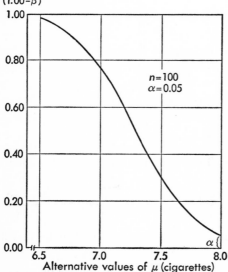

Source: Chart 11.10.

cigarettes. In Panel *A* of Chart 11.10, the regions of acceptance and rejection are presented. In the remaining Panels of that chart the β's have been graphed and computed together with the power of the test for various hypothetical values of μ. Corresponding performance and power functions have been drawn in Charts 11.11 and 11.12, respectively. In the "less than" case the performance function slopes upward and the power function downward.

11.5. MAXIMIZING POWER OF TEST

Let us recall that LUTABE could test one of the following alternative hypotheses:

A. People do *not* smoke *the same* as before, i.e., no longer smoke 8.0 cigarettes a day;

B. People smoke *more than* 8.0 cigarettes a day; or

C. People smoke *less than* 8.0 cigarettes a day.

In LUTABE'S problem the last alternative hypothesis would probably appear the most appropriate. It is easy to see that different circumstances would call for a different choice. What set of hypotheses is finally selected is of great importance; it will have an influence on our goal of maximizing the power of the test.

Regardless of what alternative hypothesis is deemed appropriate, LUTABE faces at least two dangers in reaching a decision and implementing it by action: the (corresponding) null hypothesis might be rejected at a time when its rejection is unwarranted, or it might be accepted when acceptance is unwarranted. These are our errors of Type I and Type II.

Our objective is to make a decision with a known and predetermined probability of committing an error of Type I, at the same time maximizing the power of the test, i.e., the probability of correctly rejecting H_o. Having agreed on a null and an alternative hypothesis and α, we test for the significance of the difference between the sample mean and the known or assumed mean. The result may be a rejection or an acceptance of the null hypothesis, which in turn means an acceptance or rejection of the alternative hypothesis. In our example, regardless of what set of hypotheses we selected for the test, we accepted the null hypothesis on the basis of an α of 0.05. Clearly, all three conclusions are consistent with one another.[5]

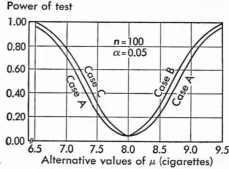

Chart 11.13 POWER FUNCTIONS (Cases A, B, and C.)

Source: Table 11.1 and Charts 11.7 and 11.10.

Thus, we have under control the risk of erroneously rejecting the null hypothesis and can move to the issue of minimizing the probability of accepting it if it is wrong, i.e., to β. Let us carefully look at the power functions of Cases A, B, and C in Chart 11.13. For any one true mean value, the higher the power function the higher the power. Thus, for the same α and same sample size, whenever the true mean is "less than" 8.0, Case C provides us with the highest power; and when the true mean is "more than" 8.0, Case B provides us with the highest power. For instance, if the true mean value is 9.0, Case A will offer us a 0.70 probability of rightly rejecting a wrong hypothesis, while Case B increases the probability to 0.77. Similarly, where the true value is 7.6, Case A affords a 0.16 probability of rejecting the wrong hypothesis while for Case C the probability is 0.23.

[5] It should be obvious that, depending on the sample mean or α value, different conclusions would be reached. For instance, retaining an α of 0.05, but assuming that the sample mean is 7.0, we would reject H_o in Cases A and C, and accept it in Case B. There is no inconsistency between the conclusions in Cases B and C. In A we conclude that, insofar as the possibility is concerned that people smoke more than before, smoking habits have not changed, and in Case C, we conclude that insofar as the possibility is concerned that people smoke less than before, smoking habits have changed.

While we have not provided proof, we have demonstrated that by establishing an alternative hypothesis of the "more than" or "less than" type (Case B or Case C), we maximize the power for a given α and sample size. This is good news.   Let us not forget, however, that this is a relative maximum in that it is consistent only with the selected α and n. It is by no means necessarily an absolute maximum, i.e., 1.0. Often we need to know how big or small the power of the test is.   For this purpose we need to construct a power function, not necessarily extending over all the possible values of μ, but only over those that we think are relevant.   In Case C, for instance, the sample data were such that we were forced to accept the null hypothesis. Looking at the power function, we could tell a management which fears that in Period 2 only an average of 7.2 to 8.0 cigarettes are smoked that the power of the test is somewhere between 0.65 and 0.05.   As a matter of fact, we would be well advised to read off the power for each and every possible value of μ between 7.2 and 8.0. Management would then know the power and the β.   The

Chart 11.14 RELATIONSHIP BETWEEN REGIONS OF REJECTION AND ACCEPTANCE AND α AND β

Small α (and regions of rejection) provides for large area of acceptance and β.

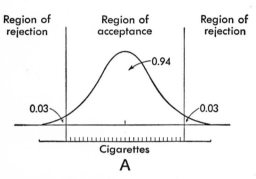

A

Large α (and regions of rejection) provides for small area of acceptance and β.

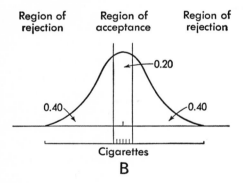

B

power is larger for a true mean of 7.2 than for a true mean of 7.9; and inversely β is smaller for a true mean of 7.2 than for one of 7.9.   However, management would be fully aware that a β of about 0.94, which goes with a μ of 7.9, is accompanied by only a minor decline in cigarette smoking habits, while the smaller β of 0.40 comes with a major decline in smoking habits that might prove ruinous.   Thus, both β and the difference must be given careful consideration.

While we now understand how to maximize the power of the test, we still remain interested in the absolute magnitude of the power. In this connection it might be helpful to remind ourselves of the relationship between α and β, i.e., the fact that the two are interdependent.

Specifically, for a given sample size the smaller an α we select the larger a β results, and vice versa. That this relationship holds can be readily understood by studying Chart 11.14. Let us forget for the moment that normal curves theoretically never reach their horizontal base. We then can say that the closer we move the two lines of demarcation of Case A to each other, the smaller the region of acceptance and the larger the regions of rejection. By having reduced the width of the region of acceptance, we also reduced the probability of committing an error of Type II. Since concomitantly we increased the totality of the regions of rejection, we also increased the probability of committing an error of Type I. The inverse would hold if we were to increase the region of acceptance. This relationship explains why, for a given sample size, the performance function is lower and the power function higher as α increases.

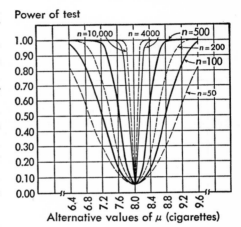

Chart 11.15 POWER FUNCTIONS CORRESPONDING TO DIFFERENT SAMPLE SIZES

Power of test

Alternative values of μ (cigarettes)

What is the effect of the sample size on the performance and power functions? For the same α in all three cases, the slope of the performance and power functions increases as the sample size increases. For a very large sample will result in powers all virtually close to 1.0, except when the value of the hypothetical parameter coincides with that in the null hypothesis, i.e., when it is 8.0 cigarettes in the case of our LUTABE example. At this point, the power of the test equals α (see Chart 11.15).

11.6. PLANNING SAMPLE SIZE

One of the first issues to be agreed upon before sampling can get under way is the proper size of the sample. Remember, in the planning stage of the estimation of confidence intervals we first calculated the proper sample size. We do the same when the objective is to provide sample information for the making of decisions.

Before we determined how large a sample was needed to estimate confidence intervals, we had to agree on the desired level of confidence and acceptable interval width, and have some knowledge about the order of magnitude of the standard deviation of the population. Similarly, in planning a sample for decision purposes a number of criteria must be agreed upon. Let us see what they are.

The very first step in planning a sample for decision purposes is to establish the hypotheses to be tested in the light of the sample information. For instance, the management of LUTABE may have a definite feeling that smoking has declined, and, as a matter of fact, on the basis of salesmen's reports and its general knowledge of the situation it may believe that people now smoke at most 8.0 but perhaps as few as 7.3 cigarettes per day. This is obviously a highly subjective assumption, but some such assumption is needed before the sample can be planned.

Chart 11.16 SAMPLE SIZE OF SPECIFIED PERFORMANCE FUNCTION (Case C.)

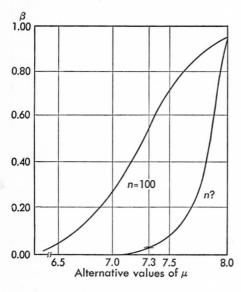

Alternative values of μ

Having made the preliminary decision within what interval the true parameter is likely to fall, we will be interested only in this interval and the performance and power functions pertaining to it. Specifically we need to find that performance (or power) function for this interval that is consistent with risks of committing errors of Type I and Type II acceptable to us. We must select an acceptable α and an acceptable β, consistent with the extreme value of the alternative hypothesis, i.e., that $\mu < 8.0 = 7.3$. There is but one sample size that will meet these requirements and it is up to us to find the corresponding n.

If, after careful consideration, LUTABE decides to settle on an α of 0.05 and β of 0.02 (and this problem has been diagrammed in Chart 11.16) we can find n by using the following formula:

$$n \doteq \left(\frac{z_\alpha + z_\beta}{\dfrac{\mu_o - \mu_a}{s}} \right)^2 , \tag{11.2}$$

where z_α is the z value of the selected α,

z_β is the z value of the selected β in case the parameter has the value indicated as extreme in H_a,

μ_o is the parameter relevant to H_o,

μ_a is the parameter relevant to H_a, and

s is an approximation of the standard deviation of the population and sample.

In this equation z_α, z_β, and $(\mu_o - \mu_a)$ are always positive. Formula 11.2 is derived from the definitions of α and β and helps to find two points on a performance curve, which meet the predetermined specifications. This formula is generally consistent with what we know about the determinants of a performance (or power) function, i.e., the larger the sample size and/or the larger α, the larger β and the higher the power of the test.

Let us stipulate that LUTABE has established the hypothesis:

$$H_o: \mu = 8.0.$$
$$H_C: \mu < 8.0.$$

The assumption is that people may smoke as few as 7.3 cigarettes per day, i.e., $\mu_a = 7.3$; $\mu_o = 8.0$. Furthermore, the company agrees that if people smoke on the average 8.0 cigarettes it is willing to reject incorrectly H_o ($\mu = 8.0$) five per cent of the time, i.e., $\alpha = 0.05$; and if people smoke on the average only 7.3 cigarettes per day the company is willing incorrectly to accept H_o ($\mu = 8.0$) 2 per cent of the time, i.e., $\beta = 0.02.$

Thus, $z_\alpha = 1.64$, $z_\beta = 2.05$, $\mu_o = 8.0$, $\mu_a = 7.3$, and $s \doteq 4.0$; and,

$$n \doteq \left(\frac{z_\alpha + z_\beta}{\mu_o - \mu_a}\right)^2 = \left(\frac{1.64 + 2.05}{\frac{8.0 - 7.3}{4.0}}\right)^2 = \left(\frac{3.69}{\frac{0.7}{4.0}}\right)^2 = (21.1)^2 = 450.$$

For the conditions agreed upon, about 450 persons would need to be included in the sample survey.

Here is another example. Let us assume that a Major League baseball club is considering dropping live television of its games. The main reason is that the old-fashioned baseball fan, who previously attended an average of 25 games a season, is now watching the game on television and comes less frequently to the ball park. To decide whether the season's attendance of the old-fashioned baseball fan has significantly fallen off, these fans are to be surveyed. The alternative hypothesis is that baseball fans now come less than 25 times a year to the park. It is agreed that if indeed fans come an average of 25 times a year to the park, management is willing to submit itself to an α of 0.05; and if fans come an average of 21 times to the park, it is willing incorrectly to accept H_o 1.5 per cent of the time, i.e., $\beta = 0.015$. The standard deviation of the population is estimated to be about 15.

With $z_\alpha = 1.64$, $z_\beta = 2.17$, $\mu_o = 25$, $\mu_a = 21$, and $s \doteq 15$,

$$n \doteq \left(\frac{1.64 + 2.17}{\frac{25 - 21}{15}}\right)^2 = \left(\frac{3.81}{\frac{4}{15}}\right)^2 = \left(\frac{57.15}{4}\right)^2 = (14.3)^2 = 200.$$

About 200 old-fashioned baseball fans need to be sampled, to make possible an intelligent decision under the indicated risks.

11.7. A SMALL SAMPLE

Sometimes one has to make decisions based on small sample data. In that case $z \doteq \dfrac{m - \mu}{s/\sqrt{n}}$ is replaced by

$$t \doteq \frac{m - \mu}{s/\sqrt{n - 1}}, \tag{11.3}$$

and we refer to a t table in place of a z table.

Let us take an example. The 1950 Census revealed that of 57 metropolitan areas, Miami, Florida, commanded the highest average monthly rent: $67 per dwelling unit. We will assume that in 1956 we sampled 26 dwelling units and found an average monthly rental of $72 with a standard deviation of $20.

Question: Did Miami rentals increase significantly between 1950 and 1956? Here are the four steps to answer this query, at an α of 0.05 (Case B):

1. $H_o: \mu = 67$.
   $H_B: \mu > 67$.
2. Reject H_o if the t value of the sample is $> +1.708$.
   Accept H_o if the t value of the sample is $< +1.708$.
3. $t \doteq \dfrac{m - \mu}{s/\sqrt{n - 1}} = \dfrac{72 - 67}{20/\sqrt{25}} = +1.2$.
4. Since the calculated t is smaller than $+1.708$ we accept the null hypothesis. We conclude that at an α of 0.05 Florida rentals did not increase significantly.

It goes without saying that the power function can be constructed without difficulty from these data. It is suggested that the reader do this as an exercise. Likewise, the reader will benefit by making the significance test, by comparing the sample mean with the mean value delineating the regions of acceptance and rejection.

11.8. SIGNIFICANCE OF DIFFERENCE BETWEEN TWO SAMPLE MEANS

"The British male over five years of age soaks himself in a hot tub on an average of 1.7 times a week in the winter . . . (and) British women average 1.5 baths a week in the winter," was a story in the San Francisco Chronicle amusingly headlined "British he's bathe more than she's." The story was based on a survey made by the Ministry of Works, which claimed to have sampled 6,000 representative British homes.

Every self-respecting British woman should ask Her Majesty's Ministry of Works: "How do you know that 1.5 female baths are significantly fewer than 1.7 male ones? Who made this decision? And, whoever he may be, how confident is he that he is right and not unjustly besmirching the reputation of the fair sex?"

This is the kind of issue that will be discussed in this section. Our discussion is an extension of the preceding pages, where we knew or assumed to know the true mean of the population.

Testing for the significance between two sample means is slightly different in detail from the significance test of the difference of a sample mean from a known or assumed mean. Let us illustrate this point in relation to the LUTABE problem. LUTABE could have sampled people as to their smoking habits prior to the news announcement and thereafter. Two sample means would be obtained, each accompanied by a sampling distribution. Having found the two sample means, we still do not know a single parameter. Instead, we can estimate confidence intervals for each mean. Our major concern is to decide whether the observed difference between the sample means is larger than random variation of the two statistics can be expected to produce. If so, the difference is significant.

How then, in practice, can we make such a significance test between two sample means? The philosophy behind the method is the same as when one mean was known or assumed, with the exception that we must allow for the possibility that the difference can be due not only to one sampling variation but to two.

We will control only the error of Type I. In principle, we take the same four steps as before. As an example we might consider the bathing habits of British males and females, set forth in the above news item. Sampling representative homes the Ministry of Works found that males in the winter go into the tub an average of 1.7 times a week; females bathed 1.5 times. We do not have the other required information; but let us assume that 9,000 males and 10,000 females were sampled and the standard deviation of the males was 1.2 and that of the females 1.0 tubs.

Now, can the British female justifiably claim that she takes as many baths per week as the British male does? The problem before us is illustrated in Chart 11.17.

We do not know μ_1 and μ_2 and, therefore, we do not know whether they are the same. However, in Chapter VII we demonstrated that the sample mean is the best estimate of the population mean. On a tentative basis, we have drawn two sampling distributions, that of females is drawn around the mean value of 1.5 and that of males around the mean value of 1.7. Both reflect their respective approximate standard errors. Theoretically, we could draw an infinitely large number of straight lines connecting midpoints, one for each distribution. By inspection it becomes clear that most of these lines will slope upward, few will be horizontal and very few will slope downward. (For simplicity's sake only one line of each type has been drawn in). While we do not know which line connects the two parameters, and therefore, do not know whether British manhood bathes just as often as, more often than, or less often than British womanhood, Chart 11.17 surmises that, with m_2 much larger than m_1 and s being small, equality in bathing habits is not very likely to prevail. To measure the probability that equal bathing habits prevail, we will present a statistical decision maker that tests whether the difference between two sample means is significant or not.

Chart 11.17 TESTING THE SIGNIFICANCE OF THE DIFFERENCE BETWEEN TWO SAMPLE MEANS

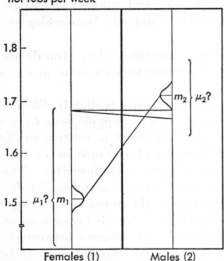

Using subscript 1 to connote female, and subscript 2 to connote male, we have the following information to work with:

$$n_1 = 10,000, \qquad n_2 = 9,000,$$
$$m_1 = 1.5, \qquad m_2 = 1.7,$$
$$s_1 = 1.0. \qquad s_2 = 1.2.$$

Let us agree that we are willing to risk incorrectly rejecting H_o in the long run twice out of 100 times and thus select an α of 0.02.

Using this information, we will indicate the four steps by which we decide whether the difference between the two sample means is significant. For the "not equal" case:

1. The null hypothesis states that the parameter pertaining to the males equals that pertaining to the females. The alternative hypothesis will be that the two parameters are not equal. In brief,

$$H_o: \mu_1 = \mu_2$$
$$H_A: \mu_1 \neq \mu_2,$$

where μ_1 is the population mean of population 1 and μ_2 that of population 2.

2. Reject H_o, if z value of sample is < -2.33 or $> +2.33$.

Accept H_o, if z value of sample falls between -2.33 and $+2.33$.

3. $z \doteq \dfrac{m_1 - m_2}{\sigma_{m_1-m_2}}.$ (11.4)

The definition of z that helps test for significance of a difference between two means is consistent with that used before, in that the numerator constitutes the difference to be tested and the denominator is the relevant standard deviation. Since we are testing for differences between sample means we will use the standard deviation—also called "standard error"— of the difference between two sample means. In examining z we realize that, while we may have little trouble in connection with m_1 and m_2, we need to learn more about $\sigma_{m_1-m_2}$. What, for instance, is the distribution of the standard error of the difference between two sample means? Remember, sample means of large samples are normally distributed around their mean. Similarly, it has been determined that in large samples the difference between two sample means is normally distributed around the mean difference: $m = m_1 - m_2$, and the standard error of the difference between the two sample means $\sigma_{m_1-m_2}$, can be approximated by

$$\sqrt{\frac{s_1^2}{n_1} + \frac{s_2^2}{n_2}}. \qquad (11.5)$$

In this bathing contest between the sexes $\sigma_{m_1-m_2} \doteq \sqrt{\dfrac{(1.0)^2}{10,000} + \dfrac{(1.2)^2}{9,000}} =$ 0.016.

With the standard error of the difference between the two sample means $\sigma_{m_1-m_2} \doteq 0.016$, we can proceed to find the z value of the sample: $z \doteq \dfrac{m_1 - m_2}{\sigma_{m_1-m_2}} = \dfrac{1.5 - 1.7}{0.016} = -12.$

4. We conclude with a 98 per cent confidence that, since the sample z (-12) is smaller than -2.33, we reject the null hypothesis that the winter bathing habits of British males and females are not significantly different. Our conclusion is that, on the basis of our criteria, there is a significant difference between the average number of hot baths British males and females take per week during the winter. While we only discussed the error of Type I, a test concerning the error of Type II could be made.

The above analysis neglects the source of bias inherent in the fact that young boys who generally detest ablutions may have brought down the male average.

WHAT WE LEARNED

1. With the future unknown, there is an advantage to making decisions of a known risk agreed upon in advance. There are statistical methods that can help make decisions carrying a calculable risk in the full sense of the word. In this chapter we were concerned primarily with deciding whether a given difference between a sample and assumed true mean was significant, i.e., due to other than random sources. We also tested the significance of a given difference between two sample means.

2. Statistical decision making calls for establishing a null hypothesis, i.e., a hypothesis of no difference, or, more generally, a hypothesis that has been enunciated with the intention of seeing whether in the light of the sample data it cannot be rejected.

3. Then, an alternative hypothesis is established. Such an alternative hypothesis, by and large, states the opposite of the null hypothesis.

4. There are three such sets of alternative hypotheses: Case A, the "not the same" case, Case B, the "more than" case, and Case C, the "less than" case.

5. In making a decision we face four situations:

I. A correct H_o is rejected and, thus, an error of Type I is committed.

II. An incorrect H_o is accepted and, thus, an error of Type II is committed.

III. A correct H_o is accepted and a good decision results.

IV. An incorrect H_o is rejected and a good decision results.

6. The probability of committing an error of Type I is called α, and the probability of committing an error of Type II is called β. The probability of rejecting an incorrect H_o is called the power of the test.

7. The general rule of a good decision is to minimize both α and β, or to minimize α and maximize the power of the test. This objective is usually accompanied by deciding on an appropriate α and selecting a method that under the circumstances maximizes the power of the test.

8. The first step in planned decision-making on the basis of sampling information is to compute the proper sample size. For this purpose it is necessary to agree upon an acceptable α, β, and interval within which the parameter is likely to fall. These three preliminary decisions are highly subjective and call for close co-operation between statistician and executive.

9. Once the proper sample size has been agreed upon, the second step is to draw a proper sample and calculate the statistics.

10. With the help of these statistics, particularly the sample mean and standard deviation, a test is made to learn whether the given difference between the sample and assumed (or true) mean is significant at the predetermined α. If in the light of the sample data we are forced to reject the null hypothesis, we conclude that at the given α the difference is significant. If, instead, we are forced to accept the null hypothesis, we may wish to learn more about the power of the test that accompanies this decision. We could then compute the power of the test and thus estimate what the β may be.

11. For a given α and sample size, Cases B and C maximize automatically the power of the test.

12. The formula for the proper sample size for testing a difference between a sample and assumed mean is $n \doteq \left(\dfrac{z_\alpha + z_\beta}{\dfrac{\mu_o - \mu_a}{s}} \right)^2$.

13. In testing for the significance of the difference between an assumed and (large) sample mean, $z = \dfrac{m - \mu}{\sigma_{\bar{x}}} \doteq \dfrac{m - \mu}{s/\sqrt{n}}$, and if the sample is small the test is made with the help of the Student-t distribution, where $t = \dfrac{m - \mu}{\sigma_{\bar{x}}} \doteq \dfrac{m - \mu}{s/\sqrt{n - 1}}$.

14. In testing for the significance of the difference between two sample means, if the sample is large,

$$z \doteq \frac{m_1 - m_2}{\sigma_{m_1-m_2}}, \text{ where } \sigma_{m_1-m_2} = \sqrt{\frac{s_1{}^2}{n_1} + \frac{s_2{}^2}{n_2}}.$$

NOW SEE WHETHER YOU CAN MAKE UP YOUR MIND ON THESE PROBLEMS:

1. In a survey of the coffee-drinking habits of the American people, 4,945 adults were sampled in each region. The per capita coffee consumption was found to be 16.1 pounds of coffee per adult per annum, with a standard deviation of 5.0 in New England, and 24.0 with a standard deviation of 10.0 in the West North Central region. At an α of 0.01, was the per capita coffee consumption in these two regions significantly different?

2. A bank in a metropolitan area has found that the average size of its checking account furnishes a good indication of the economic health of the community. Last month it sampled a random sample of 1,200 accounts and found the average balance amounting to $231. This month 1,400 accounts were sampled and found to have an average balance of $209. (The standard deviation this month was $92 and in the preceding month $97). On the basis of an α of 0.03, has a change taken place in the average balance of the bank's accounts?

3. A survey of 3,000 families from all over the United States revealed that during the third quarter of 1956 employed wage earners worked an average of 39.8 hours a week. The standard deviation was found to be 10.2 hours.

   a. Assuming that a political candidate seeking a national office claims that in the third quarter of 1956 the average employed wage earner worked 40.0 hours a week, what would be an appropriate set of hypotheses for testing the validity of the candidate's claim?

b. If you were the political opponent of the candidate who made the claim that the average work week is 40.0 hours, and were trying to show that labor's position had deteriorated, what set of hypotheses would you establish to test the validity of your claim?

c. If you were an independent observer who would like to test the validity of the 40.0 hour work week claim and were willing to assume a 6 per cent risk of incorrectly rejecting your null hypothesis, what would be your conclusion?

d. If you were an independent observer and believed that in fact the length of the average work week was somewhere between 38.8 and 40.0 hours, construct an appropriate power function.

e. If you were the political opponent of the candidate who made the claim about the work week and would select an α of 0.10, what conclusion would you reach?

f. If you were the political opponent of the claimant and believed that the average work week might be as short as 38.6 hours, what would be the corresponding power of the test?   Also get the performance function extending from a μ of 38.6 to 40.0.

g. If you were called on to make a survey about the length of the work week and agreed on the following data:
$\mu_0 = 41.0$, $\mu_2 = 39.1$, $\alpha = 0.08$, $\beta = 0.01$, $s = 11.0$, state two different objectives the survey might have and indicate how large a sample each would require.

4. Suppose the mean 1954 income per family was $4,950. However, a sample survey of 1,600 families revealed that their mean 1954 income amounted to $4,910, with a standard deviation of $1,000.

a. In case we are willing to commit an error of Type I only one time in a hundred in the long run, and neglecting for the moment the control of the error of Type II, what conclusion would we reach?

b. In case the true 1954 income per family was $4,940, how likely are we to commit an error of Type II?

c. In 1956 we think that incomes have increased since 1954 and we would like to make a sample survey to test this contention.   In case we decide that an α of 0.03 and a β of 0.01 are appropriate and the true mean lies between $4,950 and $5,000, how large a random sample is called for?

5. The Bon Mart Department Store has been greatly concerned about the fact that its stock shortages have amounted to almost 2 per cent of sales.   It realizes that one of the sources leading to stock shortages are the errors made by writing up sales checks.   The company has some information to the effect that the average shortage per sale amounted last year to 2.0 cents and would like to learn whether its training program has paid off and reduced the average shortage per sale.   Since more than 20 million sales were consummated this year, the company decides to base its decision on sample information.   Thinking that the average error may have decreased to 1.4 cents per sale, and with the standard deviation about 3.0 cents, management in discussing the risks with its statistician agrees on an α of 0.06 and a β of 0.04.   How large a sample would the statistician deem necessary?

6. The National Ladies Garment Association negotiates with a national union that insists on a 6.0 per cent wage increase, claiming that the cost of living of its workers has increased that much since the last contract was signed.   Most of the workers in the garment industry are paid piece rates and, therefore, it is not easy to know the average hourly wage.   The industry decides to learn what has happened to the average wage in the industry since the signing of the last contract.   From social security sheets, the industry statistician draws random samples of 2,600 workers, one sample for the period when the last contract was signed and a second for the most recent quarter.   The following information is thus obtained: $m_1 = \$1.03$, $s_1 = \$0.31$, $m_2 = \$1.06$, $s_2 = \$0.32$, where subscripts 1 and 2 designate the first and the second period.   Agreeing on an α of 0.01, what conclusions can be drawn?

7. Philadelphia has long been known as a city with very large dwellings.   Let us assume that the local Chamber of Commerce has decided to show that of the 57 major metropolitan areas in the United States, Philadelphia has indeed the largest dwellings.   Now somebody in Cleveland claims that it has the largest dwellings, basing the claim on the fact that the Planning Commission had surveyed each dwelling and recorded the number of rooms in it.   The average dwelling was found to have 5.7 rooms.   Philadelphia, to back up its claim, surveys a random sample of 25 dwellings, finding the average room number to be 5.8 and the standard deviation 0.80.   On the basis of an α of 0.10, is Philadelphia's claim sustained?

8. A recent survey of 2,400 workers revealed that they worked on the average 38.4 hours in the last week of March.   The standard deviation was 12.2.   It is known that in the corresponding week of the preceding year, the average work week in the United States was 40.2 hours.   At the risk of subjecting yourself to a 0.02 probability of committing an error of Type I, would you decide that the length of the work week has not changed?

9. Show why the entire α is placed in the lower tail in the "less than" or C Case.

10. In Exercise 5, the sample standard deviation was assumed to be 3 cents and at least as large as the mean.

   a. Does this relationship between mean and standard deviation point to a normal or nonnormal distribution of the population?
   b. Explain why it seems correct that the standard deviation in this example is so large in comparison to the mean?
   c. Explain why, in spite of this lopsided relation between standard deviation and mean, statistical test methods assuming normal distributions can be applied successfully?

XII

Decisions about Percentages

. . . for to say, under such circumstances, "Do not decide, but leave the
question open," is itself a passional decision,—just like deciding yes or no,—
and is attended with the same risk of losing the truth.

WILLIAM JAMES

In the preceding chapter we presented tests for the significance of differences between means. However, problems in economics and business often
call for the testing of the significance of differences between percentages,
proportions, or probabilities.[1] Two such tests, one for the difference
between a sample percentage and an assumed one, and a second for the
difference between two sample percentages (proportions or probabilities)
will be developed in the following pages.

12.1. "HALF THE BEAUTIES OF STAGE AND SCREEN PREFER GLAMORE . . . "

We can readily imagine a case in which one of the large soap manufacturers
claims that half the beauties of stage and screen prefer his brand—let us
call it "Glamore"—over all other soap brands combined. As occurs often
in reality, we can imagine in our ficticious case that competitors complained
to the Federal Trade Commission, disputing the claim's validity.

The Federal Trade Commission is the agency which by law is charged
with policing the ethics of competition. Before the Commission can act,
possibly by issuing a "cease and desist order," it must decide about the
validity of the soap manufacturer's claim. The Commission does not have

[1] From here on, what is stated about percentages will also hold for proportions and
probabilities.

200

a sufficiently large staff to contact each and every beauty in show business, ask her about her soap addiction, and thereby check the claim. Instead, it may take a sample on which its decision can be based.

Once in a lifetime, the Federal Trade Commission would have a pleasant, yes, delightful task. It could survey a random sample of, let us say, 200 beauties of stage and screen, asking them: "What is your favorite brand of soap?" Let us assume that it finds that of the 200 beauties interviewed 82, or 41 per cent, prefer Glamore over all other brands. However, the claim was that 50 per cent prefer Glamore. This calls for a test of the significance of this difference between an assumed percentage and a sample percentage.

This hypothetical case facing the Federal Trade Commission typifies decision-making in its numerous ramifications. The makers of Glamore would like the Commission to adopt a decision-making criterion, which minimizes the probability of deciding against its claim. Realizing that sampling variation can cause the sample percentage to be larger or smaller than 50 per cent, it would like to have the Commission use a criterion that would minimize the probability of the Commission's incorrectly rejecting the null hypothesis that 50 per cent of all beauties prefer Glamore, i.e., to use as small an α as possible.

The Federal Trade Commission and, of course, the competitors, on the other hand, are much concerned about an unwarranted acceptance of the null hypothesis. We know that they are interested at least as much in the error of Type II, preferring a small β. Keeping these two problems in mind, let us begin by testing the significance of the difference, using an α as 0.05.

Controlling α in terms of percentage values. This test is parallel to the one discussed in Chapter XI on testing the significance of differences between sample and assumed means. Instead of working with sampling distributions of means, we work with sampling distributions of percentages.

At the outset let us remember a very important concept, which was already discussed in Chapters IX and X, namely, that the sampling distribution of percentages can be approximated by a normal distribution in case the sample is large and the percentage is not too different from 0.50. As a matter of fact, in case the sample is very large, the approximation will be close even if the percentage does not come close to 0.50.

Here, then, is the information needed for the three steps of the test:

$$\left\{ \begin{array}{l} \pi = 0.50, \\ p = 0.41, \text{ and} \\ n = 200. \end{array} \right.$$

1. Weighing the implications of an error of Type I, we select an α of 0.05. We enunciate the null hypothesis that there is no difference between the manufacturer's claim, i.e., the assumed percentage, and the sample percentage. The alternative hypothesis states that the assumed percentage is less than the sample percentage. In brief,

$$H_o: \pi = 0.50.$$
$$H_C: \pi < 0.50.$$

2. In order to find the sample percentage values that will delineate the regions of rejection and acceptance, we will calculate the standard deviation of the sampling distribution of percentages σ_p, also called standard error of the percentage. This standard error of the percentage can be computed with the aid of Formula 9.6: $\sigma_p = \sqrt{\dfrac{\pi(1-\pi)}{n}}$, where π is the assumed percentage. We will multiply this standard error by the appropriate z value and subtract it from the assumed percentage. Thus, the line of demarcation will be at $0.50 - z\sqrt{\dfrac{\pi(1-\pi)}{n}}$, i.e., $0.50 - 1.64\sqrt{\dfrac{(0.50)(0.50)}{200}}$ or 0.44.

Drawing a normal curve around $\pi = 0.50$ to represent the sampling distribution of percentages (this is permissible because the percentage is close to 0.50 and n is reasonably large), we mark off the line of demarcation at 0.44 (see top Panel of Chart 12.1).

The criteria can also be stated as follows:

> Reject H_o, if the sample percentage < 0.44.
> Accept H_o, if the sample percentage > 0.44.

3. When we compare our sample percentage with the demarcation value, we can readily see that it lies in the region of rejection. We are therefore forced to reject the null hypothesis and conclude on the basis of an α of 0.05, that the percentage claimed by the manufacturer of Glamore is significantly larger than the sample percentage. The Federal Trade Commission could conclude that Glamore's advertisement is not consistent with the facts.

Controlling α in terms of z values. Here in brief are the four steps of this test:

1. $H_o: \pi = 0.50.$
   $H_C: \pi < 0.50.$
2. Reject H_o, if the z value of the sample data is < -1.64.
   Accept H_o, if the z value of the sample data > -1.64.

$$3.\ z = \frac{p - \pi}{\sigma_p} \doteq \frac{p - \pi}{\sqrt{\dfrac{\pi(1 - \pi)}{n}}} \tag{12.1}$$

$$\doteq \frac{0.41 - 0.50}{\sqrt{\dfrac{(0.50)(0.50)}{200}}} = -2.5.$$

4. Since the z value of the sample data is smaller than -1.64 and falls into the region of rejection, we are forced to reject the null hypothesis on the basis of an α of 0.05.

Chart 12.1 β's AND POWERS OF THE TEST
("Less than" or C Case.)

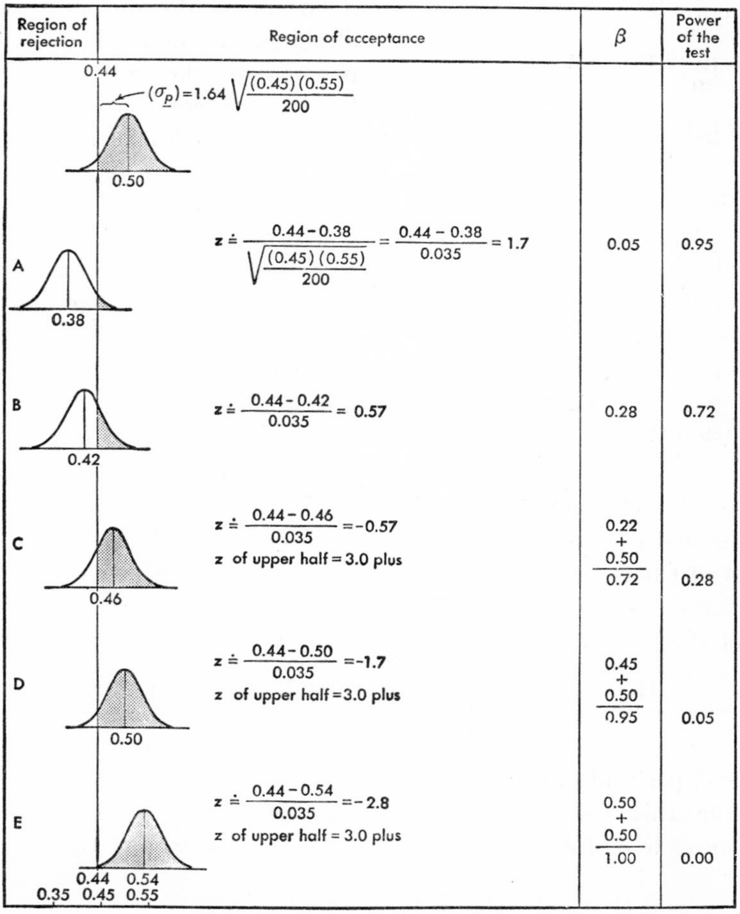

Region of rejection	Region of acceptance	β	Power of the test
0.44 $(\sigma_p)=1.64\sqrt{\dfrac{(0.45)(0.55)}{200}}$ 0.50			
A 0.38	$z \doteq \dfrac{0.44-0.38}{\sqrt{\dfrac{(0.45)(0.55)}{200}}} = \dfrac{0.44 - 0.38}{0.035} = 1.7$	0.05	0.95
B 0.42	$z \doteq \dfrac{0.44-0.42}{0.035} = 0.57$	0.28	0.72
C 0.46	$z \doteq \dfrac{0.44-0.46}{0.035} = -0.57$ z of upper half = 3.0 plus	0.22 + 0.50 ____ 0.72	0.28
D 0.50	$z \doteq \dfrac{0.44-0.50}{0.035} = -1.7$ z of upper half = 3.0 plus	0.45 + 0.50 ____ 0.95	0.05
E 0.44 0.54 0.35 0.45 0.55	$z \doteq \dfrac{0.44-0.54}{0.035} = -2.8$ z of upper half = 3.0 plus	0.50 + 0.50 ____ 1.00	0.00

Performance and power functions.   If, instead of finding a sample percentage of 0.41, we had come up with one of 0.45, our decision would have been to accept the null hypothesis.   In so doing we would have subjected ourselves to the risk of committing an error of Type II and we might want to know more about this risk and compute the performance or power functions.

What about the power of the test of this problem?   As a first step, we will find the line of demarcation, which is:

$$\pi - z\sqrt{\frac{\pi(1-\pi)}{n}} = 0.50 - 1.64\sqrt{\frac{(0.50)(0.50)}{200}} \text{ or } +0.44.$$

Now, let us suppose that those concerned with the claim of the makers of Glamore have good information which causes them to believe that, although they do not know the exact percentage, the actual percentage lies somewhere between 0.38 and 0.50.   We would, therefore, calculate performance and power functions covering the range 0.38 to 0.50.

Chart 12.2   POWER FUNCTIONS
(Cases A, B and C.)

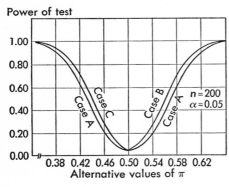

To start with, let us entertain the hypothesis that merely 38 per cent of the beauties of stage and screen prefer Glamore over all other brands. Why don't we construct a sampling distribution of percentages around $\pi = 0.38$ and see what per cent of this distribution lies in the region of acceptance?   This sampling distribution with $\pi = 0.38$ and $n = 200$ can be approximated by a normal distribution around $\pi = 0.38$, as can be seen in Panel A of Chart 12.1.   The percentage, if any, of this normal curve that lies in the region of acceptance can be readily computed by finding the z value of the interval 0.44 to 0.38 with the help of the formula that $z \doteq$

$\dfrac{p - \pi}{\sqrt{\dfrac{\pi(1-\pi)}{n}}}.$ Here $z \doteq \dfrac{0.44 - 0.38}{\sqrt{\dfrac{(0.50)(0.50)}{200}}}$ or $+1.7$.   Corresponding to a z value of

$+1.7$ is 45 per cent of the area of the normal curve, with the plus sign indicating that this area lies in the upper half of the distribution.   To the right of the lower line of demarcation lies $0.50 - 0.45$ or 0.05 of the area under the normal curve. Thus, the probability is 0.05 that the null hypothesis will be wrongly accepted; β is 0.05 and the power of the test is 0.95.

Similar computations for different hypothetical values for π (falling within the range 0.38 to 0.50) together with the relevant graphs are presented in Chart 12.1. These data have been summarized in the form of a power function together with functions for Cases A and B in Chart 12.2.

12.2. PLANNING SAMPLE SIZE

Before we can know how large a sample is needed we must make a number of subjective decisions. First of all, we must decide whether hypotheses of Type A, B, or C are called for. Next, we must select an appropriate α (the probability of incorrectly rejecting the null hypothesis) as well as an appropriate β (the probability of incorrectly accepting the null hypothesis). Finally, we must decide, on the basis of our experience and knowledge of the situation within what interval the parameter is likely to fall.

Let us make these subjective decisions in relation to the hypothetical case facing the Federal Trade Commission, and compute the desired sample size.

In case the Commission would like to check on the claim that "more beauties of stage and screen use Glamore than all other brands combined," hypotheses of "the less than" or C Case could be established. Let us furthermore agree that there is good reason to expect the actual percentage to lie between 0.40 and 0.50, and specify an α of 0.10 and β of 0.08. Here $\pi_o = 0.50$ and $\pi_a = 0.40$; $z_\alpha = 1.28$ and $z_\beta = 1.40$. We can find n using the following formula:

$$n \doteq \left(\frac{z_\alpha \sqrt{\pi_o(1.00 - \pi_o)} + z_\beta \sqrt{\pi_a(1.00 - \pi_a)}}{\pi_o - \pi_a} \right)^2, \qquad (12.2)$$

where z_α is the z value of the selected α,

z_β is the z value of the selected β in case the parameter has the value indicated as extreme in H_a,

π_o is the parameter relevant to H_o, and

π_a is the parameter relevant to H_a.

Just as in Equation 11.2, also here z_α, z_β, and the range, i.e., $\pi_o - \pi_a$ are always positive values. In our example,

$$z_\alpha = 1.28,$$
$$z_\beta = 1.40,$$
$$\pi_o = 0.50, \text{ and}$$
$$\pi_a = 0.40.$$

.50 - .90 = .10

.50 - .42 = .08

Substituting these values in Formula 12.2, we have:

$$n \doteq \left(\frac{1.28 \sqrt{(0.50)(0.50)} + 1.40 \sqrt{(0.40)(0.60)}}{0.10} \right)^2 = 180.$$

Thus, consistent with the risks the Commission is willing to assume and the information at hand, a sample of about 180 beauties of stage and screen is appropriate.

Let us take another example: One of the major electrical appliance manufacturers who has so far insisted on uniform prices throughout the country is thinking of allowing retail outlets to set their own prices. His decision will in part be influenced by the reaction of the retailers whose co-operation is considered important. He has decided not to undertake the change unless two thirds of his retail outlets favor the new system over the old one, but surmises that a mere 60 per cent will take this position. Agreeing that an α of 0.06 and a β of 0.04 are acceptable, he calculates that he needs an

$$n \doteq \left(\frac{1.56 \sqrt{(0.66)(0.34)} + 1.75 \sqrt{(0.60)(0.40)}}{0.06} \right)^2 = 700.$$

12.3. "THE HORN BLOWS AT MIDNIGHT"—IS IT KEEPING ANYONE AWAKE?

The makers of Chi-Chi chewing gum have been sponsoring for some time the television program, "The Horn Blows at Midnight." In the last meeting of the executive committee of the company, Ben Jack, the executive vice-president, expresses some doubts about the desirability of continuing this program. Says he, "I just don't think that people can stand this kind of a program for long. Oh, I liked it all right the first time, but after a while it gets boring, to put it mildly. Now mind you, this is the way I feel about it, and I am the first to admit that it is quite possible that 'The Horn Blows at Midnight' is the type of program the public goes in for. But I am just not certain and I sure hate to pour money down the drain." This statement gets Bill Willy, the enterprising vice-president in charge of sales, hot under the collar. Bill obviously thinks that the television show is a big success and brings the name of Chi-Chi chewing gum to the attention of millions of people. Finally, Robert Young White, the president, has to make some comments in the hope of cooling tempers. He points out that little harm could be done by checking the program. This should not be too difficult since when the program was first initiated a market research organization had made a Telepulse rating, i.e., estimated the percentage of viewers. "Why don't we get those boys to take a new rating and see what happens?" are his concluding remarks.

Perhaps Mr. White, the president, does not fully appreciate the nature of the problem. A comparison of Telepulse ratings in two periods is not a simple thing. It requires testing the significance of the difference between two sample percentages. Telepulse ratings are simple sample percentages, and a test of significance is needed.

Here are the results: the first survey showed that of 2,000 persons interviewed, 8 per cent were watching "The Horn Blows at Midnight"; while in the second survey of 1,800 people 7 per cent were watching. Should White conclude that apparently many people feel like his executive vice-president does, and that the interest of the television audience has significantly changed, he might be making an error of Type I. Before such a decision could be reached the significance of the difference between the two sample percentages needs testing. In order to maintain an objective position, the null hypothesis could be that the percentage of people watching the Chi-Chi chewing gum program has not changed; and the alternative hypothesis would be that there has been a change. These two hypotheses, you might say, would not prejudice the case. Mr. White, in formulating them, cannot be accused either by Jack or by Willy of taking sides before all the facts are in. Everybody is fully aware that, should the conclusion be that the show's reception by the audience has changed, and should that conclusion be unwarranted (a wrong rejection of the null hypothesis), this conclusion could lead to steps that are not in the company's best interest. Similarly, a conclusion that there has been no change, when in fact there has been a pronounced one, could prevent the company's taking corrective steps and, as Jack had put it, would pour good money down the drain. The latter point assumes that the Chi-Chi Gum Company has agreed that a Telepulse rating of 8 is the minimum that warrants a television program.

How, then, could the significance of the difference be tested? Agreeing on an α of 0.04, here are the four steps of the significance test controlling α in terms of z values:

1. $H_o: \pi_1 = \pi_2$.
   $H_A: \pi_1 \neq \pi_2$ (subscript 1 means the first and 2 the second period).
2. Reject H_o, if the z value of the sample data is < -2.05 or $> +2.05$.
   Accept H_o, if the z value of the sample data falls between -2.05 and $+2.05$.
3. $z = \dfrac{d - \delta}{\sigma_d},$ \hfill (12.3)

where d is the difference between the two sample percentages, $d = p_1 - p_2$ and δ is the difference between the two corresponding population percentages, and σ_d is the standard deviation, or standard error, of the difference between the two percentages. σ_d could also be written as $\sigma_{p_1-p_2}$. If we have large samples of size n_1 and n_2 taken from two different populations whose true proportions are π_1 and π_2, the sampling distribution of the difference between the sample percentages, i.e., $p_1 - p_2$, is closely approximated by a normal curve for which the mean is the difference between the two population percentages, i.e., $\delta = \pi_1 - \pi_2$, and the standard deviation σ_d or

$$\sigma_{p_1-p_2} = \sqrt{\frac{\pi_1(1.00 - \pi_1)}{n_1} - \frac{\pi_2(1.00 - \pi_2)}{n_2}}.$$

The two population percentages are, of course, unknown. However, we do not care about their magnitudes, except that we would like to know whether or not they are different. We established the null hypothesis that the difference between the two population percentages is 0.00. Thus, for our purposes and, whenever we test the significance of the difference between two sample percentages, proportions, ratios, or probabilities, $\delta = \pi_1 - \pi_2 = 0.00$. Under these conditions, i.e., with $\delta = 0.00$, the standard deviation of the difference between two percentages is reduced to

$$\sigma_{p_1-p_2} = \sqrt{\pi(1.00 - \pi)\left(\frac{1}{n_1} + \frac{1}{n_2}\right)}. \tag{12.4}$$

In this formula for the standard deviation of the difference between two percentages, π, the population proportion, is, of course, unknown. We approximate π, as we did before, by referring to the sample values, specifically the sample percentages. We say that

$$\pi \doteq \frac{x_1 + x_2}{n_1 + n_2} \quad \text{or} \quad \frac{p_1(n_1) + p_2(n_2)}{n_1 + n_2}, \tag{12.5}$$

where x is the number of people surveyed having a given characteristic, p is the sample proportion, n is the sample size, and the subscripts 1 and 2 pertain to the time period.

In our case,
$$p_1 = 0.08,$$
$$p_2 = 0.07,$$
$$n_1 = 2,000, \text{ and}$$
$$n_2 = 1,800;$$

so that $\pi \doteq \dfrac{p_1(n_1) + p_2(n_2)}{n_1 + n_2} = \dfrac{0.08(2,000) + 0.07(1,800)}{3,800} = 0.08$, and

$$\sigma_{p_1-p_2} = \sqrt{\pi(1.00 - \pi)\left(\frac{1}{n_1} + \frac{1}{n_2}\right)} \doteq \sqrt{0.08(0.92)\left(\frac{1}{2,000} + \frac{1}{1,800}\right)} = 0.009.$$

Now we can turn to finding $z = \dfrac{d - \delta}{\sigma_{p_1-p_2}}$. In our case, $d = p_1 - p_2 = 0.08 -$ 0.07 = 0.01; and, consistent with our null hypothesis that $\pi_1 = \pi_2$ or $\pi_1 - \pi_2 = \delta = 0.00$, we will put $\delta = 0.00$.

$$z = \frac{d - \delta}{\sigma_{p_1-p_2}} \doteq \frac{0.01 - 0.00}{0.009} = +1.1.$$

4. In conclusion, since the z value of the sample $(+1.1)$ falls between -2.05 and $+2.05$, we are forced to accept the null hypothesis that no significant change in the Telepulse rating of "The Horn Blows at Midnight" has occurred. At a risk of incorrectly rejecting the null hypothesis 4 times out of one hundred we would agree that the show sponsored by the makers of Chi-Chi chewing gum is about as popular as when it first went on the air.

This conclusion is likely to make Bill Willy, the sales vice-president, happy. Ben Jack, who initially had his doubts about the program, might well raise the question how likely the company is to accept the null hypothesis incorrectly and he may insist that a power function be calculated. We will not take the time to work through Cases B and C, but would suggest to the reader that he give some thought to them and to the power of the test.

WHAT HAS BEEN LEARNED:

1. Before we can determine how large a sample is needed to decide whether a difference between a sample and assumed percentage (proportion or probability) is significant, we must decide on how large a risk of committing an error of Type I and how large a risk of committing an error of Type II are acceptable, together with the range within which the parameter is likely to fall. Once these subjective decisions have been made, we can place these values into the following equation to find the appropriate sample size:

$$n \doteq \left(\frac{z_\alpha \sqrt{\pi_o(1.00 - \pi_o)} + z_\beta \sqrt{\pi_a(1.00 - \pi_a)}}{\pi_o - \pi_a}\right)^2.$$

2. In testing the significance of a difference between a sample and assumed percentage (proportion or probability), we make use of the following formula:

$$z = \frac{p - \pi}{\sigma_p} \doteq \frac{p - \pi}{\sqrt{\dfrac{pq}{n}}}.$$

3. We can make significance tests controlling α either in terms of percentage

values or z values.   Power and performance functions can be readily constructed in the conventional fashion.

4. In testing the significance of a difference between two sample percentages (proportions, or probabilities), we make use of the following formula:

$$z = \frac{d - \delta}{\sigma_d},$$

where if δ, the difference between π_1 and π_2, is equal to 0.00,

$$\sigma_d = \sqrt{\pi(1.00 - \pi)\left(\frac{1}{n_1} + \frac{1}{n_2}\right)}, \text{ and } \pi \doteq \frac{x_1 + x_2}{n_1 + n_2} = \frac{p_1(n_1) + p_2(n_2)}{n_1 + n_2}.$$

DECIDE FOR YOURSELF WHETHER YOU HAVE LEARNED TO MAKE DECISIONS:

1. According to law an area is declared a "labor surplus area" in case 6.0 per cent or more of its labor force is unemployed.   Once declared a "labor surplus area," the United States government accords the area preferential treatment in the letting of defense contracts.

   a. Establish the appropriate set of hypotheses for deciding whether a given area is "a labor surplus area."
   b. Discuss in relation to this decision problem the errors of Type I and Type II and what they mean to the area and to the federal government, respectively.
   c. If 2,000 members of the labor force were interviewed and 130 were found unemployed, what decision would you reach if you are willing to subject yourself to an α of 0.06?
   d. Find the power function on the assumption that the true parameter lies between 5.80 and 6.70 per cent.
   e. In the planning stage (i.e., while the information given in c is unknown), how large a sample would you think appropriate in case you settled on the following criteria:

$$\alpha = 0.06,$$
$$\beta = 0.02,$$
$$\pi_o = 0.060, \text{ and}$$
$$\pi_a = 0.067?$$

2. The Bureau of Vocational Guidance at Harvard University made a study of 4,375 men who had been discharged from various positions.   They found that only one third were lacking in ability to do the job.   Two thirds were found handicapped by destructive personality qualities that were classified under 14 different headings.   Of these two thirds, 18 per cent were handicapped by failure to co-operate, 17 per cent by unreliability, and 16 per cent by laziness.

   Assuming the sample is random, could you decide, at the risk of incorrectly rejecting a valid hypothesis in the long run 5 times out of 100, that:

   2 tailed

   a. Unreliability was just as much a handicap as failure to co-operate, and
   b. Unreliability was at least as important a handicap as laziness.

3. In the spring of 1955, 3,120 spending units were interviewed by the Survey of Consumer Finances, carried out jointly by the Federal Reserve System and the Survey Research Center of the University of Michigan. A similar survey had been made in the spring of 1954, when 3,000 spending units were sampled. On the assumption that the methods developed in this chapter were applicable, indicate whether, at an α of 0.10 and 0.02, respectively, significant changes had taken place between the early spring of 1954 and 1955 in the following items:

| | | | Difference Signi- ficant at an α of | |
Percentage of Consumers Who Intended to Buy	*1954*	*1955*	*0.10*	*0.02*
New car	7.9	8.2	NO	NO
Used car	6.4	7.5		
Furniture	11.9	12.0		
Television set	7.7	5.9		
Refrigerator	4.1	4.5		
Washing machine	3.6	5.3		

Source: Federal Reserve Bulletin, May 1955, pp. 468–469.

4. The same surveys produced also the following information, for which significance test should be made using an α of 0.04:

Money Income before Taxes in Preceding Year	*Percentage of Nonbusiness Spending Units with Zero Short-term Consumer Debt*		*Difference Significant at an α of 0.04*
	1954	*1955*	
Under $1,000	67	68	
$1,000–$2,000	56	52	
$2,000–$3,000	47	46	
$3,000–$4,000	42	37	
$4,000–$5,000	36	36	
$5,000–$7,500	37	33	
$7,500 and over	46	48	

Source: Federal Reserve Bulletin, June 1955, p. 613.

What conclusions can be drawn from these data?

5. a. In 1939 Arthur Kudner, Inc., made a survey for the Pan American Coffee Bureau designed to discover how sales of coffee might be increased. Of 4,945 persons sampled all over the United States, 46 per cent brewed coffee in a percolator and 39 per cent in a dripolator. At a 0.02 level of significance, did as many Americans use percolators as dripolators?

want to know if there is a difference only   2 tailed test

b. The survey also found that (of the, let us say, 2,400 men and 2,545 women surveyed) 82 per cent of all men and 81 per cent of all women drink coffee. At a 0.04 per cent level of significance, would you conclude that <u>as many men as women</u> over sixteen drink coffee?

6. The Kudner survey of 4,945 persons also found interesting information about the coffee-drinking habits of the adult population in various sections of the country. The per capita coffee consumption was lowest in New England—16.1 pounds per adult per annum, and highest in the West North Central region—24.0 pounds per adult per annum. At a 0.01 level of significance, was the per capita coffee consumption in the West North Central region at least as high as it was in New England? (Assume the sample standard deviations to be 14.0 and 20.0, respectively).

7. A recent study revealed that, of a sample of 5,600 cases brought to the marriage reconciliation court, the following principal causes predominated:

(1)	Excessive drinking	29.8
(2)	Unfaithfulness	24.8
(3)	Irresponsibility	12.4
(4)	Difference of temperament	12.1
(5)	In-law trouble	7.2
(6)	Sex maladjustment	5.4
(7)	Mental illness	3.0
(8)	Religious differences	2.9
(9)	Financial difficulties	0.8

a. At an α of 0.02, was excessive drinking responsible for at least 30.0 per cent of all the difficulties that finally bring couples into a marriage reconciliation court?

b. At an α of 0.03, can 12.0 per cent of the cases ending in a marriage reconciliation court be traced back to differences in temperament?

c. At an α of 0.01, can more than 8.0 per cent of the cases brought to marriage reconciliation courts be traced back to in-law trouble?

d. At an α of 0.10, can financial difficulties be assumed to be of insignificant importance insofar as causes leading to marital difficulties are concerned?

8. Five hundred twenty-nine customers of a department store were sampled as to whether they were satisfied with the store's parking facilities. Of those interviewed all but 10.0 per cent were satisfied.

a. With an α of 0.05, can we conclude that all the store's customers are satisfied with the parking facilities?

b. With an α of 0.05, construct the power function on the assumption that the true parameter may lie between 93 and 100 per cent.

c. On the basis of an α of 0.04, β of 0.02, π_o of 0.97, and π_a of 1.00, how large a sample would the store need?

9. In September, 1955, Midwest farmers on the one hand and residents of cities of 100,000 or more population on the other were surveyed to answer the following kind of question: "Are you satisfied or dissatisfied with the way the Republican Administration is handling the problem of farm prices and farm price supports?" It was reported that 33 per cent of the farmers and 35 per cent of the city dwellers were satisfied. On the assumption that 1,820 farmers and 1,930 city dwellers had

been surveyed, and on the basis of an α of 0.01, is there a significant difference between the opinion of farmers and city dwellers on the problem of farm prices? How do you explain your conclusion?

10. A brewery has been spending thousands of dollars for billboard advertising along a major highway. Lately many other breweries have been placing advertisements on the same highway, so that the company is wondering whether drivers read and remember its signs. It would like to place an interviewer near the toll station of a bridge and have him ask drivers about the billboards. Its advertising agency had claimed that 20 per cent of all drivers pay attention to the signs, yet the company is afraid that but 8 per cent see them. It is willing to work with an α of 0.10 and a β of 0.06. How large a sample is called for?

XIII

Index Numbers—Tying Up to the Hitching Post

When Roger Baldwin (long-term director of the American Civil Liberties Union and presently head of the International League for the Rights of Man) was married to Madeleine Doty, the couple used to figure their separate household obligations so minutely that sometimes a dinner guest would be embarrassed by a lively discussion about whose account should properly be charged. Baldwin's relations with his present wife are more relaxed. . . . At the outset, he told her that his income would never support her style of living. They agreed he would pay her every month just what his bachelor living expenses had been—a figure he knew to the last nickel. This is periodically adjusted according to the government cost-of-living index.[1]

DWIGHT MACDONALD

Baldwin used an *index number*, a word by which the statistician usually means a device to *measure the average movement of a group of closely related items over time relative to some base taken as 100.* Index numbers are a means of comparison; they are valuable as indirect measurements of economic magnitudes that cannot readily be measured directly. Indirect measurements are also often resorted to in the physical sciences. For example, temperature is measured indirectly on a thermometer by the size of the column of mercury; thus the scale on the thermometer may be regarded as an index number representing the movements of temperature over time.

Ever since index numbers were first compiled, their use has greatly and steadily increased and their usefulness has been amply proved. The manufacturer is aided by index numbers in setting the price policy of his firm in

[1] From an article in *The New Yorker*, July 18, 1953, p. 30.

line with changes in the general price level. Labor and management in their wage negotiations are guided by index numbers that reflect changes in the purchasing power of the take-home pay. Department stores like to compare their sales to the index of department store sales in their area so that they can be guided in their advertising policy. Many farmers when they sell to the Commodity Credit Corporation receive prices that are related to the Parity Index, which measures changes in prices of products bought by farmers. The accountant uses index numbers to measure price changes in estimating depreciation. The economist, in and out of government, constructs and watches a host of indexes to recommend fiscal and monetary policies consistent with high and stable levels of employment. These are but a few examples, testifying that index numbers have become a widely used tool. The federal government alone constructs and publishes hundreds of them and many industries and companies have their own indexes. We have good reason, thus, to examine them and acquaint ourselves with some of the more important ones.

13.1. SIMPLE INDEX NUMBERS

Let us see how Mr. Camel, the regional sales manager of LUTABE cigarettes, could establish how last week's sales figures compare with those of the past.

First, Camel compares last week's sales ($437,500) with those of the preceding week ($431,200). He is tempted to say that this week's sales are 101.5 per cent of what they were in the previous week. In comparing these two numbers he has simply given expression to relative changes by stating one of the two numbers as a percentage of the other. Such percentage changes, or percentages, are index numbers; in fact they are by far the simplest form of index numbers.

Mr. Camel is interested in merely comparing cigarette sales. For this purpose he constructs a *simple sales quantity index*, also often referred to as a *quantity relative*. Besides quantity relatives, there are *price relatives* and *value relatives*, depending on whether the comparison is one of quantity, price, or value. An example of the latter is the value of the construction awards index, which measures fluctuations in anticipated building construction (and which is published in the United States Department of Commerce's *Survey of Current Business*).

The hitching post problem. So far Mr. Camel has had an easy task. He compared sales data for but two consecutive weeks. If, however, the weekly sales data of this territory had been recorded for the last 50 years,

Mr. Camel would have quite a problem in deciding how sales compare with the past. The obvious question is: Which past? We already stated that compared with last week, this week's sales are at a 101.5 per cent level. If the sales in the same week of last year amounted to $400,000 of cigarettes, the most recent week's sales were at a 109.4 per cent level; and comparing them with 10 years back, they were at a 253 per cent level. Mr. Camel would look foolish, were he to tell his general sales manager that "sales are at a 101.5 per cent level, or perhaps at a 109.4 per cent level; or perhaps at a 253 per cent level." We got hold of the knotty problem of deciding on a

Reprinted from Louder and Funnier *by Burr Shafer, Vanguard Press.*

"However, if comparison is made with 1939 instead of 1948, I am pleased to report . . . "

hitching post. The magazine *Business Week* stated some time ago:

Every index number must have a base, a statistical hitching post from which to express the change. This hitching post, consisting of one or more years, is commonly called the *base period.*

This base period, preferably, should be recent enough so that comparisons are meaningful. In this respect [the new base of the Business Week Index] is obviously an improvement over the old. Clearly it means more to a businessman to say that production in the Dec. 26 week (of 1953) was 25.1% above 1947–49 (which is what an index of 125.1 means) than to say it was 143.6% above 1923–25.

There are other recent years besides 1947–49. We chose them because, taken together, these years represent a recent period of about average industrial activity. 1947 was a year of upswing, 1948 a relatively good year, 1949 was a year of recession and then, late in the year, a start toward recovery.

An equally important reason for choosing 1947–49 as the base years is this: In 1950, the Bureau of the Budget recommended that all federal agencies publishing indexes use these three years as a base; by now almost all important government indexes are on this base.[2]

In the construction of index numbers the selection of a proper base is all-important. The guide is to take a recent and reasonably average or normal period (whatever normal means). Once Mr. Camel has such a base, his comparative statement assumes meaning. Should he decide to go along with *Business Week* and the Bureau of the Budget, he might inform the general sales manager that this week's sales were 114 per cent above the base period 1947–49, i.e., the index stood at 214.

In summary, the construction of a simple index, for instance Camel's sales index, involves three steps:

1. A base period is chosen;
2. The sales volume of each week is divided by the sales figure of the base period; and
3. The result is multiplied by 100 (i.e., the decimal is moved two places to the right) to express sales as a percentage or index number. For instance, if the average weekly sales volume in the base period was $431,200 and sales in the week under consideration were $437,500, we find the index number for this week as follows: ($437,500 ÷ $431,200) × 100 = 101.5.

Seasonal adjustment. In constructing an index, there is another problem to be considered. Mr. Camel stated that this week's sales were 114 per cent above the base period. But could it not be that every year this particular week enjoys better than normal sales? There could be seasonal factors responsible for this high sales volume. Mr. Camel might wish to know whether the sales increase merely reflects the seasonal increases or is possibly in excess of what can be attributed to the seasonal element. By making a *seasonal adjustment*, the seasonal effects on the index are eliminated.

Retailing is an obvious example of the kind of regular fluctuations in business, pretty much the same from one year to the next, that make up a seasonal pattern and will be looked into in more detail in a later chapter. To most retailers a volume of business that would be fine for February would be terrible for December. To some extent the same holds true for Mr. Camel's case. These regular ups and downs in activity have to be ironed out before Camel can answer the general question, "How's business?" This is what a seasonal adjustment of index numbers tries to do. Should, for instance, the week under consideration be a typically slow sales week—let us

[2] The Business Week Index, *Business Week*, January 16, 1954.

say sales typically stand at only 90 per cent of what they are in the average week of the year—the 214 would be divided by 0.90 to give a seasonally adjusted index of 237.

13.2. COMPOSITE INDEX NUMBERS

There are occasions when we need an index of a single commodity and a simple index number is all that is called for. However, in the majority of cases, we want to measure the movement over time of groups of items, their prices, quantities, or values. A composite index is then needed.

Many of the problems posed by the construction of a simple index exist also in the preparation of a composite index. The fact that we are to reflect changes in the movement of a group of items gives rise to some additional problems.

Measures of relative importance—weights. Let us consider the construction of an index that we hope will measure weekly changes in over-all business activity. The *Business Week* Index, for instance, is such an index. One of the first questions that we will have to answer for ourselves is: What constitutes and affects economic activity? Electric power output, steel production, construction, are some of the factors. Next we ask: What is their relative importance? Changes in any one must be weighted by the importance of the item changing. Here are the weights of the *Business Week* Index:

Component	Weight
Electric power output	23
Steel production	17
Car loadings	29
Construction contracts awarded	7
Car and truck production	5
Machinery production	5
Transportation equipment production	5
Crude oil production	5
Paper board production	4

For this purpose, index numbers incorporate a *weighting system*. In a sense, we weight by the sampling process itself, insofar as we decide which items to include in the study and which to exclude. But within the sample it is necessary to apply appropriate weights, according to the purpose of the index. *Weights* are the importance we assign to the various components within the total index. They are the means by which in a production index, for instance, we link together tons of steel, kilowatt hours of electric output, number of automobiles, and end with a meaningful total. If we neglected to introduce weights explicitly, we would be assigning all industries equal importance. The resulting index would most likely be inappropriate.

The question remains how to select proper weights. If we are to trace changes in industrial production, we must in a general sense have the weights that reflect the relative valuations we place on the various industrial activities in the market place. A common way to do this is to use value-added figures as weights. How can we determine the value that was added to purchased materials in the process of fabricating them into finished or more nearly finished products, and do this for all the major industrial groups? To get value-added figures the Federal Reserve Monthly Index of Industrial Production has relied on United States Bureau of the Census information. The Bureau subtracts from each industry's gross value of products the cost of materials, supplies, containers, fuels, purchased electric energy, and contract work. It is in this form that the Bureau of the Census visualizes and measures each industry's unduplicated contribution to the nation's total output.[3]

The Federal Reserve Monthly Index of Industrial Production covers a total of 164 products or industries, with each industry weighted in terms of its unduplicated contribution to total output as measured by the Bureau of the Census' value-added figures. The Business Week Index incorporates but 9 main segments of industry, with the weights roughly reflecting the value added by each segment.

Weights in a consumer price index. The selection of proper weights for a price index is even more intriguing. It involves considering a wide variety of economic and sociological factors. Let us look into the weights of a consumer price index in general and of that developed by the United States Bureau of Labor Statistics in particular.

Before we can decide on proper weights, the purpose of the index must be clear. It is, therefore, best to remind ourselves of the objective that the Bureau of Labor Statistics has set itself in constructing its Consumer Price Index. It can be said that this index is designed to measure the average change in prices of goods and services customarily purchased by families of wage earners and clerical workers living in cities of the United States. The prices of the various items should, therefore, be weighted in accordance with the relative importance of each item in the budget of these families. Obviously, an index in which the price of hairpins is weighted as heavily

[3] For a more detailed discussion of the weighting system used in the Federal Reserve Monthly Index of Industrial Production see *Federal Reserve Monthly Index of Industrial Production. 1953 Revision*, Board of Governors of the Federal Reserve System (Washington, D.C., 1953), pp. 33–36.

as is the price of meat does not accurately record changes in a family's living expenses.

How can we learn about the relative importance of hairpins as against meat in the budget of the approximately two thirds of all city families who are urban wage earners and clerical workers? We must learn in fact how wage and salaried workers' families in cities spend their money. What goes into their market basket? A good way to find this out is to sample a representative group of families and learn how they spend their money.

That is exactly what the Bureau of Labor Statistics did in 1950, when it interviewed about 8,000 wage earners' and clerical workers' families in selected cities. From this survey were obtained estimates of the kinds of goods bought, quantities bought, amount spent for each article, and the quality of each article bought. (Later these estimates were adjusted to reflect 1952 conditions.)

The market basket based on the 1952 data contains eight broad classes of goods and services. These classes and their weights are reproduced in Table 13.1. According to this survey, a little less than one third of these

Table 13.1 RELATIVE IMPORTANCE OF MAJOR GROUPS INCLUDED IN THE U.S. BUREAU OF LABOR STATISTICS' CONSUMER PRICE INDEX

Group	Relative Importance
Food	30.08
Apparel	9.71
Housing	32.02
Transportation	11.00
Medical care	4.71
Personal care	2.12
Reading and recreation	5.37
Other goods and services	4.99

Source: U.S. Department of Labor, *The Consumer Price Index*, Bulletin No. 1140 (Washington, D.C., 1953), pp. 23–28.

families' expenditures goes for housing and food, respectively, with meat, poultry, and fish being the most important food group. A little more than 10 per cent goes for transportation and a little less than 10 per cent for apparel.

Each group of goods and services in the market basket, in turn, is composed of specific items, each having its own weight. For instance, Table 13.2 presents the breakdown of the list of food items, other than those eaten away from home, together with their respective weights. These weights

Table 13.2 FOOD ITEMS PRICED FOR THE CONSUMER PRICE INDEX AND THEIR 1952 RELATIVE IMPORTANCES

Item	Relative Importance	Item	Relative Importance
Cereals and bakery products	3.09	Fresh vegetables—cont.	
Cereals:		Cabbage	.07
Flour, wheat	.56	Carrots	.11
Biscuit mix	.16	Onions	.10
Corn flakes	.10	Tomatoes	.21
Rolled oats	.07	Pascal celery	.12
Corn meal	.04	Head lettuce	.22
Rice	.08	Canned fruits:	
Bakery products:		Orange juice, canned	.19
Bread, white	1.42	Peaches, canned	.17
Soda crackers	.17	Sliced pineapple, canned	.10
Vanilla cookies	.49	Fruit cocktail, canned	.09
Meats, poultry, and fish	7.99	Canned vegetables:	
Beef:		Cream style corn, canned	.13
Round steak	.98	Peas, canned	.15
Rib roast	.18	Tomatoes, canned	.20
Chuck roast	.65	Strained baby food	.14
Hamburger	.72	Frozen fruits:	
Pork:		Orange juice, concentrate frozen	.13
Pork chops	.76	Strawberries, frozen	.03
Smoked ham	.65	Frozen vegetables:	
Bacon	.81	Peas, frozen	.08
Lamb, leg	.21	Grean beans, frozen	.05
Veal cutlets	.22	Dried fruits and vegetables:	
Other meats:		Dried prunes	.08
Frankfurters	.79	Navy beans	.08
Canned luncheon meat	.27	Other food brought to be prepared at home	5.69
Poultry—frying chickens, dressed and ready-to-cook	1.17	Partially prepared foods:	
Fish and seafood:		Vegetable soup	.40
Fresh and frozen fin fish	.31	Beans with pork	.15
Canned salmon	.10	Condiments and sauces:	
Canned tuna fish	.17	Sweet gherkins	.23
Dairy products	4.19	Tomato catsup	.10
Fresh milk, sold in stores and delivered	2.49	Nonalcoholic beverages:	
Milk, evaporated	.29	Coffee	1.14
Butter	.56	Tea	.12
Ice cream	.34	Cola drinks	.33
American cheese	.51	Fats and oils:	
Fruits and vegetables	4.52	Margarine	.25
Fresh fruit:		Lard	.11
Oranges	.31	Vegetable shortening	.31
Lemons	.04	Salad dressing	.19
Grapefruit	.07	Peanut butter	.09
Apples	.25	Sugar and sweets:	
Bananas	.24	Sugar, white, granulated	.37
Peaches	.11	Corn syrup	.12
Grapes	.09	Grape jelly	.13
Strawberries	.08	Chocolate bars	.28
Watermellons	.18	Eggs, fresh	1.26
Fresh vegetables:		Miscellaneous foods:	
Potatoes	.53	Flavored gelatin dessert	.11
Sweet potatoes	.07	Total	25.48
Green beans	.10		

Source: U.S. Department of Labor, *The Consumer Price Index*, Bulletin No. 1140 (Washington, D.C., 1953), pp. 23–24.

add up to 25.48, i.e., 25.48 per cent of the entire market basket. Another 4.60 per cent is spent on food eaten away from home, making for the 30.08 per cent indicated in Table 13.1.

All in all, the Bureau of Labor Statistics has selected what it considers to be a representative list of about 300 items. These items were chosen because of their importance in family buying and because, in combination, their price movements are thought to represent well those of all goods and services.

The following might serve as a postscript to the weight problem of index numbers:

Two companies negotiate for a possible merger. The president of the larger of the two is trying to make sure that he is buying out a growing concern. Little president tells big president that his firm manufactures and sells kerosene stoves and automatic laundry dryers. Asked what he considers the outlook for the two to be in the future, he says that he expects his kerosene stove business to fall off by 80 per cent and his laundry dryer business to increase by 50 per cent within the next 5 years. Big president, taking pencil and paper, figures that 80 per cent decline is not to be offset by a 50 per cent increase and suggests that since the little president's business is on the skids he is not interested in a deal. Little president leaves depressed. When he meets his missus and broaches the news she asks him what is this year's stove business. He says: "Four million, and our laundry dryer business is $60 million." She concludes: "Then this year's business of $64 million is expected to increase to $90.8 million, isn't it?" Little president goes back to big president. The latter brings in his comptroller, who has a college degree.

Smart college graduate figures that Mrs. Little president was right and adds: "Yes, your business will then be expected to increase by a little less than 50 per cent."

Averaging. Theoretically, it is possible to construct index numbers using any measure of central tendency. In practice the mode is not used because it is very difficult to find in a series of only a few items as those involved in many index numbers, and because it depends so much on personal judgement. Similarly, the median is not a good average to use unless a large number of items are included in the sample. This leaves us with the arithmetic mean. We must remember again that the use of an average is meaningful only if there is a real central tendency. To the extent that the values tend to move together over time, the use of averages and index numbers incorporating them is legitimate; as the values tend to become more widely dispersed, the averages become less representative and the index number loses its meaning. Actually, every average should be accompanied by a measure of dispersion, but unfortunately, index numbers are seldom so accompanied. Still, dispersion should be considered, even if it means in certain cases going back to the original data.

We have already stated that in constructing a composite index we start
out by settling on a base period, weights, and a measure of central tendency
(usually the mean). Once this has been taken care of, we can derive a
meaningful index. How is this done?

Most index numbers are either *weighted aggregates* or *averages of relatives*.
Often the weighted aggregate and average of relatives methods produce the
same results; but there are times when this does not hold true and one method
is more appropriate than the other. Let us, therefore, see how to apply
these two methods in setting up a price index that relies on the weights of
the base period. Such an index—one that uses weights of the base period—
is known as a *Laspeyres* type index. In general, a Laspeyres type price
index indicates what the market basket of the *base period* would sell for in
subsequent periods and by how much its present cost would differ from that
in the base period.

Constructing a weighted aggregate price index, Laspeyres type.
As an example let us put ourselves in the position of a researcher who would
like to get a price index of fibers consumed by textile mills. We can easily
conceive of a government agency or a company desiring to know, for
instance, how the prices of fibers to mills shaped up in 1952 compared to,
let us say, the last prewar year, 1939.

We can construct a weighted aggregate price index in four steps, as
illustrated in Table 13.3:

Table 13.3 WEIGHTED AGGREGATE LASPEYRES TYPE INDEX,
FIBER PRICES TO TEXTILE MILLS, 1952
(1939 = 100)

		Dollar Price per Lb.		*Value of Mills' Purchases*	
Commodity	*Weights, 1939 Quantities in Millions of Lbs.* q_o	*1939* p_o	*1952* p_n	*1939* $(1) \times (2)$ $p_o q_o$	*1952* $(1) \times (3)$ $p_n q_o$
	1	*2*	*3*	*4*	*5*
Cotton	3,629.7	0.093	0.80	338	2,918
Wool	396.5	0.83	1.65	329	654
Silk	47.3	2.71	5.16	128	244
Synthetics	458.7	0.459	0.78	210	358
Total				1,000	4,200

Weighted aggregate Laspeyres type index for 1952: $\dfrac{4,200}{1,000} \times 100 = 420$

Source: U.S. Department of Agriculture, *Agricultural Statistics, 1953* (Washington, D.C., 1953).

1. We get the 1939 and 1952 prices of the four types of fibers, cotton, wool, silk, and synthetics, bought by mills. Likewise, we get the consumption data of these four fibers for the base year. They are the weights, which are found in Column 1.

2. We multiply the price of the base period (Column 2) by the weight (Column 1) and the price of the recent period (Column 3) by the weight (Column 1) to obtain the weighted prices, or in our case the values of the mills' purchases in the base period and in the current year, respectively (Columns 4 and 5).

3. We total these two value columns.

4. We divide the totals (the sum of Columns 4 and 5, respectively) by the total of the base period (the sum of Column 4) and multiply the result by 100. The results are two aggregate index numbers—100 for the base period and 420 for the current year. The 1952 price of textiles to mills was 420 per cent of what it was in 1939; or during this period there was an increase of 320 per cent.

Constructing an average of relatives price index, Laspeyres type. This method differs from the previous one in that the individual prices are first expressed as relatives, and then these relatives rather than the prices themselves are weighted and averaged.

The construction of an average of relatives price index is illustrated in Table 13.4:

Table 13.4   AVERAGE OF RELATIVES LASPEYRES TYPE INDEX, FIBER PRICES TO TEXTILE MILLS, 1952
(1939 = 100)

Commodity	Weights, 1939 Quantities in Millions of Lbs. q_0	Dollar Price per Lb		Price Relatives		Value Weights $(1) \times (2)$ $p_0 q_0$	Weighted Relatives	
		1939 p_0	1952 p_n	$(2) \div (2)$ $\times 100$ p_0/p_0 $\times 100$	$(3) \div (2)$ $\times 100$ p_n/p_0 $\times 100$		1939 $(4) \times (6)$ $p_0/p_0(p_0q_0)$ $\times 100$	1952 $(5) \times (6)$ $p_n/p_0(p_0q_0)$ $\times 100$
	1	*2*	*3*	*4*	*5*	*6*	*7*	*8*
Cotton	3,629.7	0.093	0.80	100	864	338	33,800	292,000
Wool	396.5	0.830	1.65	100	198	329	32,900	65,100
Silk	47.3	2.71	5.16	100	227	128	12,800	29,100
Synthetics	458.7	0.459	0.78	100	169	210	21,000	35,500
Total							100,000	420,000

Weighted average of relatives Laspeyres type index for 1952: $\dfrac{420,000}{100,000} \times 100 = 420$

Source: U.S. Department of Agriculture, *Agricultural Statistics, 1953* (Washington, D.C., 1953).

1. As before, we start by getting the prices and quantities consumed. The prices of a commodity on each date (Columns 2 and 3, respectively) are

divided by the price in the base period (Column 2) and multiplied by 100 to find price relatives of each commodity (Columns 4 and 5).

2. We multiply the base price (Column 2) by the amount consumed in the base period (Column 1) to obtain the cost of each market basket component in the base period (Column 6). These products are the weights.

3. We multiply the individual price relatives (Columns 4 and 5) by the weights obtained in Step 2 to give us the weighted relatives (Columns 7 and 8).

4. We total the weighted relatives pertaining to the base period and the recent period, respectively (Columns 7 and 8), and divide these totals by the base period total. After multiplying by 100 we come up with base and current index numbers.

The two methods have produced the same results. However, this will not always be true. To show the nature of the two methods of calculating a price index of the Laspeyres type and to realize under what conditions they produce the same results, we present the formula for each. The formula for a weighted aggregate price index of the Laspeyres type is:

$$\frac{\Sigma p_n q_o}{\Sigma p_o q_o}. \tag{13.1}$$

The formula of an average of relatives price index of the Laspeyres' type is[4]:

$$\frac{\sum \frac{p_n}{p_o} (p_o q_o)}{\Sigma p_o q_o}, \tag{13.2}$$

where, for an individual commodity,

p_o = price in the base period, e.g., 1939, or 1947–49,
p_n = price in the current year, e.g., 1952, or 1956,
q_o = quantity in the base period, and
q_n = quantity in the current year.

We know that $\Sigma p_n q_o$ could also be written as $\sum_{i=1}^{k} p_{ni} q_{oi}$. We have k commodities entering into the index. So the notation means the sum of the price of the first commodity in the current year times the base period quantity of the first commodity, plus the price of the second commodity in the current year times the base period quantity of the second commodity, etc., for all k commodities. For instance, in relation to our textile price

[4] While formulas 13.1 and 13.2 are mathematically equivalent, they are not computationally equivalent. The same holds for formulas 13.4 and 13.5, and formulas 13.6 and 13.7.

index $\Sigma p_n q_o$ or $\sum_{i=1}^{k} p_{ni} q_{oi}$ means that we sum the 1952 cotton price times the
1939 cotton consumption, the 1952 wool price times 1939 wool consumption,
the 1952 silk price times the 1939 silk consumption, and the 1952 synthetics
price times the 1939 synthetics consumption.

Examining Formulas 13.1 and 13.2, we can readily see that they are
identical in case the same base period quantities are used as weights.
Multiplying prices by base period quantities gives the same algebraic results
as multiplying price relatives by the same base period values. Only when
some other period is used as weight, and we will see such a case below, the
results of the two methods will differ.

Now we are ready to consider when each method should be used. In
general the weighted aggregate method is simpler than the average relatives
method. This is enough reason to counsel that the weighted aggregate
method should be used whenever possible.

However, there are some conditions that favor the average of relatives
index. For instance, we might wish to compare individual components of a
composite index in the form of price relatives; or the component series may
be in different units, as they often are in case of a production index with
electricity output given in kilowatts and steel ingot production in tons.
Likewise, we prefer the second method in case the weights are in value form,
e.g., value added. In other cases we might be given component series that
are in the form of relatives, and the only way to handle these components
would be in terms of averaging the relatives.

In general an index number based on the Laspeyres formula answers the
question of what the actual quantities of the commodities produced or consumed in the base year would sell for in each of the given years. Quite often
this is the comparison called for. However, the passage of time introduces
a serious problem. There are likely to be significant changes in the *regimen*
—that is, the totality of conditions in the system that is assumed constant
when the change under study is measured. Habits, methods of production,
income distribution, or quality of goods often change so much over time as
to render price comparisons meaningless. For example, a 1918 Ford is not
the same commodity as a 1957 Ford. In 1918 there was no television. In
1954 the city of Chicago was reported to have had more television sets than
bathtubs.

The further removed the given year is from the base period, the less likely
are these weights to represent the relative importance of the commodities
included in the index. This problem can in part be taken care of by using

a *Paasche* type index in place of a Laspeyres type index. The main difference between the two is that Paasche uses the current quantities as weights, whereas the Laspeyres index relies all the time on base period quantities.

We could construct a Paasche type index by using either the weighted aggregate or the average of relatives methods. The decision as to which method is preferable can be made in the same way in which it is made in connection with the Laspeyres type index. We will rely here on the simpler, the weighted aggregate index, and illustrate its application by referring to the textile price problem used before.

Constructing a weighted aggregate price index, Paasche type. What is the 1952 index number of fiber prices to mills if we use Paasche's formula and 1939 as a base? Table 13.5 illustrates the four steps that provide the answer:

Table 13.5 WEIGHTED AGGREGATE PAASCHE TYPE INDEX, FIBER PRICES TO TEXTILE MILLS, 1952 (1939 = 100)

Commodity	Weights 1952 Quantities in Millions of Lbs.	Dollar Price per Lb.		Value of Mills' Purchases	
		1939	*1952*	*1939* $(1) \times (2)$	*1952* $(1) \times (3)$
	q_n	p_o	p_n	$p_o q_n$	$p_n q_n$
	1	*2*	*3*	*4*	*5*
Cotton	4,482.6	0.093	0.80	417	3,600
Wool	466.4	0.83	1.65	387	770
Silk	12.6	2.71	5.16	34.2	65.0
Synthetics	1,214.7	0.459	0.78	588	947
Total				1,396.2	5,380

Weighted aggregate Paasche type index for 1952: $\dfrac{5,380}{1,396.2} \times 100 = 380$

Source: U.S. Department of Agriculture, *Agricultural Statistics, 1953* (Washington, D.C., 1953).

1. As before, we start by getting the prices and quantities consumed. We need the prices in the base and current period and the quantities in the current period.

2. We multiply the price of the base period (Column 2) by the weight (Column 1). In this case the weight is the quantity in the current year. Next we multiply the price of the current year (Column 3) by the weight. As a result we obtain weighted prices, i.e., the values of the mills' purchases in the base period and in the current year, respectively (Columns 4 and 5).

3. We total these two value columns.

4. We divide each of these totals by the total of the base period and, after multiplying the results by 100, obtain two aggregate index numbers—100 for the base period and 380 for the current year. We conclude that on the basis of Paasche's weighted aggregate index the 1952 fiber prices to mills were 380 per cent of what they had been in the base year of 1939. In that period the prices of fibers to mills had advanced by 280 per cent.

The Laspeyres and Paasche types of index do not necessarily give the same results, as is borne out by our example. Discrepancies are due to the different weighting systems. In the Paasche type the weights change for each different year for which an index is calculated. By this means it is hoped to overcome the difficulty of choosing representative weights when the regimen is changing. This device gives rise to a new difficulty, however. Because any given year can only be compared with the base period, two given years cannot be directly compared, as is possible with the Laspeyres index.

The general formula of a weighted aggregate price index of the Paasche type can be written as:

$$\frac{\Sigma p_n q_n}{\Sigma p_o q_n}. \qquad (13.3)$$

Quantity indexes. So far we have constructed price indexes using quantities as weights. To measure changes in economic activity over time and for many other purposes we need a composite quantity index. Quantity indexes are constructed in about the same way as price indexes, except that quantity and price are interchanged. For instance, in a weighted aggregate quantity index, the quantities consumed or produced are multiplied by price weights. In the case of a Laspeyres type index we rely on the prices of the base period as weights, while Paasche's formula calls for the use of current prices. In the average of relatives method, the quantities of the commodities are first divided by the base period quantity.

In this fashion the quantity relatives of the individual commodities are found. These relatives are then multiplied by the value (price times quantity) for the base period, if we use Laspeyres' formula, and for the current year, if we use Paasche's formula. Finally these products are totaled and each one is divided by the base period total. In broad outline, this is the method used in the construction of the Federal Reserve Monthly Index of Industrial Production.

The general formula of a weighted aggregate quantity index of the Laspeyres type can be stated as:

$$\frac{\Sigma p_o q_n}{\Sigma p_o q_o}, \qquad (13.4)$$

and of an average of relatives as:

$$\frac{\sum \frac{q_n}{q_o} (p_o q_o)}{\Sigma p_o q_o}. \qquad (13.5)$$

By the way, this last one is the formula used by the *Business Week* index. In a similar fashion, formulas of quantity indexes of the Paasche type can be developed.

Value indexes. Formulas for finding a weighted aggregate and an average of relatives value index of the Laspeyres type, respectively, are:

$$\frac{\Sigma p_n q_n}{\Sigma p_o q_o}, \qquad (13.6)$$

and

$$\frac{\sum \frac{p_n q_n}{p_o q_o} (p_o q_o)}{\Sigma p_o q_o}. \qquad (13.7)$$

Keeping index numbers accurate and relevant. The fact that index numbers attempt to measure changes of a composite of items over time, gives rise to some very knotty problems. The dispersion of prices of a group of products increases with the passage of time, principally because some prices have a long-run tendency to fall and others to rise. Basic changes in the demand and cost conditions of these items are responsible for this persistent change. The average becomes, thus, less and less representative as the distance from the base period increases.

Hand in hand with this phenomenon are changes in the regimen over time. What once was an important item in the budget of a family may today be no longer part of the budget at all. Likewise, today we spend money for articles not in existence twenty years ago.

These long-run tendencies make index number comparisons over very long periods of time unreliable and inaccurate. To overcome some of these problems, we already stated that a Paasche type index might be constructed and used in preference to a Laspeyres type formula. In addition, it is desirable to bring the items and their weights up to date. Substituting items in line with the prevailing regimen can be of great help as well as shifting the base to a more recent period.

Both steps were taken in 1953 by those responsible for the Bureau of Labor Statistics' "Consumer Price Index" and the Federal Reserve's "Monthly Index of Industrial Production." Until that time the Bureau of Labor Statistics, in calculating the consumer price index, used 200 items known to have been important in the household budget in 1934–36. It had obtained its items and their weights from the 1934–36 "Survey of Money Disbursements of Wage Earners and Clerical Workers in 42 Cities." Since early in 1953 the newly revised Consumer Price Index including 300 items is being published. The weights of these items are based on a 1950 "Consumer Expenditure Survey in 19 Cities," adjusted to reflect the 1952 expenditure pattern required to maintain the level of living characteristic of urban wage earners and clerical workers' families.

While the old index used 1935–39 as a base, the revised index is using the period 1947–49. On the basis of these two recent adjustments, the Bureau of Labor Statistics' "Consumer Price Index" is accurate and reliable in reflecting month-to-month changes in the cost of a 1952 market basket typical for urban wage earners and clerical workers' families. Every few years the food basket will be outmoded and it will be proper again to revise the list of items included and their weights. Likewise the base will have to be brought forward.

A common base. Reducing two indexes to a common base is a familiar problem and well discussed in the following quotation:

Businessmen often use the *Business Week* Index to measure how their individual companies have fared, compared with business in general, over a particular period of time. Suppose your company has been keeping a weekly index of sales on the base January, 1953 = 100. You want to compare your performance with total weekly output as measured by the BW Index. To do this, all you have to do is to convert the BW Index to a January, 1953 base by the same statistical maneuver we used to convert to a 1947–49 base: You divide all the weekly figures for 1953 by the average for January, 1953.[5]

From the above paragraph it is clear that a series can be shifted to a new base by multiplying each of its index numbers by 100/X, where X is the index number for the period selected as the new base. Since $X(100/X) =$ 100, we get the index number to be 100 in the new base period. Each old index number is multiplied by the same constant factor 100/X, and so the relative fluctuations of the series are the same in the old and the new index.

We will make an actual comparison in Table 13.6, where we present in Column 1 the index numbers of the *Business Week* Index for the four weeks of February, 1953 (1947–49 = 100), in Column 2 the revised index numbers (January, 1953 = 100) and in Column 3 the company index (January, 1953 = 100). The two indexes (Columns 2 and 3) are now readily compared and it is found that the company is ahead of the economy at large.

Shifting the base of the *Business Week* Index involved one complication

[5] *Business Week, op. cit.*, p. 4.

that is not necessarily always present. We had to take this weekly index and convert it to a monthly base.

This is readily accomplished by averaging the weekly index numbers. In our case we averaged the four weekly index numbers for January, 1953: 131.0, 134.0, 135.0, and 135.6. The January, 1953, average turned out to be 133.6. We then multiplied the February weekly index numbers by 100.0/ 133.6 or 0.7485. Comparing the indexes presented in Columns 2 and 3 we conclude that using January, 1953, as a base, the company's business at the end of February was ahead of the national average.

Table 13.6 MAKING TWO INDEXES COMPARABLE

Period	Business Week Index		Company Index
	1947–49 = 100	Jan. 1953 = 100	Jan. 1953 = 100
	1	2	3
January, 1953	133.6	100.0	100.0
February 7	135.0	101.0	106.9
14	135.0	101.0	107.8
21	135.5	101.4	109.1
28	134.8	100.9	110.2

Source: The Business Week Index, *Business Week*, January 15, 1954, p. 4.

Suppose the company wants to make a comparison over a longer period of time, and wishes to use 1947–49 as a base. The company would convert its own figures to an index with 1947–49 as base by dividing all its figures by their 1947–49 average.

Splicing. It happens frequently that we are called on to compare price or production movements over a number of years not covered by any one index. For instance, the wage contract between the International Ladies Garment Workers Union and the Associated Garment Industries of St. Louis provides for an opening of the contract in case the consumer price index has advanced by more than 10 per cent since December, 1951. At the time this contract was written the old consumer price index was published by the Bureau of Labor Statistics, but this index was discontinued in June, 1953. Since March, 1953, the revised "Consumer Price Index" has been published for St. Louis every three months.

In December, 1953, the ILGWU decided to look into the possibility that a 10 per cent increase in the consumer price index had taken place since December, 1951. In order to decide whether a 10 per cent increase had occurred, it was necessary to splice the old and the revised indexes.

Two series may be spliced together provided they are more or less comparable and are available for the same period. The old and the revised indexes of consumer prices meet the comparability test. One of the architects of the two indexes, for instance, said of them: "As the form and structure of the revised index emerge from 3 years of operational detail, it becomes clear that the outstanding fact of the revision is that the index remains essentially unchanged in purpose, in design, and in most aspects of measurement."[6]   As to availability, both have been published for March, 1953.

In order to splice the new index to the old one and carry the index numbers back to December, 1951, the value of the old index number of 190.5 in March, 1953, must be shifted to 114.7, the value of the new index for that period. The values of the old index numbers are multiplied by 114.7/190.5. This splicing is carried out in Column 3 of Table 13.7. The combined series in Column 4 represents a continuous series from December, 1951, to December, 1953, showing that there was no 10 per cent increase in the consumer price index of St. Louis. It should be clear that in this case we placed more reliance on the new index and used it to trace back the price movements. In other cases, the old index may be the one that we would like to use to reveal the movement of prices in the more recent period.

Table 13.7   SPLICING OF TWO CONSUMER PRICE INDEXES

Time	Old Index	New Index as Published	New Index as Traced Back	Spliced Series
	1	*2*	*3*	*4*
Dec., 1951	191.5		114.9	114.9
March, 1952	190.9		114.5	114.5
June, 1952	195.1		117.1	117.1
Sept., 1952	193.7		116.2	116.2
Dec., 1952	192.7		115.6	115.6
March, 1953	190.5	114.7	114.7	114.7
June, 1953		115.8		115.8
Sept., 1953		117.1		117.1
Dec., 1953		116.9		116.9

Source: Monthly Labor Review, 1952–54.

13.3. SOME IMPORTANT INDEXES

The number of indexes published is so large that covering them all would be a very great undertaking. We therefore will be satisfied with presenting Table 13.8, which lists some of the more important of the widely used

[6] Edward D. Hollander, "The Revised CPI: Some Problems in Concept and Theory," *Monthly Labor Review*, February, 1953, p. 165.

Table 13.8 SOURCES OF COMMONLY USED INDEXES*

Name of Index	Prepared by—	Frequency of Publication	Published Regularly in—
A. PRICE INDEXES			
1. Consumer Price Index	U.S. Bureau of Labor Statistics	M	SCB, FRB, MLR, Business Week, C&FC S&P, Ec. Ind.
2. Wholesale Price Index	U.S. Bureau of Labor Statistics	W, M	SCB, FRB, MLR, Dun's, N.Y. Times. Barron's, C&FC, S&P, Ec. Ind.
3. Spot Markets Prices of 22 Basic Commodities	U.S. Bureau of Labor Statistics	D, W, M	Barron's
4. Dow-Jones Commodities Futures	Dow-Jones & Co.	D	Barron's, Jour. Comm.
5. Construction Cost Indexes	American Appraisal Co.	M	SCB
6. Stock Price Averages	Dow-Jones & Co.	H, D, W, M	SCB, N.Y. Times, Barron's, S&P, Jour. Comm.
7. Stock Price Index 480 Stocks	Standard and Poor's Corporation	W, M	SCB, FRB, S&P, Ec. Ind., NICB
B. QUANTITY INDEXES			
1. Industrial Production	Federal Reserve Board	M	SCB, FRB, Dun's, N.Y. Times, S&P, Ec. Ind., NICB
2. Business Activity	New York Times	W	N.Y. Times
3. Business Index	Barron's	W	Barron's
4. Manufacturing Production-Worker Employment	U.S. Bureau of Labor Statistics	M	SCB, FRB, MLR, Dun's, S&P
5. Steel Production— Per Cent of Capacity	American Iron and Steel Institute	W, M	SCB, FRB, Business Week, N.Y. Times, Barron's, C&FC, S&P
C. VALUE INDEXES			
1. National Income	U.S. Department of Commerce	Q	SCB, FRC, N.Y. Times, S&P, Ec. Ind., NICB
2. Department Store Sales	Federal Reserve Board	W, M	SCB, FRB, N.Y. Times, Barron's, C&FC, S&P, NICB
3. Rural Sales of General Merchandise	U.S. Department of Commerce	M	SCB
4. Manufacturing Production-Worker Payrolls	U.S. Bureau of Labor Statistics	M	SCB, FRB, MLR, Dun's, S&P
5. Construction Contracts Awarded (Value)	Federal Reserve Board (from F. W. Dodge Corp. data)	M	SCB, FRB
6. Regional Trade Barometers	Dun's	M	Dun's
7. Regional Income Indexes	Business Week	M	Business Week

Source: W. A. Spurr, L. S. Kellogg, and J. H. Smith, *Business and Economic Statistics* (Homewood, Ill., Richard D. Irwin, Inc., 1954), p. 244.
* Abbreviations:
H—hourly; D—daily; W—weekly; M—monthly; Q—quarterly.
SCB—Survey of Current Business (and weekly supplement); FRB—Federal Reserve Bulletins; MLR—Monthly Labor Review; Dun's-Statistical Review; C&FC—Commercial and Financial Chronicle; S&P—Standard and Poor's Trade and Securities Service; Ec. Ind.—President's Council of Economic Advisers, Economic Indicators; NICB—National Industrial Conference Board, Business Record; Jour. Comm.—Journal of Commerce.

indexes, indicating who prepares the index, how often, and where it is published.[7]

"Think and know."   Gen. C. H. Grosvenor is reported to have stated in a speech in the House of Representatives: "Figures won't lie, but liars will figure."   He could have gone on to say "And especially watch out for index numbers; they, and comparisons based on them, can be made to dance to any man's music."

To make proper use of index numbers and detect improper uses, we are well advised to look into the following six questions:

1. How does the purpose for which the index is prepared compare to the use that is being made of it?   For example, the Bureau of Labor Statistics' "Consumer Price Index" measures changes in the cost of the market basket purchased by families of urban wage earners and clerical workers.   That is its purpose.   To compare the pay of American soldiers stationed in Japan with this index and draw inferences about the changing standard of living of American soldiers during the last 10 years would be grossly inappropriate.

2. How inclusive and appropriate are the items on which the index is based?   The *Business Week* Index includes 9 main industrial groups at a time when the Federal Reserve "Monthly Index of Industrial Production" includes 175 groups.   The latter has a much broader representation, is better balanced, and less sensitive to marginal and unimportant changes.

3. Are the weights of the index consistent with its avowed purpose?   While most indexes attempt to have appropriate up-to-date weights, they do not always succeed in attaining this objective.   As an example, we can mention illegal income, which is usually insufficiently weighted in an index of personal income.   People just do not feel like reporting their illegal income.

4. Is the index tied to the proper hitching post?   Darrell Huff examines this issue very ably.   Here are his words:

To take the simplest possible example, let's say that milk cost twenty cents a quart last year and bread was a nickel a loaf.   This year milk is down to a dime and bread has gone up to a dime.   Now what would you like to prove?   Cost of living up?   Cost of living down?   Or no change?

Consider last year as the base period. . . . Since the price of milk has since dropped to half (50 per cent) and the price of bread has doubled (200 per cent) and the average of 50 and 200 is 125, prices have gone up 25 per cent.

[7] More detailed information about these and other indexes can be found in the following references: *Survey of Current Business*, published by the U.S. Department of Commerce; *Monthly Labor Review*, published by the U.S. Department of Labor; and *Federal Reserve Bulletin*, published by the Board of Governors of the Federal Reserve System.   A full discussion is available also in R. M. Snyder, *Measuring Business Changes* (New York, John Wiley & Sons, 1955); and Federal Reserve Bank of New York, *Selected Economic Indicators* (New York, 1954).

Try it again, taking this year as base period. Milk used to cost 200 per cent as much as it does now and bread was selling for 50 per cent as much. Average: 125 per cent. Prices used to be 25 per cent higher than they are now.

To prove that the cost level hasn't changed at all we simply switch to the geometric average and use either period as the base. . . .

Take last year as the base and call its price level 100. Actually you multiply the 100 per cent for each item together and take the root, which is 100. For this year, milk being at 50 per cent of last year and bread at 200 per cent. Multiply 50 × 200 to get 10,000. The square root, which is the geometric average, is 100. Prices have not gone up *or* down.[8]

Actually Huff used both base weight and average to juggle his figures. This brings us to the next point.

5. *What kind of an average is used and is it appropriate under the circumstances?* Most indexes use an arithmetic mean to represent the numerous data that enter into the index. In a few cases a geometric mean is used. In any case, it is useful to know what measure of central tendency is used and to be aware of its possible effects on the magnitude of the index number.

6. *Is a proper index formula used?* Experts often differ on whether or not the most appropriate formula is used. Such differences of opinion do not need to disturb us.[9] Sometimes, however, a Laspeyres type index is computed solely because the weights of the base period understate the case and result in a low index number for the current period. When this is the purpose, watch out.

Consumer Price Index—CPI. Ever since 1913 the Bureau of Labor Statistics has been publishing an index of consumer prices. For the first 33 years it called its index a "Cost of Living Index." Attacked by labor and under investigation by Congress, the Bureau of Labor Statistics changed the name of its index, bringing the name closer to what the index actually measures, namely changes in consumer prices of wage earners and clerical workers' families in cities. The Bureau of Labor Statistics is fully aware, and so should all those be who use the CPI, that this index does not measure changes in the cost of living. In a rigorous sense a cost of living index would measure changes in total expenditures required in different price situations to maintain a given level of welfare, utility, or satisfaction, to use the terms of the welfare economists.

The CPI does not measure such changes, except by coincidence. Instead,

[8] Darrell Huff, *op. cit.*, pp. 118–120.
[9] An example of an honest difference of opinion concerning a very important index can be found by reading Edward D. Hollander, "The Revised CPI: Some Problems in Concept and Theory," and Lazare Teper, "An Evaluation of the Revised CPI as a Wage Deflator," *Monthly Labor Review*, February, 1953, pp. 165–172.

the index is designed primarily as a price deflator of wages. By its very definition CPI "is a measure of the average change in price of goods and services customarily purchased by families of wage earners and clerical workers living in cities of the United States."[10]

The prices included in the CPI are retail prices that consumers pay for food, clothing, household furnishings, fuel, and other goods; the fees paid to doctors and dentists; prices in barber shops, beauty parlors, and other service establishments; rents; expenses for transportation, electricity, gas,

Chart 13.1   CONSUMER PRICE INDEX
For wage-earner and clerical-worker families in U.S.
cities, 1914–56.
(1947–49 = 100)

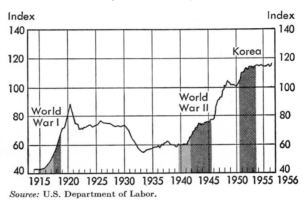

Source: U.S. Department of Labor.

and other utilities; and so on. The goods and services priced constitute the closest possible approximation of the market basket of urban wage-earner and clerical-worker families of two or more persons representing, as noted earlier, about two thirds of all city families and nearly 40 per cent of all families in the United States. The CPI for the period 1914–56 is presented in Chart 13.1.

Prices are collected regularly in 46 cities. These 46 cities are supposed to be representative of all kinds of cities, taking into consideration city characteristics that affect the way in which families spend their money, such as size, climate, density of population, size of population, and level of income of the community. Thus, of the 46 cities, 12 are the largest cities in the United States, another 9 large, another 9 medium-sized, and 16 small cities.

Only in the five largest cities are all the prices collected each month. In other cities, prices of foods, fuels, and rents are obtained every month, and prices of other goods and services are collected on a rotating cycle quarterly

[10] *The Consumer Price Index*, U.S. Department of Labor, *op. cit.*, p. 2.

in 25 large and medium-sized cities, and every four months in 16 small cities. The index for the major groups for the period 1947–54 is represented in Chart 13.2.

Chart 13.2 CONSUMER PRICE INDEX
All cities, major groups, 1947–54.
(1947–49 = 100)

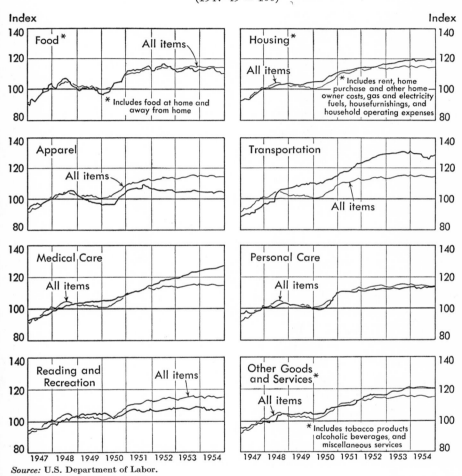

Source: U.S. Department of Labor.

Index numbers are prepared monthly for the United States and for each of the five largest cities, and quarterly for 15 additional cities. Price changes within each city are averaged and combined by a procedure which is essentially a weighted aggregate, the weights being the proportionate expenditure in the market basket for the subgroup which each item represents in the original survey of about 8,000 families. To get an index pertaining to the entire United States, the price changes for the various cities are combined by giving each city a weight proportionate to the wage-earner and clerical-worker population it represents in the index. These city weights are adjusted as new Census population figures become available.

To indicate the place that the CPI occupies, it is of interest to note that in 1951 a congressional committee termed it the "most important single statistic." The CPI has been widely used in wage negotiations. During World War II it was used as a criterion according to which the National Labor Relations Board would allow wage increases. Its most popularized use in recent years was its designation as a basis of wage-rate escalation in the 1948 wage contract between the United Automobile Workers and the General Motors Corporation which was renewed twice to run to May 1958. In this agreement provisions were made for a quarterly adjustment of wage rates of 1 cent per hour for every change of 1.14 points in the old Consumers' Price Index. When the revised CPI became available the two parties agreed to relate the escalator to the revised index. According to this accord there will be a quarterly adjustment of 1 cent per hour for each 0.6 points in the revised CPI.

Since 1948 a number of contracts have incorporated escalator clauses based on the CPI and up to four million workers had their pay adjusted every three months by the index. But there are other uses too to which this index is put. Many businesses use the CPI in market analysis and sales and advertising campaigns. In some instances long-term leases provide for adjustments based on changes in the CPI. Even payments of alimony and annuities are adjusted by it.

Because of its wide use, it is important to be aware of some of the uses to which the CPI cannot legitimately be put. So we must acquaint ourselves with some of the don'ts.

1. Do not use the CPI to testify to changes in the standard of living. The standard of living of a family changes as its income undergoes changes which in turn affect its tastes and habits. The CPI is not set up to measure such adjustments in the standard of living. As a matter of fact it assumes that tastes and habits remain the same and, therefore, relies on a constant market basket.

2. Do not use the CPI for regional comparisons. The CPI does not measure differences in the price levels between cities. A higher index number for one city does not necessarily mean that prices are higher there than in another city with a lower index number for that date. All it means is that since the base period prices in one city have risen faster than in the second.

3. Do not use the CPI to demonstrate changes in prices paid by families other than urban families of wage earners and clerical workers. Rural families, millionaires, and retired people, as examples, buy market baskets that are distinctly different from those on which the CPI is based.

4. Do not rely on the CPI to show changes in the prices paid by a particular family, even if it lives in a city and is that of a wage earner or clerical worker. We must not forget that the CPI reflects the consumption pattern of the average family and not that of a specific one.

Index of Prices Paid by Farmers, Index of Prices Received by Farmers, Parity Ratio. In the nineteen twenties general concern arose for the plight of the American farmer. At that time "equality for farmers" became an important slogan. This equality concept was translated into a policy formulation of assuring farmers prices "that will give agricultural commodities a purchasing power with respect to the articles that farmers buy equivalent to the purchasing power of agricultural commodities of the base period." This is the definition of parity that was first incorporated into federal law in the Agricultural Adjustment Act of 1933. The parity ratio is to this day the hitching post of United States farm policy. Present laws provide that farmers who conform to certain requirements can sell most staple crops to the government at a price that is a given percentage of parity. This parity ratio is calculated by the U.S. Department of Agriculture, in the form of two separate indexes, which are compared as a ratio. One is the *Index of Prices Paid by Farmers*, also often called the *Parity Index* after interest on farm mortgage debt, taxes on farm real estate, and cash wages paid to hired hands are included. This index is composed of a total of 344 price series. On a monthly basis index numbers are published for 15 subgroups. Six of these subgroups are combined to form an index of expenditures for family living; and nine are combined to form an index of expenditures for producing farm products. Bringing together these indexes results in the *Index of Prices Paid by Farmers*. (See Chart 13.3.)

When combining the prices of individual commodities, quantities are used that were derived from a survey of expenditures, by dividing the expenditure of each commodity by the average price of that commodity in 1937–41. Likewise, when subgroup and group component indexes are combined, they are weighted by the amount spent by farmers during this same base period. Unlike the CPI, this index does not measure price change alone. It is affected by changes in the quality of the commodities commonly bought by farmers as they adjust to higher or lower income levels.

The Index of Prices Received by Farmers has a very wide coverage. The 50 commodities, both crops and livestock, constitute about 95 per cent of the total cash receipts from all marketing of farm products. The prices collected are those for all grades and qualities at the point of first sale. It is a weighted aggregate index with average prices for individual commodities first made into subgroup indexes, the quantities of the commodities sold by farmers during 1937–41 being used as weights. When subgroup indexes are combined to form the all-commodity index, the weight are the percentages that cash receipts from marketing for the particular commodity

Chart 13.3   MONTHLY PRICES PAID AND RE-
CEIVED BY FARMERS, 1944–56

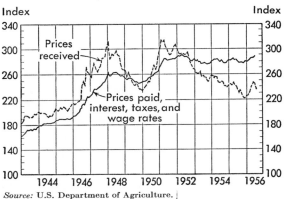

Source: U.S. Department of Agriculture.

subgroup bear to the total for the base period 1937–41. Like the *Index of Prices Paid by Farmers*, this index does not measure price changes alone.

The *Parity Ratio Index* is obtained by dividing the *Index of Prices Received by Farmers* by the *Index of Prices Paid by Farmers*. For instance, on October 15, 1955, the first index stood at 230 and the second at 280, so that the parity ratio was 82. This 82 means that on October 15, 1955, the purchasing power of agricultural commodities with respect to what farmers buy was 82 per cent of what it was in the base period.

Wholesale Price Index.   In 1902 the Bureau of Labor Statistics started to publish a *Wholesale Price Index*, which has been linked to other comparable data to provide a continuous series back to 1749. Since 1952 its base period is 1947–49. It is basically a weighted average of price relatives, with total transactions reported by the Census of Manufacturers of 1947 as weights.

The *Wholesale Price Index* measures the average rate and direction of movement in commodity prices at primary markets, i.e., at points of first commercial transaction. In spite of the name, this index does not measure changes in the prices charged by wholesalers. Instead it measures changes in the prices commodities were sold for by or to manufacturers or producers, or those in effect on organized commodity exchanges.

This index, too, is widely used in contracts, particularly among business-men. In some industries, practically all contracts by manufacturing firms with their suppliers are escalated by the *Wholesale Price Index*, or some segment of it. Many Government contracts with private industry contain escalation clauses—for example, contracts by the Navy Department and the Maritime Commission for the building of ships or the purchase of turbines. Scores of billions of dollars are involved in commercial contracts of this kind.

Since this index is constructed by the same general methods as the *Consumer Price Index*, there is no need here to go into an extended explanation of its construction. However, it is necessary to emphasize that in the last revision (1952) some major changes were made. The number of items included was increased to nearly 2,000, including many additional finished products which had not been in the old index. The purpose of this was to make it more representative of the entire business economy and to make it more useful to businessmen.

The effect of this change was to make the index as a whole more stable than it was before. The old index (before the revision) had fewer com-modities and was heavily weighted with raw materials. So it was more sensitive to changes in business conditions and moved up and down more quickly and more widely.

However, the present index is a better measure of the total price situation, while at the same time it has all the advantages of the old. Separate indexes of the price movements of commodity groups and subgroups—food, farm products, metal products, chemicals, etc. are issued. In addition, indexes for raw materials, for intermediate products, and for finished products are published. A user of the index today can readily distinguish the fast-moving price areas in the economy from the slow movers. This makes the index a better tool for the analysis of over-all business conditions. (See Chart 13.4.)

At the same time, this change has created difficult pricing problems. Farm products and other raw materials often change hands in open markets where the price is clearly defined. Finished goods are not only more specialized and less standardized, but their prices are quoted by the indi-vidual firm.

This problem has given rise to the criticism that the Bureau of Labor Statistics does not obtain the actual transaction prices of finished goods; that discounts are frequently made, but not recorded. Consequently, so the argument runs, the prices used in the index are too high and are fictitiously stable.

As a result, the index, or at least some parts of it, lags a little in catching price changes, but the lag is not very long, nor is the special discounting large enough to make a big difference.

Chart 13.4 WHOLESALE PRICE INDEX
Economic Sector Indexes, major groups, 1947–56.
(1947–49 = 100)

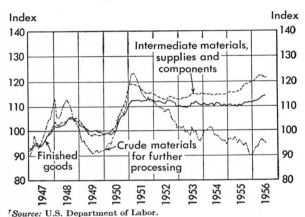

Source: U.S. Department of Labor.

Federal Reserve Monthly Index of Industrial Production. Ever since the 1920's the Board of Governors of the Federal Reserve System has published monthly data that testify to the physical output at factories and mines. It has become an increasingly important barometer of the economic weather. It answers such questions as whether production is up or down, and in what industries the increases and declines are found.

This index is based on 175 series, expressed in physical terms, reflecting the output of manufacturing and mining. The industries covered by this index account for about one third of the national income. Construction, public utilities, transportation, trade services, and agriculture are excluded.

Actually two indexes are published, one monthly and one annual. The annual index is not a simple average of the monthly ones. Instead it is separately computed. It is based on more detailed information than are the monthly indexes. Both are broken down into an index of manufactures and an index of mining. The monthly index of manufactures includes 164 industry series; the annual index about 1,370 series. The monthly index of minerals is based on 11 series and the annual index on about 70 series.

The component series are combined with weights based on value added by manufacture mainly as shown by the Census of Manufactures for 1947 and for mining as estimated by the U.S. Bureau of Labor Statistics. The composite index is calculated as a weighted average of relatives. The base period is 1947–49.

Chart 13.5 MONTHLY INDEX OF
INDUSTRIAL PRODUCTION,
1948–56
(1947–49 = 100)

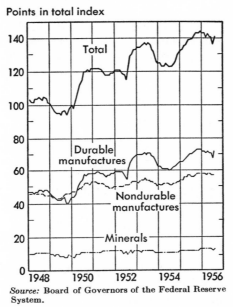

Points in total index

Source: Board of Governors of the Federal Reserve System.

The index is published for total production and the two broad classifications of manufacturing and mining, weighted 90 and 10 per cent, respectively. The manufacturing category in turn is broken down into durable and nondurable goods (see Chart 13.5). The Board of Governors also publishes indexes for 21 major manufacturing categories and 3 major mining categories, and for 175 manufacturing and mining subgroups.

WHAT WE LEARNED:

1. Index numbers measure the average movement of a group of closely related items over time relative to some base taken as 100. Most indexes are either price, quantity, or value indexes.

2. Every index must be tied to a hitching post, i.e., a base period. In the selection of an appropriate base period we try to make sure that the period is reasonably recent and "normal."

3. For many purposes we like to make seasonal adjustments in the index, so as to eliminate effects associated with seasonal phenomena.

4. Composite index numbers are always weighted. The weights reflect the importance we assign to the various components within the total index. Even if no special weights are used in the construction of the index it is weighted, i.e., equally weighted.

5. All composite index numbers are averages of one sort or another, most commonly arithmetic means.

6. We construct index numbers either as weighted aggregates or averages of relatives.

7. A Laspeyres type price index indicates what the market basket of the base period would sell for in subsequent periods and by how much its present price would differ from that in the base period.

8. The formula of a weighted aggregate price index of the Laspeyres type is

$$\frac{\Sigma p_n q_o}{\Sigma p_o q_o}.$$

The formula of an average of relatives price index of the Laspeyres type is

$$\frac{\sum \frac{p_n}{p_o} (p_o q_o)}{\Sigma p_o q_o}.$$

The formula of a weighted aggregate price index of the Paasche type is

$$\frac{\Sigma p_n q_n}{\Sigma p_o q_n},$$

where for an individual commodity

p_o = price in the base period,
p_n = price in the current year,
q_o = quantity in the base period, and
q_n = quantity in the current period.

Comparable quantity and value index formulas can be found.

9. We can make two indexes comparable by putting them on a common base.

10. In case we need to compare prices (or production, or values) over a number of years for which there is no single index in existence, we can splice two indexes to get the information.

11. Among the most important indexes are the *Consumer Price Index* and the *Wholesale Price Index* of the U.S. Bureau of Labor Statistics; the Indexes of Prices Paid by Farmers, Prices Received by Farmers, and the Parity Ratio of the U.S. Department of Agriculture; and the Federal Reserve *Monthly Index of Industrial Production*.

SEE WHAT YOU CAN MAKE OF THE FOLLOWING QUESTIONS:

1. What are some of the main difficulties in the construction of index numbers?
2. a. If you were to construct a monthly index of business activity of the State of

New York, what would be the ten most important economic activities that you would like to see reflected in the index?

b. What would guide you in the selection of a weighting system for these ten series of data?

3. Are index numbers based on the Laspeyres formula an answer to the question of what the actual quantities of the commodities produced or consumed in the base year would sell for in each of the given years? What similar question does an index number based on Paasche's formula answer?

4. Enumerate some of the changes in the regimen that make it difficult to compare consumer prices of today with those in 1944.

5. Using the following hypothetical data, calculate the 1956 index number of sales of a firm selling cigarettes, cigars, and pipe tobacco.

	In Million Cartons			
Item	*Quantity in 1947–49* q_o	*Quantity in 1956* q_n	*1956 Price in Dollars* p_n	*1947–49 Base Period* p_o
Cigarettes	7,341	7,820	1.20	0.95
Cigars	1,067	1,002	2.10	1.80
Pipe tobacco	862	870	0.90	0.80

6. The following textile data are given:

Commodity	*1939 Price (Dollars per Lb.)*	*1939 Quantity (Millions of Lbs.)*	*1941 Price (Dollars per Lb.)*	*1941 Quantity (Millions of Lbs.)*
Cotton	0.0930	3,629.7	0.139	5,187.3
Wool	0.830	396.5	1.09	652.2
Silk	2.71	47.3	2.94	25.0
Synthetics	0.4587	458.7	0.469	591.8

a. What is the 1941 index number in case you are interested in a weighted aggregate price index of the Laspeyres type?

b. What is the 1941 index number in case you are interested in an average of relatives price index of the Laspeyres type?

c. What is the 1941 index number in case you are interested in a weighted aggregate price index of the Paasche type?

7. List and discuss the major limitations of index numbers.

8. Convert the index of milk prices received by Firm X to the 1947–49 average as a base:

Year	Milk Prices Received by Firm X (1936–39 = 100)	Prices Received by Farmers (1947–49 = 100)
1945	182	76
1946	190	87
1947	200	102
1948	202	106
1949	189	92
1950	192	95
1951	220	111
1952	208	106
1953	196	95
1954	191	92

Source: U.S. Department of Agriculture, *The Marketing and Transportation Situation,* MTS-119, October, 1955, p. 14.

9. If the only information for 1942 is that Firm *X* received in that year $3.01 per 100 lbs. and the price in 1945 was $3.32 per 100 lbs., splice these figures to a new index in order to compute an index number for 1942 (make use of the data in Question 8).

10. Soon the period 1947–49 as a base for the *Consumer Price Index* will be outdated.

    a. Explain why.

    b. Explain what new period would appear to offer a good new base, in case you were called on to make a recommendation now.

    c. In case we were to revise the base of the *Consumer Price Index*, would we have completed the job of bringing it up to date? Why yes? Why no?

XIV

Association Among Quantitative Data —Regression and Correlation Analysis

14.1. SIMPLE LINEAR REGRESSION AND CORRELATION

Wrote reader Frank E. Karelsen to the Editor of the New York Times:

Giants as Market Gauge

I read with interest your excellent editorial of Sept. 15 commenting upon the survey of the stock market made by your staff correspondent A. H. Raskin.

In that editorial you quite rightly pointed out that the average professional speculator spends half his time assiduously reading the future of the market in the tea leaves of market averages.

You also advanced some other theories on the stock market speculator which were equally sound. You and Mr. Raskin, however, overlooked one gauge of the market, one which I have not seen advanced by any publication thus far; to wit: the relationship between stock market averages and the fortunes of the New York Giants baseball team.

After some research I found that when the Giants are winning the market goes up, and when the Giants are losing the market goes down. For instance, in the fall of 1951, when the Giants successfully and unexpectedly made their drive for the pennant, the market was strong. In 1952 the Giants were going well in August and the market was high. In the spring of 1953 the Giants were doing well and the market was high. Now that the Giant's team is falling to pieces, the market is falling to pieces. Perhaps further study of this relationship might be fruitful.

I have, of course, been unable to determine whether the market goes down because the Giants lose or whether the Giants lose because the market goes down. That is something that market experts and baseball magnates will have to determine. Once it is determined, it may result in either more supporters for the Giants or more supporters for the stock market.

FRANK E. KARELSEN

New York, Sept. 17, 1953

The letter on p. 247 illustrates a facetious attempt to formulate predictions on the basis of an apparent correlation between the fortunes of the New York Giants and the stock market. Another such attempt is the one, published not long ago, claiming substantial correlation between sunspots and the number of bankruptcies.

Correlation and regression techniques have been applied to more appropriate problems and in fact they usually are. While correlation analysis tests the closeness with which two (or more) phenomena co-vary, regression analysis measures the nature and extent of this relation, thus enabling us to make predictions. The term "regression" was coined by Francis Galton. His investigation of the height of about one thousand fathers and sons revealed a rather interesting relationship: Tall fathers tend to have tall sons, and short fathers short ones; but the average height of the sons of a group of tall fathers is less than that of the fathers, and the average height of the sons of a group of short fathers is greater than that of the fathers. Galton began to describe this phenomenon as one of regression, a term that soon was universally used to designate the relationship between two (or more) variates.

A problem calling for a forecast. The SOMB (Satisfied-or-Money-Back) Mail Order Company has a perennial problem that has once again become acute. S. S. Small, vice-president in charge of operations, is taking the brunt of the criticism. "If this occurs once more, you will have to look for other employment," he is told curtly by the boss, Mr. Monte G. Robust, president of SOMB. "Yesterday in the Chicago plant far too many employees were assigned to filling orders, and for the last hour and a half everyone was sitting around twiddling their thumbs on company time. Today, there weren't enough people to take care of all the orders and now, at closing time, 9,000 orders are left unfilled. It seems to me that by this time you should have some idea how many orders can be expected by our 110 plants on any particular day."

Mr. Small explains that there are wide fluctuations in the number of orders from day to day and the problem of estimating the number of orders in time to assign the proper number of help to filling them has him stumped. "My suggestion is, Mr. Robust, that the only way to lick this problem would be to hire a good management consultant for a few days and see if he can find a way of estimating the number of incoming orders."

The president wisely accepts this advice, and Mr. Jim Hamilton is hired for the job. His first step is to spend a few hours with Mr. Small discussing what makes a mail order plant tick. "This is the way we work," Small says, "all orders that reach the plant by the time the employees report for work at 8:30 A.M. must be filled at the day's end. Today's orders, for instance, came in the last three mail deliveries of yesterday and the first two of today. During the eight-hour day," Small continues, "orders are handled in 15-minute cycles; and the volume handled during each such cycle is about 1,000 orders." "Does this mean that about 1,000 orders every quarter hour, or about 32,000 orders a day, are being processed, assembled, packed, and shipped through the same operational channels and by the same personnel?" Hamilton inquires. "Not exactly," Small replies. "Actually, over the year we may handle as few as 24,000 and sometimes as many as 42,000 orders in one day in any one of our plants."

Following his discussions with Mr. Small, Hamilton visits two of the plants and watches the operation of filling a mail order step by step. Then he returns to his own office and starts thinking.

Actually, the number of letters that come in with the last three mail deliveries of the preceding day and the first two of today should reflect somehow the number of orders that will await today's processing. It shouldn't prove too difficult to find out how many orders are usually among, let's say, 100 incoming letters. But this would involve counting all incoming letters. That's too involved and expensive. It would be so much easier to weigh all incoming mail. There should be some reasonably stable number of orders per pound of incoming mail. If this is true, then the number of orders depends, at least to a certain extent, on the weight of the incoming mail. We can call the number of orders the *dependent variate*, depending as it does on the weight of the incoming mail of yesterday's three last and today's two first mail deliveries. The weight of the mail would then be the *independent variate*.

Clearly, the more mail the more orders; this means a positive relationship between orders and weight of mail. There is no reason to doubt that increases in number of orders will be proportional to the increase in the weight of the incoming mail; that is, twice as heavy a mail will tend to mean twice as many orders.

On the basis of what he has learned in the last few days in the mail order plants, Hamilton thus establishes the important hypothesis that: (1) changes in the number of orders are directly related to or brought about by changes in the weight of the incoming mail, and (2) the relationship between number of orders and weight of incoming mail is linear and positive.

This is, of course, a subjective hypothesis, no less subjective than that of the businessman who, reading that sales of fishing equipment are at a record high, considers this an infallible sign of prosperity. A union man, reading the same item might conclude, instead, that record sales of fishing equipment are an indication of rampant unemployment.

With his hypothesis Hamilton comes back to Mr. Small and inquires: "Can we get data of the number of orders filled on a given day and the weight of the incoming mail for that day, that is, the weight of the three last deliveries of the preceding day and the first two deliveries of the same day?"

Table 14.1 POUNDAGE OF MAIL AND NUMBER OF MAIL ORDERS RECEIVED BY SEVEN MAIL-ORDER PLANTS ON A GIVEN DATE

Plant	Hundreds of Pounds of Mail X	Thousands of Mail Orders Y
1	9.5	38
2	8.0	32
3	6.0	24
4	7.3	29
5	9.0	36
6	9.1	42
7	7.5	30

Source: Hypothetical data.

It turns out that SOMB has such data. by working with large masses of data

Chart 14.1 SCATTER DIAGRAM
(Poundage of mail and number of mail orders received by seven mail-order plants on a given date.)

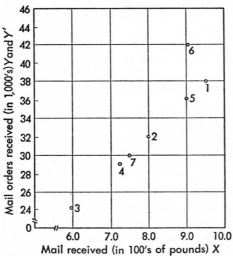

Source: Table 14.1.

So that we will not be burdened that might blur the methods of analysis, we will work with a random sample of seven of the company's 110 plants, collected on a given day. The number of mail orders are reported to the last thousand units, and mail weight to the last 10 units. In Table 14.1 we have the number of mail orders in thousands, Y, and the weight of mail in hundreds of pounds, X, of the seven sample plants. For instance, Plant 1 received on a given day 38 thousand orders weighing 9.5 hundred pounds.

Whenever we plot two variates against each other we obtain a *scatter diagram*. Orders and weight of mail of the seven sample plants are represented in scatter diagram form in Chart 14.1.

Sample Plant 1 is represented by Point 1, which is 38 thousand order units plotted on the vertical scale and 9.5 hundred weight units horizontally removed from the origin, the zero point, of the scatter diagram. Akin to the scatter diagram is the *line chart* that comes about when successive points are connected by lines.

Hamilton's subjective speculation that the number of orders is a positive, linear function of mail weight can be tested visually against the background of the scatter diagram. Apparently a straight line reasonably well represents these seven points.

A criterion is needed. In addition to this visual check a more rigorous test of the established hypothesis is called for. This test can be objective and can shed light on the quality of the relationship and its nature. In selecting such a statistical method attention must be given to the purpose of the study. Is it our purpose to predict as often as possible the exact number of orders that require filling on a given day, or is SOMB more interested in obtaining predictions which, though not necessarily correct each time, are on the average as close to the true number as humanly possible? The choice is between having a predictive mechanism that permits Mr. Small to predict precisely the incoming orders in a few plants, while he may be way off in his estimates in the rest of the plants, or a criterion that will result in predictions which when averaged over the plants, will prove as close to the actual number as possible.

SOMB's operations are sufficiently flexible so that miscalculations of 1 or 2 per cent either way cause little concern. Frequent miscalculations of large magnitudes is what Small fears most. Clearly, the second criterion, to minimize the discrepancies in predictions, is most appropriate for SOMB. Hamilton knows that *least squares correlation and regression analysis* is the statistical method that helps make predictions which, on the average, are as close as possible to the actual data. This method produces a *least squares line* which, as the name indicates, minimizes the mean squared vertical deviations from the regression line. Therefore, we call it also a "line of best fit."

What is meant by minimizing the mean squared vertical deviations from the regression line? This can be readily visualized by referring to Chart 14.2. $Y - Y'$ or d is one such deviation. The line in Chart 14.2 has been drawn so that the squares of all 7 d's are at a minimum. Let us see how such a line can be obtained.

We could start by attempting to draw a freehand line designed to minimize the mean squared deviations, also often called *error variance, s_{YX}^2*. The error variance can be written as

$$s_{YX}^2 = \frac{1}{n} \sum (Y - Y')^2, \tag{14.1}$$

and its square root, the *standard deviation of the regression coefficient,* can be written as

$$s_{YX} = \sqrt{\frac{1}{n} \sum (Y - Y')^2}. \tag{14.2}$$

In seeking freehand approximations, we must remember that the square of one large deviation is much larger than that of two deviations half that size. We must beware, therefore, not to secure an almost perfect fit with all but a few points at the expense of a few very large deviations. We will illustrate this issue, so as to obtain a better appreciation of the least squares method by fitting freehand least squares lines to four hypothetical observations. In Panel *A* of Chart 14.3 we have drawn a line through all points but Point 1, where the deviation is substantial. In Panel *B* of Chart 14.3 a flatter line was drawn, which has no large deviation from any single point.

Chart 14.2 SCATTER DIAGRAM AND REGRESSION LINE
(Poundage of mail and number of mail orders received by seven mail-order plants on a given date.)

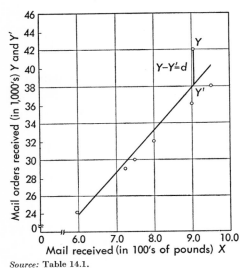

Source: Table 14.1.

To test these lines for their consistency with the least squares criterion, we will compute their trend equations. A straight line equation with two variates can be written:

$$Y' = a_{YX} + b_{YX}X,$$
or
$$Y' = a + bX, \tag{14.3}$$

where Y' is the computed or predicted value of the dependent variate;

a_{YX}, or a, the Y-intercept or height of the regression line at the origin where $X = 0$;

b_{YX}, or b, the slope of the regression line, i.e., regression coefficient; and

X the independent variate.

The a value is found by reading off the Y' value where $X = 0$.

In Panel *A* the a value of the line is 7.2. We find the slope of the line, i.e., b, by subtracting one Y' value from the preceding one and dividing this difference by the difference between the corresponding X values. Thus,

$b = \dfrac{Y_2' - Y_1'}{X_2 - X_1}$, and b of Panel A is $+0.65$, the plus sign indicating that the line slopes upward. The regression equation for the line in Panel A is therefore

$$Y' = 7.2 + 0.65X,$$

and for the line in Panel B it is

$$Y' = 7.9 + 0.45X.$$

Chart 14.3   FITTING REGRESSION LINES

A. Poor Fit   B. Relatively Good Fit

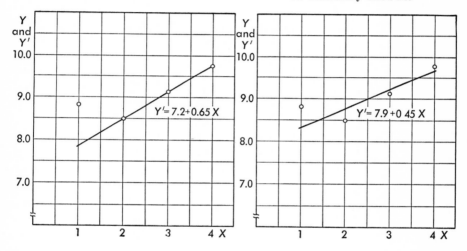

To compare the fit of these two equations, we find their error variances. In Table 14.2 we applied equation $Y' = 7.2 + 0.65X$ to find Y' values (see Column 3).

Table 14.2   LEAST SQUARES TEST OF LINE $Y' = 7.2 + 0.65X$

X	Y	Y'	$(Y - Y')$	$(Y - Y')^2$
1	*2*	*3*	*4*	*5*
1	8.92	7.8	1.1	1.2
2	8.50	8.5	0.0	0.0
3	9.12	9.1	0.0	0.0
4	9.78	9.8	0.0	0.0
Σ				1.2
$\dfrac{\Sigma}{n}$				**0.3**

For instance, for $X = 1$, $Y' = 7.2 + 0.65\,(1) = 7.8$,

for $X = 2$, $Y' = 7.2 + 0.65\,(2) = 8.5$, etc.

In Column 4 the deviations $Y - Y'$ are stated, and in Column 5 we find their squares. Adding the values in Column 5 and dividing by n gives an error variance $\dfrac{1}{n}\sum (Y - Y')^2 = 0.3$.

In Table 14.3, the same calculations are made on the basis of the equation $Y' = 7.9 + 0.45X$, and the error variance is found to be 0.08. In the light of these results we can conclude that the fit in Panel B is superior to that in Panel A.

Table 14.3   LEAST SQUARES TEST OF LINE
$Y' = 7.9 + 0.45X$

X	Y	Y'	$(Y - Y')$	$(Y - Y')^2$
1	*2*	*3*	*4*	*5*
1	8.92	8.4	0.5	0.2
2	8.50	8.8	−0.3	0.1
3	9.12	9.2	−0.1	0.0
4	9.78	9.7	0.1	0.0
Σ				0.3
$\dfrac{\Sigma}{n}$				0.08

The regression line. In order to find a "line of best fit" we need a set of equations for a and b that automatically minimize the mean squared deviations. These equations are readily derived in the following manner:

Since we assume the line of best fit to be a straight line, we can write Formula 14.3,

$$Y' = a + bX.$$

We defined the vertical deviation from the line as

$$d = Y - Y'.$$

If we insert 14.3 into $d = Y - Y'$, we obtain for the deviations,

$$d = Y - Y' = Y - (a + bX).$$

The sums of the squares of the deviations can therefore be written

$$\Sigma(Y - Y')^2 = \Sigma(Y - a - bX)^2.$$

With the help of some mathematics (differentiating and setting the first derivatives equal to zero) we can derive the following equations:

$$\Sigma Y = na + b\Sigma X$$
$$\Sigma XY = a\Sigma X + b\Sigma X^2. \qquad (14.4)$$

These two equations are called *normal equations*. They are easily remembered, as follows: To obtain the first of the two normal equations, we place a summation sign in front of every term of the original equation $Y = a + bX$, recalling that the summation of a constant is n times the constant. To obtain the second normal equation, we first multiply each term of the original equation by X and then sum.

To find a and b we would solve the two normal equations. Alternatively, we can use the following formulas for b and a:

$$b_{YX} = b = \frac{n\Sigma XY - (\Sigma X)(\Sigma Y)}{n(\Sigma X^2) - (\Sigma X)^2}, \qquad (14.5)$$

and,

$$a_{YX} = a = \bar{Y} - b\bar{X}, \qquad (14.6)$$

where $\bar{Y}$ stands for the mean of Y and $\bar{X}$ for the mean of X.

Table 14.4 WORK SHEET FOR SIMPLE LINEAR CORRELATION
(Relation between poundage of mail and number of mail orders.)
$n = 7$

X (00's Pounds of Mail)	Y (000's Mail Orders)	X²	Y²	XY
9.5	38	90.2	1,440	361
8.0	32	64.0	1,020	256
6.0	24	36.0	576	144
7.3	29	53.3	841	212
9.0	36	81.0	1,300	324
9.1	42	82.8	1,760	382
7.5	30	56.2	900	225
56.4	231	463.5	7,840	1,900

Source: Table 14.1.

When we make use of the information given in Table 14.4, we readily find that in Hamilton's case:

$$n = 7,$$
$$\Sigma X = 56.4,$$
$$\Sigma Y = 231,$$
$$\Sigma X^2 = 453.5, \text{ and}$$
$$\Sigma XY = 1,900.$$

Substituting this information in Formulas 14.5 and 14.6 we have:

$$b = \frac{7(1,900) - (56.4)(231)}{7(463.5) - (56.4)^2} = 4.69, \text{ and}$$

$$a = \frac{231}{7} - 4.69 \frac{(56.4)}{(7)} = -4.71.$$

Thus, the regression equation for the sample data of the seven plants reads:

$$Y' = -4.71 + 4.69X.$$

The regression coefficient, $b = +4.69$, can be interpreted to mean that insofar as the sample data of the seven mail order plants are concerned an increase (decrease) of 1.0 hundred pounds of mail received by one of the plants on the day considered was on the average associated with an increase (decrease) of 4.69 thousand mail orders. In general, the regression coefficient reflects the change in the dependent variate associated with unit changes in the independent variate.

Chart 14.4 PLOTTING A LINEAR RE-GRESSION
(Poundage of mail and number of mail orders received by seven mail-order plants on a given date.)

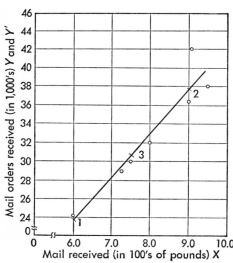

Source: Table 14.1.

No direct substantive interpretation can be given to the Y-intercept in this case. Mathematically, it indicates the value of Y' at the point where the regression line intersects the Y-axis ($X = 0$). Thus, the value of the Y-intercept pertains to the theoretical Y value that would prevail if no mail was received. This value, however, lies outside the range of observed data, and any relation that might be found to prevail within the range of observed data will not necessarily hold outside it.

So far we have discussed straight regression lines. However, there are times when curvilinear regression lines provide a better fit. The fitting of some such nonlinear regression lines will be discussed in Chapter XV.

Plotting regression lines. To plot a straight regression line we usually compute three points and place a line through them. While two points suffice to plot a straight line, working with three has the advantage of providing a check of the computations. Thus, we assume three different values for the independent variate X and place them into the regression equation, one at a time. For instance, assuming that $X = 6.0$, then $Y' = -4.71 + 4.69(6.0) = 23.4$ thousand mail orders. When $X = 9.0$, $Y' = -4.71 + 4.69(9.0) = 37.5$ orders. Finally when $X = 7.5$, $Y' = -4.71 + 4.69(7.5) = 30.5$ mail orders. We can plot these three points, as we have done in Chart 14.4, and connect them by means of a straight line extending from 600 to 950 pounds of mail. This, then, is the regression line, or "line of best fit," relating mail poundage to the number of mail orders in a sample of seven plants on a given day.

Standard deviation of regression. We measure the dispersion around a mean in terms of standard deviations. Likewise we can measure the dispersion around a regression line in terms of the *standard deviation of regression* (also sometimes called the standard error of estimate). However, very seldom would we use Formula 14.2, $s_{YX} = \sqrt{\frac{1}{n} \sum (Y - Y')^2}$, to compute the standard deviation of regression, for it presupposes knowledge of the regression equation and requires calculating all predicted values. But from it a formula can be derived that gives results much more readily, namely:

$$s_{YX} = \sqrt{\frac{\Sigma Y^2 - a\Sigma Y - b\Sigma XY}{n - 2}}. \qquad (14.7)$$

With
$$\Sigma Y^2 = 7{,}840,$$
$$a = -4.71,$$
$$\Sigma Y = 231,$$
$$b = 4.69,$$
$$\Sigma XY = 1{,}900, \text{ and}$$
$$n = 7,$$

$$s_{YX} = \sqrt{\frac{7{,}840 - (-4.71)(231) - 4.69(1{,}900)}{5}} = 1.8.$$

Quality of association—coefficients of correlation and determination. Having found the regression line, Hamilton has some indication of the relation between poundage of mail and number of mail orders for his seven plants. However, he would like to know how close the relationship is. To do so, Hamilton makes a quick analysis and finds that for the seven sample observations the *coefficient of correlation* r_{YX}, or r, is $+0.96$. As we shall soon see, correlation coefficients can assume values between $+1.0$ and -1.0. The sign of the correlation coefficient tells us whether the relationship between the two variates is positive or negative. A correlation coefficient of $+1.0$ indicates a perfect positive correlation and one of -1.0 a perfect negative correlation. Should the coefficient be zero it would mean that there is no correlation.

While the correlation coefficient tells us something about the closeness of the association in case it assumes extreme values such as 0.0 and 1.0, it does not lend itself to an easy interpretation for the majority of cases when it lies between these extremes. However, it is safe to say that the closer the correlation coefficient is to $+1.0$ or -1.0, the closer is the association of the variates.

Squaring the coefficient of correlation gives us the *coefficient of determination*, which is very useful in interpreting the closeness of the association. Here the correlation coefficient is $+0.96$ and the corresponding coefficient of determination is $(+0.96)^2$ or $(+0.92)$. We will interpret this coefficient of determination of 0.92 to mean that about 92 per cent of the daily variation in the number of mail orders received are associated with or related to changes in the weight of the daily mail.

What, then, is a coefficient of determination and why can we interpret it the way we do?

Let us examine this issue in relation to the mail orders and mail weight data of our seven plants. The least squares line for these seven data can be represented by the equation:

$Y' = -4.71 + 4.69X$, where Y' stands for the predicted value of Y. As we place different values of X in this equation, we can compute the corresponding predicted values of the dependent variate. We might wish to compare observed and predicted values of the dependent variate for the same X value. For instance, in Plant 6, 9.1 hundred pounds of mail containing 42 thousand mail orders were received at a time when our regression line would have predicted $-4.71 + 4.69(9.1)$ or 38 thousand mail orders. For an X of 9.1 hundred pounds Y is 42 and Y' is 38 thousand.

We might consider Y to be composed of two parts: Y' is the predicted part that depends on and can be explained in terms of X; and $Y - Y'$ the unrelated part and one that cannot be explained in terms of X. Thus, in our example, of the 42 thousand orders 38 thousand can be explained and predicted in terms of the weight of the mail, while another 4 thousand orders cannot be explained in terms of the weight of the mail. Apparently, there are factors other than mail weights that affect the number of orders.

We might be tempted to use this fraction Y'/Y, or here $38,000/42,000$, as a measure of the success of the equation $Y' = -4.71 + 4.69X$ in predicting the Y' of Plant 6. One of the disadvantages of such a procedure would stem from the fact that the ratio Y'/Y is strongly affected by the order of magnitude of the units in which the dependent variate is stated. This problem disappears if, instead of posing the question of what percentage of Y the equation predicts, we ask what percentage of the deviation of Y from its mean is predicted by the equation. The mean in this case is the mean of all Y values, i.e., $\bar{Y}$, which in our case is 33 thousand mail orders. The

observed number of orders in Plant 6 is 42 thousand and exceeds the mean number of orders in all seven plants by 9 thousand. $Y - \bar{Y}$, in our case 9 thousand, is the total deviation (of the orders of Plant 6 from the mean number of orders). The predicted number of orders for Plant 6 is 38 thousand, deviating from the mean by 5 thousand. We will call $Y' - \bar{Y}$, which in our case is 5 thousand, the *explained deviation*, because this deviation from the mean can be explained in terms of the independent variate, and can be predicted by the equation $Y' = -4.71 + 4.69X$. The remaining part of the total deviation, $9 - 5$ or 4 thousand mail orders for Plant 6, is a residual amount

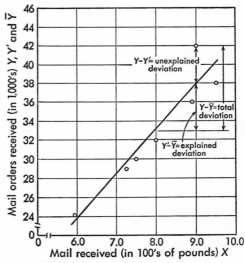

Chart 14.5 UNEXPLAINED VERSUS EXPLAINED DEVIATIONS

(Poundage of mail and number of mail orders received by seven mail-order plants on a given date.)

Source: Table 14.1.

that cannot be predicted by knowing X, and, thus, is independent of X. We call this part $Y - Y'$ the *unexplained deviation*. These three deviations have been portrayed in Chart 14.5 and computations for all plants are made in Table 14.5.

There remains the task of averaging each of these three sets of deviations, so that we can define and calculate the percentage of the explained variation that will give us a relative measure of the association. In selecting the appropriate average we must keep in mind that the explained and the unexplained variation must add up to 100 per cent. The variance fulfills this requirement, and therefore we will use it. We will average the total deviations of the seven plants to obtain the total variance, I, the explained deviations to obtain the explained variance, II, and the unexplained deviations to obtain the unexplained variance, III.

Let us see more specifically what all this means in relation to the mail order house problem.

First, there is I, the total variance of the number of mail orders received per day, and it is measured by

$$s_Y^2 = \frac{1}{n} \sum (Y - \bar{Y})^2, \qquad (14.8)$$

which is easily recognized as the variance of the Y's where $\bar{Y}$ is the mean

Table 14.5 COMPARISONS OF VARIANCES

(Poundage of mail and number of mail orders received by seven mail-order plants on a given date.)

Mail Plant	X 00's Pounds of Mail	Y 000's Mail Orders	Y' 000's Mail Orders	$(Y - \bar{Y})$ 000's Mail Orders	$(Y - \bar{Y})^2$ 000's Mail Orders	$(Y' - \bar{Y})$ 000's Mail Orders	$(Y' - \bar{Y})^2$ 000's Mail Orders	$(Y - Y')$ 000's Mail Orders	$(Y - Y')^2$ 000's Mail Orders
1	9.5	38	39.9	5	25	6.9	48.6	−1.9	3.6
2	8.0	32	32.8	−1	1	−0.2	0.04	−0.8	0.6
3	6.0	24	23.4	−9	81	−9.6	91.2	0.6	0.4
4	7.3	29	29.5	−4	16	−3.5	12.2	−0.5	0.2
5	9.0	36	37.5	3	9	4.5	20.2	−1.5	2.2
6	9.1	42	38.0	9	81	5.0	25.0	4.0	16
7	7.5	30	30.5	−3	9	−2.5	6.25	−0.5	0.2

Total					222		203		23
Mean and variance					$I = 32$ (*Total variance*)		$II = 29$ (*Explained variance*)		$III = 3$ (*Unexplained variance*)

Source: Table 14.1.

of Y.   According to Table 14.5 it is 31.7, or 32, and reflects a wide variety of factors that can cause the number of a day's orders to differ from one plant to the next.

Next there is II, the explained variance, i.e., the variance that is explainable in terms of the dependent variate.   It reflects the influence of differences in the mail poundage on the number of mail orders received per day. It is measured by

$$s_{Y'}^2 = \frac{1}{n} \sum (Y' - \bar{Y})^2, \qquad (14.9)$$

where Y' is the predicted value, and comes out to be 29.

Finally, there is III, the unexplained variance, measuring the variation of the data around the regression line.   It is measured by Formula 14.1,

$$s_{YX}^2 = \frac{1}{n} \sum (Y - Y')^2,$$

and reflects differences in the number of mail orders received that cannot be attributed to changes in mail poundage; these differences must be explained in terms of other factors. This variance is calculated in Table 14.5 to be 3.

As was stated above, the explained and unexplained variances add up to the total variance, i.e., 100 per cent of the variation:[1]

$$I = II + III \text{ or } s_Y{}^2 = s_{Y'}{}^2 + s_{YX}{}^2.$$

Now, let us return to our objective, namely, to find a measure of the closeness of the association between two variances, or a measure of the quality of the prediction. Clearly we are not interested in an absolute measure. What we need is a relative one, such as the explained variance as a percentage of the total variance. That would be $\frac{II}{I}$ or $\frac{s_{Y'}{}^2}{s_Y{}^2}$. Then, $\frac{s_{Y'}{}^2}{s_Y{}^2}$ would express the percentage of the explained variance. Clearly, the larger the percentage of the explained variance, the closer the association between the two variances and the better the quality of the prediction. This relative measure of the closeness of the association is the *coefficient of determination.*

We can now compute the coefficient of determination from the variances of Table 14.5. Our least squares equation, $Y' = -4.69 + 4.71X$, succeeds in explaining 29.0/31.7 or 92 per cent of the total variance. (Consistent with our significant digits rule we have 29.0/31.7 and not 29/32.) Ninety-two per cent of the daily variation in the number of mail orders is associated with or can be explained in terms of variations in the weight of the daily mail, and 8 per cent of the variations in the number of mail orders depends on some other factors.

In practice, the calculation of the ratio is easier than one would expect. The working equation for calculating the correlation coefficient is

$$r_{YX} = \frac{n\Sigma XY - (\Sigma X)(\Sigma Y)}{\sqrt{n\Sigma X^2 - (\Sigma X)^2}\sqrt{n\Sigma Y^2 - (\Sigma Y)^2}} \tag{14.10}$$

and can be shown to equal $s_{Y'}/s_Y$. Since $r_{YX} = s_{Y'}/s_Y$, our relative measure of the closeness of the association, also called coefficient of determination, is the square of the correlation coefficient. Thus, by squaring the coefficient of correlation we obtain a measure of the closeness of the association between the two variates. To compute r from Formula 14.10 we need to know ΣX, ΣY, ΣX^2, ΣY^2, and ΣXY. These sums are readily found from a worksheet

[1] The proof is as follows: It can be shown that

$$s_{Y'}{}^2 = r^2 s_Y{}^2 \text{ and that } s_{YX}{}^2 = (1 - r^2)s_Y{}^2.$$

Therefore,
$$r^2 s_Y{}^2 + (1 - r^2) s_Y{}^2 = s_Y{}^2$$
$$s_Y{}^2(r^2 + 1 - r^2) = s_Y{}^2$$
$$s_Y{}^2 = s_Y{}^2.$$

In our example, $s_{Y'}{}^2 = 29$, $s_{YX}{}^2 = 3$, and $s_Y{}^2 = 32$.

The sum of the first two equals the third.

of the sort presented in Table 14.4. By summing the five columns of this
typical worksheet we obtain the data to be substituted in Formula 14.10.

$$r = \frac{7(1,900) - (56.4)(231)}{\sqrt{7(463.5) - (56.4)^2} \sqrt{7(7,840) - (231)^2}} = +0.96.$$

By now the difference between the coefficients of correlation and determination should be clear. Interpretations are given best in terms of the
latter. When reading reports containing an *r* value, we would mentally
square it and think in terms of r^2.

Which came first, the hen or the egg? Even a correlation coefficient
of 1.0 or near 1.0 implies nothing about cause and effect. The greater
weight of the mail does not cause the higher number of orders, nor vice versa.

No statistical technique can establish cause and effect relationships.
What affects what is part of the hypothesis that is based on experience and
knowledge. Says Darrell Huff in his *How to Lie With Statistics:*

> Permitting statistical treatment and the hypnotic presence of numbers and deci-
> mal points to befog causal relationships is little better than superstition. And it is
> often more seriously misleading. It is rather like the conviction among the people
> of the New Hebrides that body lice produce good health. Observations over the
> centuries had taught them that people in good health usually had lice and sick people
> very often did not. The observation itself was accurate and sound, as observations
> made informally over the years surprisingly often are. Not so much can be said
> for the conclusion to which these primitive people came from their evidence: Lice
> make a man healthy. Everybody should have them.
>   . . . More sophisticated observers finally got things straightened out in the New
> Hebrides. As it turned out almost everybody in those circles had lice most of the
> time. It was, you might say, the normal condition of man. When, however, any-
> one took a fever (quite possibly carried to him by those same lice) and his body
> became too hot for comfortable habitation, the lice left. There you have cause and
> effect altogether confusingly distorted, reversed, and intermingled.[2]

All this means is that even when the coefficient of correlation is very high,
the statistical analysis cannot indicate whether or not a causal relationship
exists and, if so, in what direction it goes. Hamilton's problem is one of
association, and causation is of no concern. However, in many economic
and business problems causation is an important issue. For instance, if we
make a cross-section analysis of the relation between the level of economic
activity and automobile sales in the forty-eight states, an important question
is whether the tail wags the dog, or vice versa. This is where economics
takes over.

[2] Darrell Huff, *op. cit.*, pp. 98–99.

Adjusting for lost degrees of freedom. A scatter diagram of two observations permits a straight line to pass through both points. The two points are then right on the "line of best fit," and thus we have a perfect fit and a correlation coefficient of either $+1.0$ or -1.0, depending on the slope of the line. Does this mean that the two phenomena have perfect correlation? Let us illustrate the question by assuming that the two phenomena are number of atom bombs in United States arsenals and the size of the world's population in 1945 and 1957. We plot some such hypothetical figures (we don't know how many A bombs the United States had, but presume that in 1957 there were many more than there were in 1945) and draw a positively sloping straight line through these two points. Clearly, it would be a grave mistake to claim that, in 1945 and 1957, 100 per cent of the increase in the world's population was associated with or can be explained by increases in the United States A-bomb arsenal. Just as it would be wrong to plot the number of ministers against liquor consumption for the years 1932 and 1957, draw a straight line through the two points, and conclude that in 1932 and 1957 100 per cent of the increase in liquor consumption could be explained in terms of the increase in the number of ministers.

This is a form of *spurious* correlation, and due solely to the fact that any two points make a straight line. Spurious correlation of this sort needs to be eliminated before we can learn about the actual closeness of association. We must scale down the calculated correlation coefficient and "adjust for degrees of freedom lost." Whenever we correlate two variates by means of a linear correlation analysis, two degrees of freedom will be lost.[3]

---

[3] The degrees of freedom that are lost can be most easily established by examining the regression equation: there are as many degrees of freedom lost as there are constants in the regression equation.

Adjustments for degrees of freedom lost are readily made with the aid of the following equation:

$$r^{2*} = 1.00 - (1.00 - |r^2|)\left(\frac{n-1}{n-k}\right),$$

where the asterisk* indicates that the coefficient is adjusted for degrees of freedom lost, $|r^2|$ is the calculated value of the coefficient of determination neglecting the sign, n is the sample size, and k is the number of degrees of freedom lost.

For Hamilton's data:

$$r^{2*} = 1.00 - (1.00 - 0.92)\left(\frac{7-1}{7-2}\right)$$

$$= 1.00 - 0.08\left(\frac{6}{5}\right) = +0.90.$$

$$r^* = \sqrt{0.90} = 0.95.$$

For the sake of simplicity, we will keep using the unadjusted correlation coefficients in this text.

Is there a significant relationship? Hamilton's data, of course, are sample data and deserve to be treated as such. Now the time has come to consider the inference aspects of regression and correlation analysis. As a first step we must understand the assumptions underlying inferences about least squares correlation and regression coefficients. They are as follows:

Chart 14.6   THREE-DIMENSIONAL CHART OF REGRESSION POPULATION

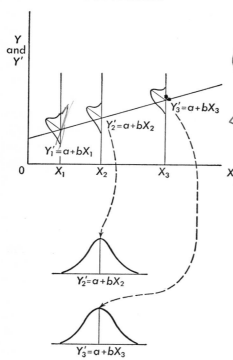

1. The values of the dependent variate of the population, i.e., the variate we want to predict, are assumed to be normally distributed around the least squares line, which thus is a line connecting the means of all these normal distributions.

2. The standard deviations of these normal population distributions are all assumed equal.

3. The observations, and their deviations from the least squares line, are assumed independent of each other.

The first two assumptions are portrayed in Chart 14.6 and the third assumption means that *successive observations should not be interdependent.* This problem of interdependence, also often referred to as *serial correlation,* will be discussed again in Chapter XV.

There are indications that, insofar as Hamilton's problem is concerned, all three conditions are met, so that he can proceed to draw inferences.

The correlation coefficient for the seven sample plants is +0.96. Let us grant that the seven plants and the day of the test are representative, and assume that the relationship indicated on the day of the test holds for all workdays. Still, the question remains whether the relationship indicated in the seven sample plants could have come about by chance, or is significant in that it exists in all 110 plants.

To decide whether a significant relationship prevailed between mail weight and orders in all 110 plants, Hamilton can test whether from seven observations, let us say at a 0.05 level of significance, a correlation coefficient of $+0.96$ could have come about by chance, or whether it is significantly different from zero. While in previous chapters we had tested for the significance of a difference of a sample mean from an assumed mean, and a sample proportion from an assumed proportion, we now would test for the difference of a sample correlation coefficient from an assumed correlation coefficient. In most cases we will put the assumed correlation equal to zero, although sometimes we might wish to test whether there is a significant difference between the sample correlation coefficient and an assumed correlation coefficient other than zero.

In principle, such a test takes the conventional form of signifiance tests. First, we establish a set of hypotheses. We start by theorizing about the nature of the relationship between mail weight and orders. Based on our best knowledge and experience, this relationship should be positive and, therefore, we would expect a population correlation coefficient that is greater than zero. Therefore, we apply the "more than" or B Case, establishing the null hypothesis that the parameter ρ (ρ, pronounced rho, is the Greek letter r) is zero and the alternative hypothesis that ρ is larger than zero. In brief,

$$H_o: \rho = 0.00.$$
$$H_B: \rho > 0.00.$$

The second step involves establishing regions and criteria of rejection and acceptance. Under certain circumstances the sampling distribution of r's, if the sample size is small, can be approximated by the student-t distribution. In finding the appropriate t value we would take into consideration the fact that in simple linear correlation two degrees of freedom are lost. Since our sample was of size 7, we look up the t value for $7 - 2$ or 5 degrees of freedom. If we insist on a level of significance of 0.05, the full 5 per cent will be placed into the upper tail of the Student-t distribution, and the appropriate t value is $+2.02$. The criteria, therefore, are in brief,

Reject H_o, if the t value of the sample data $> +2.02$.
Accept H_o, if the t value of the sample data $< +2.02$.

As a third step we calculate the t value that pertains to the sample data. As usual, t as well as z can be calculated by dividing the difference between the statistic and the parameter by the relevant standard error. In this case,

$$t = \frac{r - \rho}{\sigma_r}.$$

(14.11)

Under certain conditions, of which this is one, σ_r can be approximated by

$$\frac{1}{\sqrt{n-1}}.$$ (14.12)

For the data at hand,

$$t \doteq \frac{0.96 - 0.00}{\dfrac{1}{\sqrt{7-1}}} = +2.4.$$

Finally, we can conclude that since the t value of the sample data is larger than $+2.02$, we reject the null hypothesis and decide that in all 110 plants there is a significant relationship between mail weight and orders.

Fortunately we do not need to make all these complicated computations. Instead, much of the work has been done for us by R. A. Fisher, who has produced a table of critical correlation coefficient values (see Table IV in the Appendix). Thus, we merely compare the r pertaining to our sample data with the value in the table that corresponds to the desired level of significance and the proper degrees of freedom, i.e., $n-2$ for simple linear correlation. In Case A we would compare, if we select an α of 0.05, our r of $+0.96$ with the value 0.754, which corresponds to an α of 0.05 and $7-2$ or 5 degrees of freedom. Since the correlation coefficient of the sample data is larger than the value in the table, we reject the null hypothesis and conclude that there is a significant relationship between mail weight and orders.[4] With our set of hypotheses of the "more than" or B Case (and the same would hold for the "less than" or C Case) the critical value would even be smaller than 0.754 and a rejection of the null hypothesis is even more appropriate. While it is possible to compute performance and power functions, we will not do so.

How close is the relationship in the population? At an α of 0.05, a significant correlation between mail weight and orders was found to exist. Next, we want a confidence interval estimate of the closeness of this relationship in the population. However, such computations are very laborious. Tables have been perfected that make it possible to read off confidence intervals of population correlation coefficients, and we will rely on such a table. In the Appendix, Table V helps find the 95 per cent confidence interval of population correlation coefficients for different sample sizes. Tables for different levels of confidence can be found in F. N. David, *Tables of the Ordinates and Probability Integral of the Distribution of the Correlation Coefficient in Small Samples.*[5]

[4] In this comparison we neglect the sign of the correlation coefficient.
[5] London, The Biometrika Office.

To use Table V of the Appendix, we locate the value of the sample correlation coefficient on the horizontal axis and move vertically to the first curve with the size of the sample minus 2 written above it. In our case we locate +0.96 and move upward to the curve that has 7 − 2, or 5, written above it. From this intersection we turn horizontally either left or right, depending on which margin is closer, and read off the vertical scale the lower confidence limit of ρ, i.e., about +0.45. There is a higher curve with a 5 above it, and its intersection with the vertical line corresponding to +0.96 gives us the upper confidence limit of ρ, i.e., about +1.0. Using Table V in the Appendix, we find for an r of +0.96 and 5 degrees of freedom a 95 per cent confidence interval extending from about +0.45 to +1.0.

A correlation coefficient at the lower confidence limit of about +0.45 corresponds to a coefficient of determination at the lower limit of about (+0.45)^2 or 0.20. As a lower confidence limit, about 20 per cent of the daily variation in the number of mail orders in the 110 SOMB plants can be explained in terms of changes in the weight of the mail. Similarly, an upper confidence limit $\bar{\rho}$ and $\bar{\rho}^2$ amounting each to +1.0 means that about 100 per cent of the daily variation in the number of mail orders can be explained in terms of changes in the mail weight. Or in brief, we can assert with a 95 per cent confidence that the interval extending from 20 to 100 per cent contains the true coefficient of determination.

This interval is too wide to be of much use, particularly in view of the lower limit. The main reason for this wide interval is the very small sample size that we have been using. When we increase of the sample size, as we will do later, the precision of the estimate is improved.

Is the regression coefficient significant? If the sample data can be described by a positively (or negatively) sloping regression line, we do not yet know whether the population regression line is itself positively (or negatively) sloped or whether the slope could be due to random variation. We decide the matter with the help of a test on the significance of a difference between a given sample regression coefficient and an assumed regression coefficient of zero.

The test could proceed in the conventional way in that we first decide on a proper sample size, then decide whether on the basis of a given α the null hypothesis is to be rejected or accepted, and finally, in case we accept the null hypothesis, compute the power of the test. In most business problems that call for regression analysis, we are not given the opportunity of selecting the sample. Instead, a set of sample data are given, very often not more than 20 to 30 in number. The computation of the power of the test is somewhat involved and the interested reader can find a discussion of the matter and method of computation in a number of books.[6]   We will concern ourselves only with a test that controls the error of Type I.   Here, then, are the four steps of testing a hypothesis about the significance of a difference between a sample and an assumed regression coefficient.

We will begin by choosing an α and by establishing null and alternative hypotheses.   We select an α of 0.05 and, based on our knowledge of the situation, we would expect a positive relationship between mail weight and orders.   Our alternative hypothesis will be that we expect the population regression coefficient to be greater than zero.   Our regression coefficient is here connoted B (B, pronounced beta, is the Greek capital B that we are using here instead of β in order to avoid a mixup with the notation used previously to designate the probability of an error of Type II).

In brief,

$$H_o: B = 0.00.$$
$$H_B: B > 0.00.$$

As a second step we establish regions and criteria of rejection and acceptance.   For large samples the sampling distribution of b's is normally distributed and for small samples this distribution can be approximated by a student t distribution.   With α of 0.05 in the rejection region t is $+2.02$ (for $7 - 2$ or 5 degrees of freedom).   In brief,

Reject H_o, if the t value of the sample data $> +2.02$.
Accept H_o, if the t value of the sample data $< +2.02$.

The third step involves calculating the t value of the sample data.   For the regression coefficient z as well as

$$t = \frac{b - B}{\sigma_b}. \tag{14.13}$$

For computational purposes, it is more convenient to approximate t by using the following formula:[7]

$$t \doteq \frac{(b - B)\sqrt{\Sigma X^2 - \dfrac{(\Sigma X)^2}{n}}}{s_{YX}} \doteq \frac{(b - B)s_X \sqrt{n}}{s_{YX}}. \tag{14.14}$$

---

[6] As an example, see Acheson J. Duncan, *Quality Control and Industrial Statistics* (Homewood, Ill., Richard D. Irwin, Inc., 1953).

[7] Since $s^2 = \dfrac{\Sigma X^2}{n} - \left(\dfrac{\Sigma X}{n}\right)^2$, $ns = n\sqrt{\dfrac{\Sigma X^2}{n} - \left(\dfrac{\Sigma X}{n}\right)^2} = \sqrt{\Sigma X^2 - \dfrac{(\Sigma X)^2}{n}}.$

In our case, $s_X \sqrt{n} = \sqrt{\Sigma X^2 - \frac{(\Sigma X)^2}{n}} = \sqrt{463.5 - \frac{(56.4)^2}{7}} = 3.02.$

s_{YX} is most readily approximated from Formula 14.7, i.e.,

$$\sqrt{\frac{\Sigma Y^2 - a\Sigma Y - b\Sigma XY}{n-2}},$$

which in our case is equal to 1.8.

Placing these values in Equation 14.14, we find the t pertaining to the sample data to be approximately equal to $\frac{(4.69 - 0.00)3.02}{1.8} = 7.9.$

As our final step we conclude that since the calculated t value of the sample data is larger than $+2.02$, we reject the null hypothesis that B = 0.00. Thus, we decide at an α of 0.05 that the regression line has a significant positive slope.

What is the confidence interval of prediction? Finally, Hamilton is ready for his prediction. But what exactly is it that he wants to predict? Hamilton would like to predict with a known confidence how many orders await processing on a given day, and he bases his prediction on the weight of the mail that has been received in yesterday's three last and today's two first mail deliveries. If 9.0 hundred pounds of mail have been received, he would like to predict with a 95 per cent confidence the interval that will contain the true number of orders that await processing on that day. To make such an estimate, he would apply the following formula:

$$\bar{Y}' \doteq a + bX_o \pm t_{(n-2)}s_{YX} \sqrt{\frac{n+1}{n} + \frac{(X_o - \bar{X})^2}{ns_X^2}}, \qquad (14.15)$$

where $\bar{Y}'$ is the confidence interval of the predicted variate,

   X_o is the particular X value for which Y is to be predicted,

   $t_{(n-2)}$ is the t value corresponding to the desired α and $n-2$ degrees of freedom, and the other notations are the same as before.

This formula takes account of sampling variation due to variation of observations about the regression line, variation in the mean value of the independent variate and variation in the estimated regression coefficient.

The reader should have little difficulty in recognizing the first part of Formula 14.15, i.e., the simple linear regression equation, where the regression coefficient as well as the Y-intercept can be positive or negative. To this first part in Formula 14.15,

$$t_{(n-2)}s_{YX} \sqrt{\frac{n+1}{n} + \frac{(X_o - \bar{X})^2}{ns_X^2}},$$

i.e., t times the *standard error of prediction* is added (and subtracted) to make possible the finding of the upper (and lower) confidence limits.

Placing his data in Formula 14.15, Hamilton finds the 95 per cent confidence interval for a given day with an incoming mail of 9.0 hundred pounds:

$$\bar{Y}'_{.95} \doteq -4.71 + 4.69(9.0) \pm 2.57(1.8)$$
$$\sqrt{\frac{8}{7} + \frac{(9.0 - 8.1)^2}{9.1}} = 37.5 \pm 5.1.$$

Chart 14.7   NINETY-FIVE PER CENT PREDICTION BAND

For predicting number of mail orders received in a specific plant.

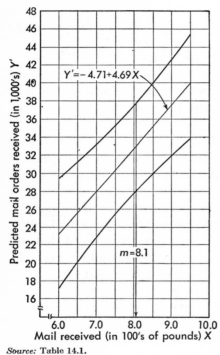

Source: Table 14.1.

Hamilton can, therefore, assert with a 95 per cent confidence that if, on a given day, 9.0 hundred pounds of mail have been received by 8:30 A.M., the interval 32 to 43 thousand mail orders will contain the number of orders that await processing that day. The confidence interval is so wide simply because the sample is very small.[8]

With the help of Formula 14.15 we can predict for any day the number of mail orders awaiting processing, by merely placing the appropriate X_o value, i.e., mail weight of that day, into the formula. We have computed a number of confidence intervals for different mail weights varying from 6.0 to 9.5 hundreds of pounds of mail, i.e., over the range of observed data. Plotting these upper and lower confidence limits around the regression line, a prediction band is obtained (see Chart 14.7). The prediction band is always narrowest where $X_o = \bar{X}$, i.e., when we want to predict Y for the mean value of the independent variate; in our case for 8.1 hundred pounds of mail.

[8] Formula 14.15 has been presented in order to make possible the prediction of specific events, e.g., number of mail orders awaiting processing on a given day on which a given poundage of mail was received. Instead of predicting individual values, it is often enough to predict mean values. Such a prediction would, for instance, involve the *mean* number of orders awaiting processing on days on which a given poundage of mail is received. Under the same circumstances the confidence interval of the mean value estimate is usually narrower than that of the individual value. To predict mean values the following formula would be used:

$$\bar{Y}' \doteq a + bX_o \pm t_{(n-2)}s_{YX}\sqrt{\frac{1}{n} + \frac{(X_o - \bar{X})^2}{ns_X^2}}.$$

Let us pause for a moment to make sure that we understand the difference between a *standard deviation of regression* and a *standard error of prediction.* The standard deviation of regression measures the dispersion of the entire population of observations about the regression line; it is a population measure and its application presupposes that all population data are given. Not so the standard error of prediction, which is a measure reflecting sample as well as population variations in the values of the regression coefficients. Since the sample regression coefficients are subject to sample variation, and thus sampling error, the sampling variance in an estimate of the average value of the dependent variate corresponding to some independent variate value is a composite of the sample variations of the regression coefficients as well as of the variation in the population. Therefore, unless we have all population data, we must predict with the help of the standard error of prediction, and not the standard deviation of regression.[9]

A larger sample. The limitations of as small a sample as Hamilton's seven observations are all too clear. Yet working with few observations has the advantage of reducing the computational work and preventing the newcomer from getting lost in the woods.

We will now draw a new sample of an order of magnitude more commonly encountered: 32. The 32 observations are summarized in Table 14.6. This time we will adopt a sequence of steps first examining the closeness of the association or the quality of the predictive mechanism and thereafter concerning ourselves with the quantitative nature of the relationship. In the future it will prove useful to use the following six steps:

I. Find the correlation coefficient.
II. Test for the significance of the correlation coefficient.
III. Estimate the confidence interval of the coefficients of correlation and determination.
IV. Find the regression coefficient and Y-intercept.
V. Test for the significance of the regression coefficient.
VI. Calculate the confidence interval of the prediction.

Step I. How to find the correlation coefficient?

$$r = \frac{n\Sigma XY - (\Sigma X)(\Sigma Y)}{\sqrt{n\Sigma X^2 - (\Sigma X)^2} \sqrt{n\Sigma Y^2 - (\Sigma Y)^2}}$$

$$= \frac{32(8,600) - (259.6)(1,042)}{\sqrt{32(2,141.2) - (259.6)^2} \sqrt{32(34,580) - (1,042)^2}}$$

$$= +0.98.$$

---

[9] Since the term "standard error" is used in relation to sampling distributions, and the standard deviation of regression is a population measure, we do not like to use the commonly used term "standard error of estimate" in its place.

Table 14.6 WORK SHEET FOR SIMPLE LINEAR CORRELATION
(Poundage of mail and number of mail orders received by seven mail-order plants
on a given date.)

X 00's Pounds of Mail	Y 000's Mail Orders	X² 00's Pounds of Mail	Y² 000's Mail Orders	XY
9.0	36	81.0	1,300	324
8.5	34	72.2	1,160	289
6.3	25	39.7	625	158
8.0	32	64.0	1,020	256
9.5	38	90.2	1,440	361
7.5	30	56.2	900	225
9.1	36	82.8	1,300	328
8.0	32	64.0	1,024	256
6.0	25	36.0	625	150
6.0	24	36.0	576	144
8.5	34	72.2	1,160	289
8.1	32	65.6	1,024	259
6.6	26	43.6	676	172
9.0	36	81.0	1,300	324
7.0	28	49.0	784	196
8.7	35	75.7	1,220	304
9.3	37	86.5	1,370	344
7.3	29	53.3	841	212
7.4	29	54.8	841	215
7.8	31	60.8	961	242
9.2	37	84.6	1,370	340
8.4	33	70.6	1,090	277
7.8	31	60.8	961	242
9.9	40	98.0	1,600	396
9.0	36	81.0	1,300	324
8.6	34	74.0	1,160	292
7.9	32	62.4	1,020	253
9.1	42	82.8	1,760	382
9.7	39	94.1	1,520	378
7.5	30	56.2	900	225
6.7	27	44.9	729	181
8.2	32	67.2	1,020	262
Total 259.6	1,042	2,141.2	34,580	8,600

Source: Hypothetical data.

Step II. Is there a significant relationship?

1. Here are the null and alternative hypotheses:

$$H_o: \rho = 0.00.$$
$$H_B: \rho > 0.00.$$

(For comparative purposes we settle once more on an α of 0.05.)

2. Reject H_o, if z value of sample data $> +1.64$.

Accept H_o, if z value of sample data $< +1.64$.

3. $z = \dfrac{r - \rho}{\sigma_r} \doteq \dfrac{r - \rho}{\dfrac{1}{\sqrt{n-1}}} = \dfrac{+0.98}{\dfrac{1}{\sqrt{32-1}}} = +5.0.$

4. Since the calculated z value pertaining to these 32 sample data is greater than $+1.64$, we reject the null hypothesis and decide that in all 110 of SOMB's plants there is a significant relationship between mail weight and orders ($\alpha = 0.05$).

The same conclusion is reached when we use Fisher's table (Table IV in the Appendix), which indicates that the critical value of the correlation coefficient is about $+0.35$ for $32 - 2$ degrees of freedom. Since the correlation coefficient in our example is greater than $+0.35$, we reject the null hypothesis that $\rho = 0.00$.

Step III. How close is the relationship?

With the help of Table V in the Appendix we find that the 95 per cent confidence interval of ρ estimated from an r of $+0.98$ and $32 - 2$ degrees extends from about $+0.95$ to $+0.98$. The corresponding coefficients of determination are $+0.90$ and $+0.96$.

Step IV. How to find the regression equation?

The regression coefficient

$$b = \frac{n\Sigma XY - (\Sigma X)(\Sigma Y)}{n(\Sigma X^2) - (\Sigma X)^2}$$
$$= \frac{32(8,600) - (259.6)(1,042)}{32(2,141.2) - (259.6)^2} = +4.2.$$

The Y-intercept $a = \bar{Y} - b\bar{X} = \dfrac{1,042}{32} - (4.2)\dfrac{259.6}{32} = -1.5.$ The regression coefficient of the 32 sample data can be interpreted as follows: In these 32 plants an increase (or decrease) of 1.0 hundred pounds of mail on a given day was on the average associated with a corresponding increase (or decrease) of 4.2 thousand mail orders.

Step V. Is the regression coefficient significant, i.e., does there exist a significant slope?

1. The null and alternative hypotheses are:

$$H_o: B = 0.00.$$
$$H_B: B > 0.00.$$

(For comparative purposes we settle once more on an α of 0.05.)

2. Reject H_o, if z value of sample data $> +1.64$.

Accept H_o, if z value of sample data $< +1.64$.

3. $z = \dfrac{b - B}{\sigma_b} \doteq \dfrac{(b - B)s_X \sqrt{n}}{s_{YX}}$,

where $s_X \sqrt{n} = \sqrt{\Sigma X^2 - \dfrac{(\Sigma X)^2}{n}} = \sqrt{2,141.2 - \dfrac{(259.6)^2}{32}} = 5.93$,

and $s_{YX} = \sqrt{\dfrac{\Sigma Y^2 - a\Sigma Y - b\Sigma XY}{n - 2}}$

$$= \sqrt{\dfrac{34,580 - (-1.5)1,042 - (4.2)8,600}{32 - 2}} = 0.82.$$

Therefore, $z \doteq \dfrac{(4.2 - 0.00)5.93}{0.82} = 30.$

4. Since the calculated z value is larger than $+1.64$, we reject the null hypothesis and decide that a regression coefficient of $+4.2$ is significantly different from zero, i.e., the regression line has a significant positive slope ($\alpha = 0.05$).

Step VI. What is the confidence interval of the prediction?

Let us assume that by 8:30 A.M., 9.0 hundred pounds of mail have been received in one of SOMB's plants, and find the 95 per cent confidence interval of the predicted number of mail orders awaiting processing.

$$\bar{Y}' \doteq a + bX_o \pm z(s_{YX}) \sqrt{\dfrac{n + 1}{n} + \dfrac{(X_o - \bar{X})^2}{ns_X^2}}$$

$$\doteq -1.5 + 4.2(9.0) \pm 1.96(0.82) \sqrt{\dfrac{33}{32} + \dfrac{(9.0 - 8.1)^2}{(5.93)^2}} = 36.3 \pm 1.66.$$

In summary, on the basis of the 32 sample observations the management of SOMB can conclude with a 95 per cent confidence that when 9.0 hundred pounds of mail are received in one of its plants by 8:30 A.M., the actual number of mail orders awaiting processing that day in the plant is between 35 and 38 thousand. This estimate is much more precise than the one we made on the basis of 7 observations, and may even be precise enough for working purposes. Increasing the size of the sample from 7 to 32 (about $4\frac{1}{2}$ times) greatly increased the definiteness of the estimate; it reduced the width of the 95 per cent confidence interval in this example from about

10 thousand to about 3 thousand mail orders. An even larger sample would further enhance the definiteness.

However, once we work with very large samples, our method becomes cumbersome and can be replaced by a method that helps to correlate grouped data. We consider this method beyond the scope of our efforts, but will indicate in a footnote some appropriate references.[10]

This method can be useful. Sears, Roebuck & Co. has been employing this method for a number of years to plan the processing of its mail orders. It found that the "quality of the mail" (by this the company means the number of mail orders per pound of mail) varies both over the season and the week. The quality of the mail was found to improve following the distribution of a new catalogue and is especially high during the Christmas season. Insofar as the weekly pattern is concerned, the quality of the mail was best on Tuesdays; on Wednesday, Thursday, Friday the quality gradually declined to a low on Monday. On the basis of this knowledge, the company computed seasonal as well as weekly indexes that closely described the pattern of these variations. By relating the quality of the mail to mail poundage, seasonal variation, and weekly variation, Sears, Roebuck had been able to perfect its method of forecasting so that by 1953 the daily estimates of the number of orders awaiting processing varied from the actual receipts by only about one half of 1 per cent.[11]

Coding—a worksaver. Instead of working with large numbers or very small ones, we can code the data by adding, subtracting, multiplying, or dividing by a constant. Then all computations are carried out with the coded data. Coefficients of correlation and determination are not affected by such coding.

The data in Table 14.1 are actually coded data. We expressed the Y's in units of 1,000, and in so doing coded the Y's, dividing them by 1,000. Similarly, the X's are coded, since they are expressed in units of 100.

However, often the coding is more complex. Take, for instance, Panel A of Table 14.7 in which Y represents the average value of farm products produced on farms in twenty Iowa counties in 1945. Instead of working with four digit numbers, coding permits us to work with but two digits in this case without much effect on the precision of the results (see Panel B of Table 14.7). To reduce all Y values to two digits we can divide each Y by

---

[10] For correlation methods of grouped data see George W. Snedecor, *Statistical Methods*, 5th ed. (Ames, Iowa State College Press, 1956); and Frederick E. Croxton and Dudley J. Cowden, *Practical Business Statistics*, second edition (New York, Prentice-Hall, Inc., 1948).

[11] C. W. Smalley, "Estimating Daily Orders from Weight of Mail," *American Statistician*, February, 1954, pp. 14–15.

100, drop the digit, and round it.   Thus, $4,605 becomes 46 and $7,988, 80, etc.   Likewise, since the X values are all greater than 100, yet smaller than 200, we can subtract from each X 100 and drop the decimal.   Then 176.3 will become 76, and 182.4, 82, etc.   In any case, we must carefully note the

Table 14.7   CODED AND UNCODED DATA OF AVERAGE VALUE OF
FARM PRODUCTS PRODUCED IN 1945 ON FARMS IN 20 IOWA
COUNTIES AND AVERAGE FARM ACREAGE

A. Uncoded Data			B. Coded Data		
County	Dollar Value Y	Acres X	County	Dollar Value Y*	Acres X†
A	4,605	176.3	A	46	76
B	7,988	182.4	B	80	82
C	8,280	168.9	C	83	69
D	7,484	163.1	D	75	63
E	8,665	190.3	E	87	90
F	2,997	171.4	F	30	71
G	5,984	162.8	G	60	63
H	6,834	186.4	H	68	86
I	7,309	181.1	I	73	81
J	8,301	181.1	J	83	81
K	3,789	150.9	K	38	51
L	3,548	146.2	L	35	46
M	4,199	173.3	M	42	73
N	6,299	170.3	N	63	70
O	8,413	184.1	O	84	84
P	8,008	182.1	P	80	82
Q	8,306	182.4	Q	83	82
R	5,848	162.6	R	58	63
S	3,881	154.6	S	39	55
T	4,601	150.2	T	46	50

* Divided by 100, digit dropped and rounded up.
† Dropped decimal and subtracted 100.

nature of the coding operation performed, because it bears on the uncoding of the results.

14.2. RANK CORRELATION

Before embarking on a correlation analysis that covers a large number of observations, it is often convenient to make a test, even if it is only a crude one, to learn whether or not there is a significant correlation.   This is readily accomplished with the help of *rank correlation*.   Unlike least squares analysis, rank correlation makes no assumptions about the shape of the distribution of the dependent variate, and therefore can be successfully applied even if the dependent variate is not normally distributed around the regression line.

Let us see how rank correlation analysis is carried out. We start by ranking, as the name indicates, the Y and X values either in ascending or descending order. Which order we select is not important as long as we are consistent. In Columns 1 and 2 of Table 14.8 we have ranked the mail

Table 14.8 WORK SHEET FOR RANK CORRELATION
(Poundage of mail and number of mail orders received by seven mail-order plants on a given date.)

X	Y	Rank of X g_X	Rank of Y g_Y	$g_X - g_Y$ or d	d^2
1	*2*	*3*	*4*	*5*	*6*
9.5	38	7	6	1	1
8.0	32	4	4	0	0
6.0	24	1	1	0	0
7.3	29	2	2	0	0
9.0	36	5	5	0	0
9.1	42	6	7	−1	1
7.5	30	3	3	0	0
	Total				2

Source: Table 14.1.

order data from Table 14.1 in ascending order in Columns 3 and 4. Since 9.5 is the highest and at the same time the 7th smallest mail receipt value, we write in Column 3 opposite 9.5 a 7. In like manner we write a 4 opposite 8.0, etc. Turning to Column 4, we write a 6 opposite 38, since 38 is the second largest or 6th smallest Y value. Opposite 32 we write 4, opposite 24 we write 1, etc. Thus, in Column 3 we have the rank of the X values, which we connote as g_X; and in Column 4 the rank of the Y values, which we connote as g_Y.

The computational formula for the rank correlation coefficient is:

$$r_r = 1.00 - \frac{(6\Sigma d^2)}{n(n^2 - 1)}, \qquad (14.16)$$

where $d = g_X - g_Y$.

In Column 5 we have written the difference in the rank of the two variates, i.e., $g_X - g_Y = d$, and in Column 6 this difference has been squared. The sum of these squares is 2, which is placed in Formula 14.16:

$$r_r = 1.00 - \frac{6(2)}{7(49 - 1)} \text{ or } +0.96.$$

Instead of making a regular significance test, we can compare the computed value of the rank correlation coefficient with some critical values, as have been reproduced in Table VI of the Appendix. In this table are given critical rank correlation values for α's of 0.05 and 0.01, respectively, for sample sizes 4 through 30. For instance, the critical value corresponding to an α of 0.05 and a sample size of 7 is 0.714. Since (neglecting signs) the calculated rank correlation coefficient is larger than the critical value of Table VI, we reject the null hypothesis, and conclude that the rank correlation coefficient of $+0.96$ is significant.

On the basis of this rank correlation analysis, we would be inclined to embark on a least squares regression and correlation analysis. It should be pointed out, however, that in only very few instances will rank and least squares correlation coefficients have the same magnitude, as is the case in our example.

Rank correlation analysis has additional applications. Whenever one or both of the variates are not readily quantified, but instead can only be ranked qualitatively, rank correlation is useful. For instance, we might want to learn about the consistency with which cars participating in the Memorial Day speedway races in Indianapolis occupied positions during various stages of the race. Is there a relationship between a driver's position during the race and his final position? For instance, is the winning car usually leading during most of the race, or is it only in the last few laps that the winner usually pulls to the front?

To answer this question we could test for the consistency with which cars maintained their position throughout the race. We could rank the position of, let us say, the first twenty cars every tenth lap and compute the rank correlation coefficient.

There are also important applications of rank correlation analysis to market research. Many market variates are inherently qualitative. In a consumer preference survey we might want to ask the consumer for his preference among different brands. After arranging the items according to consumer preference and, let us say, price, we could compute the rank correlation coefficient that will attest to the closeness of this relationship.

14.3. MULTIPLE CORRELATION

In the preceding pages we discussed the relation between the average value of products produced on farms in 20 Iowa counties and the farm size. The coefficient of correlation for these 20 data in Table 14.7 is +0.71, or (ignoring the inference aspects of the problem) about 50 per cent of the difference in value produced, county by county, was associated with the size of the farm. What about the other 50 per cent? They were associated with other factors. For instance, the fertility of the soil might have affected the value of the output. We can get some idea about soil fertility by using data on yield per acre. Calculation of the correlation coefficient between average value of farm products and corn yield per acre reveals a coefficient of +0.29. If we connote the dependent variate, average value of farm products, by X_1, one independent variate, acreage, by X_2, and the second independent variate, average yield of corn per acre, by X_3, we can say $r_{X_1X_2}$ or, for short $r_{12} = +0.71$ and $r_{13} = +0.29$.

However, what is the combined association of these three variates? For this purpose we calculate a *coefficient of multiple correlation*, $R_{1.23}$, or its square, the *coefficient of multiple determination*, $R_{1.23}^2$.

Before we compute $R_{1.23}$ we must find one other (simple) correlation coefficient, i.e., r_{23}, which testifies to the relation between the independent variates. In the example on hand $r_{23} = -0.036$. Knowing r_{12}, r_{13}, and r_{23}, we can find $R_{1.23}$ with the help of the equation

$$R_{1.23} = \sqrt{\frac{r_{12}^2 + r_{13}^2 - 2r_{12}r_{13}r_{23}}{1 - r_{23}^2}}. \tag{14.17}$$

Instead of computing $R_{1.23}$ from Formula 14.17 we can make use of a nomograph, which was developed by Frederic M. Lord and is reproduced in Table VII of the Appendix.

For the year 1945,

$$r_{12} = +0.71,$$
$$r_{13} = +0.29, \text{ and}$$
$$r_{23} = -0.036.$$

Placing these values in Formula 14.17, we find that $R_{1.23} = +0.78$, the same result as would be obtained by using the nomograph.

If we neglect the inference aspects of the problem and square 0.78 to get the coefficient of multiple determination, we could interpret the finding as follows: In these 20 counties about 61 per cent of the differences in the average value of farm products produced in 1945 were associated with differences in size of farm and corn yield per acre.

The area of multiple correlation and regression has many more interesting facets which, however, we consider beyond the scope of this book. Likewise it should be obvious that we could correlate more than two independent variates with the dependent variate. Clearly, the more variates we have the more complicated the computations. But this should not discourage such studies. Nowadays, high speed electronic computers can handle most complicated correlation problems rapidly. For instance, the research department of the Rayco Company, an integrated firm in the seat cover industry, made a multiple correlation analysis covering 55 variates to decide on the location of new stores.[12] Electronic computing machines solved the equations in a few hours.

WE HAVE LEARNED THAT:

1. Simple linear regression and correlation analysis makes possible predictions which on the average are as little off as possible.
2. The assumptions underlying such an analysis are:
   a. The dependent variate of the population is normally distributed around the least squares line,
   b. The standard deviations of these normal populations are all of equal magnitude, and
   c. The observations, and their deviations from the least squares line, are all independent of one another.
3. The correlation coefficient as well as the coefficient of determination testify to the closeness of the association between two phenomena.
4. The correlation coefficient can be computed with the help of the following formula:

$$r = \frac{n\Sigma XY - (\Sigma X)(\Sigma Y)}{\sqrt{n\Sigma X^2 - (\Sigma X)^2}\,\sqrt{n\Sigma Y^2 - (\Sigma Y)^2}}.$$

5. The coefficient of determination can be computed by squaring r.
6. The coefficient of determination can assume values from -1.0 to $+1.0$, expressing the percentage of the variation of the dependent variate that is associated with variations in the independent variate.
7. The significance of a sample correlation coefficient can be readily tested. One method is to compare the sample value with the critical value of the correlation coefficient relative to a given α and degrees of freedom (see Table IV in the Appendix).
8. Confidence intervals of sample correlation coefficients are readily found with the help of Table V in the Appendix.
9. Correlation analysis cannot indicate whether a causal relationship exists between the variates. This problem lies outside the field of statistics.

[12] "Using a Computer to Run a Business," *Business Week*, May 14, 1955.

10. The simple linear regression equation can be written as: $Y' = a + bX$, where a is the Y-intercept and b the regression coefficient.

11. The regression coefficient can be computed with the help of the following formula:

$$b = \frac{n\Sigma XY - (\Sigma X)(\Sigma Y)}{n(\Sigma X^2) - (\Sigma X)^2}.$$

12. The Y-intercept can be computed with the help of the following formula: $a = \bar{Y} - b\bar{X}. \quad \left(a = \bar{Y} - b\bar{X} \right)$

13. If the sample is large, the sampling distribution of b's is about normally distributed around B. In that case,

$$z = \frac{b - B}{\sigma_b} \doteq \frac{(b - B)\sqrt{\Sigma X^2 - \frac{(\Sigma X)^2}{n}}}{s_{YX}},$$

where

$$s_{YX} = \sqrt{\frac{\Sigma Y^2 - a\Sigma Y - b\Sigma XY}{n - 2}}.$$

14. Confidence interval predictions of specific values are made with the help of the following formula:

$$\bar{Y}' \doteq a + bX_0 \pm t_{(n-2)} s_{YX} \sqrt{\frac{n + 1}{n} + \frac{(X_0 - \bar{X})^2}{ns_X^2}},$$

where $\bar{Y}'$ is the confidence interval of the predicted variate, X_o is the particular X value for which Y is to be predicted, and $t_{(n-2)}$ is the t value corresponding to the desired α and $n - 2$ degrees of freedom.

15. The prediction band is narrowest at the mean value of the independent variate, making predictions far removed from it indefinite. Yet, the larger the sample the narrower the prediction band will tend to be.

16. The rank correlation coefficient can be computed with the help of the following formula: $r_r = 1.00 - \frac{(6\Sigma d^2)}{n(n^2 - 1)}.$

17. The computations in both regression and correlation analysis can be greatly simplified if the data are first coded.

18. A multiple correlation coefficient measures the combined association between a number of independent variates and the dependent one. Its value can either be read off a nomograph or calculated with the help of the formula:

$$R_{1.23} = \sqrt{\frac{r_{12}^2 + r_{13}^2 - 2r_{12}r_{13}r_{23}}{1 - r_{23}^2}}.$$

HOW WOULD YOU SOLVE THESE:

1. Using the sales and acreage data for the 20 Iowa counties given in Table 14.7A,
   a. Find the correlation coefficient.
   b. Adjust the correlation coefficient for degrees of freedom.

c. Test the significance of the correlation coefficient using an α of 0.01.
d. Estimate the 95 per cent confidence interval.
e. Find the simple linear regression equation and plot the regression line.
f. Test the significance of the regression coefficient using an α of 0.05.
g. Estimate the dollar sales for a 137-acre farm with an 80 per cent confidence.
h. Calculate and plot the 80 per cent band by making the necessary calculations for five farm sizes of your choosing.

2. Find the rank correlation for the sales and acreage data given in Table 14.7B and test for its significance at an α of 0.01.

3. A national chain of department stores administers a test before it hires sales personnel. The test score ranges from 0 to 100, with the latter a perfect score. Recently, it was decided to inquire into the effectiveness of this test in forecasting successful salesmanship. The test score was correlated with mean daily sales in the ready-to-wear department. Of the thousands of employees, we have selected a random sample of 36 and present below their test scores and mean daily sales:

Number	Test Score	Mean Daily Sales in Dollars	Number	Test Score	Mean Daily Sales in Dollars
1	42	78	21	92	80
2	59	83	22	58	79
3	87	99	23	51	76
4	63	64	24	73	85
5	79	87	25	86	91
6	45	67	26	95	98
7	67	78	27	74	81
8	78	87	28	79	84
9	99	98	29	61	68
10	47	63	30	47	52
11	53	75	31	74	83
12	46	69	32	74	81
13	79	89	33	87	95
14	52	72	34	83	89
15	61	80	35	47	56
16	79	88	36	76	85
17	75	82			
18	76	82			
19	84	89			
20	41	61			

a. Find the rank correlation coefficient and test for its significance at an α of 0.05.
b. Compute the least squares correlation coefficient and the coefficient of determination.
c. Test for the significance of the least squares correlation coefficient and, in case it is appropriate, find the 95 per cent confidence interval.

d. Compute the regression equation pertaining to these sample data and test their significance at an α of 0.06. In case it is appropriate, estimate with a 98 per cent confidence the mean daily sales that could be expected to have been made by a salesperson with a 72 test score.

4. Correlating the 1953 expenditures of each of the 48 states for higher education with their 1952 income payments produced a coefficient of determination of +0.90.

a. Interpret the meaning of this r^2 of +0.90 and carefully explain why a coefficient of determination can be interpreted the way you did.

b. What light, if any, does this analysis shed on the question of the relationship between states' expenditures for higher education and the people's ability to pay?

c. A similar analysis, relating expenditures for higher education to the population of the various states, produced a coefficient of determination of +0.79. Interpret the +0.79 after testing its significance.

d. On the basis of the information given, could you decide whether in the 48 states ability to pay or need (i.e., size of the population) is the more important factor, having determined states' expenditures for higher education in 1953? If not, what additional information would you need, and why?

r^2 - coefficient of determination

XV

Time Series Analysis—Prophecy Galore

In the space of one hundred and seventy-six years the lower Mississippi has shortened itself two hundred and forty-two miles. That is an average of a trifle over one mile and a third per year. Therefore, any calm person, who is not blind or idiotic, can see that in the Old Oolitic Silurian Period, just a million years ago next November, the Lower Mississippi River was upward of one million three hundred thousand miles long, and stuck out over the Gulf of Mexico like a fishing-rod. And by the same token any person can see that seven hundred and forty-two years from now the Lower Mississippi will be only a mile and three-quarters long, and Cairo and New Orleans will have joined their streets together, and be plodding comfortably along under a single mayor and a mutual board of aldermen. There is something fascinating about science. One gets such wholesale returns of conjecture out of such a trifling investment of fact.

MARK TWAIN

15.1. A MOVING PICTURE

A main objective in analyzing time series is to understand, interpret, and evaluate changes in economic phenomena in the hope of more correctly anticipating the course of future events. By studying the past pattern of changes, the business executive can appraise his firm's position and obtain the type of information upon which he can base policies. The same holds on a larger scale for the policy-maker in government, who is concerned, directly or indirectly, with maintaining a gradually rising, but otherwise stable, level of economic activity.

The analysis of time series by the economic statistician is also sometimes carried out with a view toward forecasting the future. In the popular mind this is perhaps his most important single function, one fraught with many hidden dangers. Government and business, with huge sums at stake, have widely enlisted the help of the statistician for support in penetrating the future; but often our statistical tools are far from adequate. Some statisticians are highly skeptical of our ability to forecast. For instance, this position is well expressed by M. J. Moroney, who said,

> Economic forecasting, like weather forecasting in England, is only valid for the next six hours or so. Beyond that it is sheer guesswork.[1]

Should government and bussiness executives subscribe to this view they might be driven back into the dark ages when prediction was the business of the astrologer, palm reader, and fortuneteller.

A *time series* is a sequence of values of the same variate corresponding to successive points in time. Thus, for instance, the daily quotations of the Dow-Jones Industrial Average on the New York Stock Exchange constitute

Chart 15.1 DOW-JONES INDUSTRIAL AVERAGE, 1952–56

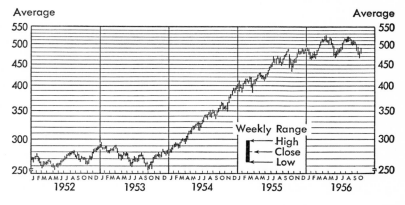

a time series, which is presented in Chart 15.1. Likewise, the monthly data of the Federal Reserve Board's *Index of Industrial Production* can be looked upon as a time series.

It is not sufficient for a researcher or businessman to observe merely the pattern of change in time series. Instead, the forces that produce the changes need to be analyzed, measured, and appraised. For instance was the 6 per cent increase in the level of industrial production that took place between July and August, 1954, due to what might be considered the normal

[1] M. J. Moroney, *Facts from Figures* (Harmondsworth, Penguin Books, 1951), p. 324.

growth of the American economy, was it attributable to a seasonal pickup in demand, or was it explainable as a cyclical business boom? Before one can answer this question one must examine what particular phenomenon can be held responsible for the increase. A careful analysis reveals that practically the entire 6 per cent increase was seasonal in nature. There also appears to be wide unanimity in attributing much of the credit for the increased business activity of the fall of 1954 to the early changeover by the

Cartoon by George Lichty reproduced by permission of the Chicago Sun-Times Syndicate.

"You get around the building, Gus . . . how do the other
charts look? . . . Is business up or down?"

automobile industry to new models. Thus, time series analysis is useful not only for forecasting, but also for understanding the past, which in turn helps appraise the future.

Trend.   An early step in time series analysis is to examine carefully the possible forces that might underlie its movement. The temporal behavior of an economic indicator is merely a reflection of various underlying factors. Some of these forces have a tendency to persist. Population has been growing steadily, just as the productivity and production of the United States (expressed as a percentage of the average 1923–28 production) increased on the average 3.4 per cent per year. In brief, there was a *secular* (upward) *trend* in United States production. *By trend, sometimes also called secular trend, we mean the long run gradual growth or decline in a series which is an expression of such fundamental forces as population growth, improvements in know-how and productivity, increases in the supply of capital equipment, and changes in consumption habits.*

Some phenomena have an upward and others a downward trend. Also, the pace of secular growth or decline varies. For instance, in most countries there exists a pronounced downward trend in the length of the work week.

Since the turn of the century agricultural output has increased at a substantially slower pace than industrial output. Not all secular changes have been at a constant pace. Plotted in time series Chart 15.2, the secular upward trend in the total experienced United States labor force is linear

Chart 15.3 TREND IN GROSS NATIONAL PRODUCT, 1929–56

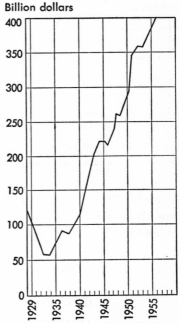

Billion dollars

Source: U.S. Bureau of Labor Statistics, *Economic Forces in the U.S.A.* (Washington D.C., 1954), p. 45, and Federal Reserve Bulletin, 1956.

Chart 15.2 TREND IN TOTAL EXPERIENCED UNITED STATES LABOR FORCE, 1870–56.

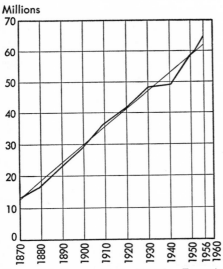

Millions

Source: U.S. Bureau of Labor Statistics, *Economic Forces in the U.S.A.* (Washington, D.C., 1954), p. 24, and *Monthly Labor Review*, Dec., 1956.

between 1870 and 1956. Yet the growth in gross national product appears to follow a curvilinear trend between 1929 and 1956 (see Chart 15.3).

Some trends have a rather complex form. Cotton production from 1800 to 1950 portrayed in Chart 15.4 follows a flat S-shaped trend. Such a trend is often referred to as following the pattern of a growth curve. Many firms and industries start slowly, then expand rapidly, and finally their growth levels off.

Periodic variations. It is no secret that department store sales, tourist trade, demand deposits, and money in circulation show large-scale changes over the year. Interestingly enough, these changes exhibit a rather stable pattern.   Nature and custom are responsible for the pronounced and regular seasonal pattern of many economic phenomena.   *Seasonal—or more generally, periodic—variations are the recurrent pattern of change within the period that results from the operation of forces connected with climate or custom at different times of the period.*   De-partment store sales expand before Easter and particularly before Christ-mas.   Knowing the rhythm of the department store business can be useful to management as well as to the economist who watches depart-ment store sales as possible indicators of business fluctuations.   For in-stance, if it is known that there is usually a seasonal pickup in sales before Easter and before Christmas, and if a reasonably good estimate of its magnitude is available, the per-sonnel department can plan in time to provide for the proper number of saleswomen and delivery boys.   At the same time, the store's purchasing agent is helped in ascertaining the proper amount and flow of wrapping and packing material.

Chart 15.4 FLAT S-SHAPED TREND
(Cotton production in million bales, United States, 1800–1950.)

Million bales

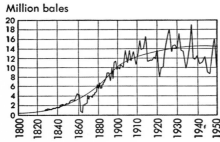

Source: Data from 1800–1945 from *Historical Statistics of the United States, 1789–1945*, pp. 108–109; data from 1945 to 1950 from *Statistical Abstract of the United States*, 1953, p. 652.

Chart 15.5   SEASONAL PATTERN OF DE-MAND DEPOSITS, 1946–54

Billion dollars

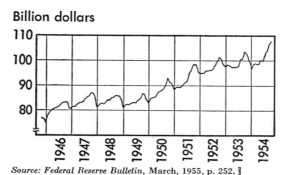

Source: Federal Reserve Bulletin, March, 1955, p. 252.

There is also a pronounced seasonal pattern in monthly deposits held by banks during the year.   Chart 15.5 presents monthly demand deposits from 1946 to 1954.[2]   Generally speaking, in the summer and fall demand

[2] These demand deposit data have been adjusted to exclude interbank and U.S. govern-ment deposits as well as cash items in the process of collection.

deposits tend to expand, reaching a peak in December, and then to contract during the first part of the following year. This rhythm is a reflection of the fact that during the latter part of the year marketing of agricultural commodities as well as retail sales usually reach a peak, leading to a general increase in business activity. To finance these transactions demand deposits are built up during the second half of the year. Another factor, though admittedly not of major importance, which also helps reduce demand deposits in the first half of the year is institutional in nature: since 1951 a progressively larger share of corporate income tax payments have been due in the first half of the year.

In following demand deposit data one might easily reach conclusions that neglect the seasonal rhythm. To conclude that people are dissaving and that there are cyclical deflationary forces at work may be a mistake, when the spring decline in demand deposits could be accounted for in terms of the typical seasonal rhythm.

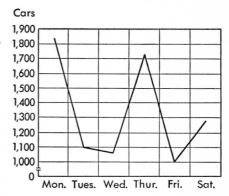

Chart 15.6 WEEKLY VARIATION IN CUSTOMER PARKING IN GARAGE OF DEPARTMENT STORE, 1954

Besides monthly variations there are also weekly and daily variations. Department store sales have not only seasonal but also *weekly variations.* In Chart 15.6 we portray the weekly variations of car parking in the customer service garage of a major department store. The parking rhythm runs parallel to the more important sales rhythm. Monday and Thursday figures are high because on those days the store is open three additional night hours. Saturday is a high-volume day, because many people are off work and have time to do their shopping.

An example of *daily variations* is hourly water consumption in the summer months. During the night relatively little water is used; as the day progresses more and more people water their yards, an activity that reaches its peak in the late afternoon hours.

The traffic across the Oakland-San Francisco Bay Bridge is heaviest between 7 and 9 A.M. and 4 and 6 P.M., when many people go to or return from work. To alleviate this daily variation, which has the disadvantages of leading to traffic congestion in the two periods, a number of proposals have been made. One plan contemplates charging higher toll fees during the rush hours, so as to discourage those who can travel earlier or later from slowing down traffic during the rush hours.

Also of some interest are *hourly variations*. Telepulse ratings of TV programs can be affected by the fact that there are more people watching television on the hour or half hour than at any other time. These are the times when programs change. As the program proceeds it is not uncommon for listeners to get bored or disinterested and to turn it off.

Trend and seasonal variations of a number of economic phenomena are stable. Once we succeed in measuring these past relations we can gain a better understanding of the phenomena; and should this convince us that the past relations are likely to endure, forecasts of the future can be attempted.

Cycle. The other two time series components—*cyclical variation* and *irregular variation*—have no stable pattern.

The oscillatory movement upward and downward of a series of data that results from alternating levels of economic activity is often referred to by the economist as the "business cycle." By its very nature it has four successive stages: Inflation, recession, depression, and recovery. While these four stages are essentially present in any cycle, the duration of the cycle and its amplitude are the imponderables.

Irregular variations. The irregular variations are often looked upon as the residuals that cannot be explained in terms of the other three components. They have no definite pattern. The forces that produce such irregularities can be legislation, such as a tax cut; the outcome of an election, for instance, the 1952 presidential election, which imbued businessmen with hopeful confidence; the outbreak of war; labor unrest, as in the case of the steel strike in 1951; or natural calamities—for example, the San Francisco earthquake early this century. However, if we deal with aggregate data, e.g., world wheat production or gross national product, irregular variations tend to cancel each other. A short wheat crop in one area often goes hand in hand with a good crop elsewhere.

All components. In brief then, the fluctuations that appear in time series, and that may cause forecasters to age prematurely, can be secular, periodic, cyclical, or irregular. These are the four components of a time series. One way, and a very common one, of looking at a time series is to consider the series to be the product of these four components. If O is used to symbolize the original time series data—for instance, a month's daily closing quotations of a certain stock—T connotes the trend, S the seasonal or periodic variation, C the cycle, and I the irregular component, the relationship may be stated as follows:

$$O = T \times S \times C \times I. \tag{15.1}$$

We might say that the task of the statistician is to take a time series and isolate and measure those parts of the variation that are traceable to the influence of each of these four factors. If his efforts are successful the quality of forecasts can be enhanced; also, it becomes easier to assess and measure the position of the firm, industry, or economy. Such questions as "Are sales slipping?" "Are we getting our share of the seasonal upturn?" or "Is industrial production in the United States still falling once we reflect the seasonal pattern of production?" can be answered more authoritatively, if stable relations in the time series have been ascertained.

15.2. TREND—THE LONG RUN PULL

Edit of annual data. Before we can start measuring trends and the other components of time series we need to study carefully the nature of the data at hand. In trying to reveal and measure the regular and persistent movements we should not be misled by irrelevant and extraneous causes of variations. We must be on the lookout for such distorting factors.

Here is an example of what we have in mind. Government sources show that since 1939 the take-home pay of workers increased more than two and one-half times. If we were to take this series of data and fit a trend line, would we be in a position to make some useful statements about the trend in the well-being of American labor? Most people would agree that these data are not very meaningful for the called-for objective. Well-being does not vary directly with the size of the pay envelope, but with the purchasing power of the pay check.

In order to learn about changes in the well-being of American labor, we must *deflate* our time series. We can deflate the weekly take-home pay or net spendable income data by dividing them by some index that reflects changes in the prices of the items bought by most American workers and their families. The *Consumer Price Index* of the Bureau of Labor Statistics is one obvious choice. By dividing the average annual take-home pay data by the year's consumer price index we have the "real" net spendable weekly earnings figure for the year under consideration. Deflating converts money income into real income or income of a constant dollar value. This brings up the question as to what year's dollar value we want to see maintained. Since the period 1947–49 has been chosen as normal for index number purposes, we might settle for the same period. We thus use as the deflator an index that has 1947–49 as its base. For instance, in 1939 the weekly take-home pay of the average worker with three dependents was $23.62, and the consumer price index stood at 45.1. Dividing the first figure by the second and multiplying by 100, we convert a $23.62 money income into a $39.76 real income in 1947–49 dollars.

Chart 15.7 shows both the net spendable weekly earnings of the average American worker (with three dependents) in current dollars and the "real" net spendable weekly earnings of the same worker in 1947–49 dollars for the period 1939 to 1953. The trend of the money income data is sharply upward during these 15 years. In 1947–49 dollars the picture is very different.

Chart 15.7 NET SPENDABLE WEEKLY EARNINGS IN CUR- RENT DOLLARS AND "REAL" NET SPENDABLE WEEKLY EARNINGS IN 1947–49 DOLLARS, 1939–53

Chart 15.8 WORLD GOLD PRODUC- TION OUTSIDE SOVIET RUSSIA, 1919–39

Source: U.S. Bureau of Labor Statistics, *Economic Forces in the U.S.A.* (Washington, D.C., 1954), p. 34.

Source: Survey of Current Business, Annual Supple- ment, 1940, p. 59, 1913–1938, 1939 data from *Federal Reserve Bulletin*, June, 1941, p. 585.

From 1939 to the end of World War II the real income and money income trends run more or less parallel. In 1945 both series decline. Thereafter, the money income series continues to advance at about the same rate as during the war, while the real income series increases at a substantially slower pace. Altogether during these 15 years money income advanced about 290 per cent, yet real income advanced only about 155 per cent. Quite a difference, isn't it? In wage negotiations, using the first would greatly confuse the issue.

We must watch out for possible changes in the units of the series. Units should be comparable. The importance of this is readily appreciated by considering the volume of gold production in dollars outside Soviet Russia between 1913 and 1939 (Chart 15.8). In 1933–34 gold production seems to have greatly increased. It almost doubled within a year's period. While part of this increase can be explained as being stimulated by lower gold production costs, which went hand in hand with a lowering in the general price level, there is a further point that needs consideration. It should be remembered that the price of gold was raised in 1933 from $20.67 an ounce to $35.00. Until 1933 each ounce of gold mined was recorded at a price of $20.67. An ounce of gold produced after 1933 carried extra duty; it was recorded at $35.00. The changes in the gold price are reflected in Chart 15.8 and to no small extent they are responsible for the steep slope of the series from 1934 on. Yet we are interested in the physical volume of gold production and the picture should not be distorted by such extraneous factors as changes in the price of gold. We must deflate the series, starting with 1934, so as to express the entire series in terms of $20.67 for an ounce of gold.

The broken line of the period 1934–39 represents the deflated gold production figures. Using these data, we can conclude that gold production increased at a reasonably steady pace since the early 1920's.

Table 15.1 WINTER LETTUCE PRODUCTION, UNITED STATES, 1918–52

Year	Winter Lettuce Production in Million Crates	Year	Winter Lettuce Production in Million Crates
1918	1.64	1938	4.45
1919	1.23	1939	5.19
1920	3.50	1940	4.61
1921	2.54	1941	5.30
1922	3.01	1942	5.73
1923	4.21	1943	5.80
1924	4.92	1944	7.31
1925	4.84	1945	7.55
1926	5.02	1946	8.92
1927	5.16	1947	8.50
1928	5.85	1948	9.12
1929	6.26	1949	9.78
1930	5.74	1950	9.52
1931	5.35	1951	9.29
1932	4.83	1952	10.58
1933	4.49		
1934	3.83		
1935	4.07		
1936	4.45		
1937	4.65		

Source: S. S. Hoos, "*Statistical Analysis of the Annual Farm Prices for Seasonal Types of Commercial Head Lettuce, 1918–47,*" *Giannini Foundation of Agricultural Economics Report* 92, 1948, and Industry Sources.

Where to start and where to end? The selection of the period under study can greatly affect the outcome of a trend analysis. Let us examine Table 15.1 and Chart 15.9 which present commercial winter lettuce production in the United States from 1918 to 1952. A trend line fitted to the 1918–1930 data will be quite different from one fitted to those for the years 1928–1935. The first will have a positive and the second a negative slope.

Actually neither one is necessarily a trend line, since it covers so short a period of years.

The period covered should be reasonably long, although no simple rule can be given to determine the proper length. Often also, when we find ourselves concerned with a young firm or industry, our data cover only a few years. Should we succumb to the temptation of making a trend analysis on the basis of a few annual readings, we should not forget the limitations of the results. Economists have not always heeded this advice.

Chart 15.9   WINTER LETTUCE PRODUCTION, UNITED STATES, 1918–52

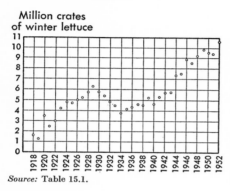

Source: Table 15.1.

Perhaps the most famous example is the "secular stagnation" thesis advanced in the middle 1930's. This thesis, the formulation of which was undoubtedly affected by the great depression of that period, suggested that because of certain elements inherent in the capitalistic system, the level of economic activity in the United States was likely to decline in the long run. In a sense, the secular stagnation thesis was formulated on the basis of too short a time series. Whether the same holds true for the "secular inflation" thesis widely accepted at present remains to be seen.

In selecting the period for the fitting of a trend we should attempt to have the series start and end in about the same phase of the business cycle. In prosperous times we should start our series in a period that was also reasonably prosperous, because, should we start in a depression, our trend line is likely to be steeper than conditions warrant.

If distinct and abrupt changes take place that affect the series, it is usually best to break the series into two parts and fit separate curves. Changes that reverse a trend are not common. However, they may be brought about by the introduction of new products and creation of new habits.

Methods of measuring trend. Once we have decided that there is a significant trend we want to determine its nature and measure it. To accomplish this objective at least four different methods have been developed: (1) the graphic "freehand" fit, (2) the "semiaverage" fit, (3) the moving average fit, and (4) the least squares fit.

Chart 15.10 SCATTER DIAGRAM
(United States total labor force, 1929–55.)

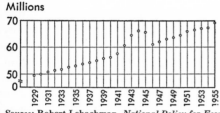

Chart 15.11 LINE CHART
(United States total labor force, 1929–55.)

Source: Robert Lekachman, *National Policy for Economic Welfare at Home and Abroad* (New York; Doubleday & Co., 1955) p. 148.

Before either method is applied it is good practice to plot the time series data in the form of a *scatter diagram* or *line chart*, which differ only in the fact that in the second chart successive points are connected by lines (see Charts 15.10 and 15.11).

These charts can have either an *arithmetic* or *ratio scale*. The arithmetic scale, as used in Charts 15.10 and 15.11, is easier for the beginner to use, but there are many cases where the trend involves a virtually stable percentage change and then the ratio scale is more appropriate and should therefore be used.

For instance, hourly earnings of steel workers presented in Chart 15.12 appear to have increased at a stable percentage. Under the circumstances a ratio scale, also called a semilogarithmic scale, appears appropriate. Whenever an analysis

Chart 15.12 SEMILOGARITHMIC TREND
(Hourly earnings of workers in the iron and steel industry, United States, 1940–56.)

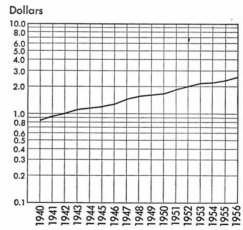

Source: American Iron and Steel Institute, *Charting Steel's Progress* (New York, 1956), p. 56.

of relative rather than absolute variations is needed the ratio or semi-logarithmic scale is employed.[3]

In the construction of a semilogarithmic scale chart, the units along the vertical scale are expressed in logarithms. This has been done in Chart 15.12, where the hourly earnings of iron and steel workers appear to have enjoyed a reasonably stable percentage increase between 1940 and 1956.

Arithmetic and semilogarithmic scales give distinctly different graphic descriptions of the same data, as can be seen in Chart 15.13. In *A* we have a dependent variate rising by $10,000 a year, following a straight line on an arithmetic scale. In *B* the same data are plotted on a semilogarithmic scale and describe a concave curve. In *C* the dependent variate increases by 34.6 per cent a year and describes a concave curve on an arithmetic scale. Plotted on semilogarithmic scale, the data fall along a straight line (*D*). *E* through *H* have a negative slope and can be explained in a similar manner.

The graphic "freehand" fit. When the *graphic freehand* method is relied on for measuring a trend, the original data are first plotted as a scatter diagram, and through the series a smooth line is drawn which in the analyst's best judgment properly describes the secular movement. In drawing this straight or curvilinear line a transparent ruler, French curve, or an engineer's flexible spine rule may be used. In general the trend should be drawn so that the vertical deviations of observations above the line are equal to those of observations below it, with this equality holding in different sections of the chart.

An experienced analyst can do an admirable job with the freehand method. He can neglect extremes that his experience makes him believe to be unimportant and atypical. He will be guided by his subjective evaluation of events bearing on the problem. In a sense subjectivity is the strength and limitation of the method. Seldom, if ever, will two analysts draw the same freehand fit through the same set of data. The analyst will often be tempted to juggle the line even so as to make his extrapolation less than smooth.

The semiaverage fit. When a straight line trend appears to fit the data well, the data may be divided into two equal parts and arithmetic means calculated for the first and second half. By plotting these two points and drawing a straight line through them a *semiaverage fit* is obtained. If there is an odd number of years the middle year may be omitted.

If we were to use the semiaverage method to fit a trend line to the 1918–52

[3] Sometimes we scale both axes logarithmically and we then obtain a double logarithmic scale.

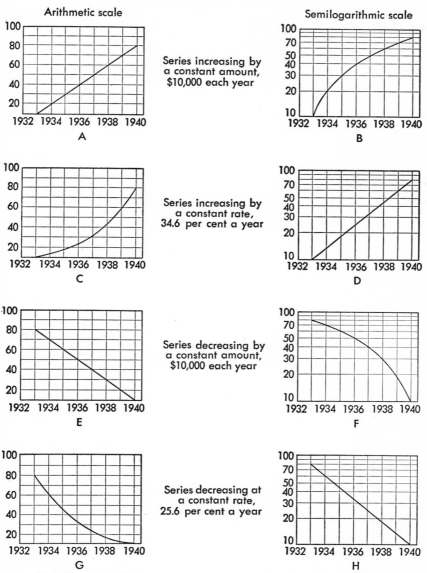

Source: W. A. Neiswanger, *Elementary Statistical Methods*, Revised Edition (New York, The Macmillan Company, 1956), p. 209.

lettuce data of Table 15.1 we would omit the year 1935 and find the (arithmetic) mean of winter lettuce production for the periods 1918–34 and

Chart 15.14   SEMIAVERAGE TREND
(Winter lettuce production in million
crates, United States, 1918–52.)

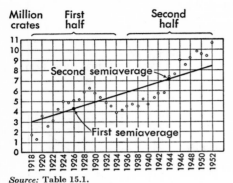

Source: Table 15.1.

1936–52.   The first is 4.26 and the
second 7.10 million crates.   The
means are plotted by centering them
in their respective periods.   Finally
a straight line is drawn through these
two points (see Chart 15.14).

The semiaverage method is simple
and, compared to the freehand
method, it is objective.   However,
it assumes a straight line relationship
and because of its reliance on arithmetic means it can be unduly affected
by extreme values of the series.

The moving average fit.   A *moving average* is a series of overlapping
means that automatically cancel out high and low values.   In a time series

Table 15.2   THREE-YEAR MOVING AVERAGE

Year	Production in Millions	Three-Year Moving Total	Three-Year Moving Average
1	2	3	4
1943	10		
1944	13	39	13
1945	16	42	14
1946	13	45	15
1947	16	48	16
1948	19	51	17
1949	16	54	18
1950	19	57	19
1951	22	60	20
1952	19	63	21
1953	22	66	22
1954	25	69	23
1955	22		

Source: Hypothetical data.

of annual data alternative highs and lows often reflect the business cycle, which under certain conditions will be leveled by the moving average to produce a smooth trend. The moving average method will, however, yield a smooth trend only if the time series incorporates variations that are essentially of stable duration and amplitude, and the trend is basically linear. When the basic trend is curvilinear a bias appears, namely, if the series is concave upward the values of the moving average will be too high; if convex upward the values will be too low.

Chart 15.15 THREE-YEAR MOVING AVERAGE

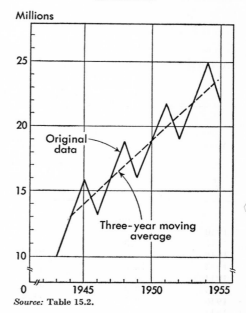

Source: Table 15.2.

In Table 15.2 and Chart 15.15 we have presented some hypothetical production data. Within a three-year interval the data pass from trough to peak and down again. There is a stable three-year duration as well as stability in the amplitude of the variations. The basic trend is linear. Thus, this series incorporates all the conditions required for the successful use of the moving average to produce a trend.

Since the data reach a peak or trough every third year, a three-year moving average is clearly indicated. It is a general rule that the number of overlapping periods for which an arithmetic mean will be calculated corresponds to the average length of the cycle in the data. Should we select a period shorter than the length of the cycle, part of the cycle will remain in the moving average.

The computations of the three-year moving average are carried out in Table 15.2: In Column 2 we have the original data, which are added, and three-year totals are recorded in Column 3. This total is divided by 3 and recorded in Column 4 as the 3-year moving average. After we have the 3-year moving average for 1943–45, we return to the data in Column 2, drop the 1943 figure, and add the 1946 figure to find the three-year moving total and average for 1944–46, and so on down the line.

Both the original and the three-year moving average data have been plotted in Chart 15.15. Because the data incorporated a cycle of stable duration and amplitude and the trend was basically linear, we should be little surprised to end up with a straight trend line.   While this method has produced a very good fit, the fact remains that it stops one year short of the most recent period.   That no averages can be computed for the limits of the series is a disadvantage of the method.

Such ideal conditions as those incorporated in the data given in Table 15.2 are seldom met by most economic series.   The cyclical variation is rarely so uniform.   However, sometimes a series approximates these ideal conditions as, for instance, the number of sows farrowing in spring.   The 1940–53 data of this series are given in Table 15.3.   These data reach a peak every fourth year.   The amplitude of the variations is not very stable.   Nevertheless, we will apply the moving average method.   The computations are carried out in Table 15.3.

Table 15.3   FOUR-YEAR MOVING AVERAGE
(Sows farrowing in spring, United States, 1940–53.)

Year	Sows Farrowing in Spring	Four-year Moving Total	Four-year Moving Average	Centered Four-year Moving Average
1	*2*	*3*	*4*	*5*
	Millions	*Millions*	*Millions*	*Millions*
1940	8.2			
1941	7.8			
1942	9.7	37.9	9.48	9.60
1943	12.2	38.9	9.72	9.79
1944	9.2	39.4	9.85	9.65
1945	8.3	37.8	9.45	9.05
1946	8.1	34.2	8.65	8.42
1947	8.6	32.8	8.20	8.26
1948	7.8	33.3	8.32	8.46
1949	8.8	34.4	8.60	8.72
1950	9.2	35.4	8.85	8.94
1951	9.6	36.1	9.02	8.85
1952	8.5	34.7	8.68	
1953	7.4			

Source: U.S. Department of Agriculture, *Agricultural Statistics*, (Washington, D.C., 1953), p. 349.

Unlike the production data of Table 15.2, the data in Table 15.3 call for a moving average of an even number of years.   When the average, 9.5 million sows, is taken for the first 4 years, 1940–43, it falls in the middle of this time interval, i.e., between December 31, 1941 and January 1, 1942.   The average should, however, be centered in the middle of the year to which it relates.   It is, therefore, necessary to add the first and second four-year moving averages, 9.4 + 9.72, and divide the sum by 2 to get the mean of 9.60 million sows, which falls in the middle of the year 1942.   This process is known as "centering the moving average" and is carried out in Column 5 of Table 15.3. The original and the centered four-year moving average data are plotted in Chart 15.16.

The least squares fit. The *least squares method* gives rise to a straight or curvilinear trend line from which the mean of the squared vertical deviations of the observed values is a minimum. In this sense, then, it is a line of "best fit." However, as will be remembered from Chapter XIV, inference aspects of the least squares method are based on a number of assumptions that are seldom met by time series data. The method is most appropriate when the values of the dependent variate of the population, i.e., of the variate we want to predict, are normally distributed around the least squares line, which thus is a line connecting the means of all these normal distributions. Also, the variances of these normal population distributions are assumed uniform, and the observations and their deviations from the least squares line are independent of each other.

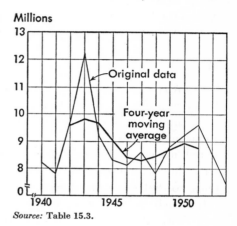

Chart 15.16 FOUR-YEAR MOVING AVERAGE
Sows farrowing in spring, United States, 1940–53.)

Source: Table 15.3.

This last assumption, particularly, is rarely met by time series data. For instance, the price of 1956 automobiles is closely related to that of 1955 automobiles. Time series data are often distinctly interdependent. Yet, even if all assumptions were met the trend would only be valid over the range of the observed data and not for extrapolation into the future.

Because of the interdependence of time series data, we will treat them as population data and refrain from making inferences.

Before the least squares method is applied we must decide on how long a period we want to cover, whether the trend is up or down, and whether a straight or curvilinear line plotted on an arithmetic or semilogarithmic scale best describes the data. Following these decisions we select the proper set of equations to compute the trend line.

We can write our linear trend equation as

$$Y' = a + bX, \qquad (15.2)$$

where Y' is the predicted dependent variate, trend value, a is the height of the trend line at the origin where $X = 0$; b is the slope of the trend line, or trend regression coefficient; and X is the independent variate, i.e., time expressed in years. In line with the least squares regression techniques discussed in Chapter XIV, we need to find a and b values that minimize the mean squared deviations. However, there are some short cuts that can be employed in fitting trend lines as shown below.

An example. If we were to find the trend of winter lettuce production from the data in Table 15.4, Y' would be the predicted annual trend value of winter lettuce production in millions of crates, and X would represent time in terms of years with the year 1918 = 0.

Using the formulas

$$b = \frac{N\Sigma XY - (\Sigma X)(\Sigma Y)}{N(\Sigma X^2) - (\Sigma X)^2},\tag{15.3}$$

and

$$a = \bar{Y} - b\bar{X},\tag{15.4}$$

which automatically minimize the mean squared deviations, we would calculate the appropriate values to put into the trend equation $Y' = a + bX$.

This method is, however, somewhat laborious and we are fortunate that we can make use of a short-cut. In a trend analysis the X's are usually ordered according to their magnitude. They run 0, 1, 2, 3, . . . , N. Under these circumstances, we can readily subtract a constant from all X values, so that the mean is zero. We know that if we adjust the X values so that their mean is zero, the sum of all adjusted X values will also be zero. We will denote the thus adjusted X values by x.[4]

In Table 15.4 the data extend from 1918 to 1952. Of those 35 years the 17th year, 1935, is the middle year. We will connote 1935 as year 0, and then have 1936 as year $+1$, 1937 as year $+2$, etc., and 1934 as year -1, 1933 as year -2, etc. The data are presented in this form in Table 15.4.

When Σx or $\dfrac{\Sigma x}{N} = 0$, the formulas for b and a reduce to

$$b = \frac{\Sigma x Y}{\Sigma x^2},\tag{15.5}$$

and

$$a = \bar{Y}.\tag{15.6}$$

Substituting in the equations the information from Table 15.4, we have

$$b = \frac{\Sigma x Y}{\Sigma x^2} = \frac{687.20}{3,570} = +0.193$$

$$a = \bar{Y} = \frac{197.24}{35} = +5.64.$$

[4] If $\dfrac{1}{N}\sum x = 0$, also $\Sigma x = 0$.

Table 15.4 SHORT-CUT LEAST SQUARES METHOD FOR FINDING
TREND OVER ODD NUMBER OF YEARS
(Winter lettuce production in million crates, United States, 1918–52.)

Year	Y in Million Crates	x 1935 = 0	x^2	xY
1918	1.64	−17		
1919	1.23	−16		
1920	3.50	−15		
1921	2.54	−14		
1922	3.01	−13		
1923	4.21	−12		
1924	4.92	−11		
1925	4.84	−10		
1926	5.02	− 9		
1927	5.16	− 8		
1928	5.85	− 7		
1929	6.26	− 6		
1930	5.74	− 5		
1931	5.35	− 4		
1932	4.83	− 3		
1933	4.49	− 2		
1934	3.83	− 1		
1935	4.07	0		
1936	4.45	1		
1937	4.65	2		
1938	4.45	3		
1939	5.19	4		
1940	4.61	5		
1941	5.30	6		
1942	5.73	7		
1943	5.80	8		
1944	7.31	9		
1945	7.55	10		
1946	8.92	11		
1947	8.50	12		
1948	9.12	13		
1949	9.78	14		
1950	9.52	15		
1951	9.29	16		
1952	10.58	17		
Total	197.24	0	3,570	687.2

Source: Table 15.1.

Thus, our trend equation for the 1918–52 winter lettuce production, $Y' = a + bx$, is $Y' = 5.64 + 0.193x$.

What is the meaning of $a = +5.64$ and $b = +0.193$? Remember that Y is stated in millions of crates. An a of 5.64 means that in the base year of 1935, the line of best fit would predict a 5.64 million crate production of winter lettuce. (Compared to the actual 1935 production of 4.07 million crates, this prediction is substantially too high.) b of $+0.193$ means that on the basis of the 1918–52 least squares trend line, winter lettuce production increased an average of 193,000 crates a year.

To draw the trend line we take three values of x, e.g., -17, 0, and $+17$, and place them into the trend equation, one at a time. For $x = -17$, we find a Y' value of $+5.64 + 0.193 (-17)$ or 2.36; for $x = 0$ the Y' value is $+5.64 + 0.193 (0)$ or 5.64, and for $x = +17$ the Y' value is $+5.64 + 0.193 (+17)$ or 8.92. Plotting these three points and connecting them by a straight line extending from the year -17 to the year $+17$ gives us the trend line of commercial winter lettuce production in the United States for 1918–52.

Trends in aggregates. Policy-makers in and out of government are concerned about changes in such macroeconomic or aggregate variates as consumption, investment, and production. These aggregates are commonly measured in the form of specially constructed indexes. Once the index is given, we can treat the index number like any other number and measure the trend.

As an illustration we have selected an index of agricultural production and an index of industrial production. The data are presented in Table 15.5. Applying the short-cut method to the 1899–1937 index numbers (the base year being 1899), we find the following trend regression equation pertaining to agricultural output: $Y' = 125 + 1.19x$. During 1899–1937 the index of agricultural output (1899 = 100) increased an average of 1.19 per cent per year.

The trend equation for industrial output covering the same period is $Y' = 223 + 5.96x$.

Testing for curvilinearity. Is a straight line trend most appropriate? In some cases our experience and knowledge of the situation help us to establish a hypothesis about the nature of the trend. Whether we have such a hypothesis or not, it is sometimes useful to make a mechanical check as to whether perhaps another type of trend line would not offer a better fit. For this purpose we can calculate the deviations from the line of best fit, either by reading them off the chart or by calculating them with the help of the trend equation, and plot them.

Table 15.5 LEAST SQUARES TREND—AGRICULTURAL AND
MANUFACTURING OUTPUT, UNITED STATES, 1899–1937
(1899 = 100)

Year	Ya	Ym	x	X^2	xYa	xYm
1899	100	100	−19	361	−1900	−1900
1900	101	102	−18	324	−1818	−1836
1901	99	115	−17	289	−1683	−1955
1902	103	129	−16	256	−1648	−2064
1903	104	132	−15	225	−1560	−1980
1904	109	124	−14	196	−1526	−1736
1905	108	148	−13	169	−1404	−1924
1906	118	159	−12	144	−1416	−1908
1907	110	167	−11	121	−1210	−1771
1908	112	133	−10	100	−1120	−1330
1909	111	158	− 9	81	− 999	−1422
1910	114	168	− 8	64	− 912	−1344
1911	117	161	− 7	49	− 819	−1127
1912	123	185	− 6	36	− 738	−1110
1913	119	198	− 5	25	− 595	− 990
1914	129	186	− 4	16	− 516	− 744
1915	129	218	− 3	9	− 387	− 654
1916	119	259	− 2	4	− 238	− 518
1917	124	257	− 1	1	− 124	− 257
1918	130	254	0	0	0	0
1919	125	222	1	1	125	222
1920	130	242	2	4	260	484
1921	118	194	3	9	354	582
1922	130	249	4	16	520	996
1923	132	280	5	25	660	1400
1924	137	266	6	36	822	1596
1925	138	298	7	49	966	2086
1926	146	316	8	64	1168	2528
1927	141	317	9	81	1269	2853
1928	147	332	10	100	1470	3320
1929	144	364	11	121	1584	4004
1930	145	311	12	144	1740	3732
1931	150	262	13	169	1950	3406
1932	144	197	14	196	2016	2758
1933	140	228	15	225	2100	3420
1934	120	252	16	256	1920	4032
1935	133	301	17	289	2261	5117
1936	134	353	18	324	2412	6354
1937	153	376	19	361	2907	7144
Total	4,886	8,707	0	4,940	5,891	29,464

Source: H. Berger and H. H. Landsberg, *American Agriculture, 1899–1939* (New York,
National Bureau of Economic Research, 1942), p. 21 and Solomon Fabricant, *The Output of
Manufacturing Industries, 1899–1937* (New York, National Bureau of Economic Research,
1940), p. 44.

Where Y_a = agricultural output, and
$\quad\quad Y_m$ = manufacturing output.

$$a = \bar{Y}_a = 125.28 \quad\quad\quad\quad a = \bar{Y}_m = 223.26$$

$$b = \frac{\Sigma_x Y_a}{\Sigma x^2} = \frac{5,891}{4,940} = +1.19. \quad\quad b = \frac{\Sigma_x Y_m}{\Sigma x^2} = \frac{29,464}{4,940} = +5.96.$$

In Table 15.6 we present the original and predicted values as well as the deviations. While there are refined methods, we will merely decide on the basis of our inspection whether the data reveal a curvilinear pattern. In our case the deviations appear to lack a distinct curvilinear pattern and we conclude that a straight trend line appears appropriate. Had we found

Table 15.6 DEVIATIONS OF UNITED STATES AGRICULTURAL
OUTPUT FROM TREND, 1899–1937
(1899 = 100)

Year	Ya	Y'a	Ya − Y'a	Year	Ya	Y'a	Ya − Y'a
1899	100	103	−3	1919	125	126	−1
1900	101	104	−3	1920	130	128	+2
1901	99	105	−6	1921	118	129	−11
1902	103	106	−3	1922	130	130	0
1903	104	107	−3	1923	132	131	+1
1904	109	109	0	1924	137	132	+5
1905	108	110	−2	1925	138	134	+4
1906	118	111	+7	1926	146	135	+11
1907	110	112	−2	1927	141	136	+5
1908	112	113	−1	1928	147	137	+10
1909	111	115	−4	1929	144	138	+6
1910	114	116	−2	1930	145	140	+5
1911	117	117	0	1931	150	141	+9
1912	123	118	+5	1932	144	142	+2
1913	119	119	0	1933	140	143	−3
1914	129	121	+8	1934	120	144	−24
1915	129	122	+7	1935	133	146	−13
1916	119	123	−4	1936	134	147	−13
1917	124	124	0	1937	153	148	+5
1918	130	125	+5				

Source: Table 15.5.

a curvilinear pattern, a curvilinear trend line could be fitted to the original data; more will be said about this below.

Not all things are odd. With series of 35 and 39 years we had little trouble finding the middle year of the period and calling it 0. What would we do if the total number of years for which information is available is an even number? Let us look at Table 15.7 where we added lettuce data for 1953. We have information for a total of 36 years, an even number, and we would like to apply the short-cut method of trend finding.

To use the short-cut method for estimating trends when the number of years is even calls for some extra manipulations. Here we have 36 years and we know that we can shorten our computations if we select the origin

Table 15.7 SHORT-CUT LEAST SQUARES METHOD FOR FINDING
TREND OVER EVEN NUMBER OF YEARS
(Winter lettuce production in million crates, United States, 1918–53.)

Year	Y in Million Crates	x	x^2	xY
1918	1.64	−35		
1919	1.23	−33		
1920	3.50	−31		
1921	2.54	−29		
1922	3.01	−27		
1923	4.21	−25		
1924	4.92	−23		
1925	4.84	−21		
1926	5.02	−19		
1927	5.16	−17		
1928	5.85	−15		
1929	6.26	−13		
1930	5.74	−11		
1931	5.35	− 9		
1932	4.83	− 7		
1933	4.49	− 5		
1934	3.83	− 3		
1935	4.07	− 1		
1936	4.45	1		
1937	4.65	3		
1938	4.45	5		
1939	5.19	7		
1940	4.61	9		
1941	5.30	11		
1942	5.73	13		
1943	5.80	15		
1944	7.31	17		
1945	7.55	19		
1946	8.92	21		
1947	8.50	23		
1948	9.12	25		
1949	9.78	27		
1950	9.52	29		
1951	9.29	31		
1952	10.58	33		
1953	10.77	35		
Total	208.11	0	15,540	1,554.21

Source: Table 15.1.

307

of x so that the summation of all the x's is 0.   The middle of the 1918–53 period falls between 1935 and 1936.   From the beginning of 1936, it is 1/2 year to the middle of 1936.   We could assign x values to the different years beginning with -17.5 for 1918 and ending with $+17.5$ for 1953.   Few people like to work with fractions in computations.   Therefore, one unit of the independent variate is taken to represent a six-month period.   That is why in Table 15.7 1935 is labeled -1 and 1936 $+1$.   Since there is an interval of two six-month periods between any two points of time a year apart, 1937 is shown as $+3$, 1938 as $+5$, and so on.

The trend equation for the data in Table 15.7 is: $Y' = 5.78 + 0.10x$, with the beginning of 1936 the origin and the x values expressed in units of 1/2 year.   With the help of this information we can compute, for instance, the total winter lettuce predicted for 1953 by adding 35 times 0.10 to 5.78: $Y'_{35} = 5.78 + 0.10\,(35)$ or 9.28 million crates.   We multiply 0.10 by 35, since 35 times six months have elapsed from the beginning of 1936, the origin of the x's.   (The figure of 9.28 million crates might be compared with 10.77 million crates of lettuce that were produced in 1953.)

Converting annual trend data into monthly ones.   The statistical department of one of the foremost chain stores in the United States recently calculated that since the company's existence its annual sales volume has increased on the average by about $60 million per annum.   The corresponding trend equation looks about like this: $Y' = 100,000 + 60,000,000x$, where Y' represents the predicted annual sales in dollars and x is a one-year period. $60 million is the annual increment of the annual data.   But now management asks the question: "By how much did our sales increase on the average per month?"   Don't divide $60 million by 12 because that will not give the correct answer.   Dividing $60 million by 12 will reduce the annual trend increment of the annual data to a monthly trend increment of the annual data.   It tells us that on the average there was a $5 million annual increase in sales per month.   Management's question concerns the average *monthly* sales increase *per month*.   To answer this, we must divide the $60 million by 144.   Monthly sales have increased an average of $60 million/ 144 or by $0.42 million per month.

To reduce an annual trend increment of annual data to a monthly trend increment of monthly data the regression coefficient is divided by 144.   In case we wish to change the annual regression equation to represent monthly increments in monthly magnitudes, we divide the Y-intercept, a, by 12 and the regression coefficient, b, by 144.   Thus the monthly regression equation is:

$$Y'_m = \frac{a}{12} + \frac{b}{144}\, x_m, \tag{15.7}$$

where the subscript m indicates that the data are monthly and not annual. Then the chain store's equation would read $Y'_m = \dfrac{100,000}{12} + \dfrac{60,000,000}{144} x_m.$

There are other ways to calculate monthly increases per month. For one, monthly data could be used. However, if the data have a seasonal pattern, it will be necessary first to prepare the monthly data for the regression analysis by removing the seasonal pattern.

Problems associated with periodic variation in general and seasonal variations in particular will be taken up shortly. But before we move into the field of seasonal variation, we would like to address ourselves to fitting curvilinear trend lines.

The trend may not be linear—parabola. After a careful look at the line chart of 1918–52 winter lettuce production we might wonder whether the trend was really a straight line. We might detect some curvature and decide to fit a curve instead.

One of the simplest curves is the parabola, the general shape of which reminds one of an automobile headlight reflector, pointing either up or down. A section of the parabola might well describe the trend of a set of data. Sometimes a more complicated curve will be more appropriate. While the equation of a parabola is a second-degree equation—X is raised to the second power—a third- or fourth-degree equation could be tried. Usually we will refrain from using other than first- and second-degree equations, since they call for very complicated and laborious calculations and their complex form might not be too useful for predictive purposes.

We will write the equation of a parabola as

$$Y' = a + bX + cX^2, \tag{15.8}$$

or

$$Y' = a + bx + cx^2, \tag{15.9}$$

when the origin is placed at the middle year. Instead of the two unknowns of a straight line equation, this equation has three unknowns, a, b, and c.

We will use the short-cut method and, therefore, the second equation. With the x origin centered, a will be the height of the curve in the middle year of the time series, b is the slope of the curve at this Y-intercept, and c will reflect the amount and direction of curvature.

To solve for the three unknowns we have the following three normal equations:

$$\begin{aligned}
\Sigma Y &= Na + c\Sigma x^2 \\
\Sigma xY &= b\Sigma x^2 \\
\Sigma x^2 Y &= a\Sigma x^2 + c\Sigma x^4.
\end{aligned} \tag{15.10}$$

With the help of a work sheet we get ΣY, $\Sigma x Y$, Σx^2, and Σx^4, which we place into the three normal equations and solve them by the easiest method available to us. One simple method is to calculate b from the middle, equation, i.e., $b = \dfrac{\Sigma x Y}{\Sigma x^2}$. Thereafter, a and c are easily calculated from the first and third equations.

Let us fit a parabola to the winter lettuce production data, 1918–52. The trend equation will be found to read: $Y' = 5.12 + 0.193x + 0.00052x^2$, in terms of millions of crates of winter lettuce. With the origin at 1935, we would replace the x in the equation by 18 to make a forecast for the year 1953. In this way we have: $Y' = 5.12 + 0.193(18) + 0.00052(18)^2$, and the forecast for 1953 would be 8.8 (see Table 15.8).

If we plot both the straight line and curvilinear trend to the 1918–52 winter lettuce data, we can test which line gives a better fit. Two tests suggest themselves. One would call for measuring the vertical differences of each and every observation from the trend line and plotting these differences on a graph, with a zero line in the middle. Positive differences would lie above and negative differences below the zero line.

By inspection we can decide whether there appears to be any curvilinearity in these residuals. If we fitted a straight line trend and the residuals exhibit linearity, we can conclude that it might be desirable to fit a curvilinear trend. After doing so we might again plot the residuals, this time from the curvilinear trend line. If the residuals are about randomly distributed around the zero line we can conclude that the curvilinear trend line is a better fit than the linear one.

The second method calls for calculating a correlation coefficient that reflects the quality of the fit the least squares line accords. Whatever line offers the best fit will also tend to have the highest correlation coefficient, after adjusting for degrees of freedom and sampling variation.

A curvilinear trend can become linear—logarithmic straight line. From time to time we get data that appear to incorporate a comparatively fixed growth rate. Fitting a semilogarithmic straight line could then prove appropriate; and often a curvilinear relationship on an arithmetic scale can be reduced to a straight line relationship on a semilogarithmic scale. The semilogarithmic straight line equation can be written as

$$\log Y' = a + bX, \tag{15.11}$$

or

$$\log Y' = a + bx, \tag{15.12}$$

when the x origin is centered.

Table 15.8 CURVILINEAR LEAST SQUARES TREND (PARABOLA)
(Winter lettuce production in million crates, United States, 1918–52.)

Year	Y in Million Crates	x 1935 = 0	xY	x^2	x^4	x^2Y
1918	1.64	−17				
1919	1.23	−16				
1920	3.50	−15				
1921	2.54	−14				
1922	3.01	−13				
1923	4.21	−12				
1924	4.92	−11				
1925	4.84	−10				
1926	5.02	− 9				
1927	5.16	− 8				
1928	5.85	− 7				
1929	6.26	− 6				
1930	5.74	− 5				
1931	5.35	− 4				
1932	4.83	− 3				
1933	4.49	− 2				
1934	3.83	− 1				
1935	4.07	0				
1936	4.45	1				
1937	4.65	2				
1938	4.45	3				
1939	5.19	4				
1940	4.61	5				
1941	5.30	6				
1942	5.73	7				
1943	5.80	8				
1944	7.31	9				
1945	7.55	10				
1946	8.92	11				
1947	8.50	12				
1948	9.12	13				
1949	9.78	14				
1950	9.52	15				
1951	9.29	16				
1952	10.58	17				
Total	197.24	0	687.2	3,570	654,738	21,633

Source: Table 15.1.

I. $\Sigma Y = Na + c\Sigma x^2$

II. $\Sigma xY = b\Sigma x^2$

III. $\Sigma x^2 Y = a\Sigma x^2 + c\Sigma x^4$

$$\text{I.} \quad 197.24 = 35a + 3{,}570c$$
$$\text{II.} \quad 21{,}633 = 3{,}570a + 654{,}738c$$
$$-(105) \; \text{I} = \text{I}' \quad -20{,}118 = -3{,}570a - 364{,}140c$$
$$\text{II} - \text{I}' \quad 1{,}515 = 290{,}598c$$
$$c = 0.0052$$

$$b = \frac{\Sigma xY}{\Sigma x^2} = \frac{687.2}{3{,}570} = 0.193$$

$$a = \frac{197.24}{35} = \frac{3{,}570(0.052)}{35} = 5.12$$

Therefore, $Y' = 5.12 + 0.193x + 0.0052x^2$.

311

The fitting of a semilogarithmic trend line starts by converting the Y data into logarithms. Table 15.9 is a worksheet that helps find the summations needed for fitting a semilogarithmic trend line. We take the summations from this table and place them into the two equations:

$$b = \frac{\Sigma x \log Y}{\Sigma x^2}, \qquad (15.13)$$

and

$$a = \frac{\Sigma \log Y}{N}. \qquad (15.14)$$

For the lettuce data,

$$b = \frac{58.061293}{3,570} = +0.016, \text{ and}$$

$$a = \frac{24.858666}{35} = +0.710.$$

Thus, the straight line semilogarithmic trend equation reads: $\log Y' = 0.710 + 0.016x$, which has been plotted in Chart 15.17. A forecast for 1953

Chart 15.17 SEMILOGARITHMIC LEAST
SQUARES TREND
(Winter lettuce production in million crates, United
States, 1918–52.)
$(1935 = 0)$

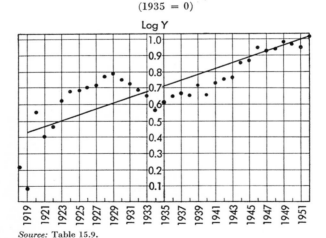

Source: Table 15.9.

could be made by substituting for $x + 18$, so that $\log Y'$ for 1953 is $0.710 + 0.016(18)$ or 0.998. By finding the antilog of log 0.998 we have a Y' of 9.96 million crates for 1953.[5]

[5] To appraise the relative appropriateness of a simple linear versus a straight line semilogarithmic trend line we can calculate the correlation coefficients for the two cases. The coefficient in the first case is $+0.85$ and in the second $+0.81$. To the extent that one is more appropriate than the other, the advantage lies with the simple straight line.

Table 15.9 SEMILOGARITHMIC LEAST SQUARES TREND
(Winter lettuce production in million crates, United States, 1918–52.)

Year	x	Y	Log Y	x^2	x log Y
1918	−17	1.64	.214844		
1919	−16	1.23	.089905		
1920	−15	3.50	.544068		
1921	−14	2.54	.404834		
1922	−13	3.01	.478566		
1923	−12	4.21	.624282		
1924	−11	4.92	.691965		
1925	−10	4.84	.684845		
1926	− 9	5.02	.700704		
1927	− 8	5.16	.712650		
1928	− 7	5.85	.767156		
1929	− 6	6.26	.796574		
1930	− 5	5.74	.758912		
1931	− 4	5.35	.728354		
1932	− 3	4.83	.683947		
1933	− 2	4.49	.652246		
1934	− 1	3.83	.583199		
1935	0	4.07	.609594		
1936	1	4.45	.648360		
1937	2	4.65	.667453		
1938	3	4.45	.648360		
1939	4	5.19	.715167		
1940	5	4.61	.663701		
1941	6	5.30	.724276		
1942	7	5.73	.758155		
1943	8	5.80	.763428		
1944	9	7.31	.863917		
1945	10	7.55	.877947		
1946	11	8.92	.950365		
1947	12	8.50	.929419		
1948	13	9.12	.959995		
1949	14	9.78	.990339		
1950	15	9.52	.978637		
1951	16	9.29	.968016		
1952	17	10.58	1.024486		
Total	0		24.858666	3,570	58.061293

Source: Table 15.1.

313

A warning. Time series analysis in general and trend analysis in particular should never become a blind obsession with the mathematical fitting of curves. Much knowledge of what is behind the data is needed before sound results can be obtained. These thoughts have been particularly well stated by W. S. Woytinsky:

In the 1890's a mathematician and astronomer, N. S. Pritchett, . . . offered a formula for predicting the population of the United States. His formula was a third degree parabola fitted to census data from 1790 to 1890. The fit was excellent and Pritchett did not hesitate to extrapolate this formula in the next millenium. Thus, he found that by 2900 our population will reach 41 billion, in round numbers . . . three things were wrong with this projection: first, the contention that the growth of population in a country can be expressed by a mathematical formula; second, the assumption that such a formula must present the future population as a function of a single variable—time; third, the belief that the shape of this formula for the coming millenium is revealed by the experience of the preceding century. . . . This case . . . is typical of what happens when too much mathematics is combined with too little nonmathematical observation.[6]

These remarks are not designed to sell statistical trend analysis short. Since it is so difficult to make long range forecasts, all possible sources of help need to be pooled. The trend analysis that has been discussed above, if regarded in the proper perspective, has usefulness that cannot be denied. However, it would be a mistake to rely exclusively on mathematical methods. Instead, we should regard these results as first approximations and modify them by whatever additional information can be brought to bear on the issue.

15.3. IS THERE A SIGNIFICANT TREND?

When we come to the problem of establishing whether or not there is a significant trend we find that to this day no powerful tried and proved inference method has been developed that is generally applicable to time series, although much promising research on the problem is being carried out. The main difficulty that makes inferences of the sort developed in Chapter XIV for least squares coefficients inapplicable here is that deviations of time series observations from their population means are dependent upon one another. Or, we can say that the observations are serially correlated. *Serial correlation* refers to correlation among successive values in a series. In a time series the smallest and largest observations are most

[6] W. S. Woytinsky, "Limits of Mathematics in Statistics," *The American Statistician*, February, 1954, pp. 6–10.

unlikely to be consecutive. An additional observation taken between two sample observations will not produce much additional information, for in the presence of serial correlation little, if any, new light is thrown by having adjacent values. Close agreement at one point is most likely followed by close agreement at adjacent points in time. What appears as several agreements may be a single instant observed by us a number of times. For this reason serially correlated data are redundant and uninformative. Clearly the standard error of the correlation coefficient would under the circumstances not be reduced much even if the sample were greatly increased in size.

Some methods have been developed that make possible the testing for a significant trend and that under certain conditions can produce reliable results. One such test is the *first differences test for trend.* This test reasons that there is no trend if there are as many annual increases as decreases in a time series of annual data. Inversely we would expect to have a trend if we find a significantly larger number of increases than decreases, or vice versa. To claim the presence or absence of a trend with an assessable confidence we need a significance test. This test should be able to indicate whether a given ratio of increases to decreases could, at a known risk, be attributable to sample variation or whether it reflects a genuine difference between the number of increases and decreases.

The first differences test does just that. It is a nonparametric test—one that makes no assumption about the normalcy of the distribution. A first difference of a time series is the difference between one observation and the one chronologically succeeding it. If we use the data in Table 15.1, for instance, we see that winter lettuce production in 1918 was 1.64 million crates and in 1919 1.23 million crates. Production declined from 1918 to 1919; the first difference between the 1918 and 1919 data is negative. The independent variate can be ordered and represented by $X_1, X_2, X_3, \ldots,$ X_n and the first differences by $d_1 = X_2 - X_1,$ $d_2 = X_3 - X_2,$ $d_3 = X_4 - X_3, \ldots, d_n = X_n - X_{n-1}.$ Thus, for the 1918–52 lettuce production data we have 34 first differences, 13 negative and 21 positive (see Table 15.10).

The significance test takes the usual form.

1. The set of hypotheses: Our null hypothesis would be that there is no trend in the series of data, i.e., there are as many positive as negative first differences. The alternative hypothesis would be that there is a trend, i.e., that there are more positive (or more negative) first differences. Depending on circumstances, cases A, B, or C would be applicable. We will deal here with Case B and leave it up to the reader to apply cases A and C.

In brief, H_o: The number of positive first differences in the population is

Table 15.10 FIRST DIFFERENCES TEST FOR TREND
(Winter lettuce production in million crates, United States, 1918–52.)

Year	Winter Lettuce Production in Million Crates Y	Sign of First Difference
1918	1.64	
1919	1.23	−
1920	3.50	+
1921	2.54	−
1922	3.01	+
1923	4.21	+
1924	4.92	+
1925	4.84	−
1926	5.02	+
1927	5.16	+
1928	5.85	+
1929	6.26	+
1930	5.74	−
1931	5.35	−
1932	4.83	−
1933	4.49	−
1934	3.83	−
1935	4.07	+
1936	4.45	+
1937	4.65	+
1938	4.45	−
1939	5.19	+
1940	4.61	−
1941	5.30	+
1942	5.73	+
1943	5.80	+
1944	7.31	+
1945	7.55	+
1946	8.92	+
1947	8.50	−
1948	9.12	+
1949	9.78	+
1950	9.52	−
1951	9.29	−
1952	10.58	+

Source: Table 15.1.

316

equal to the number of negative first differences in the population, i.e., there is no trend.

H_B: The number of positive first differences in the population is larger than the number of negative first differences in the population, i.e., there is a trend.

2. Criteria and regions of rejection and acceptance: We have a normal distribution of first differences and therefore we can state, using a 0.05 level of significance:

Reject H_o if z value of sample $> +1.64$.

Accept H_o if z value of sample $< +1.64$.

3. Calculating the sample z value we make use of the following formula:[7]

$$z = \frac{(m - \mu) - \frac{1}{2}}{\sigma}, \tag{15.15}$$

where m is the observed number of plus (or minus) signs [positive (or negative) first differences] in the sample, μ is the expected number of plus (or minus) signs in the population if the observations are random in order, and σ is the standard error of the number of plus (or minus) signs. If the observations are random in order the expected number of plus or minus signs is about one half of all observations, i.e.,

$$\mu \doteq \frac{(n - 1)}{2}, \tag{15.16}$$

and the standard deviation of the number of plus or minus signs

$$\sigma \doteq \sqrt{\frac{(n + 1)}{12}}. \tag{15.17}$$

For large samples the distribution is about normal.

Using the winter lettuce production data of Table 15.10, there are 21 increases and 13 decreases, or 21 plus and 13 minus signs.

$$\mu \doteq \frac{(n - 1)}{2} = \frac{34}{2} = 17.$$

$$\sigma \doteq \sqrt{\frac{(n + 1)}{12}} = \sqrt{\frac{36}{12}} = \sqrt{3.0} = 1.73.$$

Therefore, $$z = \frac{(m - \mu) - \frac{1}{2}}{\sigma} \doteq \frac{21 - 17 - .5}{1.73} = 2.0.$$

4. We conclude that, since the z value of the sample is greater than $+1.64$, we reject the null hypothesis and assert with a 95 per cent confidence

[7] We adjust the difference between the observed and expected number of plus or minus signs for continuity by subtracting $1/2$.

that the data in Table 15.10 exhibit a significant positive trend. This statement neglects the error of Type II. A power function can be derived, but we will not do so here.

A warning must be sounded, however. The first differences test for trend is concerned with order. Basically it tests whether the positive and negative differences are about randomly distributed. It altogether neglects the order of magnitude of the differences. Thus, we can conceive of cases where there are about as many positive as negative differences, yet the former are much larger in order and lead to a clear-cut upward trend. Or, we might find a significantly larger number of positive than negative first differences. Yet the order of magnitude of the former is on the average so much smaller than that of the latter that in fact no trend exists. These are some of the extreme cases for which the test is not suited.

WE LEARNED:

1. A time series is a sequence of values of the same variate corresponding to successive points in time.

2. It is common to look upon a time series as being composed of the following four components: secular trend, periodic variations, cyclical variations, and irregular variations.

3. The secular trend, or in short, trend, is the long-run gradual growth or decline in a series that is an expression of such fundamental forces as population growth, improvements in know-how and productivity, increases in the supply of capital, and changes in consumption habits.

4. Periodic variations, or more specifically seasonal variations, are the recurrent pattern of change within the period that results from the operation of forces connected with climate or custom.

5. Cyclical variations are the oscillatory movements upward and downward that result from alternating levels of economic activity.

6. Irregular variations have no specific pattern.

7. The original time series data can be looked upon as being the product of the four components: $O = T \times S \times C \times I$.

8. Trend may be measured for any of the following three purposes: (1) long-term forecasting, (2) study of past trends, and (3) elimination of trend influence to isolate cyclical variations.

9. While long-term forecasting calls for extrapolation, careful consideration must be given to whether extrapolating past movements is warranted.

10. Before the annual data can be subjected to trend analysis, it is often appropriate to edit the data, so that they become comparable and consistent. Thus, for instance, money wages will be deflated by dividing them by an index reflecting the price level to give real wages, which will be comparable over time and not affected by changes in the price level.

11. Great care must be exercised in selecting the beginning and end of the time series that is to be subjected to a trend analysis. This subjective decision should be

guided by the rule that the series should begin and end in about the same phase of the business cycle.

12. Before a trend analysis is undertaken it is usually proper to test for a significant trend. While there are a number of possible trend tests, we have presented the first differences test, a nonparametric test.

13. There are four main methods for fitting a trend line: the graphical freehand fit, semiaverage fit, moving average fit, and the least squares fit.

14. To fit a trend line by the graphical freehand method, we make use of a transparent ruler so as to equalize the deviations above and below the line.

15. The semiaverage method connects the means of the two halves of the data by a straight line.

16. In the moving average method a series of overlapping means that approximate the trend (by canceling out any regular cycles having the same period as the average) are connected by a curve.

17. The method of least squares fits a straight or curvilinear line to the data so that the mean of the squared vertical deviations of the observed values from this line of best fit is smaller than that for any other curve of the same type. Within limits, this method is both accurate and objective. Inferences about the least squares trend line are usually not possible, since time series data are serially correlated.

18. The least squares linear regression method makes use of formulas with the help of which the Y-intercept, a, and the regression coefficient, b, are found, so that they can be placed into the trend equation: $Y' = a + bX$.

19. The trend regression coefficient $b = \dfrac{N\Sigma XY - (\Sigma X)(\Sigma Y)}{N(\Sigma X^2) - (\Sigma X)^2}$ and the Y-intercept $a = \bar{Y} - b\bar{X}$, in the long method.

20. In the short-cut method in which the X values are so adjusted that their mean is 0, the regression coefficient $b = \dfrac{\Sigma xY}{\Sigma x^2}$, and the Y intercept $a = \bar{Y}$.

21. The equation of a parabola (using the short-cut notations) is $Y' = a + bx + cx^2$, and we can use the following three normal equations to solve for the three unknowns in the equation:

$$\Sigma Y = Na + c\Sigma x^2$$
$$\Sigma xY = b\Sigma x^2$$
$$\Sigma x^2 Y = a\Sigma x^2 + c\Sigma x^4.$$

22. The equation of a semilogarithmic straight line is $\log Y' = a + bx$ (using again short-cut notations). In this case the regression coefficient b is defined as $\dfrac{\Sigma x \log Y}{\Sigma x^2}$ and the Y-intercept as $\dfrac{\Sigma \log Y}{N}$.

23. To convert an annual regression equation to an equation in terms of monthly increments in monthly magnitudes, we divide a by 12 and b by 144.

SEE WHETHER YOU CAN FIT THE TREND:

1. The following is a series of gross private domestic investment in new construction (in billions of dollars in 1953 prices):

1929	19.8	1935	6.0	1945	7.1
		1936	8.4	1946	16.2
1930	14.7	1937	10.1	1947	18.5
1931	10.3	1938	8.9	1948	21.4
1932	5.6	1939	13.1	1949	21.1
1933	4.0				
1934	4.5	1940	14.5	1950	26.1
		1941	16.4	1951	24.7
		1942	8.8	1952	24.1
		1943	5.2	1953	25.1
		1944	5.4		

Using a level of significance of 0.01, decide whether between 1929 and 1953 there was a significant positive trend in gross private domestic investment in new construction.

2. Fit a freehand line to the data given in Problem 1.

3. Attempt a semiaverage fit of the data given in Problem 1.

4. Attempt a moving average fit of the data given in Problem 1 and discuss whether this method is appropriate in solving the problem at hand.

5. Fit a least squares line on an arithmetic scale to the data given in Problem 1.

6. Fit a least squares line on a ratio scale to the data given in Problem 1.

7. Plot the various trend lines that you have obtained on the same graph, and expound the advantages and disadvantages of the various results.   Carefully discuss the series of data and the problems they pose.   Finally, interpret the results of the trend analysis in a language understandable to the novice in statistical techniques.

8. The following is a series of disposable personal income per capita in current prices:

1933	$360	1940	573 +	1950	1,357 +
1934	408 +	1941	690 +	1951	1,458 +
		1942	866 +	1952	1,497 +
1935	455 +	1943	968 +	1953	1,553 +
1936	516 +	1944	1,062 +		
1937	551 +				
1938	504 −	1945	.1,080 +		
1939	536 +	1946	1,124 +		
		1947	1,176 +		
		1948	1,285 +		
		1949	1,255 −		

a. Using a level of significance of 0.05 decide whether there is a significant trend.

b. Plot the data on arithmetic graph paper and draw a freehand line.

c. Fit a linear least squares trend using the short-cut method, and present the results in common sense terms.

d. Fit a linear least squares trend for the period 1934–53.

e. Carefully appraise the limitations of the series and the least squares trend analysis.

XVI

Time Series Analysis—Prophecy Galore (*Continued*)

16.1. SEASONAL VARIATIONS

According to *The New Yorker*, the following letter was received by a Rochester firm from the business manager of the American Funeral Directors:

> With the low death-rate months behind us . . . and the high-death months just ahead, we now head into the up-curve on business in the funeral field.
>
> This normal seasonal upswing is sufficient in itself to spurt buying. This fall and winter, however, may even be better than recent years since "close" buying in the past has resulted in substantially shrunken inventories.
>
> Little wonder authorities in the funeral field look forward to a good fall and winter season!
>
> If you want some of the business, therefore, now is the time for you to go after it.[1]

This informative letter is an example of management's interest in seasonal business rhythms. Measures of the average seasonal behavior of demand, supply, inventories, and prices are indispensable in understanding the typical fluctuations in over-all economic activity as well as in a company's business over the year. With the help of such seasonal measures it becomes possible to evaluate current figures, and decide whether, for instance, an increase in employment between March and April of this year was more or less than the usual seasonal amount. Such measures also help to answer questions as to what the typical variation in the "orders at hand" is between two months, or how much the volume of shell eggs in cold storage normally changes from month to month, etc.

[1] *The New Yorker*, October 2, 1954, p. 61.

Often we need to find the typical seasonal variation so that we can extract it from a time series and obtain a clearer idea of cyclical and secular movements. Dividing monthly data by their typical seasonal pattern, we are left with the trend, cycle, and irregular elements. Such government publications as the *Federal Reserve Bulletin* and the *Survey of Current Business* issue seasonally adjusted data on gross national product, national income, personal income, savings, industrial production, department store sales, department store stocks, business inventories, manufacturers' orders, advertising volume, freight carloadings, construction contract awards, and employment, to mention only some of the more important ones.

Edit of monthly data. Often the original data need editing to eliminate peculiarities of our calendar. If we are interested, for instance, in an analysis of retail sales, we would have to consider that there are fewer days in

Table 16.1 MONTHLY ADJUSTMENT FACTORS FOR NUMBER OF CALENDAR DAYS PER MONTH

Month	Calendar Days	Ratio of Actual to Average Calendar Days	Reciprocal of the Ratio in Column 2
	1	2	3
Jan.	31	1.01918	0.98118
Feb.	28	0.92055	1.08631
March	31	1.01918	0.98118
April	30	0.98630	1.01389
May	31	1.01918	0.98118
June	30	0.98630	1.01389
July	31	1.01918	0.98118
Aug.	31	1.01918	0.98118
Sept.	30	0.98630	1.01389
Oct.	31	1.01918	0.98118
Nov.	30	0.98630	1.01389
Dec.	31	1.01918	0.98118

February than there are in October. In such a case the data might be adjusted on the basis of calendar days. Such an adjustment is readily made. A factor is calculated that raises or lowers the values of each month, assuming an average of 30.4167 days per month (365/12). Adjustment factors for all 12 months of the year have been calculated in Table 16.1. In Column 1 are the calendar days, in Column 2 the ratios of actual to average calendar days, i.e., actual calendar days of each month divided by 30.4167, and in Column 3 the reciprocals of the ratio of actual to average number of calendar days in each month. To adjust the original data for differences in the length of different months we multiply the original data by the adjustment factor in Column 3.

In many cases it is not the calendar days that count, but instead, working days. Adjustment for differences in working days can be made only in view of the special character of the problem. Some enterprises work all seven days of the week, others only five and again others 5.5 days. Thus, adjustment of a final series showing stock sales would need to be different from one on electric power production.

Floating holidays introduce complications. In 1948, Easter was in March; usually it is in April. Easter business will make it difficult to compare March, 1948, with March, 1949, retail sales figures.

Another problem comes about when the seasonal pattern changes abruptly. For instance, instead of bringing out the 1955 car models in January or February, as in previous years, the industry came out with the new models in November of 1954 and even earlier. As a result, annual production, employment, and sales patterns of the automobile industry changed. This caused repercussions in the production, employment, and sales patterns of those industries that supply the automobile manufacturers. Since automobile manufacture and its associated industries are an important segment of the United States economy, the over-all production and employment patterns of the economy were likely to be affected by this change. It will be difficult, therefore, to compare November or December production data of 1953 with those of 1954. However, should new models continue to be introduced in November and not in January in succeeding years, it will be best to break the time series into two or more parts, and calculate a typical seasonal index for each part separately. The second part could start with 1954.

If our interest is in weekly or monthly values not affected by the length of the period, e.g., total number of cases of shell eggs held in cold storage, the original data can be used as such. Most adjustments are needed if we are concerned with rates of activity that characterize the week or month, e.g., weekly coal production.

An example of seasonal rhythm. Year in and year out, the egg remains the mainstay of the American breakfast. We eat eggs at the annual rate of about 400 eggs per person. Hens lay nearly 55 billion eggs a year, at the average rate of 17 eggs every 30 days. Although egg consumption is fairly stable over the year, egg production is heaviest in spring and somewhat less in early summer. Thereafter it falls off considerably. In most years there is a surplus of fresh eggs during spring and early summer and a relative shortage during the rest of the year. Resourceful enterpreneurs have long recognized this seasonal pattern and placed substantial amounts of eggs in cold storage in periods of plentiful supply, to be taken out of storage when

Table 16.2 MONTHLY SHELL EGGS COLD-STORAGE HOLDINGS IN MILLION CASES, UNITED STATES, 1948–54

Date	1948	1949	1950	1951	1952	1953	1954
Jan. 1	0.20	0.16	0.11	0.03	0.14	0.15	0.09
Feb. 1	0.27	0.15	0.38	0.08	0.24	0.12	0.08
March 1	0.37	0.14	0.74	0.16	0.94	0.25	0.14
April 1	1.17	0.53	1.30	0.31	1.60	0.38	0.44
May 1	3.09	0.95	2.15	0.97	2.18	0.82	0.72
June 1	4.90	1.94	3.41	2.08	3.18	1.43	1.31
July 1	5.77	2.29	3.67	2.43	3.36	1.51	1.64
Aug. 1	5.52	1.94	3.16	2.27	2.73	1.20	1.44
Sept. 1	4.61	1.43	2.56	1.61	2.17	0.83	1.03
Oct. 1	3.79	0.81	1.56	0.96	1.71	0.49	0.83
Nov. 1	1.68	0.50	0.50	0.53	1.00	0.29	0.63
Dec. 1	0.44	0.25	0.06	0.23	0.39	0.14	0.33

Source: U.S. Department of Agriculture, *Agricultural Statistics, 1953* (Washington, D.C., 1954), p. 427.

hens show signs of becoming lazy. These actions are reflected in the seasonal pattern of cold-storage holdings of shell eggs, which are recorded by the U.S. Department of Agriculture on the first of each month.

Table 16.2 and Chart 16.1 portray the monthly cold-storage holdings of

Chart 16.1 SEASONAL PATTERN OF MONTHLY SHELL EGGS COLD-STORAGE HOLDINGS IN MILLION CASES, 1948–54.

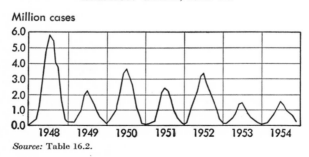

Source: Table 16.2.

shell eggs for the period 1948–54. That there is a pronounced and reasonably stable seasonal rhythm cannot be denied. Holdings reach a high in July and then decline to a low in January-February.

Knowing the typical seasonal pattern of cold-storage holdings of shell eggs is of help to many who trade in eggs or use eggs commercially. Those who trade egg contracts on organized commodity exchanges tend to speculate on seasonal price changes.

The egg trade often wishes to know whether a change in cold-storage holdings that took place during a particular month can be considered to be more or less than seasonal. Also, many traders try to foresee what holdings will amount to a month or two hence. For these purposes, a seasonal index is computed, and we will develop two methods—the *simple average method* and the *ratio to moving-average method*—to calculate the typical seasonal pattern.

Simple average method. Not infrequently we are interested in applying as simple a method as possible, so that we can obtain results without investing much effort. For the sake of speed we are sometimes willing to sacrifice quality.

The application of the simple average method to the cold-storage data of shell eggs is illustrated in Table 16.3. The first 7 columns of this table represent the monthly cold-storage holdings for the 7 years under consideration. Column 8 records the monthly totals, obtained by adding horizontally for each month the 7 figures to the left of Column 8. Column 9 contains the averages of the monthly totals and is obtained by dividing each total in Column 8 by 7, our number of years. The data in Column 10 are trend adjustments, which, as we will see later, were calculated by the least squares method. They could have been computed by any of the four methods of trend fitting discussed in Chapter XV. According to our trend analysis, cold-storage holdings of eggs during 1948–54 declined an average of 0.0085 million cases a month. Therefore, we write in Column 10 for January 0, for February -0.0085, for March -0.0170, etc.

In order not to confuse trend with seasonal variations we must eliminate the trend before we can evaluate the seasonal pattern. To eliminate the trend we add the monthly trend changes to the averages in Column 9. Keeping the January average fixed, we add 0.0085 once to the February average of 0.1100, twice to the March average of 0.2283, three times to the April average of 0.4775, etc. Thus, we obtain in Column 11 monthly averages that have been adjusted for trend. The data in Column 11 are those in Column 9 plus those of Column 10.

Let us remind ourselves what we are after, namely, an index that compares each month's cold-storage holdings with the over-all monthly average of the entire year. With this objective in mind we will compute the over-all monthly average of our data, a figure that is obtained by adding the data in Column 11 and dividing the total by 12. Dividing the total of this column, i.e., 16.2883, by 12 we find that the average monthly holdings (after trend has been eliminated) are 1.35736 million cases of shell eggs. Multiplying each

Table 16.3 SIMPLE AVERAGE METHOD FOR FINDING SEASONAL INDEX
(Monthly shell egg cold-storage holdings in million cases, 1948–54.)

	1948	1949	1950	1951	1952	1953	1954	Monthly Totals	Monthly Averages (Col. 8 ÷ 7)	Trend Adjustment	Seasonally Adjusted for Trend (Col. 9 + Col. 10)	Seasonal Index (Col. 11 ÷ 1.35736 × 100)
	1	2	3	4	5	6	7	8	9	10	11	12
Jan. 1	0.20	0.16	0.11	0.03	0.14	0.15	0.09	0.88	0.1257	0.0000	0.1257	9.26
Feb. 1	0.27	0.15	0.38	0.08	0.24	0.12	0.08	1.32	0.1886	0.0085	0.1971	14.5
March 1	0.37	0.14	0.74	0.16	0.94	0.25	0.14	2.74	0.3914	0.0170	0.4084	30.1
April 1	1.17	0.53	1.30	0.31	1.60	0.38	0.44	5.73	0.8186	0.0255	0.8441	62.2
May 1	3.09	0.95	2.15	0.97	2.18	0.82	0.72	10.88	1.5543	0.0340	1.5883	117.0
June 1	4.90	1.94	3.41	2.08	3.18	1.43	1.31	18.25	2.6071	0.0425	2.6496	195.2
July 1	5.77	2.29	3.67	2.43	3.36	1.51	1.64	20.67	2.9529	0.0510	3.0039	221.3
Aug. 1	5.52	1.94	3.16	2.27	2.73	1.20	1.44	18.26	2.6086	0.0595	2.6681	196.6
Sept. 1	4.61	1.43	2.56	1.61	2.17	0.83	1.03	14.24	2.0343	0.0680	2.1023	154.9
Oct. 1	3.79	0.81	1.56	0.96	1.71	0.49	0.83	10.15	1.4500	0.0765	1.5265	112.5
Nov. 1	1.68	0.50	0.50	0.52	1.00	0.29	0.63	5.13	0.7329	0.0850	0.8179	60.3
Dec. 1	0.44	0.25	0.06	0.23	0.39	0.14	0.33	1.84	0.2629	0.0935	0.3564	26.3

$$m = \frac{\Sigma x}{N} = \frac{16.2883}{12} = 1.35736$$

Source: Table 16.2.

figure of Column 11 by 100 and dividing the product by their mean, e.g., by 1.35736, we come up with the seasonal index reproduced in Column 12.

According to this index cold-storage holdings of shell eggs in January, for instance, were 9.3 per cent of those in the average month during 1948–54. Likewise, holdings in February were 14.5 per cent of those of the average month, etc.

Ratio to moving average method. For certain purposes the simple method given above is adequate. Not infrequently, however, a more refined and reliable method is called for. The United States Bureau of the Census as well as the Federal Reserve Board use the *ratio to moving average method*, and since this method is in general use we will present it here. We know that a moving average smooths out all variations that are uniform in duration and amplitude. Since most seasonal variations meet this condition, a moving average covering a year at a time irons out much of the seasonal element in the series. The other three elements are retained. By dividing the original data by the moving average, as the name indicates, the ratio to moving average method eliminates from the original data most of the influences of trend, cycle, and irregular factors.

In short, the method assumes that ratios of the original observations to a 12-month moving average include the seasonal and irregular component of a series, but not the trend and cyclical components. It further assumes that the averages of the ratios for each of the 12 months measure the seasonal component alone.

The derivation of a seasonal index by the ratio to moving average method is shown in Table 16.4. The computation proceeds in three steps.

Step 1 is to compute a 12-month moving average. This can be done in a number of intermediary steps, as has been shown in Chapter XV. First, we calculate the 12-month moving totals. It involves adding the first 12 monthly figures and writing the total into Column 3 of Table 16.4 in the middle of the space to which they refer, e.g., between June and July. Here 31.81 is the first 12-month moving total. To find the second 12-month moving total we drop the original data for January 1948, 0.20, and add the January 1949, original data, 0.16. The total amounts to 31.77 and is written between July and August. In this fashion the entire Column 3 is completed. As with all moving totals of averages of monthly data, the last figure in Column 3 will be 6 months removed from the most recent month for which data are available.

Next the moving average is calculated by dividing the moving total by 12 and placing the results in Column 4. Thus, for instance, the first moving total of 31.81 is divided by 12, which gives 2.650, which in turn is placed in

Table 16.4 RATIO TO MOVING AVERAGE METHOD FOR FINDING SEASONAL INDEX

(Monthly shell egg cold-storage holdings in million cases, 1948–54.)

Year and Month	Original Data	12-Month Moving Total	12-Month Moving Average (Col. 3 ÷ 12)	12-Month Moving Total (from Col. 4)	Centered 12-Month Average (Col. 5 ÷ 2)	% of Centered 12-Month Moving Average (Col. 2 ÷ Col. 6 × 100)
1	2	3	4	5	6	7
1948 Jan.	0.20					
Feb.	0.27					
March	0.37					
April	1.17					
May	3.09					
June	4.90					
		31.81	2.650			
July	5.77			5.292	2.646	218.1
		31.77	2.642			
Aug.	5.52			5.280	2.640	209.1
		31.65	2.638			
Sept.	4.61			5.256	2.628	175.4
		31.42	2.618			
Oct.	3.79			5.183	2.592	146.2
		30.78	2.565			
Nov.	1.68			4.952	2.476	67.9
		28.64	2.387			
Dec.	0.44			4.572	2.286	19.2
		25.68	2.185			
1949 Jan.	0.16			3.990	1.995	8.0
		22.20	1.850			
Feb.	0.15			3.402	1.701	8.8
		18.62	1.552			
March	0.14			2.839	1.420	9.9
		15.44	1.287			
April	0.53			2.325	1.163	45.6
		12.46	1.038			
May	0.95			1.978	0.989	|96.1
		11.28	0.940			
June	1.94			1.864	0.932	208.2
		11.09	0.924			
July	2.29			1.844	0.922	248.4
		11.04	0.920			
Aug.	1.94			1.859	0.930	208.6
		11.27	0.939			
Sept.	1.43			1.928	0.964	148.3
		11.87	0.989			
Oct.	0.81			2.042	1.021	79.3
		12.64	1.053			
Nov.	0.50			2.206	1.103	45.3
		13.84	1.153			
Dec.	0.25			2.429	1.215	20.6
		15.31	1.276			
1950 Jan.	0.11			2.667	1.334	8.2
		16.69	1.391			

Table 16.4 RATIO TO MOVING AVERAGE METHOD FOR FINDING SEASONAL INDEX (*Continued*)

Year and Month	Original Data	12-Month Moving Total	12-Month Moving Average (Col. 3 ÷ 12)	12-Month Moving Total (from Col. 4)	Centered 12-Month Average (Col. 5 ÷ 2)	% of Centered 12-Month Moving Average (Col. 2 ÷ Col. 6 × 100)
1	2	3	4	5	6	7
Feb.	0.38			2.883	1.442	26.4
		17.91	1.492			
March	0.74			3.079	1.540	48.1
		19.04	1.587			
April	1.30			3.236	1.618	80.3
		19.79	1.649			
May	2.15			3.298	1.649	130.4
		19.79	1.649			
June	3.41			3.282	1.641	207.8
		19.60	1.633			
July	3.67			3.260	1.630	225.2
		19.52	1.627			
Aug.	3.16			3.229	1.615	195.7
		19.22	1.602			
Sept.	2.56			3.155	1.578	162.2
		18.64	1.553			
Oct.	1.56			3.024	1.512	103.2
		17.65	1.471			
Nov.	0.50			2.843	1.422	35.2
		16.47	1.372			
Dec.	0.06			2.634	1.317	4.6
		15.14	1.262			
1951 Jan.	0.03			2.420	1.210	2.5
		13.90	1.158			
Feb.	0.08			2.242	1.121	7.1
		13.01	1.084			
March	0.16			2.089	1.045	15.3
		12.06	1.005			
April	0.31			1.960	0.980	31.6
		11.46	0.955			
May	0.97			1.912	0.956	101.5
		11.49	0.957			
June	2.08			1.929	0.965	215.5
		11.66	0.972			
July	2.43			1.953	0.977	248.7
		11.77	0.981			
Aug.	2.27			1.975	0.988	229.8
		11.93	0.994			
Sept.	1.61			2.053	1.027	156.8
		12.71	1.059			
Oct.	0.96			2.226	1.113	86.3
		14.00	1.167			
Nov.	0.53			2.434	1.217	43.5
		15.21	1.267			

Table 16.4 RATIO TO MOVING AVERAGE METHOD FOR FINDING
SEASONAL INDEX (*Continued*)

Year and Month	Original Data	12-Month Moving Total	12-Month Moving Average (Col. 3 ÷ 12)	12-Month Moving Total (from Col. 4)	Centered 12-Month Average (Col. 5 ÷ 2)	% of Centered 12-Month Moving Average (Col. 2 ÷ Col. 6 × 100)
1	*2*	*3*	*4*	*5*	*6*	*7*
Dec.	0.23			2.626	1.313	17.5
		16.31	1.359			
1952 Jan.	0.14			2.796	1.398	10.0
		17.24	1.437			
Feb.	0.24			2.912	1.456	16.5
		17.70	1.475			
March	0.94			2.997	1.499	62.7
		18.26	1.522			
April	1.60			3.106	1.553	103.0
		19.01	1.584			
May	2.18			3.207	1.604	135.9
		19.48	1.623			
June	3.18			3.260	1.630	195.1
		19.64	1.637			
July	3.36			3.274	1.637	205.3
		19.65	1.627			
Aug.	2.73			3.264	1.632	167.3
		19.53	1.627			
Sept.	2.17			3.197	1.599	135.7
		18.84	1.570			
Oct.	1.71			3.038	1.519	112.6
		17.62	1.468			
Nov.	1.00			2.823	1.412	70.8
		16.26	1.355			
Dec.	0.39			2.564	1.282	30.4
		14.51	1.209			
1953 Jan.	0.15			2.264	1.132	13.3
		12.66	1.055			
Feb.	0.912			1.982	0.991	12.1
		11.13	0.927			
March	0.25			1.743	0.872	28.7
		9.79	0.816			
April	0.38			1.530	0.765	49.7
		8.57	0.714			
May	0.82			1.369	0.685	119.7
		7.86	0.655			
June	1.43			1.289	1.645	221.7
		7.61	0.634			
July	1.51			1.263	0.632	238.9
		7.55	0.629			
Aug.	1.20			1.255	0.628	191.1
		7.51	0.626			
Sept.	0.83			1.243	0.622	133.4
		7.40	0.617			

Table 16.4 RATIO TO MOVING AVERAGE METHOD FOR FINDING SEASONAL INDEX (*Continued*)

Year and Month	Original Data	12-Month Moving Total	12-Month Moving Average (Col. 3 ÷ 12)	12-Month Moving Total (from Col. 4)	Centered 12-Month Average (Col. 5 ÷ 2)	% of Centered 12-Month Moving Average (Col. 2 ÷ Col. 6 × 100)
1	2	3	4	5	6	7
Oct.	0.49			1.239	0.620	79.0
		7.46	0.622			
Nov.	0.29			1.235	0.618	46.9
		7.36	0.613			
Dec.	0.14			1.216	0.608	23.0
		7.24	0.603			
1954 Jan.	0.09			1.217	0.608	14.8
		7.37	0.614			
Feb.	0.08			1.248	0.624	12.8
		7.61	0.634			
March	0.14			1.285	0.642	66.2
		7.81	0.651			
April	0.44			1.330	0.665	103.7
		8.15	0.679			
May	0.72			1.387	0.694	183.2
		8.49	0.708			
June	1.31			1.430	0.715	
		8.67	0.722			
July	1.64					
Aug.	1.44					
Sept.	1.03					
Oct.	0.83					
Nov.	0.63					
Dec.	0.32					

Source: Table 16.1.

Column 4 opposite the corresponding 12-month moving total. Column 4 contains averages of every consecutive 12-month period.

Since an even number of months, 12, are employed in the calculation of a seasonal moving average, the averages need centering. When the first 12-month moving total is taken for the period July, 1948, to June, 1949, the average falls in the middle of this period: January 1, 1949. In order that data be typical of a given month they need to be plotted to the middle of this month. We must find the value of the moving average for January 15, 1949, i.e., we must center the moving averages. This is done by averaging two successive uncentered moving averages. Specifically, we add the first and second uncentered moving average from Column 4 and write them in

Column 5 as a 2-month moving total in the space between the two first 12-month moving averages, i.e., opposite July, 1948. The 2.650 and 2.642 of Column 4 add up to 5.292, which we write in Column 5. Exactly the same is done with all the other 12-month moving averages. The centering operation is completed by dividing the 2-month moving total that is found in Column 5 by 2 to get the centered 12-month moving average, which is written in Column 6.[2]

Step 2 calls for doing what the name of the method says: finding the ratio (of the original data) to moving averages. We divide the original data by the 12-month centered moving average. Specifically, we take the July, 1948, figure in Column 2 and divide it by the corresponding July figure in Column 6: 5.77 divided by 2.646 is 2.181, or 218.1 per cent, which we place in Column 7. Thus, the original July, 1948, figure is 218.1 per cent of the corresponding 12-month centered moving average.

By dividing the original data by the centered 12-month moving average, they in effect have been divided by trend and cycle. The percentages in Column 7 reflect seasonal and, to some degree, irregular influences:

$$\frac{T \times S \times C \times I}{T \times C} = S \times I.$$

Step 3 is the one in which we get from these numerous percentages of centered 12-month moving averages a set of typical, average, or normal percentages, or, in brief, a typical seasonal index. In seeking a *typical seasonal index* we hope to leave behind influences of the irregular factors as well as possible errors that may be present because of a failure of the centering process to accomplish its objective. We can either take an average of all the observations or (and we will do this especially when the period covers many years) we can use a *positional mean*, which discards all but a few middle values.

We will use both methods in turn, so that we can acquaint ourselves with both of them. In Table 16.5 we find the seasonal index using all the readings. We first find the January totals, February totals, etc., and then divide each total by 6, giving us the January means, February means, etc. For instance, the January mean is 9.47 per cent.

To complete the computation we will make sure that when the seasonal index is plotted the 100 per cent value will pass through the middle of the series. *Leveling* makes the average ratios equal to 100. Here is how the leveling is accomplished. We add up the unleveled seasonal index, i.e., we

---

[2] As more experience is gained, operations in a number of columns can be combined, e.g., those in Columns 3–5.

Table 16.5 SEASONAL INDEX (AVERAGE OF ALL VALUES)
(Monthly shell egg cold-storage holdings in million cases, 1948–54.)

	Jan.	Feb.	March	April	May	June	July	Aug.	Sept.	Oct.	Nov.	Dec.	Total
1948	.....	.....	.....	.....	.....	.....	218.1	209.1	175.4	146.2	67.9	19.2	
1949	8.0	8.8	9.9	45.6	96.1	208.2	248.4	208.6	148.3	79.3	45.3	20.6	
1950	8.2	26.4	48.1	80.3	130.4	207.8	225.2	195.7	162.2	103.2	35.2	4.6	
1951	2.5	7.1	15.3	31.6	101.5	215.5	248.7	229.8	156.8	86.3	43.5	17.5	
1952	10.0	16.5	62.7	103.0	135.9	195.1	205.3	167.3	135.7	112.6	70.8	30.4	
1953	13.3	12.1	28.7	49.7	119.7	221.7	238.9	191.1	133.4	79.0	46.9	23.0	
1954	14.8	12.8	21.8	66.2	103.7	183.2	.....	.....	.....	.....	.....	.....	
Total	56.8	83.7	186.5	376.3	687.3	1,231.5	1,384.6	1,201.6	911.8	606.6	309.6	115.3	1,191.95
Mean	9.47	13.95	31.08	62.73	114.55	205.25	230.77	200.27	151.97	101.10	51.60	19.22	
Leveled Mean	9.54	14.05	31.30	63.17	115.35	206.69	232.39	201.67	153.03	101.81	51.96	19.35	

Correction coefficient: $\dfrac{1,200}{1,191.95} = 1.007$

Source: Table 16.4.

add 9.47 to 13.95, and so on.   If these mean values add up to 1,200 per cent,
i.e., 12 times 100 per cent, we have
proof that their mean is 100 per
cent and no special leveling is
needed.   But if the sum is not
1,200, this sum needs to be divided
into 1,200 to provide a correction
factor by which each unleveled
mean is multiplied so that we get
the leveled seasonal index.

Chart 16.2 SEASONAL INDEX (AVER-
AGE OF ALL VALUES)
(Monthly shell egg cold-storage holdings in
million cases, United States, 1948–54.)

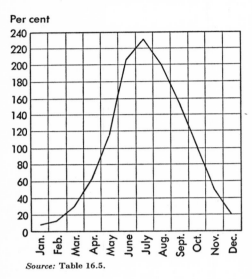

Source: Table 16.5.

Here in the cold-storage problem
under consideration the 12 unleveled seasonal index numbers
add up to 1,191.95.   The adjustment factor, therefore, is 1,200/1,
191.95 or 1.007 and by it we multiply each unleveled index number.
For instance, the January figure of
9.47 per cent we multiply by 1.007
giving us the leveled seasonal index
for January of 9.54 per cent.   This
means that, for instance, January

cold-storage holdings of shell eggs are ordinarily about 9.54 per cent of those
of the average month.   The
leveled seasonal index is presented
in the last line of Table 16.5 and is
plotted in Chart 16.2.

We might feel that the (leveled)
seasonal index of Table 16.5 is too
strongly influenced by irregular
forces that caused the moving average of a given month to be too high
in some years and too low in others.
Having data for but seven years
(actually only for six years since we
have no moving average for the
first and last six months) we might
still prefer a positional mean to an
over-all mean.   We have plotted

Chart 16.3 SEASONAL INDEX (POSI-
TIONAL MEAN)
(Monthly shell egg cold-storage holdings in
million cases, United States, 1948–54.)

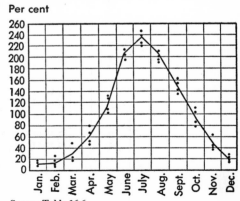

Source: Table 16.6.

the percentages of the 12-month moving averages for 1948–54 in Chart 16.3.

Table 16.6 SEASONAL INDEX (Positional Mean)
(Monthly shell egg cold-storage holdings in million cases, 1948–54.)

	Jan.	Feb.	March	April	May	June	July	Aug.	Sept.	Oct.	Nov.	Dec.	Total
1948	.....	......	......	......	......	......	218.1	209.1	~~175.4~~	~~146.2~~	67.9	19.2	
1949	8.0	8.8	~~9.9~~	45.6	~~96.1~~	208.2	248.4	208.6	148.3	79.3	45.3	20.6	
1950	8.2	~~26.4~~	48.1	80.3	130.4	207.8	225.2	195.7	162.2	103.2	~~25.2~~	~~4.6~~	
1951	~~2.5~~	~~7.1~~	15.3	~~31.6~~	101.5	215.5	~~248.7~~	~~229.8~~	156.8	86.3	43.5	17.5	
1952	10.0	16.5	~~62.7~~	~~103.0~~	~~135.9~~	195.1	~~205.8~~	~~167.3~~	135.7	112.26	~~70.8~~	~~30.4~~	
1953	13.3	12.1	28.7	49.7	119.7	~~221.7~~	238.9	191.1	~~133.4~~	~~79.0~~	46.9	23.0	
1954	~~14.7~~	12.8	21.8	66.2	103.7	~~183.2~~	......	......	......	......	......	......	
Total	39.5	50.2	113.9	241.8	455.3	826.6	930.6	804.5	60.30	381.4	203.6	80.3	1,182.68
Mean	9.875	12.55	28.475	60.450	113.825	206.65	232.65	201.12	150.75	95.350	50.900	20.08	
Leveled	10.0	12.7	28.9	61.4	115.5	209.8	236.1	204.1	153.0	96.8	51.7	20.4	

Correction coefficient: $\dfrac{1,200}{1,182.68} = 1.015$

Source: Table 16.4.

It appears desirable to drop the highest and the lowest percentage figure for each month and calculate a positional mean from the remaining four percentages. The totals and the positional means for the 12 months are presented in Table 16.6. Since the 12 averages add up to 1,182.68, we level the data with the help of the correction coefficient 1,200/1,182.68 or 1.015. The (leveled) seasonal index based on positional mean values is given in the last line of Table 16.6. These index data are not very different from those in Table 16.5, which are not based on a positional mean. When we have as few years as we do in the cold-storage example, we usually would not compute a positional mean. However, when the period covers, let us say, 25 years, we can drop the lowest and the highest 10 readings, respectively, and compute a positional mean from the middle 5 readings.

Applying the seasonal index. Let us look into some of the applications. On August 1, 1954, the government announced that 1.44 million cases of shell eggs were in cold storage. At that time many traders may have been eager to know whether the change in cold-storage holdings from July 1, 1954, to August 1, 1954, had been normal or abnormal. Merely because holdings decreased during the month of July from 1.64 to 1.44 million cases, i.e., by 12 per cent, no intelligent trader would have concluded that the decline was necessarily abnormal and for this reason, for instance, have taken a "long" position on the Chicago Mercantile Exchange.

The trader would have been well advised to ask himself whether this decline was more than the usual seasonal July decline. To find an answer to this question he would have been helped by having a seasonal index of the sort that we computed. He could then have calculated what the cold-storage holdings of shell eggs would have been on July 1, 1954, and August 1, 1954, respectively, if the seasonal influence were removed. He could have "deseasonalized" the July and August figures by dividing each of the two original data by the corresponding index number. For July it would have meant dividing 1,640,000 by 2.361 (from Table 16.6), which is 695,000, and for August we would have divided 1,440,000 by 2.041, which is 706,000. Comparing the two deseasonalized figures, the trader would have decided that, on the assumption that there was no sampling variation, the decline in cold-storage holdings during July, 1954, was slightly less than seasonal.

Or, let us look for a moment at the July 1, 1951, and August 1, 1951, data. Holdings declined from 2.43 million cases to 2.27 million cases. Deseasonalizing these two figures, we learn that reduction in cold-storage holdings of shell eggs was substantially smaller than the normal seasonal decline.

All this is useful information to the man in the egg trade. But having answered one question, a second suggests itself. If the decline in cold-storage holdings of shell eggs during July, 1954, was less than seasonal, what is responsible for this departure from normal? If no irregular forces could be pinpointed, trend or cyclical variation would need to be investigated.

We can be sure that there were many traders who, on August 1, 1954, were curious to know what the cold storage holdings of shell eggs were likely to be one month hence. One way for them to get an idea about this would have been to pursue the following reasoning: During the next 30 days seasonal factors are likely to dominate in shaping changes in cold-storage holdings. Thus, at least initially, trend and cyclical factors could be neglected. A preliminary forecast could be made by assuming that the average seasonal pattern of the last 7 years would persist in the short run. The preliminary forecast could then be adjusted for irregular and cyclical factors to the extent that information about them is available.

On this basis the forecast would take the following form: Knowing the August 1, 1954, cold-storage holdings, and assuming that changes are solely seasonal in nature and consistent with the pattern of the past, the August 1 holdings could be multiplied by the ratio of the September to August seasonal index. Since the August 1, 1954, holdings were 1.44 million cases, the seasonal index for September and August, respectively, was 153.0 and 204.1; the September 1, 1954, forecast would be (1.44)153/204 or 1.08 million cases. This figure could have been adjusted upward or downward, depending on whether, and what kind of, additional information was available. As it turned out, the forecast proved correct, since September 1, 1954, holdings in fact were 1.03 million cases.

Often a forecast into a somewhat more distant future is needed. For instance, traders might wish to know in August, 1954, how large cold-storage holdings of shell eggs are likely to be on December 1, 1954. While it is not easy to make forecasts 30 days in advance, it is even more difficult to peep farther into the future. Should we be convinced that pronounced seasonal and secular forces are present, we would attempt to measure them. We could use the short-cut method and find the trend of the monthly data. This is done in Table 16.7 for the 1948–54 cold-storage egg data, with July 1, 1951, as the origin. The trend equation is $Y' = 1.31 - 0.0085x$. Assuming that the past trend will prevail, trend alone would tend to reduce December 1, 1954, cold-storage holdings to 0.61 million cases. Insofar as the typical seasonal rhythm is concerned, December 1 cold-storage holdings are but 20 per cent of the average month of the year. By modifying the

Table 16.7 MONTHLY LEAST SQUARES TREND
(Shell egg cold-storage holdings in million cases, 1948–52.)

Date	Y	x	x^2	xY	Date	Y	x	x^2	xY
1948 Jan.	0.20	−83			1951 July	2.43	+ 1		
Feb.	0.27	−81			Aug.	2.27	+ 3		
March	0.37	−79			Sept.	1.61	+ 5		
April	1.17	−77			Oct.	0.96	+ 7		
May	3.09	−75			Nov.	0.53	+ 9		
June	4.90	−73			Dec.	0.23	+11		
July	5.77	−71							
Aug.	5.52	−69			1952 Jan.	0.14	+13		
Sept.	4.61	−67			Feb.	0.24	+15		
Oct.	3.79	−65			March	0.94	+17		
Nov.	1.68	−63			April	1.60	+19		
Dec.	0.44	−61			May	2.18	+21		
					June	3.18	+23		
1949 Jan.	0.16	−59			July	3.36	+25		
Feb.	0.15	−57			Aug.	2.73	+27		
March	0.14	−55			Sept.	2.17	+29		
April	0.53	−53			Oct.	1.71	+31		
May	0.95	−51			Nov.	1.00	+33		
June	1.94	−49			Dec.	0.39	+35		
July	2.29	−47							
Aug.	1.94	−45			1953 Jan.	0.15	+37		
Sept.	1.43	−43			Feb.	0.12	+39		
Oct.	0.81	−41			March	0.25	+41		
Nov.	0.50	−39			April	0.38	+43		
Dec.	0.25	−37			May	0.82	+45		
					June	1.43	+47		
1950 Jan.	0.11	−35			July	1.51	+49		
Feb.	0.38	−33			Aug.	1.20	+51		
March	0.74	−31			Sept.	0.83	+53		
April	1.30	−29			Oct.	0.49	+55		
May	2.15	−27			Nov.	0.29	+57		
June	3.41	−25			Dec.	0.14	+59		
July	3.67	−23							
Aug.	3.16	−21			1954 Jan.	0.09	+61		
Sept.	2.56	−19			Feb.	0.08	+63		
Oct.	1.56	−17			March	0.14	+65		
Nov.	0.50	−15			April	0.44	+67		
Dec.	0.06	−13			May	0.72	+69		
					June	1.31	+71		
1951 Jan.	0.03	−11			July	1.64	+73		
Feb.	0.08	− 9			Aug.	1.44	+75		
March	0.16	− 7			Sept.	1.03	+77		
April	0.31	− 5			Oct.	0.83	+79		
May	0.97	− 3			Nov.	0.63	+81		
June	2.08	− 1			Dec.	0.32	+83		
					Total	110.08	0	197,540	−1,668.44

Source: Table 16.2.

$$b = \frac{\Sigma xY}{\Sigma x^2} = \frac{-1,668.44}{197,540} = -0.0085$$

$$a = \frac{\Sigma Y}{N} = \frac{110.08}{84} = 1.31.$$

trend forecast by the seasonal index we would estimate December 1, 1954, holdings to amount to 0.61 × 0.20 or about 0.12 million cases.[3]

This estimate of about 120,000 cases of shell eggs turns out to be sub-

[3] We could also use another method that is less time-consuming, but often less reliable. Instead of working with monthly data, we could use annual averages, find the annual trend equation, and adjust it. In this case we would divide the trend regression coefficient of the annual data by 144.

stantially below the actual December figures. There can be many reasons for this poor estimate. As we will see below in our discussion of cyclical variations, the main culprit is the cyclical rhythm, which we have so far neglected. Also, irregular variation plays its part.

Seasonal computations by electronics. In 1954 the Bureau of the Census perfected techniques that enable it to use a high-speed electronic computer to compute seasonal indexes and adjust time series data for seasonality. These computations are being made at the speed of about one minute for a ten-year monthly series, and at a cost of about two dollars.

The computer performs arithmetic computations at a very high rate of speed. Its operation is virtually completely automatic, checking circuits preventing the propagation of errors. This type of computer is at its best in performing operations involving long series of sequential computations on relatively small numbers of original observations. The computation of seasonal indexes and seasonally adjusted series fit this requirement very well. The method programmed by the Bureau of the Census for the computer is an adaption of the ratio to moving average method discussed above, though containing many refinements.

In computing a seasonal index, the computer computes first a 12-month moving average and then centers it. The resulting seasonal index is moving rather than constant. Furthermore, two sets of seasonal indexes and two seasonally adjusted series are computed by the Bureau of the Census. The first set of indexes is based upon ratios to the 12-month moving average of the original observations. Since this moving average sometimes provides an inadequate measure of the underlying cyclical movement of the series, a second set of moving seasonal indexes, based upon ratios of the original observations to a 5-month moving average of the first seasonally adjusted series, is computed and used to adjust the original observations.

The electronic computer also makes tests of the soundness of its seasonal adjustments. The seasonally adjusted figures for each month are divided by an average of the adjusted figures for the preceding and following months. When values above or below 1.00 are found in an adjusted series for a particular month in a number of consecutive years, the adjusted series is reviewed by analysts for residual seasonality. One further test is made. An uncentered 12-month moving average of the seasonally adjusted observations is divided by an uncentered moving average of the original data. This test shows whether the seasonal adjustment has resulted in substantial differences between the averages of the adjusted data and the averages of the unadjusted data for any 12-month period.

Finally, computer prints the results. Altogether it produces nineteen tables, showing the original observations, five different moving averages, two sets of ratios to moving averages, two centered and two uncentered sets of moving seasonal factors, two seasonally adjusted series, and five tests of the work.

16.2. CYCLICAL VARIATIONS

The incalculable Up-and-Down of Time.

SIDNEY LANIER

Perhaps the two most important characteristics of the dynamics of the American economy are the gradual changes over long periods and those creating short run cyclical fluctuations. The latter, insofar as the over-all economy is concerned, are business cycles. They consist in recurring alternations of expansion and contraction in aggregate economic activity. These alternating movements are self-reinforced and pervade virtually all parts of the economy. There is nothing periodic about the cyclical movement. In some cycles the upswing lasts longer and in others the downswing. We have cycles in economic activity because the economy appears incapable of remaining on an even keel. Actually, if we take time to think about it we will be little surprised. Why should the economy remain on an even keel? Such stability would be well-nigh an exception to the rule.

In the past, business cycles in the United States have lasted from two to eleven years. Fluctuations must be cumulative to constitute business cycles. Since the development of a cumulative movement takes time to work itself out, a cycle is not likely to be of less than two-year duration. At the other extreme, the inherent recuperative powers of the cycle and particularly the social consciousness of the government prevent cycles from lasting very many years.

The National Bureau of Economic Research has done perhaps more work in this area than has any other group. It has found business cycles in the period 1854 to 1949 that were as brief as twenty-seven months (1919–21) and as long as ninety-nine months (1870–79). In the last four cycles presented in Table 16.8 the duration was at least four years. In the 1929–33 cycle the contraction phase was dominant, while in the other three the expansion period dominated.

In reviewing Table 16.8 it is well to recognize that the diversity between cycles is greater than this table suggests. Only one of the two dimensions of the cycle is represented. Not only are the differences in duration substantial but so is the diversity in amplitude.

Many workers in this field subdivide business cycles into two types, major and minor. The former extend over a period of six to eleven years and have a relatively wide amplitude. They often are claimed to be the result of important changes in business expectations regarding the profitability of long-term investment. The shorter, minor cycles tend to be associated with changes in short-term business expectations and minor maladjustments.

Table 16.8 TURNING POINTS AND DURATIONS OF AMERICAN
BUSINESS CYCLES, 1854–1955

Dates of Turning Points		Duration in Months		
Peak	Trough	Expansion*	Contraction†	Full Cycle
	Dec., 1854			
June, 1857	Dec., 1858	30	18	48
Oct., 1860	June, 1861	22	8	30
April, 1865	Dec., 1867	46	32	78
June, 1869	Dec., 1870	18	18	36
Oct., 1873	March, 1879	34	65	99
March, 1882	May, 1885	36	38	74
March, 1887	April, 1888	22	13	35
July, 1890	May, 1891	27	10	37
Jan., 1893	June, 1894	20	17	37
Dec., 1895	June, 1897	18	18	36
June, 1899	Dec., 1900	24	18	42
Sept., 1902	Aug., 1904	21	23	44
May, 1907	June, 1908	33	13	46
Jan., 1910	Jan., 1912	19	24	43
Jan., 1913	Dec., 1914	12	23	35
Aug., 1918	April, 1919	44	8	52
Jan., 1920	July, 1921	9	18	27
May, 1923	July, 1924	22	14	36
Oct., 1926	Nov., 1927	27	13	40
June, 1929	March, 1933	19	45	64
May, 1937	June, 1938	50	13	63
Feb., 1945	Oct., 1945	80	8	88
Nov., 1948	Oct., 1949	37	11	48
July, 1953	Aug., 1954	45	13	58

Source: R. A. Gordon, *Business Fluctuations* (New York, Harper & Bros., 1952), p. 216.
* Measured from trough on preceding line to peak.
† From peak to trough on same line.

Sometimes a minor and major cycle occur simultaneously. For instance, the course of business activity in the United States between 1921 and 1933 appeared to trace out a major cycle covering the entire period. Minor cycles with peaks in 1923 and 1926 and troughs in 1924 and 1927 were superimposed on this major cycle.

Cycles in aggregate economic activity are reflected, although to differing degrees, in cyclical changes in individual firms and industries. While the

Table 16.9 RESIDUAL METHOD FOR ISOLATING CYCLICAL
VARIATIONS IN ANNUAL DATA
(Winter lettuce production in million cases, 1918–52.)
(1935 = 0)

Year	x	$Y = 0$	$Y' = T$	$Y/Y' = 0/T = C \times I$
1	2	3	4	5
1918	−17	1.64	2.36	0.69
1919	−16	1.23	2.56	0.48
1920	−15	3.50	2.75	1.27
1921	−14	2.54	2.94	0.86
1922	−13	3.01	3.13	0.96
1923	−12	4.21	3.32	1.27
1924	−11	4.92	3.52	1.40
1925	−10	4.84	3.71	1.30
1926	− 9	5.02	3.90	1.29
1927	− 8	5.16	4.10	1.26
1928	− 7	5.85	4.29	1.36
1929	− 6	6.26	4.48	1.40
1930	− 5	5.74	4.67	1.23
1931	− 4	5.35	4.86	1.10
1932	− 3	4.83	5.06	0.95
1933	− 2	4.49	5.25	0.86
1934	− 1	3.83	5.44	0.71
1935	0	4.07	5.64	0.72
1936	1	4.45	5.83	0.76
1937	2	4.65	6.02	0.77
1938	3	4.45	6.21	0.72
1939	4	5.19	6.40	0.80
1940	5	4.61	6.60	0.70
1941	6	5.30	6.79	0.78
1942	7	5.73	6.98	0.82
1943	8	5.80	7.18	0.81
1944	9	7.31	7.37	0.99
1945	10	7.55	7.56	1.00
1946	11	8.92	7.75	1.15
1947	12	8.50	7.94	1.07
1948	13	9.12	8.14	1.12
1949	14	9.78	8.33	1.17
1950	15	9.52	8.52	1.12
1951	16	9.29	8.72	1.07
1952	17	10.58	8.91	1.20

Source: Table 16.1.

various cyclical patterns have some common features, they exhibit many dissimilarities. The cycles differ as to timing. The agricultural sector is often the first to incur declines in income. In amplitude there are numerous differences too, with the production of nondurable consumers' goods, for instance, much more stable than that of durable consumers' goods.

Cyclical variations as a residual. As of today we do not have a completely satisfactory technique for separating cyclical variations from the other components of a time series. The difficulty lies in the interdependence of cyclical variations and trend. Cyclical forces influence secular fluctuations, and, in turn, the kind of trend we choose to eliminate helps to determine the shape of the resulting cyclical variations. The method that calculates the trend as a residual divides the seasonally adjusted monthly data or the annual data, if we are dealing with such, by the corresponding trend values.

Let us apply the residual method to the winter lettuce data of Chapter XV.

Earlier in our discussion we pointed out that we may consider a time series to be composed of trend, cyclical,

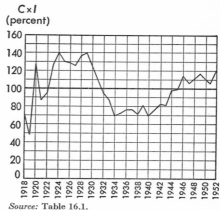

Chart 16.4 CYCLICAL-IRREGULAR VARIATIONS OF ANNUAL DATA
(Winter lettuce production in million crates, 1918–52.)

Source: Table 16.1.

seasonal, and irregular elements. Since we are concerned here with annual data, they cannot contain a seasonal element. We may, therefore, look upon our lettuce data as representing the product of trend, cyclical, and irregular elements. In short, $O = T \times C \times I$. If we were to divide our original data by the trend data of the corresponding years, we would be left with the cyclical-irregular aspects of the series. To learn about the cyclical characteristics of the winter lettuce industry, we would only have to smooth out the irregular elements.

These steps are shown in Table 16.9, where first the original data (Y or O of Column 3) are divided by the calculated trend data (Y' or T of Column 4). The results (Y/Y' or O/T or $C \times I$) are given in Column 5. The data containing only the cyclical-irregular variation in percentage terms are plotted in Chart 16.4. Either by a freehand or moving average method we could eliminate much of the irregular variation so that we would be left with the cyclical pattern.

In the early part of the period under analysis, winter lettuce production apparently went through a cyclical upswing, reaching a peak during 1924–29; in the early 1930's production turned down, reaching a trough in 1934; after some vaccilation production turned up and was still increasing cyclically in 1952.

As a further example, we will eliminate the trend from the American Telephone and Telegraph *Index of Industrial Activity.* Chart 16.5 shows

Chart 16.5 AMERICAN TELEPHONE AND TELEGRAPH COMPANY'S INDEX OF IN-DUSTRIAL ACTIVITY BEFORE AND AFTER CORRECTION FOR TREND, 1899–56*

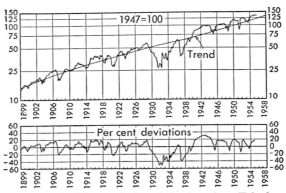

* This chart is reproduced with permission of the American Telephone and Telegraph Company, who constructs this Index of Industrial Activity for information of Bell System personnel and not for general distribution.

the original data plus the trend line. In the lower part of Chart 16.5 the original data divided by the trend values have been plotted. Cycle plus irregular variations fluctuate now around a horizontal line.

Decomposing a time series of monthly data is somewhat more complex. We must "eliminate" the seasonal and secular movements, and will be left with cyclical-irregular fluctuations expressed as percentages. There are a number of ways to eliminate the seasonal and secular elements of the series. We will illustrate one method in relation to the cold-storage data of shell eggs. At the start we use the least squares correlation method to fit a straight line trend to our monthly egg data. The trend equation turns out to be $Y' = 1.31 - 0.00846x$, with July, 1951 = +1. With the help of this trend equation, which we have checked and found to have a significant slope, we calculate the predicted trend values for all 84 months (see Table 16.10). In Column 4 we have the seasonal index copied from Table 16.6. We multiply the trend values from Column 3 by the seasonal values in Column 5 and have the results in Column 5. In a sense the monthly data in Column 5 reflect the combined seasonal and secular movement, which we will divide into our original data in Column 2, and multiply the result by 100 to come up in Column 6 with the cyclical-irregular fluctuations expressed in percentage terms. We might wish to eliminate parts of the irregular movements, which can be done by using a 2- or 3-month moving average or by freehand.

After eliminating the seasonal and secular movements, we have left the cyclical-irregular fluctuations in percentage terms. These residual cyclical movements are sometimes looked upon as representing deviations from "normal." Sometimes they are considered to represent departures from the equilibrium position portrayed by the secular-seasonal movement that has been eliminated. Unfortunately, these statements have little justification. The base line from which we measure cyclical fluctuations represents in only a very limited sense "normality." In no sense is it an equilibrium expansion path. Anyhow, there is little agreement as to what is "normal." Whatever our concept of normal, there is little reason to consider trend times seasonal variations, from which we measure cyclical deviations, as representing a normal situation.

Chart 16.6 CYCLICAL-IRREGULAR VARIATIONS OF MONTHLY DATA (Shell egg cold-storage holdings in million cases, 1948–54.)

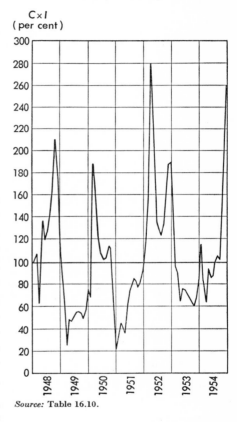

Source: Table 16.10.

To avoid misconceptions, it is better not to think of business cycles as fluctuating around some determinable "normal" level. This is not to deny the late Professor Schumpeter's position that businessmen have a rough-and-ready idea of "normal business" with which they compare current cyclical fluctuations.[4]

Let us examine for a moment the cyclical-irregular elements of the 1948–54 egg cold-storage series printed in Chart 16.6. Troughs are reached in 1949, 1951, and 1953; peaks are reached in 1948, 1950, and 1952. By and large

[4] J. A. Schumpeter, *Business Cycles* (New York, McGraw-Hill, 1939) vol. 1, chap. 1.

Table 16.10 RESIDUAL METHOD FOR ISOLATING CYCLICAL VARIATIONS IN MONTHLY DATA
(Monthly shell egg cold-storage holdings in million cases, 1948–54.)

	Y	Y'	S	$Y'S$	$\dfrac{Y}{Y'S} \times 100 = C \times I$
	1	2	3	4	5	6
1948 Jan.	0.20	2.011	0.100	0.2011	99.5
Feb.	0.27	1.995	0.127	0.2534	107
March	0.37	1.978	0.289	0.5716	64.7
April	1.17	1.961	0.614	1.204	97.2
May	3.09	1.944	1.155	2.2453	137.6
June	4.90	1.927	2.098	4.0429	121.2
July	5.77	1.910	2.361	4.5095	128.0
Aug.	5.52	1.893	2.041	3.8636	142.9
Sept.	4.61	1.876	1.530	2.8703	160.6
Oct.	3.79	1.859	0.968	1.800	210.6
Nov.	1.68	1.842	0.517	0.9523	176.4
Dec.	0.44	1.825	0.204	0.3723	118
1949 Jan.	0.16	1.808	0.100	0.1808	88.5
Feb.	0.15	1.791	0.127	0.2275	65.9
March	0.14	1.775	0.289	0.5130	27.3
April	0.53	1.758	0.614	1.079	49.1
May	0.95	1.741	1.155	2.0109	47.2
June	1.94	1.724	2.098	3.6170	53.64
July	2.29	1.707	2.361	4.0302	56.82
Aug.	1.94	1.690	2.041	3.4493	56.24
Sept.	1.43	1.673	1.530	2.5597	55.87
Oct.	0.81	1.656	0.968	1.603	50.5
Nov.	0.50	1.639	0.517	0.8474	59.0
Dec.	0.25	1.622	0.204	0.3309	75.6
1950 Jan.	0.11	1.605	0.100	0.1605	68.5
Feb.	0.38	1.588	0.127	0.2017	188
March	0.74	1.572	0.289	0.4543	163
April	1.30	1.555	0.614	0.9548	136.2
May	2.15	1.538	1.155	1.7764	121.0
June	3.41	1.521	2.098	3.1911	106.9
July	3.67	1.504	2.361	3.5509	103.4
Aug.	3.16	1.487	2.041	3.0350	104.1
Sept.	2.56	1.470	1.530	2.2491	113.8
Oct.	1.56	1.453	0.968	1.407	110.9
Nov.	0.50	1.437	0.517	0.7429	67.3
Dec.	0.06	1.419	0.204	0.2895	21
1951 Jan.	0.03	1.402	0.100	0.1402	21
Feb.	0.08	1.385	0.127	0.1759	46
March	0.16	1.368	0.289	0.3954	40.5
April	0.31	1.352	0.614	0.8301	37.3
May	0.97	1.335	1.155	1.5419	62.9
June	2.08	1.318	2.098	2.7652	74.22

Table 16.10 RESIDUAL METHOD FOR ISOLATING CYCLICAL
VARIATIONS IN MONTHLY DATA (*Continued*)
(Monthly shell egg cold storage holdings in million cases, 1948–54.)

		Y	Y'	S	$Y'S$	$\dfrac{Y}{Y'S} \times 100 = C \times I$
		1	*2*	*3*	*4*	*5*	*6*
1951	July	2.43	1.301	2.361	3.0717	79.11
	Aug.	2.27	1.284	2.041	2.6206	86.62
	Sept.	1.61	1.267	1.530	1.9385	83.05
	Oct.	0.96	1.250	0.968	1.210	79.3
	Nov.	0.53	1.233	0.517	0.6375	83.1
	Dec.	0.23	1.216	0.204	0.2481	92.7
1952	Jan.	0.14	1.119	0.100	0.1199	117
	Feb.	0.24	1.182	0.127	0.1501	160
	March	0.94	1.165	0.289	0.3367	279
	April	1.60	1.148	0.614	0.7049	227.0
	May	2.18	1.135	1.155	1.3109	166.3
	June	3.18	1.115	2.098	2.3393	135.9
	July	3.36	1.098	2.361	2.5924	129.6
	Aug.	2.73	1.081	2.041	2.2063	123.7
	Sept.	2.17	1.064	1.530	1.6279	133.3
	Oct.	1.71	1.047	0.968	1.014	168.6
	Nov.	1.00	1.030	0.517	0.5325	187.8
	Dec.	0.39	1.013	0.204	0.2067	189
1953	Jan.	0.15	0.9962	0.100	0.09962	151
	Feb.	0.12	0.9792	0.127	0.1244	96.5
	March	0.25	0.9623	0.289	0.2781	89.9
	April	0.38	0.9454	0.614	0.5805	65.5
	May	0.82	0.9285	1.155	1.0724	76.5
	June	1.43	0.9116	2.098	1.9125	74.77
	July	1.51	0.8946	2.361	2.1122	71.49
	Aug.	1.20	0.8777	2.041	1.7914	66.99
	Sept.	0.83	0.8608	1.530	1.3170	63.0
	Oct.	0.49	0.8439	0.968	0.8169	60.0
	Nov.	0.29	0.8269	0.517	0.4275	67.8
	Dec.	0.14	0.8100	0.204	0.1652	84.8
1954	Jan.	0.09	0.7931	0.100	0.07931	114
	Feb.	0.08	0.7762	0.127	0.09858	81.2
	March	0.14	0.7593	0.289	0.2194	63.8
	April	0.44	0.7423	0.614	0.4558	96.5
	May	0.72	0.7254	1.155	0.83784	85.9
	June	1.31	0.7085	2.098	1.4864	88.13
	July	1.64	0.6916	2.361	1.6329	100.4
	Aug.	1.44	0.6746	2.041	1.3769	104.6
	Sept.	1.03	0.6577	1.530	1.0063	102.4
	Oct.	0.83	0.6408	0.968	0.6203	134
	Nov.	0.63	0.6239	0.517	0.3226	195
	Dec.	0.32	0.6070	0.204	0.1238	259

Source: Tables 16.2 and 16.6.

the series incorporates a two-year cycle. Why would cold-storage holdings of eggs go through a two-year cycle? Agricultural economists have developed the "cobweb theorem," which, in brief, claims that high prices induce the atomistic producers of an agricultural commodity to increase next year's production. Unless demand conditions are greatly changed, the increased supply will tend to depress prices, which in turn will tend to persuade many a farmer to plan on a smaller crop in the coming year. The small output will tend to raise prices and the cycle will start all over again. Our egg data may be analyzed in these terms.

The National Bureau's method of measuring typical cyclical behavior. The residual method simply tends to extract the cyclical element of a time series. Yet often knowledge of the average or typical behavior of cycles is called for. By far the most exhaustive study of typical cyclical patterns has been made by the National Bureau of Economic Research.[5] Their method is as follows:

1. The original monthly data are adjusted for seasonal variation by the ratio to moving average method.

2. The deseasonalized data are charted on a ratio grid, and the trough of each cycle is selected by inspection.

3. The average level of the series is computed for each cycle, and the monthly figures are expressed as percentages of this base. In doing so the data for all series and all cycles are reduced to a common unit so as to make for convenient comparability. The resulting percentages are referred to as "specific-cycle relatives."

4. Next, each and every cycle is separated into nine stages. Stage I covers the three months centered on the initial trough, Stage V the three months centered on the peak, and Stage IX the three months centered on the terminal trough. Stages II, III, and IV cover successive thirds of the period of expansion; and Stages VI, VII, and VIII the successive thirds of the periods of contraction. The average of the relatives is computed for each stage, producing a nine-point pattern for each cycle.

5. Finally, each of the nine stages is averaged for all cycles so as to result in the "specific-cycle pattern" of the typical cycle.

6. The series is marked off at the months representing the troughs in general business activity rather than the troughs in the series itself. On these data the same operations are performed as above to yield a "reference-cycle pattern" showing the typical behavior of the series in the period occupied by a general business cycle.

---

[5] Arthur F. Burns and Wesley C. Mitchell, *Measuring Business Cycles* (New York, National Bureau of Economic Research, 1946), chap. 2.

7. Finally, mean deviations are computed for various averages to indicate the variation from cycle to cycle. A number of other measures, such as lags, leads, conformity, etc., are computed.

The method of the National Bureau is perhaps best illustrated by reproducing the sample chart that gives the typical patterns in coke production,

Chart 16.7 REFERENCE AND SPECIFIC CYCLE PATTERNS FOR COKE PRODUCTION

T stands for trough and *P* for peak.

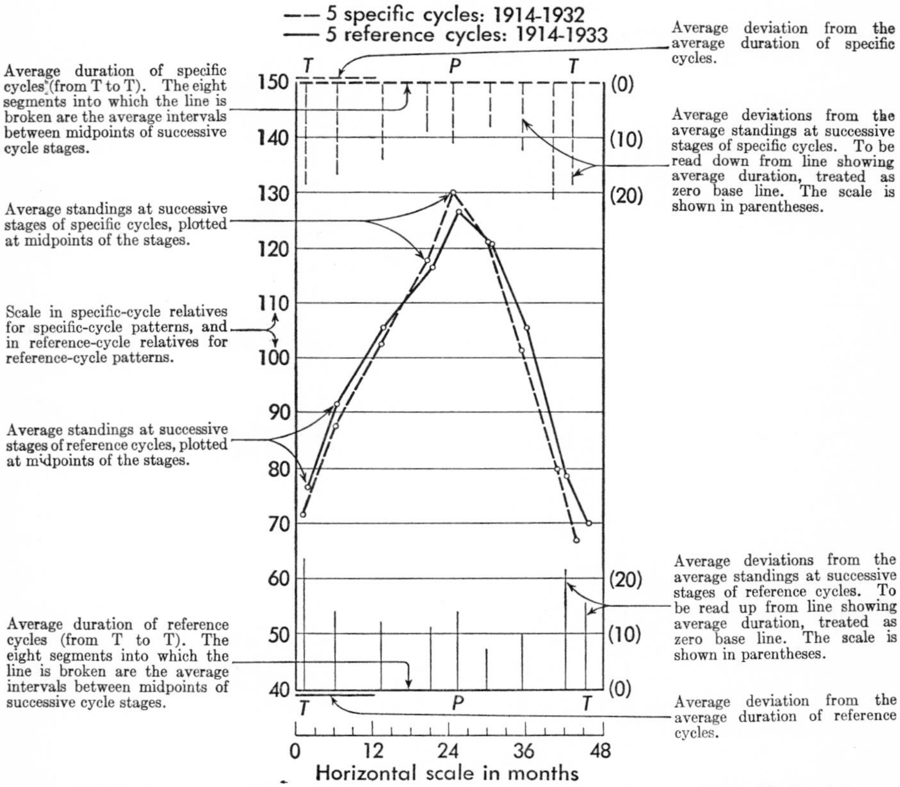

Source: Arthur F. Burns and Wesley C. Mitchell, *Measuring Business Cycles* (New York, National Bureau of Economic Research, 1946), p. 35.

1914–33 (Chart 16.7). Changes in coke production are highly correlated with those in the aggregate economic activity. As a result the specific-cycle and the reference-cycle curves are not far apart from each other. According to the solid curve, coke production typically increases from about 77 to 127 per cent of its cycle average during a typical expansion period in aggregate economic activity. It then drops rather abruptly to about 71 at the end. While the solid curve refers to the reference cycles, the broken curve represents the specific cycles. The vertical lines at the top and bottom of the chart show the mean deviations of the individual cycle standing in each stage. They show considerable variation from cycle to cycle in most series.

16.3. IS THERE A SIGNIFICANT OSCILLATING PATTERN?

To learn whether there is a pattern of alternating highs and lows, we can test whether the data move consecutively in the same direction significantly more often than would be the case with independent observations moving at random. Our main concern is with the persistence of movements in one and the same direction. We can test whether or not the duration of suc-

Table 16.11   FIRST DIFFERENCES TEST FOR SEASONAL PATTERN
(Monthly shell eggs cold-storage holdings in million cases, 1948–54.)

Year and Month	Original Data	Sign	Year and Month	Original Data	Sign	Year and Month	Original Data	Sign
1	2	3	1	2	3	1	2	3
1948 Jan.	0.20		May	2.15		Sept.	2.17	−
Feb.	0.27	+	June	3.41	+	Oct.	1.71	−
Mar.	0.37	+	July	3.67	+	Nov.	1.00	−
Apr.	1.17	+	Aug.	3.16	−	Dec.	0.39	−
May	3.09	+	Sept.	2.56	−	1953 Jan.	0.15	−
June	4.90	+	Oct.	1.56	−	Feb.	0.12	−
July	5.77	+	Nov.	0.50	−	Mar.	0.25	+
Aug.	5.52	−	Dec.	0.06	−	Apr.	0.38	+
Sept.	4.61	−	1951 Jan.	0.03	−	May	0.82	+
Oct.	3.79	−	Feb.	0.08	+	June	1.43	+
Nov.	1.68	−	Mar.	0.16	+	July	1.51	+
Dec.	0.44	−	Apr.	0.31	+	Aug.	1.20	−
1949 Jan.	0.16	−	May	0.97	+	Sept.	0.83	−
Feb.	0.15	−	June	2.08	+	Oct.	0.49	−
Mar.	0.14	−	July	2.43	+	Nov.	0.29	−
Apr.	0.53	+	Aug.	2.27	−	Dec.	0.14	−
May	0.95	+	Sept.	1.61	−	1954 Jan.	0.09	−
June	1.94	+	Oct.	0.96	−	Feb.	0.08	−
July	2.29	+	Nov.	0.53	−	Mar.	0.14	+
Aug.	1.94	−	Dec.	0.23	−	Apr.	0.44	+
Sept.	1.43	−	1952 Jan.	0.14	−	May	0.72	+
Oct.	0.81	−	Feb.	0.24	+	June	1.31	+
Nov.	0.50	−	Mar.	0.94	+	July	1.64	+
Dec.	0.25	−	Apr.	1.60	+	Aug.	1.44	−
1950 Jan.	0.11	−	May	2.18	+	Sept.	1.03	−
Feb.	0.38	+	June	3.18	+	Oct.	0.83	−
Mar.	0.74	+	July	3.36	+	Nov.	0.63	−
Apr.	1.30	+	Aug.	2.73	−	Dec.	0.32	−
		+						

Source: Table 16.2.

cessive upturns and downturns, as measured by the sequence of like signs in the first differences between successive observations, is significantly different from a random pattern. A sequence of identical signs, followed and preceded either by a different sign or no sign at all, is called a *run*. (In addition to runs of signs there are also runs of letters.) If there is a systematically oscillating pattern, be it periodic or cyclical, positive and negative signs are likely to occur in bunches, and we have reasonably long runs of like signs. In a random pattern few like signs will tend to follow one another and we have short runs.

If we look at the monthly cold-storage holdings of shell eggs in Table 16.11 we find in early 1948 that cold storage holdings increased for six successive months before they reached their peak on July 1. Thereafter, holdings declined for eight successive months until they reached a trough on March 1, 1949. Between the July, 1948, peak and the March, 1949, trough we have eight negative first differences or minus signs. We might say that the first full phase of our storage data extended over eight months. Eight is the number of intervals (months) between the first set of successive turning points. Likewise, we find that four is the number in the second set of turning points, and so on.

The first step in the test for an oscillating pattern involves a listing in order of the signs of the first differences between successive items. Let us do this for the monthly shell egg cold-storage holdings in 1948–54 given in Table 16.11. The runs can be summarized as follows:

$$+ + + + + + | - - - - - - - - | + + + + | - - - - - - | + + + + + + |$$
$$\quad 6 \qquad\qquad 8 \qquad\qquad 4 \qquad\quad 6 \qquad\qquad 6$$

$$- - - - - - | + + + + + + | - - - - - - | + + + + + + | - - - - - - - |$$
$$\quad 6 \qquad\qquad 6 \qquad\qquad 6 \qquad\qquad 6 \qquad\qquad 7$$

$$+ + + + + | - - - - - - - | + + + + + | - - - - - .$$
$$\quad 5 \qquad\qquad 7 \qquad\qquad 5 \qquad\quad 5$$

The first six pluses and the last five minuses do not represent a complete run. This leaves us with twelve complete runs, Ru. In total we have seventy-two first differences and signs, always one less than the total number of observations, n.

The details of the test are as follows:

1. The null hypothesis is that the data do not conform to an oscillating pattern; and the alternative hypothesis is that there are fewer runs than indicated by the null hypothesis so that the data conform to an oscillating pattern.

2. The statistic is about normally distributed. On the basis of an α of 0.05 we

reject the null hypothesis if $z < -1.64$,

and accept the null hypothesis if $z > -1.64$.

3.

$$z \doteq \frac{3Ru - 2n + 2.5}{\sqrt{\dfrac{16n - 29}{10}}} \tag{16.1}$$

$$= \frac{3(12) - 2(73) + 2.5}{\sqrt{\dfrac{16(73) - 29}{10}}} = -10.$$

4. With the z value of our sample data smaller than -1.64 we reject the null hypothesis and conclude that the data conform to an oscillating pattern.

There are more tests of this sort, although it appears that the two that we have given suffice for our purposes. Likewise, we consider a discussion of the limitations of this and other test beyond the scope of our efforts.

WHAT WE HAVE LEARNED:

1. Monthly data often need editing before they can be properly deseasonalized or before a seasonal index can be computed.

2. By editing the data we can adjust for peculiarities of the calendar, i.e., months of differing length, floating holidays, etc.

3. When the seasonal pattern changes abruptly, it may become necessary to divide the series into two.

4. With the help of a significance test it becomes possible to decide with a known confidence whether there is a pattern of alternating highs and lows.

5. A fast, although crude, method for finding the seasonal variation is the simple average method for finding the seasonal index. Its application calls for calculating the means of all 12 months, adjusting each mean for trend, and computing an index number for each of the 12 months.

6. The ratio to moving average method for finding the seasonal index is perhaps the most commonly used and most adequate method presently available. This method calls for the use of 12-month moving averages, their centering, averaging, and the computing of an index.

7. Cyclical variations can be isolated by dividing original, unadjusted data by trend and seasonal variations and then smoothing out the smaller irregularities.

8. In addition to isolating cyclical variations, there is much interest in measuring typical cyclical behavior; one such method has been presented.

CAN YOU FIND SEASONAL PATTERNS AND ISOLATE CYCLES?

1. The following are residential construction contract data for the Eighth Federal Reserve District (in million dollars):

	'45	'46	'47	'48	'49	'50	'51	'52	53	'54
Jan.	0.6	3.9	12.5	15.5	8.3	19.0	23.8	15.1	19.7	22.7
Feb.	0.7	4.8	9.1	9.2	11.4	14.5	25.4	24.8	26.8	24.8
Mar.	1.7	10.7	7.1	14.8	15.8	23.8	38.3	30.5	33.8	30.1
April	3.5	18.8	14.9	16.5	15.9	33.3	28.6	57.6	40.1	41.0
May	3.8	15.2	15.9	17.6	18.8	41.4	38.7	49.6	35.9	37.5
June	2.2	20.2	14.3	16.8	22.1	32.7	28.7	40.8	21.4	37.3
July	3.0	17.4	11.9	26.1	20.6	33.0	31.8	33.0	28.2	45.3
Aug.	2.8	12.3	13.7	19.5	21.5	39.6	38.4	32.6	32.9	39.9
Sept.	2.3	9.7	17.2	16.8	24.0	45.3	25.9	20.3	25.8	53.1
Oct.	1.9	11.3	21.4	17.3	23.0	28.3	30.3	28.4	38.4	36.5
Nov.	3.0	11.3	15.8	15.2	20.4	22.0	26.1	23.5	22.0	31.5
Dec.	4.5	8.3	13.1	13.7	26.0	17.5	26.8	36.3	23.1	57.1

    a. Plot the time series as a line chart.
    b. Using an α of 0.05, is there a significant trend?
    c. Using an α of 0.05, is there a significant seasonal pattern?
    d. Find the semiaverage trend fit.
    e. Find the least squares fit.
    f. With the help of the simple average method, find the seasonal index.
    g. Using the residual method for finding cyclical variations, isolate the cycle.
    h. With the help of the ratio to moving average method for finding the seasonal index find the seasonal index, and applying the residual method for finding cyclical variations isolate the cycle.
2. Discuss the purpose of selecting a positional mean in seasonal analyses.
3. Explain how in the ratio to moving-average method for finding the seasonal index an adjustment for trend is made.
4. The following are index numbers of seasonal variation of pork production and prices received by farmers for hogs in the postwar period:

Month	Production	Price
Jan.	130	96
Feb.	94	98
Mar.	97	100
Apr.	91	96
May	94	96
Jun.	97	99
Jul.	85	106
Aug.	79	108
Sept.	78	111
Oct.	99	104
Nov.	120	95
Dec.	136	91

Source: Frederick V. Waugh, *Graphic Analysis* (Washington, D.C., U.S. Department of Agriculture, 1955), p. 23.

    a. Make line charts of the two series using the same piece of graph paper.
    b. Examining your charts, what economic conclusions do you reach?
    c. Describe three problems where knowledge of the index of seasonal variations of pork production can prove invaluable.

XVII

Association Among Qualitative Data

17.1. CHI-SQUARE ANALYSIS

Not infrequently we are interested in the relationship between phenomena that are different in nature rather than in degree, or in which the degree of difference cannot readily be quantified. For instance, a recent A.P. dispatch stated that two psychologists reported to the British Association for the Advancement of Science, that fat boys show less suspicion and resentment than thin boys. Least squares analysis cannot be applied to suspicion and resentment, since such data are not readily quantified. If the data are qualitative in nature a rank correlation analysis can sometimes be successfully applied. In other cases a *chi-square* analysis can prove appropriate.

Let us see how the chi-square method is used in the following example:

Avocados were introduced to this country fairly recently. The avocado industry has, therefore, been engaged in a publicity campaign designed to acquaint more people with its product and break down some of the resistance to the taste and texture of the alligator pear. The growers would like to concentrate their efforts on that region of the United States where the fine qualities of this fruit are likely to be most appreciated as a new addition to the diet.

One problem this raises is whether acceptance of avocados is related to geographical areas. Suppose that an appropriate probability sample of people in the East, West, and Midwest were visited, given avocados, and their reactions ascertained, which were then classified as like, indifferent, or dislike. The results of the survey are presented in Table 17.1.

A first examination of Table 17.1 will leave most of us uncertain as to whether acceptance of the avocado as a new fruit is related to geographical

354

areas. However, the chi-square test helps to shed light on the question. Here is the philosophy underlying this test:

If we knew the cell frequencies that could be expected in the absence of any relationship between the two variates, could we not compare this *expected frequency* and the *observed frequency* of each cell, and after subtracting the first from the second, test whether this difference is significantly different

Table 17.1 THREE-BY-THREE TABLE
(Like and dislike for avocados in different geographical areas.)

	Like	Indifferent	Dislike	Row Totals
East	240	170	20	430
West	100	100	50	250
Midwest	140	170	10	320
Column totals	480	440	80	

Source: Hypothetical data.

Table 17.2 CONTINGENCY TABLE OF EXPECTED FREQUENCIES

	A_1	A_2	A_3	A_4	A_b	Row Totals
B_1	e_{11}	e_{12}	e_{13}	e_{14}	e_{1b}	$e_1.$
B_2	e_{21}	e_{22}	e_{23}	e_{24}	e_{2b}	$e_2.$
B_3	e_{31}	e_{32}	e_{33}	e_{34}	e_{3b}	$e_3.$
B_4	e_{41}	e_{42}	e_{43}	e_{44}	e_{4b}	$e_4.$
B_b	e_{a1}	e_{a2}	e_{a3}	e_{a4}	e_{ab}	$e_a.$
Column totals	$e._1$	$e._2$	$e._3$	$e._4$	$e._b$	

from zero? That is what we will do. We will first find for each cell the frequency that we could expect under the assumption that the two variates are altogether unrelated. We will call these the *expected frequencies* of each cell, or for short e_{ij}, where subscript i refers to the row and j to the column to which the respective cell belongs.

Theoretically, with A and B the two variates and A_1, A_2, A_3, A_4, . . . , A_a and B_1, B_2, B_3, B_4, . . . , B_b categories into which variates A and B are subdivided, respectively, we can conceive of the following *contingency table* of expected frequencies. The total of the first row is denoted as e_1. In general the total of the ith row will be e_i. Also, the total of the jth column will be e_j (see Table 17.2).

Similarly, we can conceive of the following contingency table of *observed* frequencies, where the total of the first row is denoted as n_1. The total of the ith row would be n_i, the total of the jth column e_j, and the grand total, the size of the sample, n (see Table 17.3).

Table 17.3   CONTINGENCY TABLE OF OBSERVED FREQUENCIES

	A_1	A_2	A_3	A_4	A_b	Row Totals
B_1	n_{11}	n_{12}	n_{13}	n_{14}	n_{1b}	$n_{1.}$
B_2	n_{21}	n_{22}	n_{23}	n_{24}	n_{2b}	$n_{3.}$
B_3	n_{31}	n_{32}	n_{33}	n_{34}	n_{3b}	$n_{3.}$
B_4	n_{41}	n_{42}	n_{43}	n_{44}	n_{4b}	$n_{4.}$
B_b	n_{a1}	n_{a2}	n_{a3}	n_{a4}	n_{ab}	$n_{a.}$
Column totals	$n_{.1}$	$n_{.2}$	$n_{.3}$	$n_{.4}$	$n_{.b}$	n

In our example,

$$A_1 = \text{Like avocados}$$
$$A_2 = \text{Indifferent to avocados}$$
$$A_3 = \text{Dislike avocados}$$
$$B_1 = \text{East}$$
$$B_2 = \text{West}$$
$$B_3 = \text{Midwest.}$$

For instance, e_{32} indicates how many people of our sample we could expect to find indifferent to avocados in the Midwest, on the assumption that there was no relation between where people live and their like or dislike of avocados. n_{32} would be the corresponding observed frequency; in our example $n_{32} = 170$.

Before comparing the n_{ij}'s and e_{ij}'s, let us see how we can calculate the e_{ij}'s. In Table 17.4 we left the cells blank, putting down only the row and column totals. To fill in expected frequencies we could make use of the multiplication law of probabilities, which the reader will remember from Chapter V. We know from the totals of our table that $430/1,000$ or 43 per cent of our sample consisted of Easterners. Similarly, the percentage of those who like avocados is $480/1,000$ or 48 per cent. Assuming that location and acceptance are independent, i.e., that the two variates are unrelated, we multiply 0.43 by 0.48, which is 0.206. Multiplying this percentage by the sample size 1,000 we conclude that we could expect to find in our sample 206 Easterners who like avocados, $e_{11} = 206$.[1]

---

[1] In practice we would find the expected frequency of 206 by multiplying $\dfrac{430}{1,000}$ by 480.

We can do the same for all e_{ij}'s, making use of the formula that $e_{ij} =$

$$\frac{(n_j)(n_i)}{n}. \tag{17.1}$$

Using this formula, we find that the expected number of Westerners in our sample who like avocados is

$$e_{21} = \frac{(480)(250)}{1,000} \text{ or } 120.$$

Table 17.4 CONTINGENCY TABLE WITH ROW AND COLUMN TOTALS

	Like	*Indifferent*	*Dislike*	*Row Totals*
East				430
West				250
Midwest				320
Column totals	480	440	80	

Source: Table 17.1.

We could also use Formula 17.1 to calculate the expected frequency of Midwesterners liking avocados. But we can save ourselves some work by remembering that both expected and actual total frequencies are the same. 480 people are known to have liked avocados. The expected frequencies of the Easterners was calculated to be 206 and that of the Westerners 120. That of the Midwesterners is $480 - (206 + 120)$ or 154. In our case we could use Formula 17.1 to calculate only e_{11}, e_{12}, e_{21}, and e_{22}. All the other expected frequencies could be found by subtracting those that we have calculated from the known totals, although it is best to perform the computation both ways as a check.

In Table 17.5 we present the actual cell frequencies and, in brackets, the expected frequencies.

Let us pause and reflect for a moment before we proceed. The expected frequencies were calculated on the assumption that the two variates are unrelated. Should the observed frequencies closely agree with those we might have expected in the absence of a relationship, we will be inclined to think that the data reveal little if any correlation. The smaller the discrepancies between the n_{ij}'s and e_{ij}'s the smaller the probability that the variates are correlated; and vice versa, the greater the discrepancies the better the chances of close correlation.

To decide about the significance of the correlation of qualitative data some decision criteria and a significance test are needed. *Chi square*, χ^2, is such a criterion. It is defined as:

$$\chi^2 = \sum \frac{(n_{ij} - e_{ij})^2}{e_{ij}}. \qquad (17.2)$$

If the agreement between observed and expected data is close, χ^2 will be
small, and vice versa.   On the assumption that the two variates under
consideration are independent of one another the sampling distribution of χ^2
is closely approximated by a so-called χ^2 distribution.   While we saw that
each different sample size and p has a binomial distribution of distinct shape,
χ^2 distributions assume different shapes depending on the number of
degrees of freedom, (d.f.).

Table 17.5   CONTINGENCY TABLE OF EXPECTED AND
OBSERVED FREQUENCIES

	Like	*Indifferent*	*Dislike*	*Row Totals*
East	240 (206)	170 (189)	20 (35)	430
West	100 (120)	100 (110)	50 (20)	250
Midwest	140 (154)	170 (141)	10 (25)	320
Column totals	480	440	80	

Source: Table 17.1.

What are the degrees of freedom in a chi-square analysis?   In computing
the expected frequencies of our three-by-three table, we found that, after
calculating four of the expected cell frequencies with the help of the relation
$e_{ij} = \dfrac{(n_{.j})(n_{i.})}{n}$, the rest could be found by subtracting each calculated
expected frequency from the respective row or column totals.   If, as in our
case, four of the expected cell frequencies are calculated or known, we have
no more freedom in filling the remaining cells.   From the very beginning our
three-by-three table afforded us but four degrees of freedom.   Instead of
going through this lengthy reasoning process we can make use of the
following formula:

$$d.f. = (\text{number of columns} -1)(\text{number of rows} -1). \qquad (17.3)$$

Let us try our hand at using Formula 17.3.   For a three-by-three table,

d.f. = $(3 - 1)(3 - 1)$ or 4. For a six-by-five table, *d.f.* = $(6 - 1)(5 - 1)$ or 20. For a nine-by-seven table, *d.f.* = $(9 - 1)(7 - 1)$ or 48.

Now we are ready for the significance test. Here are the four steps applied to our example:

1. The null and alternative hypotheses:

H_o: There is no significant relationship between the place of residence of the consumer and his acceptance of avocado as a new fruit.

H_A: There is a significant relationship between these two phenomena.

2. Regions and criteria of rejection and acceptance:

After agreeing on an appropriate α and determining the number of degrees of freedom, we can look up in Table VIII of the Appendix the chi-square value corresponding to those conditions. In our example, let us agree on an α of 0.05. In a three-by-three table *d.f.* = 4, and the corresponding chi-square value is 11.14.

Therefore, we will reject H_o, in case the χ^2 value of the sample is >11.14. Otherwise, we will accept H_o.

3. Calculation of the χ^2 value of the sample data:

$$\chi^2 = \sum \frac{(n_{ij} - e_{ij})^2}{e_{ij}}$$

and has been calculated in Table 17.6 to be 79.

Table 17.6 WORK SHEET FOR CHI-SQUARE ANALYSIS
(Like and dislike for avocados in different geographical areas.)

n_{ij}	e_{ij}	$n_{ij} - e_{ij}$	$(n_{ij} - e_{ij})^2$	$\dfrac{(n_{ij} - e_{ij})^2}{e_{ij}}$
1	*2*	*3*	*4*	*5*
240	206	+34	1,160	5.63
170	189	−19	361	1.91
20	35	−15	225	6.43
100	120	−20	400	3.33
100	110	−10	100	0.909
50	20	+30	900	45.0
140	154	−14	196	1.27
170	141	+29	841	5.96
10	25	−15	225	9.00

Total: $\sum \dfrac{(n_{ij} - e_{ij})^2}{e_{ij}}$ 79

Source: Table 17.5.

4. We conclude, therefore, that since the calculated χ^2 value is larger than 11.14, we are forced to reject H_o.[2] Neglecting the error of Type II, we reach the conclusion that, on the basis of an α of 0.05, the acceptance of avocados is related to the geographical area in which the consumer lives.

To pass judgment on how close is the relationship between these qualitative data, we can make use of the chi-square to find a relative measure of association, the *contingency coefficient*.

The contingency coefficient

$$C = \sqrt{\frac{\chi^2}{\chi^2 + n}},\qquad(17.4)$$

where n is the sample size. In our example $C = \sqrt{\dfrac{79}{79 + 1,000}} = 0.27$.

The contingency coefficient can be interpreted in about the same way we interpret the least squares correlation coefficient. However, there is one major difference: while the maximum value of r is in all cases 1.0, the contingency coefficient of small contingency tables can never be that large. For instance, in case of a three-by-three table C can never be larger than 0.816, which in turn can be interpreted as perfect correlation. The C for a two-by-two table cannot exceed 0.707 and that for a four-by-four-table 0.866.[3] While there are significance tests for contingency coefficients, we consider them beyond the scope of our efforts.

We will apply chi-square analysis to another example. The McCall Corporation made a qualitative study of magazines in 1946. In one aspect of this study, a sample of women, who had indicated an interest in home management and home decoration and in whose houses copies of specified magazines were found, were asked whether they were keenly interested in receiving certain magazines. The results of this survey are given in Table 17.7 (data not in brackets) and we will test whether, on the basis of an α of 0.10, interest in these eight magazines is significantly related to the women's marital status. Here is the test:

1. Our null hypothesis is that there is no significant relationship between marital status and interest in these eight magazines. The alternative hypothesis is that there is a significant relation.

2. With $(8 - 1)(3 - 1)$ or 14 degrees of freedom the critical χ^2 value for an α of 0.10 is 23.68 (see Table VIII in the Appendix). We will reject H_o, in case χ^2 of the sample is > 23.68. Otherwise, we will accept H_o.

[2] It is important to realize that the chi-square test is applicable only in cases where the values of the individual expected cell frequencies exceed four.

[3] For a table having the same number of columns as rows, the maximum value of C can be computed with the help of the following formula: $\sqrt{\dfrac{\text{number of columns} - 1}{\text{number of columns}}}$.

3. To find the χ^2 value of the sample data we start by computing the expected frequencies for the 24 cells of the eight-by-three contingency table. Assuming, for instance, that interest in the specified magazine is correlated with women's marital status, we would expect to find $598/7,037 \times 5,544/7,037 \times 7,037$, or 471, women interested in receiving *The American*

Table 17.7 CONTINGENCY TABLE OF EXPECTED AND
OBSERVED FREQUENCIES
(Interest in magazines by women of differing marital status.)

	Married	*Single*	*Widowed*	*Row Totals*
The American Home	493 [471]	53 [70]	52 [57]	598
Better Homes and Gardens	930 [882]	81 [131]	109 [107]	1,120
Good Housekeeping	965 [979]	147 [145]	131 [119]	1,243
Ladies' Home Journal	1,030 [1,071]	183 [159]	147 [130]	1,360
McCall's Magazine	782 [803]	139 [119]	98 [97]	1,019
Redbook Magazine	310 [301]	46 [45]	26 [36]	382
Woman's Day	274 [264]	40 [39]	21 [32]	335
Woman's Home Companion	760 [772]	132 [114]	88 [94]	980
Column totals	5,544	821	672	7,037

Source: By permission from Robert Ferber, *Statistical Techniques in Market Research,* copyright 1949, McGraw-Hill Book Company, Inc., p. 271.

Home. Similar expected frequencies have been computed for all 24 cells and are presented in Table 17.7 (in brackets) together with the corresponding observed frequencies. The chi-square of these data is calculated in Table 17.8 and found to be 50.6.

4. With the calculated χ^2 substantially larger then 23.68, we are forced to reject H_o and conclude, on the basis of an α of 0.10, that interest in these eight magazines is related to the marital status of women.

The chi-square method has proved useful in many fields. For example, it helped medical science finally dispose of the old idea that a coated tongue indicates illness. Seven hundred fifty children were studied and the condition of their tongues (clean, partly furred, furred) was correlated with a large number of diseases from digestive upsets to bowlegs and obesity. No association was found, and the time is at hand when doctors will no longer ask a patient to stick out his tongue.

Table 17.8 WORK SHEET FOR CHI-SQUARE ANALYSIS
(Interest in magazines by women of differing marital status.)

n_{ij}	e_{ij}	$n_{ij} - e_{ij}$	$(n_{ij} - e_{ij})^2$	$\dfrac{(n_{ij} - e_{ij})^2}{e_{ij}}$
493	471	+22	484	1.03
930	882	+48	2,300	2.60
965	979	−14	196	0.200
1,030	1,071	−41	1,680	1.56
782	803	−21	441	0.549
310	301	+9	81	0.269
274	264	+10	100	0.379
760	772	−12	144	0.186
53	70	−17	289	4.13
81	131	−50	2,500	19.08
147	145	+2	4	0.0275
183	159	+24	576	3.623
139	119	+20	400	3.361
46	45	+1	1	0.0222
40	39	+1	1	0.0256
132	114	+18	324	2.842
52	57	−5	25	0.438
109	107	+2	4	0.0373
131	119	+12	144	1.210
147	130	+17	289	2.223
98	97	+1	1	0.0103
26	36	−10	100	2.778
21	32	−11	121	3.781
88	94	−6	36	0.383

Total: $\sum \dfrac{(n_{ij} - e_{ij})^2}{e_{ij}}$ 50.6

Source: Table 17.7.

WE KNOW:

1. Chi-square analysis makes possible the correlation of qualitative data.

2. Chi-square, $\chi^2 = \sum \dfrac{(n_{ij} - e_{ij})^2}{e_{ij}}$, where n_{ij} are the observed frequencies and e_{ij} the expected frequencies.

3. The significance of the chi-square value is tested by making comparisons with critical chi-square values relative to a given α and sample size (see Table VIII in the Appendix).

4. The closeness of the association between the qualitative data is assessed with the help of the contingency coefficient, which can be computed by the following formula:

$$C = \sqrt{\frac{x^2}{x^2 + n}}.$$

SEE WHETHER THERE IS AN ASSOCIATION:

1. Under what circumstances would you apply a least squares analysis in preference to a chi-square analysis?

2. Relate the concept of "degrees of freedom lost" in least squares correlation to that of "degrees of freedom" in chi-square analysis.

3. A representative sample of white and nonwhite families was questioned about desegregation of the school system. Assume the following to be the results of the survey:

	Strongly Oppose Desegregation	Oppose Desegregation	Indifferent	Favor Desegregation	Strongly Favor Desegregation
White	421	327	29	416	673
Nonwhite	3	20	63	74	125

a. At an α of 0.10, is there a significant difference between the attitude of the white and nonwhite population in regard to the problem of the desegregation of the school system?

b. How close is the relationship between racial background and opinions on school desegregation?

4. The Bon-Toe Shoe Company, makers of shoes for children and teen-agers, believes that children of different ages prefer different shoe styles. If such a relation exists the company would like to know about it, so that it can properly gauge its advertising and production policies. It divides children into three groups, those attending elementary school, junior high, and high school and classifies shoes as oxfords, saddle shoes, loafers, and others. A probability sample of 1,312 children is interviewed and the following results are obtained:

	Elementary School Students	Junior High School Students	High School Students
Oxfords	250	302	205
Saddle shoes	56	68	91
Loafers	13	26	112
Others	121	43	25

a. At an α of 0.05 is there a significant difference in shoe style preferences between children of different ages?

b. What is the contingency coefficient?

5. In the late spring of 1956 a probability sample of 356 high school seniors attending private, county parochial, county public, city parochial and city public high schools in the St. Louis metropolitan area were interviewed about their intention to attend college, and the following results were obtained:

	Private High Schools	County Parochial High Schools	County Public High Schools	City Parochial High Schools	City Public High Schools
Intend to attend college	14	23	79	24	28
Undecided	0	0	15	2	12
Do not intend to attend college	3	18	74	34	30

The order in which the high schools are stated reflects to some extent the financial ability of the parents of the pupils, the wealthiest families sending their children to private high schools and the poorest families relying on city public high schools.

a. With an α of 0.10, is there a significant relationship between the type of high schools attended by a pupil and his intention to go to college?

b. Compute the contingency coefficient.

XVIII

Decisions by Control Charts

Without quality control you, as a producer or purchaser, are in the same position as the man who bets on a horse race—with one exception, the odds are not posted.

F. M. STEADMAN

18.1. CHANCE VERSUS ASSIGNABLE CAUSES

Today's business executive is at the helm of increasingly complex and vast operations. Statistics, as we have shown, can assist him in gaining the proper information with the help of which his decisions can be improved and facilitated. In addition, statistics can even help relieve the executive of some decisions: statistical quality control makes it possible for the executive to delegate the responsibility for what is otherwise a very time-consuming field of managerial concern. Once a control system has been set up, its supervision becomes a mere routine and can be assigned to an assistant, who will consult with the executive only when the system is out of control.

Not only can the introduction of statistical control methods reduce the load of the executive, but it can also increase the uniformity and standardization of processes and their end products. It was the need for vast quantities of highly standardized products in World War II that give the field of statistical control its impetus. However, while the engineer has been very successful in recognizing the opportunities offered by quality control, business and economics have been slow in applying this important principle to their problems. As we will see below, statistical control methods permit the control of operations on a sample basis, a task which otherwise would prove uneconomical or outright impossible.

The kind of repetitive operation to which statistical control techniques can be applied is exemplified by a machine manufacturing large numbers of supposedly "identical" pieces—nuts, plastic discs, frames, tin cans, light bulbs, etc.   In addition to controlling the quality of manufactured items, statistical control has been used for other purposes—to control the performance of a sales force, of fleets of taxicabs and delivery trucks, to keep a running check of charge accounts, shortages in stores, orders received, consumer acceptance of new products—in short, almost any repetitive phenomenon composed of distinct units under reasonably stable conditions.

The innumerable activities in our intricate production and marketing system have in common that they change, even if only slightly.   Were we to measure the dimensions of the discs produced by a machine that operates to very high tolerances, we would find (depending upon the quality of our measuring instruments) small changes from disc to disc.   Whenever we measure the quality of a product, process, or service, we are likely to discover a stable pattern of *random* or *chance variation*.   This chance variation reflects a host of minor influences underlying a particular measurement or result we happen to obtain.   To illustrate this, we might consider the machining of a gear shaft.   There are bound to be slight differences in diameter from one angular direction to another, and from one piece to another.   The rotational speed, the depth of the cut, and pressure of the lathe will tend to vary, as will the coolant, lubrication, and angle of the holding device.   The hardness of the metal will differ from shaft to shaft and even within a particular shaft.   The measurements by the inspector will be affected by the measuring device, the presence of oil and dust on the shaft, and the angle from which the reading is made.

These forces exist even if we try as hard as humanly possible to hold all conditions constant.   Each one has only a minor effect.   All together they make for a stable pattern of variation that can be considered natural and inherent in the process and, to some extent, in the tools of measurement. This variation is said to be due to *chance* or *random causes*.

There can, however, be another type of variation, reflecting the presence of *assignable causes*, which either temporarily or permanently tend to bring about changes in the process and throw it out of kilter.   In a sense, the basic conditions and, thus, the population have changed.   In the machining of a gear shaft an assignable cause might be a new lot of castings made of harder stock than prescribed, a change in the position of the holding device, a sudden defect in the cutter, lack of lubricant, or neglect on behalf of the operator, to mention but a few.   The presence of any one of these causes could lead to an end product that is not up to standard.

If it were possible to measure each and every unit produced, we could separate the defectives from those that come up to specifications. Since this is usually either too expensive or time-consuming, and in some cases the test itself is destructive, statistical quality and performance control relies on measuring at fixed intervals, let us say every hour, a sample cluster of fixed size. On the basis of the sample information thus obtained, the null hypothesis, that the process is "in control," is tested. A decision is reached as to whether a high or low sample value obtained by the inspector is an indication of the presence of an assignable cause of change in the process, which then is sought and corrected, or whether this statistic is likely to have come about by chance alone. The basic concern of statistical control is to determine with a predetermined risk when we should declare a process out of control and seek out an assignable cause so that it can be corrected; and when to keep our hands off. This decision can be made with great speed, so that we can detect defects or mistakes soon after they have occurred and prevent their repetition.

Clearly, such a sampling plan entails two risks. First, there is the risk that an acceptable lot will yield a bad sample and we will incorrectly reject a good lot and sound a false alarm. In so doing we would commit an error of Type I, and the producer's interest would be harmed. For this reason we call this the *producer's risk*. Second, there is the risk that an inacceptable lot will yield a good sample. We may incorrectly accept a bad lot and commit an error of Type II, which would damage the interest of the buyer or consumer. This is the *consumer's risk.*

It is thus evident that by and large statistical quality and performance control is but a special case and application of statistical decision making discussed in Chapters XI and XII. A sampling plan can be developed after settling on acceptable α's and β's. Or, looking at the problem from a different angle, we can evaluate a particular sampling plan by computing the probabilities of the two types of error. A certain quality is defined as acceptable, and the probability is calculated that a lot or process of this quality would produce a sample leading to rejection. Another quality is defined as rejectable—there is a zone of comparative indifference between the acceptable and rejectable quality levels—and the probability is calculated that a lot or process of this quality will produce a sample leading to acceptance. These two probabilities measure the producer's and consumer's risks. With the help of methods developed in Chapters XI and XII, performance and power functions can be constructed.

In quality control work in the United States it is common to use an α of 0.003, i.e., a z of 3.0. While it is true that the determination of the risks that appear as acceptable should be based on the costs that can accompany errors of types I and II as well as the inspection work in each particular case, industry has preferred simplicity and standardization to a careful examination of the risks in each problem. A width of 3 standard errors is considered to constitute a conservative decision criterion, leading to merely three false alarms in a thousand, which is not excessive.

There is a very good argument in favor of conservatism. It is related to the possible skewness of the sampling distribution. We will see that some distributions are not entirely normal. The departure from normality need not be very great to change the three false alarms in a thousand to twenty or even more in a thousand.

However, we need not be unduly concerned about this danger. The nineteenth-century Russian mathematician Pafnuti Lvovitch Tchebycheff discovered a rule that is commonly referred to as *Tchebycheff's inequality*. According to this rule, regardless of how badly skewed a distribution is, not more than a fraction, $1/K^2$, of the observations in a population can lie more than K times the standard deviation away from the mean. Thus, no more than 1/9 or 11 per cent of the observations in any population can be over three standard deviations away from the mean. This rule, by the way, concerns the proportion of the observations in the population falling outside the limits $\mu \pm K\sigma$ and not the proportion in any one sample.

18.2. PROCESS CONTROL

It is common to separate statistical quality control into two distinct fields. On the one hand there is *process control*, which is designed to control the quality of a product or service being produced in many successive units. On the other hand, *acceptance sampling* verifies the quality of a product or service before being shipped or accepted.

In this section we will discuss process control, which, depending upon the objective and nature of the product, can take a number of forms. We will illustrate this by referring to the example of the Hobby-Bobby Toy Company, initially introduced in Chapter IX, which produces rubber balls. In Chapter IX we referred to control of the *attribute*, percentage of defectives, often also called *fraction defectives*. By counting the number of items that are defective, and relating this number to that of nondefectives, the company learns about its fraction defectives.

In the control of the attribute fraction defective we need to determine whether a given unit falls into one of two categories, e.g., defective versus nondefective. In instances where a unit can have more than one defect, we might want to control the number of *defects*, which is another attribute.

For instance, a rubber ball might have defects in its color, shape, firmness, finish, etc. Or, an electric shaver can have scores of different defects. While in both cases we seek to control attributes, in the first we *control fraction defectives* and in the second we *control defects*.

Table 18.1 SAMPLE LOT INSPECTION DATA ON RUBBER BALLS
(28 lots of 200 balls each.)

Sample Lot Numbers	Number Defectives	Fraction Defective
1	4	0.020
2	3	0.015
3	2	0.010
4	3	0.015
5	1	0.005
6	4	0.020
7	13	0.065
8	5	0.025
9	7	0.035
10	8	0.040
11	10	0.050
12	6	0.030
13	12	0.060
14	5	0.025
15	15	0.075
16	14	0.070
17	8	0.040
18	6	0.030
19	4	0.020
20	21	0.105
21	11	0.055
22	7	0.035
23	10	0.050
24	14	0.070
25	4	0.020
26	3	0.015
27	10	0.050
28	14	0.070
Total	224	

Source: Hypothetical data.

But our toy manufacturer has some products for which certain numerical quality characteristics need to be measured and controlled. In this connection the company would seek to *control* a *measurement*, often also referred to as variable, perhaps in terms of hundredth of an inch. For instance, the company may be manufacturing a solid rubber ball that is to be hammered by a child through a round opening in a box. If the ball is too small it will fall through the hole before the child has a chance to hit it; and if the ball is too big frustration will also ensue. The control of measurements can be one of *means* or *ranges*, although sometimes measurements can be checked as attributes and a control system of attributes may then be applied.

The p chart. In Chapter IX, when we introduced the problem of the Hobby-Bobby Toy Company in controlling the quality of its rubber balls, we considered the binomial distribution and showed how with its help we can calculate the probability of various numbers of defectives being found in a cluster of samples. Once we can do this we have the basis for setting up a control system that will tell whether, consistent with the risks that we are willing to assume, a process or performance is "in control" or "out of control." Specifically, for this purpose a *p* chart is developed that helps control the fraction defectives.

In Chapter IX, for convenience' sake, we assumed that the control system involved checking a sample lot of five rubber balls every hour. Actually, for reasons which will be discussed below, we usually prefer to work with larger sample lots. For instance, let us draw a sample lot of 200 rubber balls, count the defectives, and plot the fraction defective pertaining to this sample in the control chart. In a control chart we have percentage values on the vertical axis and on the horizontal axis we have a series of integers, beginning with 1, to represent the sequence of sample lots. Thus, in Table 18.1 we have 28 successive sample percentages, the first one being 2 per cent, since we found 4 duds among the first 200 balls tested. We have plotted these values in Chart 18.1.

Chart 18.1 *p* CHART FOR RUBBER BALL MANUFACTURER
(28 lots of 200 balls each.)

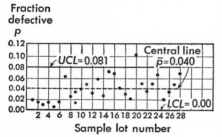

The *p* chart which controls the proportion of units that are defective in a given attribute has its theoretical basis in the *binomial distribution*, which was discussed in Chapter IX. As was noted at that time, the sampling distribution of fractions (of defectives) approximates normality when the sample is large and the fraction of defectives is not too different from that of nondefectives. For this reason among others we usually prefer to work in the control of fraction defectives with samples of 50 *su*'s or more.

Chart 18.2 portrays the relationship between a control chart and a normal distribution with p values tending to be normally distributed around the value of the parameter. At that value, or its approximation, $\bar{p}$, a *central line* is placed. The average fraction defective $\bar{p}$ is found by summing the number of defectives and dividing them by the total number inspected. For the data in Table 18.1, $\bar{p} = 224/5{,}600$ or 0.040.

As we have mentioned earlier, in most control work we use an α of 0.003 which means a z of 3.0. At $\bar{p} - 3\sigma_p$ we draw a line parallel to the central line, to delineate the *lower control limit*, *LCL*, and at $\bar{p} + 3\sigma_p$ we draw the *upper control limit*, *UCL* (see Chart 18.1).

Chart 18.2 CONTROL CHART AND NORMAL DISTRIBUTION

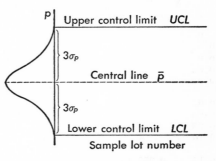

Let us reflect on this three-sigma range. If the process is in control we will nevertheless sound three false alarms in a thousand. The producer's risk is pretty small. If the parameter changes, the normal distribution will shift vertically and the probability of a sample percentage falling outside the limits is increased. In the presence of an assignable cause, there is then a given probability of finding the process "out of control." However, we might find points inside the control limits in spite of a changed parameter, and commit an error of Type II. We can quantify this risk by constructing the performance function that will have its peak at the central line value.

The control limits are $3\sigma_p$ away from the central line.

With

$$\sigma_p \doteq \sqrt{\frac{pq}{n}} \tag{9.7}$$

$$= \sqrt{\frac{(0.040)(0.960)}{200}}$$

$$= 0.0138.$$

$3\sigma_p = 0.041$ and therefore,

$$LCL_p = \bar{p} - 3\sigma_p \doteq 0.040 - 0.041 = -0.001.$$
$$UCL_p = \bar{p} + 3\sigma_p \doteq 0.040 + 0.041 = 0.081.$$

Since it is impossible to have -0.001 per cent defectives, we place the lower control limit at zero.

Examining the control chart (Chart 18.1) we find that the process had been in control all the time except when sample lot 20 was taken. At that time the process appears to have been "out of control." If a cause can be assigned and held responsible for the excessive number of defectives and this trouble is corrected, we can recalculate the central line and control limits and use the new lines as the basis for the control of future production.

Sometimes we can detect the source of the trouble by carefully analyzing the control chart. For instance, if in a manufacturing process successive

Table 18.2 PERFORMANCE FUNCTION FOR p CHART
$$(LCL_p = 0.064, \ UCL_p = 0.430, \ n = 50.)$$

π	$\sqrt{\dfrac{\pi(1-\pi)}{n}} \ \sigma_p^2 \doteq \sqrt{\dfrac{\pi(1-\pi)}{n}}$		$z \doteq \dfrac{0.430 - \pi}{\sigma_p}$	$z \doteq \dfrac{0.064 - \pi}{\sigma_p}$	β
0					0
0.01					0.002
0.02					0.02
0.03					0.07
0.04					0.14
		Based on the Poisson distribution			
0.05					0.24
0.06					0.35
0.08					0.57
0.10					0.73
0.15	0.357	0.0505	5.54	−1.70	0.95
0.25	0.433	0.0612	2.94	−3.04	0.997
0.30	0.458	0.0648	2.01	−3.64	0.98
0.35	0.477	0.0675	1.19	. . . . . .	0.88
0.40	0.490	0.0693	0.43	. . . . . .	0.67
0.43	. . . . .	. . . . . .	0	. . . . . .	0.50
0.50	0.500	0.0707	−0.99	. . . . . .	0.16
0.55	0.498	0.0704	−1.70	. . . . . .	0.04
0.60	0.490	0.0693	−2.45	. . . . . .	0.01

Source: Acheson J. Duncan, *op. cit.*, p. 266.

points on the control chart fall along an upward sloping line, the chances are that machinery or tools are gradually wearing out.

We will present one further example to illustrate the performance function in quality control. Acheson J. Duncan constructed a p chart for the production of railway-car side frames by a foundry.[1] A random sample of 50 frames was taken from each day's output and $\bar{p}$ was found to be 0.247. Thus,

$$LCL_p = 0.247 - 3\sqrt{\frac{(0.247)(0.753)}{50}} = 0.064.$$

$$UCL_p = 0.247 + 3\sqrt{\frac{(0.247)(0.753)}{50}} = 0.430.$$

[1] Acheson J. Duncan, *Quality Control and Industrial Statistics* (Homewood, Ill., Richard D. Irwin, Inc., 1953), pp. 254–268.

The consumer's risk is an important consideration in this case. The performance function is found by computing the probabilities of a sample value falling within the control limits when in fact the fraction defectives are various assumed values of π.

The method of computing the β's is by and large the same as was developed in Chapters XI and XII. However, we will not be able to use normal curve methods unless the assumed π value is larger than 0.10. Otherwise we use the Poisson distribution which will be referred to again below.

Let us illustrate the computation of β for the case of $\pi = 0.60$. Then,

$$z \doteq \frac{(p - \pi)}{\sqrt{\dfrac{\pi(1 - \pi)}{n}}} = \frac{0.430 - 0.60}{\sqrt{\dfrac{(0.247)(0.753)}{50}}} = -2.8.$$

Less than 1 per cent falls into the area of acceptance, i.e., β is about zero.

Results of similar computations for other assumed π values are presented in Table 18.2, while for π values of 0.10 or less only the results (based on the Poisson distribution) are given. The performance function is plotted in Chart 18.3, and the fact that it is not symmetrical can be explained in part by the skewness of the sampling distribution.

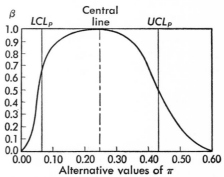

Chart 18.3 PERFORMANCE FUNCTION FOR p CHART
($LCL_p = 0.064$, $UCL_p = 0.430$, $n = 50$.)

Source: Table 18.2.

Control of defects. In the control of fraction defectives, we are concerned with the percentage of the units in a given production or marketing process that do not come up to standard. When the unit itself can be subdivided into subunits, each one either coming up to standard or not coming up to standard, we might want to *control defects*. For instance, a mail-order company stocks its merchandise in different departments according to type of merchandise. The order system uses a ticket for each catalog number order. The order is scheduled after a ticket is placed for each item on the customer's order slip. The individual items are selected by departments, which send them by conveyor belt to a checking station prior to the final consolidation in the shipping department. Since many persons participate in the filling of this multi-item order, there are many opportunities for errors. The mail-order company cannot be satisfied with controlling the percentage of orders that are incorrectly filled. An incorrectly filled order may contain one error or many.   Thus, the mail-order house would be interested in controlling the number of errors per order.   It would wish to control the attribute: number of errors (or defects) and apply a *c chart*.

The *c* chart is based on the *Poisson distribution*, which we owe to the work of the nineteenth-century French mathematician Simeon Poisson.   This distribution is applicable in cases where the probability of success is either very high or very low.   A detailed discussion of the *c* chart and its construction can be found in books referred to in Footnote 2, this chapter.

Control of means and $\bar{x}$ chart.   So far we have discussed charts to control attributes, be they fraction defectives or defects.   In many processes we want to control measurements, i.e., mean or range.

We will discuss the control of means and the $\bar{x}$ chart in relation to the problem of controlling the performance of a department store's sales force. In writing a sales check and filling an order a salesman can make more than a dozen different types of mistakes, some of them entailing substantial financial losses to the company.   For this reason department stores have shown a desire to control the mean loss per sale.   To accomplish this, every 2 hours a sample cluster of 15 sales, let us say, is checked and the magnitude of the mistake is recorded in cents.   In Table 18.3 the means and ranges of 22 successive sample clusters are presented.   We next compute the central line by adding the 22 sample means and dividing by 22.

$$\bar{m} = \frac{\Sigma m}{n}$$

$$= -\frac{33}{22} = -1.5.$$

We will take this value, at least tentatively, as our approximation of the population mean and location of the central line.

To obtain the upper and lower control limits we must find $3\sigma_{\bar{x}}$, which is arrived at after calculating the mean range, $\bar{R}$, and reading from Table IX in the Appendix A_2, the factor for control limits of means.

In brief,

$$3\sigma_{\bar{x}} = A_2\bar{R}. \tag{18.1}$$

For 15 *su*'s in a sample lot, $A_2 = 0.223$; and from Table 18.3 we find that the mean range

$$\bar{R} = \frac{\Sigma R}{n} = \frac{458}{22} = 21.$$

Thus,

$$3\sigma_{\bar{x}} = A_2\bar{R} = 0.223(21) = 4.7.$$
$$LCL_{\bar{x}} = \bar{m} - 3\sigma_{\bar{x}} = -1.5 - 4.7 = -6.2.$$
$$UCL_{\bar{x}} = \bar{m} + 3\sigma_{\bar{x}} = -1.5 + 4.7 = 3.2.$$

Table 18.3 MEANS AND RANGES OF MISTAKES MADE BY THE SALES FORCE OF A DEPARTMENT STORE IN CENTS, 22 SAMPLE CLUSTERS OF 15 SALES EACH

Sample Cluster Number	Mean	Range
1	−6	22
2	4	32
3	0	23
4	1	15
5	−4	18
6	−7	14
7	3	18
8	1	25
9	2	10
10	−7	35
11	−5	10
12	2	18
13	3	24
14	−7	16
15	1	26
16	−4	22
17	−6	14
18	1	25
19	4	15
20	−5	37
21	3	24
22	−7	15
Total	−33	458

Drawing the center line and the control limits into the control chart, we find that not all points are within the control limits (see Chart 18.4). If we can find an "assignable cause" and eliminate the source of the trouble we would then neglect these points, recalculate the central line and control limits, and use the revised chart for future decisions.

Control of variability and R chart. Although the $\bar{x}$ chart helps control variability to some extent, sometimes special control charts for variability are used. Variability is measured in terms of the range, R, and the

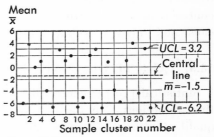

Chart 18.4 $\bar{x}$ CHART FOR MISTAKES MADE BY THE SALES FORCE OF A DEPARTMENT STORE, IN CENTS (22 Sample clusters of 15 sales each.)

Source: Table 18.3.

R chart reflects variations in the ranges of samples. In a few instances the standard deviation is used in place of the range. The sampling distribution of ranges is not normal; it has some positive skewness. Nevertheless, when the samples are reasonably large it works well to use $3\sigma_R$ limits about the average range as control limits. Only if the samples are small will the skewness cause difficulties. Under such conditions the lower control limit can become negative. Since the range value cannot logically be negative we set the lower control limit in such a case at zero.

Chart 18.5 R CHART FOR MIS-
TAKES MADE BY THE SALES
FORCE OF A DEPARTMENT
STORE, IN CENTS
(22 sample clusters of 15 sales each.)

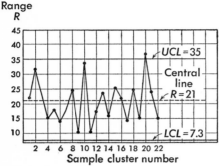

Source: Table 18.3.

The construction of the R chart is greatly facilitated when we make use of factors for control limits of ranges presented in Table IX of the Appendix. We will demonstrate their use in relation to the department store performance data given in Table 18.3, where the mean range, $\bar{R}$, was found to be 21. Therefore, we place the central line of our R chart at 21.

$$LCL_R = \bar{R} - 3\sigma_R = D_3\bar{R} \qquad (18.2)$$

and

$$UCL_R = \bar{R} + 3\sigma_R = D_4\bar{R}. \qquad (18.3)$$

With 15 su's in each sample lot $D_3 = 0.348$ and $D_4 = 1.652$. Therefore, we find

$$LCL_R = 0.348(21) = 7.3, \text{ and}$$
$$UCL_R = 1.652(21) = 35.$$

The R chart is presented in Chart 18.5, where we find that the performance of the sales force was "out of control" twice during the period of the 22 control readings. As with other control charts, we could seek an assignable cause and in case it is found, adjust the chart.

18.3. TAKE IT OR LEAVE IT—ACCEPTANCE SAMPLING

Statistical process control discussed so far may be considered to fulfill three functions. In the first place, it helps specify the performance or quality that exists as well as that which we consider appropriate. In addition, statistical process control, whether of attributes or measurements, is an important instrument in obtaining the performance or quality goal once it has been set.   Finally, it makes it possible to decide with a predetermined or assessable risk whether or not the goal has been attained.   However, at many points in our complicated production and marketing channels, it becomes necessary to decide whether a given shipment comes up to specifications and can be accepted.   Before accepting a shipment and paying for it, *acceptance sampling* can play an important role.

The reasons for having to decide whether to accept a shipment on the basis of sampling information (in preference to a complete canvas) are all too clear.   In most cases sampling provides answers much faster and is much less expensive.   If the test is destructive, sampling is the only means.

We will not concern ourselves with the problems and methods of acceptance sampling, except to indicate briefly three of the main methods: the *single-sampling plan, double-sampling plan, and sequential sampling plan.*[2]

In the *single-sample* plan we decide on the proper sample size and calculate the number of defective units that will delineate regions of rejection and acceptance.   If a smaller number of defectives is found than the critical number, the entire lot is accepted and assumed to come up to standards. In the opposite case the lot is rejected.

In order to give the lot a second chance, double sampling is often relied upon.   To begin with, a relatively small sample—smaller than in the single-sample plan—is taken and critical c_1 and c_2 values are computed. If the sample produces less than c_1 defective units, the lot is unequivocally accepted; if it produces more than c_2 defective units, the lot is rejected. However, if somewhere between c_1 and c_2 defectives are contained in the lot, a second sample is taken.   This second sample is larger than the first.   If after the second sample has been taken the combined number of defectives in the two samples is c_2 or smaller, the lot is accepted; otherwise it is rejected.

Perhaps the most recent addition to the arsenal of acceptance sampling plans is *sequential sampling*, a technique closely associated with the name of the late Abraham Wald.   In sequential sampling we do not determine the size of the sample in advance.   Instead, we decide after each sample observation or group of observations whether to accept, to reject, or to reserve judgment and continue sampling until a decision is finally reached. Very often, the final decision is reached after fewer samples have been taken than would be needed by a single- or double-sampling plan.

[2] A detailed discussion of acceptance sampling can be found in A. J. Duncan, *Quality Control and Industrial Statistics* (Homewood, Ill., Richard D. Irwin, Inc., 1953), pp. 131–240, and E. L. Grant, *Statistical Quality Control*, 2d ed. (New York, McGraw-Hill Book Company, 1952), pp. 285–437.   For a discussion of sequential sampling with possible applications to business research, see Robert Ferber, *Statistical Techniques in Market Research* (New York, McGraw-Hill Book Company, 1949) pp. 155–183.

WHAT YOU LEARNED:

1. Statistical quality and performance control is the application of statistical decision-making to distinguish between chance variation, on the one hand, and assignable variation, on the other.   Process control is designed to control the quality of a product or service as it is produced, while acceptance sampling verifies the quality of a product or service before it is shipped or accepted.

2. Chance variation is inherent in every process and it reflects the host of minor influences underlying a particular measurement that we happen to obtain.   It follows a stable pattern, closely approximating a normal distribution.

3. Assignable variation is caused by a distinct change in the process.   It constitutes a change in the population.

4. With the help of a control system it becomes possible to decide with a predetermined risk of being wrong whether assignable causes are present.

5. In quality and performance control we test the null hypothesis that the process is "in control," i.e., that no assignable causes are present.

6. The null hypothesis in quality and performance control is tested with the help of a control chart, with a central line placed at a value approximating the parameter and a lower and upper control limit, respectively, 3 standard errors away from that line.

7. By using a width of three standard errors to constitute the producer's risk, the manufacturer subjects himself to three false alarms in a thousand in the long run, in case the sampling distribution is normal.   A performance function can be derived reflecting the consumer's risk.

8. p charts have been developed to control fraction defectives.

9. In case the unit can have a number of defects we can apply a c chart, which is used to control defects.

10. The $\bar{x}$ chart is useful if the mean of a quality characteristic of units produced is to be controlled.

11. To control the range of a quality characteristic we employ the R chart.

12. To set up a control chart we usually check sample lots of fixed size at fixed intervals, and plot the statistics on a chart that has along its vertical axis the units in which the statistic is recorded and along its horizontal axis the number of sample lots.   After a number of sample lots have been inspected, values for the central line and lower and upper control limits are computed and these three lines are drawn into the scatter diagram or line chart.   In case all observations lie within the control limits, this control chart is ready for use to control the process in the future, assuming that past specifications are retained.   If one or more observations lie outside the limits, assignable causes are sought and, if found and corrected, the central line and lower and upper control limits can be recalculated and used.

13. In acceptance sampling the objective is to decide with a predetermined risk whether the quality of a population of completed products comes up to a predetermined standard or not.

14. Three methods of acceptance sampling have been developed: the single-sampling plan, double-sampling plan, and sequential-sampling plan.

SEE WHETHER THE PROCESS IS "IN CONTROL."

1. The following data pertaining to incandescent lamps represent the average life and range for 32 sample lots of 5 lamps each, with the data given in hours:

Sample Lot Number	$\bar{x}$	R	Sample Lot Number	$\bar{x}$	R
1	1,080	420	17	1,270	420
2	1,390	670	18	1,580	470
3	1,460	180	19	1,560	650
4	1,380	320	20	750	580
5	1,090	70	21	1,200	590
6	1,230	690	22	1,080	360
7	1,370	950	23	1,730	190
8	1,310	380	24	1,170	310
9	1,630	1,080	25	1,260	760
10	2,120	350	26	1,420	340
11	1,230	580	27	1,290	160
12	1,600	680	28	1,500	360
13	2,290	470	29	1,210	940
14	2,050	270	30	1,940	540
15	1,580	170	31	760	670
16	1,510	670	32	1,150	480

Source: Warren R. Purcell, "Saving Time in Testing Life," *Industrial Quality Control*, p. 16 (March, 1947).

   a. Use the first 20 sample lots to set up an $\bar{x}$ chart and plot the next 12 sets of data to see if the process continues "in control."

   b. Plot the performance function based upon the data of the first 20 lots.

   c. Use the first 20 sample lots to set up an R chart and plot the next 12 data to see if the process is "in control."

   d. What is the null hypothesis and the alternative hypothesis that are being tested?

   e. What different aspects of the quality of lamps is controlled by the $\bar{x}$ chart and which by the R chart?

2. The National Providence and Confidence Trust Company considers the percentage of checks exceeding \$1,000 a sensitive indication of the status of capital spending in the community. The bank examines the first 400 checks that reach it on the eighth and sixteenth business days of the month. The following are the percentages of checks in excess of \$1,000 found by the bank during the first year of checking:

Sample Number	Per Cent of Checks in Excess of $1,000	Sample Number	Per Cent of Checks in Excess of $1,000
1	1.00	13	0.75
2	0.50	14	4.50
3	2.50	15	2.25
4	3.00	16	2.00
5	0.75	17	1.75
6	0.25	18	3.00
7	4.75	19	3.50
8	3.50	20	0.50
9	1.25	21	1.75
10	2.50	22	2.75
11	1.75	23	4.00
12	3.75	24	2.75

a. Use the first 18 samples to set up a p chart and plot the next 6 data to see whether capital spending continues "in control."

b. Based on all 24 data, construct a p chart to see whether capital spending is "in control" or "out of control."

c. Draw the performance function for all 24 data.

d. Would you expect the sampling distribution of p's to be normal or not? Why?

3. Discuss the difference between statistical process control and statistical decision making developed in Chapters XI and XII.

4. Assume that the trouble causing some readings to lie outside the limits of Chart 18.1 have been corrected and compute the adjusted central line and lower and upper control limits.

XIX

The Statistician in the Age of Electronics

Oh, the years we waste and the tears we waste
And the work of our head and hand . . .
RUDYARD KIPLING

19.1. 16,600 ADDITIONS A SECOND

In 1956 the contract negotiations between the steel industry and the AFL-CIO United Steel workers were of especially great complexity. It was reported in the press that both sides used research staffs and electronic computers to analyze every item discussed. Electronic computing devices were employed in making intricate calculations involving a myriad of job classifications in an industry requiring highly developed techniques.

This is only one of an increasing number of examples which show that executives in business, as well as labor leaders and high government officials, are availing themselves of the assistance of high-speed automatic data processing machines. Only a few years ago, a well-known mathematician remarked with regard to meteorological data processing: "Even if we had all the necessary information about today's weather today, it would take us two weeks to carry out all the calculations needed to predict tomorrow's weather from that information." Similarly, before the availability of high-speed computers, management frequently had to act without the benefit of certain types of data, because it took too long to process them.

Electronic computation may, in a way, be looked upon as automation for a certain part of the work of management. The uses of electronic computers in business and industry are numerous, but usually they can be

381

divided into two main ones.   On the one hand, there is the high-speed processing of business data to provide management early with information of broad scope and facilitate its task of decision-making.   For instance, a large electrical manufacturer recently set up an electronic data-processing center in its home office.   The large electronic computer was installed and linked by special Western Union wires with the company's plants, sales offices, and warehouses in fifty-one cities throughout the United States. This computing system makes it possible for all offices to feed their business transactions data by wire into the center and have them processed there at enormous speeds.   Thus, it can provide management almost instantaneously with general accounting records, financial reports, departmental expense reports, production cost reports, inventory reports, to mention only some of the more important ones.   For marketing strategy, the computer can prepare statements of sales, cost of goods sold, gross profit by products, order analyses, etc.   It can also rapidly procure an over-all sales analysis, calling upon the sales data of as many past years as might be considered pertinent.   In addition, electronic computers have been successfully applied to such business routines as payroll accounting, customer billing, insurance policy servicing, inventory control, records of air transportation, and many others.

Cartoon by George Lichty reproduced by permission of the Chicago Sun-Times Syndicate.

"Come in, come in, Truffle! . . . We're just processing your request for a raise! . . . "

On the other hand, there are the scientific applications.   For example, a refinery can be run in any number of ways.   Many different kinds of crude oil flow into the plant and their mixture can be varied.   The process can be directed to produce various kinds of end products and in varying proportions.   Finding a plan of operations that will yield the best and economically most advantageous combination is by no means an easy task.   Electronic computers have been successfully put to use in evaluating scientific solutions for this and similar problems.   Scientists in several of the country's largest oil companies have been employing electronic computers to help increase the efficiency of refining operations.

The work of business statisticians, of course, can benefit greatly from the use of these machines.   For instance, a large research department undertook to analyse the sales for each month of the year for 12 years of 28 basic lines of merchandise.   The first step was to compute seasonal indexes; from these, least squares trend lines were computed for each month.   Twelve trend lines for each of the 28 lines of merchandise, or a total of 336 trend lines, were thus calculated.   If electric desk calculators had been used, computing these 336 trend lines would have required an estimated 200 man-hours.   The high-speed electronic computer, however, completed all the computations in 3.5 minutes.[1]

Also, multiple regression and correlation analyses with scores of independent variates are no longer an impossibility.   Programs have been devised for one giant electronic computer that make possible regression and correlation analyses where the variates are as many as 138 with up to 1,022 observations of each.[2]   One such complicated regression and correlation analysis was made by a seat cover manufacturer to help determine optimum store locations.[3]

Operations Research, which attempts to apply scientific analysis and mathematical and statistical techniques to the problem of managing a business (or an economy) is greatly benefiting from high-speed computers and in many instances could not be successfully carried out without such help.   In Operations Research, as a first step, the problem at hand is expressed in the form of a mathematical abstraction, or model.   As a second step, empirical information is analyzed in terms of the model.   This is accomplished with the help of statistical techniques.   Because of the complexity of many of the models and the large volume of data it would often require many man-years of desk calculator computations before the quantitative results could be obtained.   Electronic computers can do the work in a few minutes or hours.

The opportunities electronic computers offer to policy-makers in government are by no means less far-reaching than those in business and industry. The men who formulate economic policy in the White House, the marble

[1] Edward H. Burgeson, "A Sales Forecast for '54," *Systems*, 18:17–18 (January, 1954).
[2] F. S. Beckman and D. A. Quarles, Jr., "Multiple Regression and Correlation Analysis on the IBM Type 701 and Type 704 Electronic Data Processing Machines," *The American Statistician*, 10:6–8, 16 (February, 1956).
[3] *Business Week*, May 14, 1955.

halls of the Federal Reserve Board, in the Bureau of the Budget and the Treasury Department and on Capitol Hill have in the past had to reach decisions on the basis of relatively meager and often out-dated information. For instance, one of the means of counteracting inflationary forces in the economy is for the Federal Reserve Board to raise its discount rates.   To help the Board decide whether, when, and by how much to tighten credit, a wealth of data has to be gathered and interpreted rapidly.   Modern survey techniques can give the Board an early indication of changes in the financial position of consumers, and even their future plans as well as their spending and saving behavior.   Both the consumer's attitude toward his personal financial status and prospects and the prospects of the country as a whole can be promptly sounded.   By the same method, information can become available on short notice regarding the financial position of business and industry and their investment plans for the near future.   On the other hand, electronic computers operate at such high speeds that the data thus collected can be processed and results obtained without delay, and placed on the desks of executives as background information for their early action.

These are great achievements, which are likely to revolutionize policy-making in government and elsewhere.   In addition, electronic computers can help make certain types of decisions, and in some cases, assist in supervising their implementation.[4]

19.2. THE COMPUTER AT WORK

How statisticians can make use of computers to analyze business and economic problems and find their solution is illustrated in Chart 19.1 with its nine steps.

Programming.   An electronic computing system is a figure factory that can manipulate data at enormously high speeds: by 1957 computers were able to make up to 16,600 additions a second, and there is no doubt that as time goes on still faster machines will become available.   Yet a machine does not have the initiative to start, nor does it know what to do unless its master—man—has given it instructions.   These robots become useful only once man has charted their steps, a process known as "programming."   We should remember that high-speed data processing can be both a blessing and a curse.   If the machine has been properly pro-

---

[4] An interesting example of what computers can do in this field is the U.S. Air Force plan for using electronic computers in logistics.   This is discussed in U.S. Air Force, Logistical Systems, *An Outline Plan for Modernizing USAF Logistics Utilizing Electronic Data Processing* (Wright-Patterson Air Force Base, U.S. Air Force, Logistical Systems Research and Planning Office, 1955).

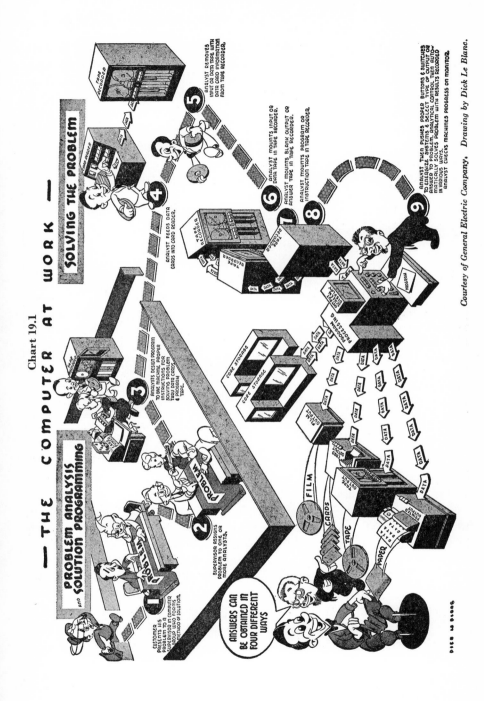

Chart 19.1

— THE COMPUTER AT WORK —

PROBLEM ANALYSIS and SOLUTION PROGRAMMING

SOLVING THE PROBLEM

Courtesy of General Electric Company. Drawing by Dick Le Blanc.

385

grammed, results flow out at a rapid pace. If the program or the data are faulty, mistakes are turned out at a speed never before dreamed of.

Programming means setting up a plan for processing data through a computer; the program is a set of instructions that specify the operations that the computer is to perform as well as their sequence. Depending upon the complexity of the task, it is often helpful to state the problem in the form of a mathematical formula and then portray the sequence of operations by way of a diagram.

Chart 19.2 PUNCHED CARD

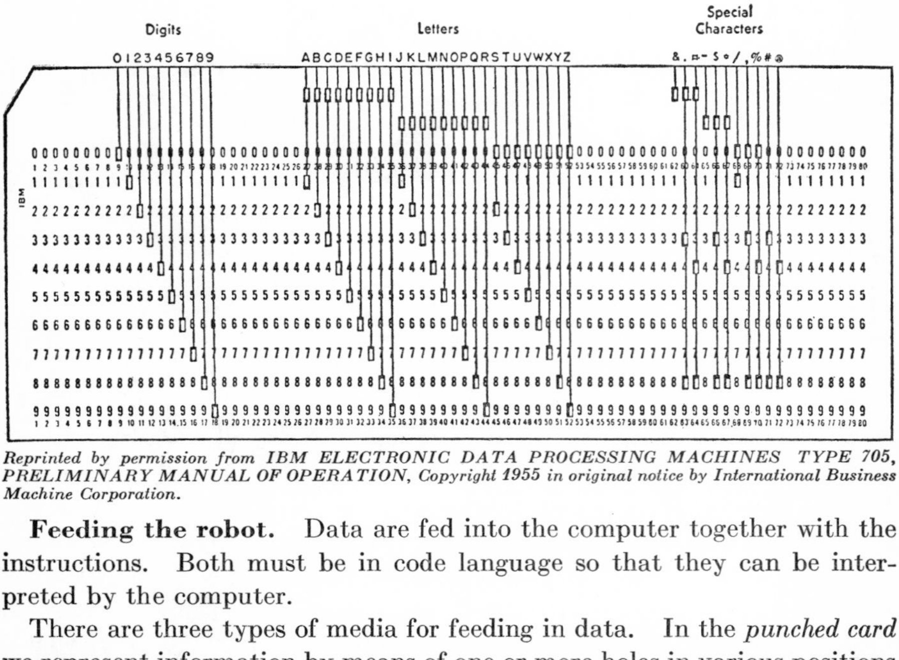

Digits	Letters	Special Characters
0123456789	ABCDEFGHIJKLMNOPQRSTUVWXYZ	&.¤‑$¢/,%#@

```
00000000 0 0 0 0 0 0 0 0
0000000000                                              0 0 0
000000000        000000000             000000000000  000000000  00000000
1111111111       111111111             1          1  1111111111 11111111
2222222222       222222222    2        2           2 2222222222 22222222
3333333333       333333333    33       3 3           3333333333 33333333
4444444444       444444444    444      44            4444444444 44444444
5555555555       555555555    5555     555           5555555555 55555555
6666666666       666666666    66666    6666          6666666666 66666666
7777777777       777777777    777777   77777         7777777777 77777777
8888888888       888888888    8888888  888888        8888888888 88888888
9999999999       999999999    99999999 9999999       9999999999 99999999
```

Reprinted by permission from IBM ELECTRONIC DATA PROCESSING MACHINES TYPE 705, PRELIMINARY MANUAL OF OPERATION, Copyright 1955 in original notice by International Business Machine Corporation.

Feeding the robot. Data are fed into the computer together with the instructions. Both must be in code language so that they can be interpreted by the computer.

There are three types of media for feeding in data. In the *punched card* we represent information by means of one or more holes in various positions in the vertical column of a paper card. Various card punches have been perfected, which permit typing the information on a regular typewriter keyboard and turning out cards punched with the desired information (see Chart 19.2). Another medium is the *paper tape*, where the coding of a character takes the form of holes or inked dots across the width of the tape, or in channels running the length of the tape. A number of codes are in use with between five and eight channels taking up the width of the tape. *Magnetic tapes*, which vary from 1/4 inch to 3 inches in width, are either metallic or plastic covered with a magnetizable material. Magnetic "spots" placed laterally on the tape by pulses emanating from small electromagnets represent characters, with 200 or more to each linear inch (see enlargement in Chart 19.3).

These media are prepared by special *input preparation equipment.* Once the medium is ready, it is passed through an *input reading device,* which translates data and instructions into a language understood by the processing unit. All reading devices work on the same principle: as the medium moves through the device the information on the medium is translated into electronic equivalents that are fed into the processing unit. Punched-card reading devices read at speeds of up to 1,200 characters per second, paper tape readers up to 1,000, and magnetic tape readers up to 56,000.

Chart 19.3   MAGNETIC TAPE

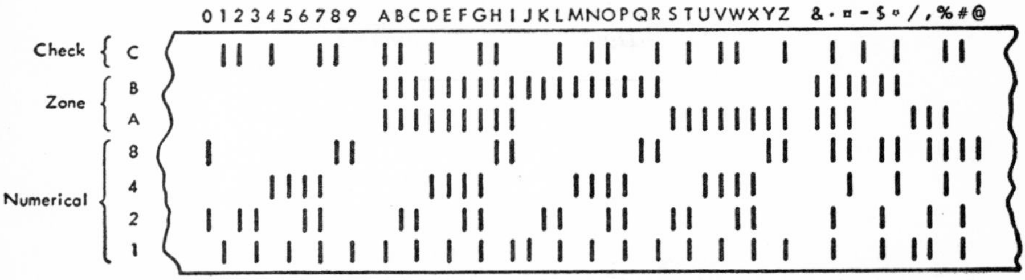

```
        0 1 2 3 4 5 6 7 8 9   A B C D E F G H I J K L M N O P Q R S T U V W X Y Z   & · ¤ - $ ° / , % # @
Check { C    || |   || | || | || | || | || | || | || | || |
Zone  [ B          |||||||||||||||||||||||          ||||||
      [ A          |||||||||||||          |||||||||| |||    |||
      [ 8    |      ||       ||       ||       ||  || || ||||
Numerical { 4    ||||    ||||    ||||    ||||   |   |   ||
          { 2  | ||  ||   || ||  || ||  || ||  || ||   |   |  || 
          [ 1    | | | | | | | | | | || | | | | | | | | |  |  | || |
```

Reprinted by permission from IBM ELECTRONIC DATA PROCESSING MACHINES TYPE 705 PRELIMINARY MANUAL OF OPERATION, Copyright 1955 in original notice by International Business Machine Corporation.

Electronic computers do not speak English, Russian, or French. They speak an electronic language, perhaps the simplest language known to man. An electronic pulse is either present—"pulse"—or it is absent—"no pulse." We must therefore find a system that can translate the characters of our alphabet as well as numbers into the "flip-flop" language of electronic circuits, in the same way as the Morse code was invented as a language for the electric telegraph. For computers we have, for instance, the *binary system,* in which all numbers, letters, and other characters are represented by sets of two symbols, let us say 0 and 1. Most computers use the so-called 8-4-2-1 or binary coded decimal system, which requires a maximum of four binary digits to represent one decimal digit.

We can visualize this system in the following way: There are four circuits, one next to the other. Each one can have a pulse, 1, or no pulse, 0. If none has a pulse, i.e., all four binary digits are 0, 0 0 0 0, the decimal digit is 0. If the circuit farthest to the right has a pulse and the other three have no pulse, 0 0 0 1, the decimal digit is 1; if only the second farthest circuit to the right has a pulse, 0 0 1 0, the decimal digit is 2; and if only the third farthest has a pulse, 0 1 0 0, the decimal digit is 4, etc. These and all the other possible arrangements are summarized in Table 19.1, which also helps to understand why the system has the name 8-4-2-1.   For example, decimal 48 is written: 0100 1000.   Decimal 931 is written: 1001 0011 0001.

Alphabetic characters and other symbols are represented by combining two additional binary digits with the four needed for the binary coded decimal digits.   For instance, the binary notation for *A* is 01 0001, for *B* it is 01 0010, for $ 11 1011, and so forth.   Such a group of six binary digits gives us 64 combinations, more than we need to represent our 10 decimal digits and 26 alphabetic characters.   Some of the remaining 28 choices have been used to represent standard punctuation marks and abbreviations.

Table 19.1 DECIMAL DIGITS AND BINARY NOTATIONS

Decimal Digit	Binary Notation
	8 4 2 1
0	0 0 0 0
1	0 0 0 1
2	0 0 1 0
3	0 0 1 1
4	0 1 0 0
5	0 1 0 1
6	0 1 1 0
7	0 1 1 1
8	1 0 0 0
9	1 0 0 1

Controlling the robot.   The data and instructions are fed into the processing unit, which is the heart of the computing system.   It consists of a control unit, a memory unit, and an arithmetic and logic unit.   The control unit interprets the instructions and directs the processing of the data.   It can readily be seen that one of our major tasks in the use of computers is the preparation of the instructions, which are then fed into the memory part of the processing unit in planned sequence.

Certain instructions are given manually.   For this purpose there is a keyboard on the operator's console.   From this keyboard instructions to read in the data are issued.   Once the processing routine is in progress it can be monitored by watching the lights on the console and, if necessary, it can be altered by manipulating certain keys, buttons, and switches, and further instructions can be added.

The robot's memory.   Data fed into the processing unit go first to a storage device and so do the instructions with them.   There are various types of storage media, but all receive the information coming from the input unit and hold it until introduced into the processing routine. At the completion of the processing some of the results may be returned to the storage device. Realizing that information enters and leaves the memory unit in huge amounts and at very high speeds, it is clear that no information can be permitted to float freely in the system. Instead, all data and instructions are assigned to specified locations: in computer parlance, "addresses" in the system.

The main types of storage media are vacuum tubes, cathode ray tubes, magnetic cores, acoustic delay lines, magnetic drums, and magnetic tapes. The speed with which the computer processes information depends to no small extent on the time required to find data and instructions in the memory unit. Speed of access to storage together with storage capacity are among the main factors affecting the capacity of the computing system. The speed of access is greatest if the information is stored in magnetic cores, cathode ray tubes, and vacuum tubes. For example, one of the giants among the computers takes only 12 millionths of a second to find any given number in its magnetic core memory.

The robot's logic. We are now ready to inquire into the method used by an electronic computer to manipulate information that reaches it in the form of flip-flop language. The types of manipulations involved are:

> addition,
> subtraction,
> multiplication,
> division, and
> decisions.

The basic manipulation is addition, where the electronic computer counts pulses. It subtracts, multiplies, and divides with the help of the well-known principle that all arithmetic operations can be carried out as variations of the process of addition. Thus, the computer subtracts by adding complements, it multiplies by successive addition, and divides by successive subtraction.

Logical decisions take the form of comparing numbers or other characters. This is accomplished by subtracting one number or characteristic from another and determining whether or not the result is zero. Based upon the outcome of this examination, the computer takes one of several alternative courses of action.

All these manipulations go on at electronic speed in the arithmetic and logic unit of the computer. The results can be turned over to memory, or retained for further manipulation, or both.

Robot records output.   We used input units to get information from the outside world into the computer and now we need equipment to get information from the computer back into the outside world.   Often we can use the same equipment that reads information into the computer also as an output unit.   The processing unit sends its output in binary coded form to an output unit, which transfers the information to punched cards or to paper or magnetic tape, or the results may be sent to a high-speed printer directly from memory.[5]   Information on these media can become the input in subsequent computer work or can be printed out as a final report document.

19.3. COMPUTER, STATISTICIAN, AND EXECUTIVE

It is hoped that the above discussion has given the reader some basis for judging what an electronic computing machine can do.   But it should also be apparent that there are many of the present-day functions both of management and of statisticians that we cannot expect even the most complicated machine to perform.

A machine has no judgment of men, of the subtleties of the business world, or of values.   The results of statistical investigations are scientific and impersonal, and correct calculations can only give one answer.   Yet the result yielded by the robots can be no better than the data and instructions fed into them; and these again depend to a certain extent on underlying assumptions that influenced the formulation of the problem.   Statisticians and mathematicians are still responsible for the organization of data and instructions; but they must collaborate closely with management, which alone has the judgment necessary to formulate the assumptions.

The increasing use of computers will offer statistician and executive new challenges.   The statistician will be expected to develop new tools of analysis that can utilize the high speed with which data can be processed for obtaining useful information and decisions.   Management, too, will have to be on its toes to make the fullest use of these machines.

19.4. THE FRONTIERS OF BUSINESS AND ECONOMIC STATISTICS

Linear programming.   Statistics is a dynamic field of inquiry, where new and often important contributions are made at a rapid pace.   In recent

[5] Still another mode of output recording, one which bears great promise for the future, consists of displaying results on the face of a cathode ray tube similar to a television picture tube (see the screen in the lower middle of Chart 19.1).   This display may be in the form of curves or letters and numbers, traced at very high speed.   A camera can take pictures of the screen so that the results are preserved for future scrutiny and reference.

years much progress has been made in sampling theory and methods as well as in measuring association. Some very promising new tools have been added to the kit of the statistician and in some cases they have been applied with great success. Perhaps the two most interesting of these are *linear programming* and *input-output analysis.*

Linear programming was launched when in 1947 G. B. Dantzig developed the "simplex method," and with its aid it has become possible to specify the most profitable or least costly mode of operations for a variety of problems. Here are some of the problems to which this method can be applied:

1. How much of what items should be produced to result in maximum profit?

2. What product mix and how much of it should be shipped and sold at what price to yield maximum profit?

3. What allocation of what types of labor to what jobs will minimize labor requirements or costs?

4. From what plants should what quantity of products be shipped to what outlets so as to minimize shipping costs?

5. What quantities of what ingredients (be they gasoline blending stocks or animal feeds) should be blended to meet specifications at minimum cost?

Let us consider a problem that was referred to by Robert Dorfman.[6] One large newsprint company with six mills widely scattered throughout Canada and some two hundred customers located in various parts of the United States faces a serious transportation and freight problem. Freight is a major element in the cost of newsprint. One of the company's main problems is to decide how much newsprint to ship from each mill to each customer so as, first, to meet the contract requirements of each customer; second, to stay within the capacity limits of each mill; and third, to keep the total freight bill at a minimum. With the six shipment origins and two hundred destinations, this problem involves a total of 6×200 or 1,200 variates.

While 1,200 variates may appear at first glance to make the problem unmanageable, electronic computers render the solution economically feasible. A standard program for as many as 50×100 variates has been designed and carried through on a giant electronic computer.[7] The solution of a problem with 18×34 or 612 variates took just twenty minutes.

Most manufacturing and transportation operations are highly complex

---

[6] Robert Dorfman, "Mathematical, or 'Linear,' Programming," *The American Economic Review*, 43:820–821 (December, 1953).

[7] Kurt Eisemann, "Linear Programming," *Quarterly of Applied Mathematics*, 8:231–232 (October, 1955).

and interdependent upon one another. Thus, a change in one operating characteristic usually generates adjustments in related factors. To trace and measure them is virtually impossible by trial and error; linear programming does it systematically. Usually, the manufacturing operation is carried out under conditions that are somewhat restrictive. For instance, a company manufacturing newsprint has plants of given capacities, raw materials are available in given amounts at given locations, and so are storage facilities and customer demands. Also, by and large, transportation facilities and freight rates are given. Linear programming methods make it possible to express these relationships and restrictions in mathematical form and, after they have been formed into tables, to manipulate them algebraically. The rules of manipulation are then simple and routine, and enable us to determine out of an infinite number of possible solutions that unique solution which makes a certain profit, quality, or volume function a maximum, or cost function a minimum. When the manipulations are completed, the best possible program for the stipulated conditions will result.

Input–output analysis. *Input–output analysis* was developed largely by Wassily W. Leontief. In 1941 he described and first applied his method to the United States economy.[8] Much progress has been made subsequently, and government and business researchers are now applying the method to their problems. Here are some of the problems in which input–output analysis can be useful:

1. What will be the effect on the railroad industry of the 1956 highway building act?

2. What will be the market for electronic computers?

3. How will regional and industrial developments affect freight hauling by trucks, railroads, and planes and by how much must their facilities be expanded?

4. How does government spending each year break down into demand for the products of specific industries?

5. What will be the demand for domestically produced crude oil, iron ore, and aluminum, and how adequate will be the existing sources of supply?

To provide answers to such questions an input–output table is constructed which shows the way goods flow from one industry (output) to another (input). This table describes the interrelationship of the various sectors of the economy and makes possible forecasts of what effects changes somewhere in the system will have on its various sectors.

An input–output table is a sort of double-entry table not unlike the mileage

---

[8] Wassily W. Leontief, *The Structure of the American Economy*, 2d ed. (New York, Oxford University Press, 1951).

table on a road map. Along its left side are listed the separate industries of the economy, each industry occupying one row. Across the top of the table the same industries are repeated, with each at the head of a single column. Every cell in the table stands for either an input or an output. From the standpoint of its position in the column, the number in the cell represents the input to the industry whose name appears at the top of the column; while from the standpoint of its position in the row, it is the output specified at the left of the row. When government, consumers, and foreign trades sectors are added, the table portrays the total flow of goods and services in the national economy.

Table 19.2 is such an input-output table and pertains to the United States economy of 1939. For instance, the total net output of agriculture and foods amounted to 16,964 million dollars. Of this, 555 million dollars' worth were used by the textile, leather, and rubber industries, 643 million dollars' worth were exported, 14,522 million dollars' worth were destined for direct household consumption, etc.

From such an input-output table a table of input-output technical coefficients is derived. These coefficients are obtained from the original table by dividing each cell in an industry's column by the output of that industry.

These tables can be used to indicate the way specific developments will affect the system. For instance, we can change the output values of a specific industry and work back to see the effect upon input requirements, i.e., output of industries supplying the particular industry. In this form we can work out, for example, by how much the input requirements of the automobile industry will increase as a result of a 1.2-billion-dollar increase in automobile output. Likewise, it is possible to show by how much the output of industries supplying the automobile industry, e.g., steel, glass, rubber, and paint industries, will increase. This would be the primary effect, which in turn will generate a secondary effect, i.e., increases in output required by industries supplying the suppliers of the automobile industry.

These two new tools were developed by mathematicians and economists well trained in mathematics. It is the mathematician and the mathematically trained statistician and economist who push ahead the frontiers of statistics and develop methods that may become useful in business and economic research. Most of these contributions have been made in an abstract framework. Sometimes the mathematics are worked out years and even decades before any practical application is discovered.

Game theory. Some theoretical contributions await further work before they can be applied to business and economic problems. Perhaps

Table 19.2 INPUT-OUTPUT TABLE, UNITED STATES, 1939

Distribution of Outlays (Input) of Classes Listed at Top of Table	Distribution of Output of Classes Listed at Left of Table											
	1 Agriculture and foods	*2* Minerals	*3* Metal Fabricating	*4* Fuel and Power	*5* Textiles, Leather, and Rubber	*6* Railroad Transportation	*7* Foreign Trade (Exports)	*8* Industries n.e.c.	*9* Government	*10* All Other Industries	*11* Household	*12* Total Net Output
1. Agriculture and foods	.....	.....	.....	.....	555	.....	643	585	9	650	14,522	16,964
2. Minerals	112	.....	1,190	12	4	.....	190	1,250	.....	856	149	3,763
3. Metal fabricating	718	69	.....	342	118	302	1,070	2,142	337	4,186	3,020	12,304
4. Fuel and power	417	282	355	.....	138	265	700	402	195	2,581	3,541	8,876
5. Textiles, leather, and rubber	82	.....	315	5	.....	6	197	95	27	824	5,442	6,993
6. Railroad transportation	1,294	346	368	971	17	.....	.....	514	100	4	689	4,303
7. Foreign trade (imports)	967	366	46	81	238	.....	.....	488	.....	647	.....	2,833
8. Industries n.e.c.	853	77	352	1,033	459	630	376	.....	4,623	5,198	5,625	19,226
9. Government (taxes)	1,073	.....	185	191	8	32	.....	53	.....	9,659	2,594	13,795
10. All other industries	8,155	1,490	3,366	3,099	3,149	723	88	9,078	2,812	.....	28,937	60,896
11. Household	4,167	1,106	6,653	3,563	2,890	2,548	.....	5,532	7,897	34,492	.....	68,848
Total net outlays (input)	17,838	3,736	12,830	9,297	7,576	4,506	3,264	20,139	16,000	58,745	64,519	

Source: Wassily W. Leontief, *The Structure of the American Economy, 1919–1939,* 2d ed. (New York, Oxford University Press, 1951) p. 140. All figures are in millions of dollars and, in addition to manufactures' value, include transportation costs, but exclude trade margins.

the most famous example is *game theory*, associated with the names of the mathematician John von Neumann and the economist Oskar Morgenstern.[9] It is the mathematical approach to the selection of an optimum strategy against an opponent who has a strategy of his own. In the pricing of products in different market situations and in collective bargaining it appears to have possible applications.

An afterthought. The addition of such promising tools to the statistician's tool kit and the availability of machines that render complex computations economically feasible make the future look bright. The climate is becoming increasingly favorable to the making of decisions on the basis of reliable information and with the help of scientific methods. It is widely recognized that scientific planning is the basis for intelligent decisions by policy-makers in business, labor, and government.

We may be on the threshold of an age when statistician and policy-maker, both utilizing the services of electronic computers, are entering into a partnership. The technological advances of our century, together with the ever-increasing complexity of our society and economy, require closer ties between managerial ability and knowledge of statistical principles and techniques. There can be no doubt that the field of activity of the statistician is expanding.

[9] John von Neumann and Oskar Morgenstern, *Theory of Games and Economic Behavior*, 3d ed. (Princeton, Princeton University Press, 1953).

(handwritten annotations at top)

99% C.C.   2.57 z value
90% C.C.   1.65   "   "
95% C.C.   1.96   "   "
97% C.C.   2.17   "   "

Appendix

Table I   NORMAL CURVE AREAS*

An entry in this table is the fraction of the area under the entire normal curve that is between $z = 0$ and a positive value of z.   For instance, the area between $z = 0$ and $z = +1.64$ is 0.4495.   Since the normal curve is symmetrical, the area between $z = 0$ and $z = -1.64$ is also 0.4495.   The area between -1.64 and $+1.64$ is 0.8990 and that in the tails of the curve beyond ±1.64 is 0.1010.

This table shows the black area:

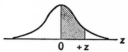

z	.00	.01	.02	.03	.04	.05	.06	.07	.08	.09
0.0	.0000	.0040	.0080	.0120	.0160	.0199	.0239	.0279	.0319	.0359
0.1	.0398	.0438	.0478	.0517	.0557	.0596	.0636	.0675	.0714	.0753
0.2	.0793	.0832	.0871	.0910	.0948	.0987	.1026	.1064	.1103	.1141
0.3	.1179	.1217	.1255	.1293	.1331	.1368	.1406	.1443	.1480	.1517
0.4	.1554	.1591	.1628	.1664	.1700	.1736	.1772	.1808	.1844	.1879
0.5	.1915	.1950	.1985	.2019	.2054	.2088	.2123	.2157	.2190	.2224
0.6	.2257	.2291	.2324	.2357	.2389	.2422	.2454	.2486	.2517	.2549
0.7	.2589	.2611	.2642	.2673	.2704	.2734	.2764	.2794	.2823	.2852
0.8	.2281	.2910	.2939	.2967	.2995	.3023	.3051	.3078	.3106	.3133
0.9	.3159	.3186	.3212	.3238	.3264	.3289	.3315	.3340	.3365	.3389
1.0	.3413	.3438	.3461	.3485	.3508	.3531	.3554	.3577	.3599	.3621
1.1	.3643	.3665	.3686	.3708	.3729	.3749	.3770	.3790	.3810	.3830
1.2	.3849	.3869	.3888	.3907	.3925	.3944	.3962	.3980	.3997	.4015
1.3	.4032	.4049	.4066	.4082	.4099	.4115	.4131	.4147	.4162	.4177
1.4	.4192	.4207	.4222	.4236	.4251	.4265	.4279	.4292	.4306	.4319
1.5	.4332	.4345	.4357	.4370	.4382	.4394	.4406	.4418	.4429	.4441
1.6	.4452	.4463	.4474	.4484	.4495	.4505	.4515	.4525	.4535	.4545
1.7	.4554	.4564	.4573	.4582	.4591	.4599	.4608	.4616	.4625	.4633
1.8	.4641	.4649	.4656	.4664	.4671	.4678	.4686	.4693	.4699	.4706
1.9	.4713	.4719	.4726	.4732	.4738	.4744	.4750	.4756	.4761	.4767
2.0	.4772	.4778	.4783	.4788	.4793	.4798	.4803	.4808	.4812	.4817
2.1	.4821	.4826	.4830	.4834	.4838	.4842	.4846	.4850	.4854	.4857
2.2	.4861	.4864	.4868	.4871	.4875	.4878	.4881	.4884	.4887	.4890
2.3	.4893	.4896	.4898	.4901	.4904	.4906	.4909	.4911	.4913	.4916
2.4	.4919	.4920	.4922	.4925	.4927	.4929	.4931	.4932	.4934	.4936
2.5	.4938	.4940	.4941	.4943	.4945	.4946	.4948	.4949	.4951	.4952
2.6	.4953	.4955	.4956	.4957	.4959	.4960	.4961	.4962	.4963	.4964
2.7	.4965	.4966	.4967	.4968	.4969	.4970	.4971	.4972	.4973	.4974
2.8	.4974	.4975	.4976	.4977	.4977	.4978	.4979	.4979	.4980	.4981
2.9	.4981	.4982	.4982	.4983	.4984	.4984	.4985	.4985	.4986	.4986
3.0	.4987	.4987	.4987	.4988	.4988	.4989	.4989	.4989	.4990	.4990

(handwritten margin notes)

+332
.4332
.866

* Table I is reproduced with the permission of the publishers from J. Neyman, *First Course in Probability and Statistics* (New York, Henry Holt and Company, Inc., 1950).

Table II CRITICAL VALUES OF t*

An entry in this table is the value of t (for given degrees of freedom, or sample size -1) beyond which we find the given percentage of the area under the curve. For instance, we denote t above (or below) which we find the highest (or lowest) 2.5 per cent as $t_{.025}$ and for 20 degrees of freedom its value is 2.086. In the lower tail below $t_{.025}$ lies 2.5 per cent of the curve, and in the upper tail above $t_{.025}$ lies another 2.5 per cent. Thus, a t value of 2.086 for 20 degrees of freedom corresponds to a 95 per cent confidence level.

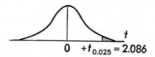

$0 \quad +t_{0.025} = 2.086$

AMT. IN ONE TAIL

90% 95%

Sample Size	$t_{.100}$	$t_{.050}$	$t_{.025}$	$t_{.010}$	$t_{.005}$	Degrees of Freedom
2	3.078	6.314	12.706	31.821	63.657	1
3	1.886	2.920	4.303	6.965	9.925	2
4	1.638	2.353	3.182	4.541	5.841	3
5	1.533	2.132	2.776	3.747	4.604	4
6	1.476	2.015	2.571	3.365	4.032	5
7	1.440	1.943	2.447	3.143	3.707	6
8	1.415	1.895	2.365	2.998	3.499	7
9	1.397	1.860	2.306	2.896	3.355	8
10	1.383	1.833	2.262	2.821	3.250	9
11	1.372	1.812	2.228	2.764	3.169	10
12	1.363	1.796	2.201	2.718	3.106	11
13	1.356	1.782	2.179	2.681	3.055	12
14	1.350	1.771	2.160	2.650	3.012	13
15	1.345	1.761	2.145	2.624	2.977	14
16	1.341	1.753	2.131	2.602	2.947	15
17	1.337	1.746	2.120	2.583	2.921	16
18	1.333	1.740	2.110	2.567	2.898	17
19	1.330	1.734	2.101	2.552	2.878	18
20	1.328	1.729	2.093	2.539	2.861	19
21	1.325	1.725	2.086	2.528	2.845	20
22	1.323	1.721	2.080	2.518	2.831	21
23	1.321	1.717	2.074	2.508	2.819	22
24	1.319	1.714	2.069	2.500	2.807	23
25	1.318	1.711	2.064	2.492	2.797	24
26	1.316	1.708	2.060	2.485	2.787	25
27	1.315	1.706	2.056	2.479	2.779	26
28	1.314	1.703	2.052	2.473	2.771	27
29	1.313	1.701	2.048	2.467	2.763	28
30	1.311	1.699	2.045	2.462	2.756	29
inf.	1.282	1.645	1.960	2.326	2.576	inf.

*Table II is abridged from Table IV of R. A. Fisher, *Statistical Methods for Research Workers*, published by Oliver & Boyd Ltd., Edinburgh, by permission of the author and publishers.

Table III 95 PER CENT CONFIDENCE INTERVAL (PER CENT) FOR BINOMIAL DISTRIBUTION*

Entries in this table are values of lower and upper 95 per cent confidence limits of percentages for a given sample percentage.

Number Observed X	Size of Sample 10		Size of Sample 15		Size of Sample 20		Size of Sample 30		Size of Sample 50		Size of Sample 100†		Fraction Observed X/n	Size of Sample 250‡		Size of Sample 1000‡	
0	0	31	0	22	0	17	0	12	0	07	0	4	.00	0	1	0	0
1	0	45	0	32	0	25	0	17	0	11	0	5	.01	0	4	0	2
2	3	56	2	40	1	31	1	22	0	14	0	7	.02	1	5	1	3
3	7	65	4	48	3	38	2	27	1	17	1	8	.03	1	6	2	4
4	12	74	8	55	6	44	4	31	2	19	1	10	.04	2	7	3	5
5	19	81	12	62	9	49	6	35	3	22	2	11	.05	3	9	4	7
6	26	88	16	68	12	54	8	39	5	24	2	12	.06	3	10	5	8
7	35	93	21	73	15	59	10	43	6	27	3	14	.07	4	11	6	9
8	44	97	27	79	19	64	12	46	7	29	4	15	.08	5	12	6	10
9	55	100	32	84	23	68	15	50	9	31	4	16	.09	6	13	7	11
10	69	100	38	88	27	73	17	53	10	34	5	18	.10	7	14	8	12
11			45	92	32	77	20	56	12	36	5	19	.11	7	16	9	13
12			52	96	36	81	23	60	13	38	6	20	.12	8	17	10	14
13			60	98	41	85	25	63	15	41	7	21	.13	9	18	11	15
14			68	100	46	88	28	66	16	43	8	22	.14	10	19	12	16
15			78	100	51	91	31	69	18	44	9	24	.15	10	20	13	17
16					56	94	34	72	20	46	9	25	.16	11	21	14	18
17					62	97	37	75	21	48	10	26	.17	12	22	15	19
18					69	99	40	77	23	50	11	27	.18	13	23	16	21
19					75	100	44	80	25	53	12	28	.19	14	24	17	22
20					83	100	47	83	27	55	13	29	.20	15	26	18	23
21							50	85	28	57	14	30	.21	16	27	19	24
22							54	88	30	59	14	31	.22	17	28	19	25
23							57	90	32	61	15	32	.23	18	29	20	26
24							61	92	34	63	16	33	.24	19	30	21	27
25							65	94	36	64	17	35	.25	20	31	22	28
26							69	96	37	66	18	36	.26	20	32	23	29
27							73	98	39	68	19	37	.27	21	33	24	30
28							78	99	41	70	19	38	.28	22	34	25	31
29							83	100	43	72	20	39	.29	23	35	26	32
30							88	100	45	73	21	40	.30	24	36	27	33
31									47	75	22	41	.31	25	37	28	34
32									50	77	23	42	.32	26	38	29	35
33									52	79	24	43	.33	27	39	30	36
34									54	80	25	44	.34	28	40	31	37
35									56	82	26	45	.35	29	41	32	38
36									57	84	27	46	.36	30	42	33	39
37									59	85	28	47	.37	31	43	34	40
38									62	87	28	48	.38	32	44	35	41
39									64	88	29	49	.39	33	45	36	42
40									66	90	30	50	.40	34	46	37	43
41									69	91	31	51	.41	35	47	38	44
42									71	93	32	52	.42	36	48	39	45
43									73	94	33	53	.43	37	49	40	46
44									76	95	34	54	.44	38	50	41	47
45									78	97	35	55	.45	39	51	42	48
46									81	98	36	56	.46	40	52	43	49
47									83	99	37	57	.47	41	53	44	50
48									86	100	38	58	.48	42	54	45	51
49									89	100	39	59	.49	43	55	46	52
50									93	100	40	60	.50	44	56	47	53

* Table III is reproduced with permission of the author and publisher from Table 1.3.1 of G. W. Snedecor, *Statistical Methods*, 5th ed. (Ames, Iowa State College Press, 1956), pp. 4–5.
† If X exceeds 50, read $100 - X$, number observed, and subtract each confidence limit from 100.
‡ If X/n exceeds 0.50, read $1.00 - X/n$, fraction observed, and subtract each confidence limit from 100.

Table IV CRITICAL VALUES OF THE LEAST SQUARES
CORRELATION COEFFICIENT*

An entry to this table is the value of the correlation coefficient r which, for a given number of degrees of freedom, is exceeded with the given α (in the two tails of the curve).

Degrees of Freedom	α of 0.05	α of 0.01	Degrees of Freedom	α of 0.05	α of 0.01
1	.997	1.000	24	.388	.496
2	.950	.990	25	.381	.487
3	.878	.959	26	.374	.478
4	.811	.917	27	.367	.470
5	.754	.874	28	.361	.463
6	.707	.834	29	.355	.456
7	.666	.798	30	.349	.449
8	.632	.765	35	.325	.418
9	.602	.735	40	.304	.393
10	.576	.708	45	.288	.372
11	.553	.684	50	.273	.354
12	.532	.661	60	.250	.325
13	.514	.641	70	.232	.302
14	.497	.623	80	.217	.283
15	.482	.606	90	.205	.267
16	.468	.590	100	.195	.254
17	.456	.575	125	.174	.228
18	.444	.561	150	.159	.208
19	.433	.549	200	.138	.181
20	.423	.537	300	.113	.148
21	.413	.526	400	.098	.128
22	.404	.515	500	.088	.115
23	.396	.505	1,000	.062	.081

* Portions of Table IV were abridged from Table VI of Fisher and Yates, *Statistical Tables for Biological, Agricultural, and Medical Research*, published by Oliver & Boyd Ltd., Edinburgh, by permission of the authors and publishers.

*any value below critical value —
any difference in 2 variables
due to sampling variation*

Table V 95 PER CENT CONFIDENCE LIMITS FOR THE CORRELATION COEFFICIENT

To find the 95 per cent confidence interval for the coefficient of correlation: (1) Locate the sample value of r along the lower horizontal scale; (2) Move up vertically until you cross the curve which has your sample size written above it.   The ρ value of the intersection (the vertical scale at the left and right) is the value of the lower confidence limit, ρ. (3) Move up once more vertically at the sample value of r until you cross the second curve that carries your sample size above it.   The value at this intersection is the value of the upper confidence limit, $\bar{\rho}$.

Table V 95 PER CENT CONFIDENCE LIMITS FOR THE COEFFICIENT OF CORRELATION

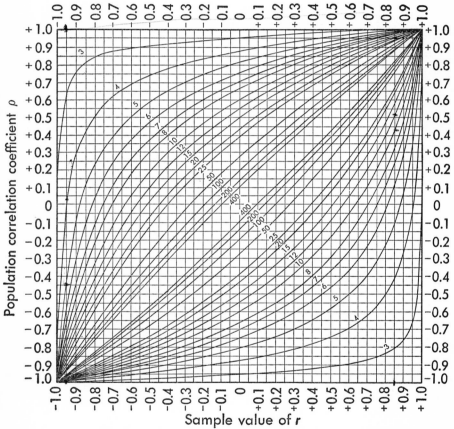

* Table V is reproduced from F. N. David, *Tables of the Ordinates and Probability Integral of the Distribution of the Correlation in Small Samples*, The Biometrika Office, London, by permission of Professor E. S. Pearson.

Table VI CRITICAL VALUES OF RANK CORRELATION COEFFICIENT*

An entry in this table is the value of the rank correlation coefficient r_r which, for a given sample size, is exceeded with the given α (in the two tails of the curve).

n	α of 0.05	α of 0.01	n	α of 0.05	α of 0.01
4	1.000	. . . . .	16	0.425	0.601
5	0.900	1.000	18	0.399	0.564
6	0.829	0.943	20	0.377	0.534
7	0.714	0.893	22	0.359	0.508
8	0.643	0.833	24	0.343	0.485
9	0.600	0.783	26	0.329	0.465
10	0.564	0.746	28	0.317	0.448
12	0.506	0.712	30	0.306	0.432
14	0.456	0.645			

* Table VI is abridged from Edwin G. Olds, "Distributions of Sums of Squares of Rank Differences for Small Numbers of Individuals," *Annals of Mathematical Statistics*, 9:133–148 (1938), and reproduced with the permission of the author and the Institute of Mathematical Statistics.

Table VII NOMOGRAPH FOR COMPUTING MULTIPLE CORRELATION COEFFICIENTS
(Two independent variates.)

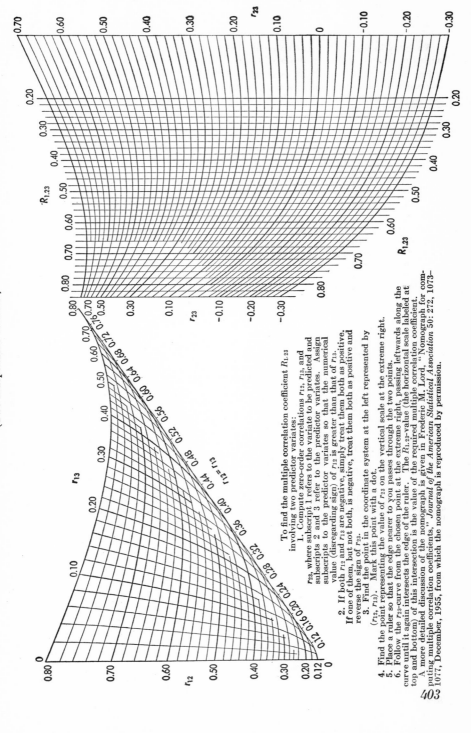

To find the multiple correlation coefficient $R_{1.23}$ involving two predictor variates:

1. Compute zero-order correlations r_{12}, r_{13}, and r_{23}, where subscript 1 refers to the variate to be predicted and subscripts 2 and 3 refer to the predictor variates. Assign subscripts to the predictor variates so that the numerical value (disregarding sign) of r_{12} is greater than that of r_{13}.

2. If both r_{12} and r_{13} are negative, simply treat them both as positive. If one of them, but not both, is negative, treat them both as positive and reverse the sign of r_{23}.

3. Find the point in the coordinate system at the left represented by (r_{13}, r_{12}). Mark this point with a dot.

4. Find the point representing the value of r_{23} on the vertical scale at the extreme right.

5. Place a ruler so that the edge nearer to you passes through the two points.

6. Follow the r_{23}-curve from the chosen point at the extreme right, passing leftwards along the curve until it again intersects the edge of the ruler. The $R_{1.23}$-value (the horizontal scale labeled at top and bottom) of this intersection is the value of the required multiple correlation coefficient.

A more detailed discussion of the nomograph is given in Frederic M. Lord, "Nomograph for computing multiple correlation coefficients," *Journal of the American Statistical Association* 50: 272, 1073–1077, December, 1955, from which the nomograph is reproduced by permission.

Table VIII CRITICAL VALUES OF χ^2*

An entry in this table is the value of χ^2 which, for given degrees of freedom, is exceeded with the given α in the two tails of the curve.

For larger values of n, the expression $\sqrt{2\chi^2} - \sqrt{2n-1}$ may be used as a normal deviate with standard deviation equal to 1, remembering that the probability for χ^2 corresponds with that of a single tail of the normal curve.

Degrees of Freedom	α of 0.10	α of 0.05	α of 0.025	α of 0.01	α of 0.005
1	2.71	3.84	5.02	6.63	7.88
2	4.61	5.99	7.38	9.21	10.60
3	6.25	7.81	9.35	11.34	12.84
4	7.78	9.49	11.14	13.28	14.86
5	9.24	11.07	12.83	15.09	16.75
6	10.64	12.59	14.45	16.81	18.55
7	12.02	14.07	16.01	18.48	20.28
8	13.36	15.51	17.53	20.09	21.96
9	14.68	16.92	19.02	21.67	23.59
10	15.99	18.31	20.48	23.21	25.19
11	17.28	19.68	21.92	24.73	26.76
12	18.55	21.03	23.34	26.22	28.30
13	19.81	22.36	24.74	27.69	29.82
14	21.06	23.68	26.12	29.14	31.32
15	22.31	25.00	27.49	30.58	32.80
16	23.54	26.30	28.85	32.00	34.27
18	25.99	28.87	31.53	34.81	37.16
20	28.41	31.41	34.17	37.57	40.00
24	33.20	36.42	39.36	42.98	45.56
30	40.26	43.77	46.98	50.89	53.67
40	51.81	55.76	59.34	63.69	66.77
60	74.40	79.08	83.30	88.38	91.95
120	140.23	146.57	152.21	158.95	163.64

* Table VIII is abridged from Table IV of Fisher and Yates, *Statistical Tables for Biological, Agricultural, and Medical Research*, published by Oliver & Boyd, Ltd., Edinburgh, by permission of the authors and publishers.

Table IX FACTORS FOR CONTROL LIMITS OF MEANS AND RANGES*
An entry in this table is the value of a factor for control limits of means and ranges for a given number of units in the sample lot.

| | | Factors for | |
Number of Units in Sample Lot	Factors for Control Limits of Means A_2	Lower Control Limit of Ranges D_3	Upper Control Limit of Ranges D_4
2	1.880	0	3.267
3	1.023	0	2.575
4	0.729	0	2.282
5	0.577	0	2.115
6	0.483	0	2.004
7	0.419	0.076	1.924
8	0.373	0.136	1.864
9	0.337	0.184	1.816
10	0.308	0.223	1.777
11	0.285	0.256	1.744
12	0.266	0.284	1.716
13	0.249	0.308	1.692
14	0.235	0.329	1.671
15	0.223	0.348	1.652

* Table IX is abridged from Table M in the Appendix of Acheson J. Duncan, *Quality Control and Industrial Statistics* (Homewood, Illinois, Richard D. Irwin, Inc., 1953) p. 628, and is reproduced with the permission of the author and publisher, and of the American Society for Testing Materials, *Manual on Quality Control of Materials.*

Table X SQUARES, SQUARE ROOTS, AND RECIPROCALS 1-1,000*

N	N²	√N	√10N	1/N
1	1	1.000 000	3.162 278	1.0000000
2	4	1.414 214	4.472 136	.5000000
3	9	1.732 051	5.477 226	.3333333
4	16	2.000 000	6.324 555	.2500000
5	25	2.236 068	7.071 068	.2000000
6	36	2.449 490	7.745 967	.1666667
7	49	2.645 751	8.366 600	.1428571
8	64	2.828 427	8.944 272	.1250000
9	81	3.000 000	9.486 833	.1111111
10	100	3.162 278	10.00000	.1000000
11	121	3.316 625	10.48809	.09090909
12	144	3.464 102	10.95445	.08333333
13	169	3.605 551	11.40175	.07692308
14	196	3.741 657	11.83216	.07142857
15	225	3.872 983	12.24745	.06666667
16	256	4.000 000	12.64911	.06250000
17	289	4.123 106	13.03840	.05882353
18	324	4.242 641	13.41641	.05555556
19	361	4.358 899	13.78405	.05263158
20	400	4.472 136	14.14214	.05000000
21	441	4.582 576	14.49138	.04761905
22	484	4.690 416	14.83240	.04545455
23	529	4.795 832	15.16575	.04347826
24	576	4.898 979	15.49193	.04166667
25	625	5.000 000	15.81139	.04000000
26	676	5.099 020	16.12452	.03846154
27	729	5.196 152	16.43168	.03703704
28	784	5.291 503	16.73320	.03571429
29	841	5.385 165	17.02939	.03448276
30	900	5.477 226	17.32051	.03333333
31	961	5.567 764	17.60682	.03225806
32	1 024	5.656 854	17.88854	.03125000
33	1 089	5.744 563	18.16590	.03030303
34	1 156	5.830 952	18.43909	.02941176
35	1 225	5.916 080	18.70829	.02857143
36	1 296	6.000 000	18.97367	.02777778
37	1 369	6.082 763	19.23538	.02702703
38	1 444	6.164 414	19.49359	.02631579
39	1 521	6.244 998	19.74842	.02564103
40	1 600	6.324 555	20.00000	.02500000
41	1 681	6.403 124	20.24846	.02439024
42	1 764	6.480 741	20.49390	.02380952
43	1 849	6.557 439	20.73644	.02325581
44	1 936	6.633 250	20.97618	.02272727
45	2 025	6.708 204	21.21320	.02222222
46	2 116	6.782 330	21.44761	.02173913
47	2 209	6.855 655	21.67948	.02127660
48	2 304	6.928 203	21.90890	.02083333
49	2 401	7.000 000	22.13594	.02040816
50	2 500	7.071 068	22.36068	.02000000

N	N²	√N	√10N	1/N .0
50	2 500	7.071 068	22.36068	2000000
51	2 601	7.141 428	22.58318	1960784
52	2 704	7.211 103	22.80351	1923077
53	2 809	7.280 110	23.02173	1886792
54	2 916	7.348 469	23.23790	1851852
55	3 025	7.416 198	23.45208	1818182
56	3 136	7.483 315	23.66432	1785714
57	3 249	7.549 834	23.87467	1754386
58	3 364	7.615 773	24.08319	1724138
59	3 481	7.681 146	24.28992	1694915
60	3 600	7.745 967	24.49490	1666667
61	3 721	7.810 250	24.69818	1639344
62	3 844	7.874 008	24.89980	1612903
63	3 969	7.937 254	25.09980	1587302
64	4 096	8.000 000	25.29822	1562500
65	4 225	8.062 258	25.49510	1538462
66	4 356	8.124 038	25.69047	1515152
67	4 489	8.185 353	25.88436	1492537
68	4 624	8.246 211	26.07661	1470588
69	4 761	8.306 624	26.26785	1449275
70	4 900	8.366 600	26.45751	1428571
71	5 041	8.426 150	26.64583	1408451
72	5 184	8.485 281	26.83282	1388889
73	5 329	8.544 004	27.01851	1369863
74	5 476	8.602 325	27.20294	1351351
75	5 625	8.660 254	27.38613	1333333
76	5 776	8.717 798	27.56810	1315789
77	5 929	8.774 964	27.74887	1298701
78	6 084	8.831 761	27.92848	1282051
79	6 241	8.888 194	28.10694	1265823
80	6 400	8.944 272	28.28427	1250000
81	6 561	9.000 000	28.46050	1234568
82	6 724	9.055 385	28.63564	1219512
83	6 889	9.110 434	28.80972	1204819
84	7 056	9.165 151	28.98275	1190476
85	7 225	9.219 544	29.15476	1176471
86	7 396	9.273 618	29.32576	1162791
87	7 569	9.327 379	29.49576	1149425
88	7 744	9.380 832	29.66479	1136364
89	7 921	9.433 981	29.83287	1123596
90	8 100	9.486 833	30.00000	1111111
91	8 281	9.539 392	30.16621	1098901
92	8 464	9.591 663	30.33150	1086957
93	8 649	9.643 651	30.49590	1075269
94	8 836	9.695 360	30.65942	1063830
95	9 025	9.746 794	30.82207	1052632
96	9 216	9.797 959	30.98387	1041667
97	9 409	9.848 858	31.14482	1030928
98	9 604	9.899 495	31.30495	1020408
99	9 801	9.949 874	31.46427	1010101
100	10 000	10.00000	31.62278	1000000

* From Frederick E. Croxton and Dudley J. Cowden, *Practical Business Statistics*, 2d ed. (Copyright, 1939, 1955, by Prentice-Hall, Inc., Englewood Cliffs, N.J.), pp. 766–775. Reproduced by permission of the publisher.

Table X SQUARES, SQUARE ROOTS, AND RECIPROCALS 1–1,000 (*Continued*)

N	N²	$\sqrt{N}$	$\sqrt{10N}$	1/N .0	N	N²	$\sqrt{N}$	$\sqrt{10N}$	1/N .00
100	10 000	10.00000	31.62278	10000000	150	22 500	12.24745	38.72983	6666667
101	10 201	10.04988	31.78050	09900990	151	22 801	12.28821	38.85872	6622517
102	10 404	10.09950	31.93744	09803922	152	23 104	12.32883	38.98718	6578947
103	10 609	10.14889	32.09361	09708738	153	23 409	12.36932	39.11521	6535948
104	10 816	10.19804	32.24903	09615385	154	23 716	12.40967	39.24283	6493506
105	11 025	10.24695	32.40370	09523810	155	24 025	12.44990	39.37004	6451613
106	11 236	10.29563	32.55764	09433962	156	24 336	12.49000	39.49684	6410256
107	11 449	10.34408	32.71085	09345794	157	24 649	12.52996	39.62323	6369427
108	11 664	10.39230	32.86335	09259259	158	24 964	12.56981	39.74921	6329114
109	11 881	10.44031	33.01515	09174312	159	25 281	12.60952	39.87480	6289308
110	12 100	10.48809	33.16625	09090909	160	25 600	12.64911	40.00000	6250000
111	12 321	10.53565	33.31666	09009009	161	25 921	12.68858	40.12481	6211180
112	12 544	10.58301	33.46640	08928571	162	26 244	12.72792	40.24922	6172840
113	12 769	10.63015	33.61547	08849558	163	26 569	12.76715	40.37326	6134969
114	12 996	10.67708	33.76389	08771930	164	26 896	12.80625	40.49691	6097561
115	13 225	10.72381	33.91165	08695652	165	27 225	12.84523	40.62019	6060606
116	13 456	10.77033	34.05877	08620690	166	27 556	12.88410	40.74310	6024096
117	13 689	10.81665	34.20526	08547009	167	27 889	12.92285	40.86563	5988024
118	13 924	10.86278	34.35113	08474576	168	28 224	12.96148	40.98780	5952381
119	14 161	10.90871	34.49638	08403361	169	28 561	13.00000	41.10961	5917160
120	14 400	10.95445	34.64102	08333333	170	28 900	13.03840	41.23106	5882353
121	14 641	11.00000	34.78505	08264463	171	29 241	13.07670	41.35215	5847953
122	14 884	11.04536	34.92850	08196721	172	29 584	13.11488	41.47288	5813953
123	15 129	11.09054	35.07136	08130081	173	29 929	13.15295	41.59327	5780347
124	15 376	11.13553	35.21363	08064516	174	30 276	13.19091	41.71331	5747126
125	15 625	11.18034	35.35534	08000000	175	30 625	13.22876	41.83300	5714286
126	15 876	11.22497	35.49648	07936508	176	30 976	13.26650	41.95235	5681818
127	16 129	11.26943	35.63706	07874016	177	31 329	13.30413	42.07137	5649718
128	16 384	11.31371	35.77709	07812500	178	31 684	13.34166	42.19005	5617978
129	16 641	11.35782	35.91657	07751938	179	32 041	13.37909	42.30839	5586592
130	16 900	11.40175	36.05551	07692308	180	32 400	13.41641	42.42641	5555556
131	17 161	11.44552	36.19392	07633588	181	32 761	13.45362	42.54409	5524862
132	17 424	11.48913	36.33180	07575758	182	33 124	13.49074	42.66146	5494505
133	17 689	11.53256	36.46917	07518797	183	33 489	13.52775	42.77850	5464481
134	17 956	11.57584	36.60601	07462687	184	33 856	13.56466	42.89522	5434783
135	18 225	11.61895	36.74235	07407407	185	34 225	13.60147	43.01163	5405405
136	18 496	11.66190	36.87818	07352941	186	34 596	13.63818	43.12772	5376344
137	18 769	11.70470	37.01351	07299270	187	34 969	13.67479	43.24350	5347594
138	19 044	11.74734	37.14835	07246377	188	35 344	13.71131	43.35897	5319149
139	19 321	11.78983	37.28270	07194245	189	35 721	13.74773	43.47413	5291005
140	19 600	11.83216	37.41657	07142857	190	36 100	13.78405	43.58899	5263158
141	19 881	11.87434	37.54997	07092199	191	36 481	13.82027	43.70355	5235602
142	20 164	11.91638	37.68289	07042254	192	36 864	13.85641	43.81780	5208333
143	20 449	11.95826	37.81534	06993007	193	37 249	13.89244	43.93177	5181347
144	20 736	12.00000	37.94733	06944444	194	37 636	13.92839	44.04543	5154639
145	21 025	12.04159	38.07887	06896552	195	38 025	13.96424	44.15880	5128205
146	21 316	12.08305	38.20995	06849315	196	38 416	14.00000	44.27189	5102041
147	21 609	12.12436	38.34058	06802721	197	38 809	14.03567	44.38468	5076142
148	21 904	12.16553	38.47077	06756757	198	39 204	14.07125	44.49719	5050505
149	22 201	12.20656	38.60052	06711409	199	39 601	14.10674	44.60942	5025126
150	22 500	12.24745	38.72983	06666667	200	40 000	14.14214	44.72136	5000000

Table X SQUARES, SQUARE ROOTS, AND RECIPROCALS, 1–1,000 (*Continued*)

N	N²	√N	√10N	1/N .00	N	N²	√N	√10N	1/N .00
200	40 000	14.14214	44.72136	5000000	250	62 500	15.81139	50.00000	4000000
201	40 401	14.17745	44.83302	4975124	251	63 001	15.84298	50.09990	3984064
202	40 804	14.21267	44.94441	4950495	252	63 504	15.87451	50.19960	3968254
203	41 209	14.24781	45.05552	4926108	253	64 009	15.90597	50.29911	3952569
204	41 616	14.28286	45.16636	4901961	254	64 516	15.93738	50.39841	3937008
205	42 025	14.31782	45.27693	4878049	255	65 025	15.96872	50.49752	3921569
206	42 436	14.35270	45.38722	4854369	256	65 536	16.00000	50.59644	3906250
207	42 849	14.38749	45.49725	4830918	257	66 049	16.03122	50.69517	3891051
208	43 264	14.42221	45.60702	4807692	258	66 564	16.06238	50.79370	3875969
209	43 681	14.45683	45.71652	4784689	259	67 081	16.09348	50.89204	3861004
210	44 100	14.49138	45.82576	4761905	260	67 600	16.12452	50.99020	3846154
211	44 521	14.52584	45.93474	4739336	261	68 121	16.15549	51.08816	3831418
212	44 944	14.56022	46.04346	4716981	262	68 644	16.18641	51.18594	3816794
213	45 369	14.59452	46.15192	4694836	263	69 169	16.21727	51.28353	3802281
214	45 796	14.62874	46.26013	4672897	264	69 696	16.24808	51.38093	3787879
215	46 225	14.66288	46.36809	4651163	265	70 225	16.27882	51.47815	3773585
216	46 656	14.69694	46.47580	4629630	266	70 756	16.30951	51.57519	3759398
217	47 089	14.73092	46.58326	4608295	267	71 289	16.34013	51.67204	3745318
218	47 524	14.76482	46.69047	4587156	268	71 824	16.37071	51.76872	3731343
219	47 961	14.79865	46.79744	4566210	269	72 361	16.40122	51.86521	3717472
220	48 400	14.83240	46.90416	4545455	270	72 900	16.43168	51.96152	3703704
221	48 841	14.86607	47.01064	4524887	271	73 441	16.46208	52.05766	3690037
222	49 284	14.89966	47.11688	4504505	272	73 984	16.49242	52.15362	3676471
223	49 729	14.93318	47.22288	4484305	273	74 529	16.52271	52.24940	3663004
224	50 176	14.96663	47.32864	4464286	274	75 076	16.55295	52.34501	3649635
225	50 625	15.00000	47.43416	4444444	275	75 625	16.58312	52.44044	3636364
226	51 076	15.03330	47.53946	4424779	276	76 176	16.61325	52.53570	3623188
227	51 529	15.06652	47.64452	4405286	277	76 729	16.64332	52.63079	3610108
228	51 984	15.09967	47.74935	4385965	278	77 284	16.67333	52.72571	3597122
229	52 441	15.13275	47.85394	4366812	279	77 841	16.70329	52.82045	3584229
230	52 900	15.16575	47.95832	4347826	280	78 400	16.73320	52.91503	3571429
231	53 361	15.19868	48.06246	4329004	281	78 961	16.76305	53.00943	3558719
232	53 824	15.23155	48.16638	4310345	282	79 524	16.79286	53.10367	3546099
233	54 289	15.26434	48.27007	4291845	283	80 089	16.82260	53.19774	3533569
234	54 756	15.29706	48.37355	4273504	284	80 656	16.85230	53.29165	3521127
235	55 225	15.32971	48.47680	4255319	285	81 225	16.88194	53.38539	3508772
236	55 696	15.36229	48.57983	4237288	286	81 796	16.91153	53.47897	3496503
237	56 169	15.39480	48.68265	4219409	287	82 369	16.94107	53.57238	3484321
238	56 644	15.42725	48.78524	4201681	288	82 944	16.97056	53.66563	3472222
239	57 121	15.45962	48.88763	4184100	289	83 521	17.00000	53.75872	3460208
240	57 600	15.49193	48.98979	4166667	290	84 100	17.02939	53.85165	3448276
241	58 081	15.52417	49.09175	4149378	291	84 681	17.05872	53.94442	3436426
242	58 564	15.55635	49.19350	4132231	292	85 264	17.08801	54.03702	3424658
243	59 049	15.58846	49.29503	4115226	293	85 849	17.11724	54.12947	3412969
244	59 536	15.62050	49.39636	4098361	294	86 436	17.14643	54.22177	3401361
245	60 025	15.65248	49.49747	4081633	295	87 025	17.17556	54.31390	3389831
246	60 516	15.68439	49.59839	4065041	296	87 616	17.20465	54.40588	3378378
247	61 009	15.71623	49.69909	4048583	297	88 209	17.23369	54.49771	3367003
248	61 504	15.74802	49.79960	4032258	298	88 804	17.26268	54.58938	3355705
249	62 001	15.77973	49.89990	4016064	299	89 401	17.29162	54.68089	3344482
250	62 500	15.81139	50.00000	4000000	300	90 000	17.32051	54.77226	3333333

Table X   SQUARES, SQUARE ROOTS, AND RECIPROCALS, 1–1,000 (*Continued*)

N	N²	√N	√10N	1/N .00	N	N²	√N	√10N	1/N .00
300	90 000	17.32051	54.77226	3333333	350	122 500	18.70829	59.16080	2857143
301	90 601	17.34935	54.86347	3322259	351	123 201	18.73499	59.24525	2849003
302	91 204	17.37815	54.95453	3311258	352	123 904	18.76166	59.32959	2840909
303	91 809	17.40690	55.04544	3300330	353	124 609	18.78829	59.41380	2832861
304	92 416	17.43560	55.13620	3289474	354	125 316	18.81489	59.49790	2824859
305	93 025	17.46425	55.22681	3278689	355	126 025	18.84144	59.58188	2816901
306	93 636	17.49286	55.31727	3267974	356	126 736	18.86796	59.66574	2808989
307	94 249	17.52142	55.40758	3257329	357	127 449	18.89444	59.74948	2801120
308	94 864	17.54993	55.49775	3246753	358	128 164	18.92089	59.83310	2793296
309	95 481	17.57840	55.58777	3236246	359	128 881	18.94730	59.91661	2785515
310	96 100	17.60682	55.67764	3225806	360	129 600	18.97367	60.00000	2777778
311	96 721	17.63519	55.76737	3215434	361	130 321	19.00000	60.08328	2770083
312	97 344	17.66352	55.85696	3205128	362	131 044	19.02630	60.16644	2762431
313	97 969	17.69181	55.94640	3194888	363	131 769	19.05256	60.24948	2754821
314	98 596	17.72005	56.03570	3184713	364	132 496	19.07878	60.33241	2747253
315	99 225	17.74824	56.12486	3174603	365	133 225	19.10497	60.41523	2739726
316	99 856	17.77639	56.21388	3164557	366	133 956	19.13113	60.49793	2732240
317	100 489	17.80449	56.30275	3154574	367	134 689	19.15724	60.58052	2724796
318	101 124	17.83255	56.39149	3144654	368	135 424	19.18333	60.66300	2717391
319	101 761	17.86057	56.48008	3134796	369	136 161	19.20937	60.74537	2710027
320	102 400	17.88854	56.56854	3125000	370	136 900	19.23538	60.82763	2702703
321	103 041	17.91647	56.65686	3115265	371	137 641	19.26136	60.90977	2695418
322	103 684	17.94436	56.74504	3105590	372	138 384	19.28730	60.99180	2688172
323	104 329	17.97220	56.83309	3095975	373	139 129	19.31321	61.07373	2680965
324	104 976	18.00000	56.92100	3086420	374	139 876	19.33908	61.15554	2673797
325	105 625	18.02776	57.00877	3076923	375	140 625	19.36492	61.23724	2666667
326	106 276	18.05547	57.09641	3067485	376	141 376	19.39072	61.31884	2659574
327	106 929	18.08314	57.18391	3058104	377	142 129	19.41649	61.40033	2652520
328	107 584	18.11077	57.27128	3048780	378	142 884	19.44222	61.48170	2645503
329	108 241	18.13836	57.35852	3039514	379	143 641	19.46792	61.56298	2638522
330	108 900	18.16590	57.44563	3030303	380	144 400	19.49359	61.64414	2631579
331	109 561	18.19341	57.53260	3021148	381	145 161	19.51922	61.72520	2624672
332	110 224	18 22087	57.61944	3012048	382	145 924	19.54483	61.80615	2617801
333	110 889	18.24829	57.70615	3003003	383	146 689	19.57039	61.88699	2610966
334	111 556	18.27567	57.79273	2994012	384	147 456	19.59592	61.96773	2604167
335	112 225	18.30301	57.87918	2985075	385	148 225	19.62142	62.04837	2597403
336	112 896	18.33030	57.96551	2976190	386	148 996	19.64688	62.12890	2590674
337	113 569	18.35756	58.05170	2967359	387	149 769	19.67232	62.20932	2583979
338	114 244	18.38478	58.13777	2958580	388	150 544	19.69772	62.28965	2577320
339	114 921	18.41195	58.22371	2949853	389	151 321	19.72308	62.36986	2570694
340	115 600	18.43909	58.30952	2941176	390	152 100	19.74842	62.44998	2564103
341	116 281	18.46619	58.39521	2932551	391	152 881	19.77372	62.52999	2557545
342	116 964	18.49324	58.48077	2923977	392	153 664	19.79899	62.60990	2551020
343	117 649	18.52026	58.56620	2915452	393	154 449	19.82423	62.68971	2544529
344	118 336	18.54724	58.65151	2906977	394	155 236	19.84943	62.76942	2538071
345	119 025	18.57418	58.73670	2898551	395	156 025	19.87461	62.84903	2531646
346	119 716	18.60108	58.82176	2890173	396	156 816	19.89975	62.92853	2525253
347	120 409	18.62794	58.90671	2881844	397	157 609	19.92486	63.00794	2518892
348	121 104	18.65476	58.99152	2873563	398	158 404	19.94994	63.08724	2512563
349	121 801	18.68154	59.07622	2865330	399	159 201	19.97498	63.16645	2506266
350	122 500	18.70829	59.16080	2857143	400	160 000	20.00000	63.24555	2500000

Table X SQUARES, SQUARE ROOTS, AND RECIPROCALS 1–1,000 *(Continued)*

N	N^2	$\sqrt{N}$	$\sqrt{10N}$	$1/N$ .00	N	N^2	$\sqrt{N}$	$\sqrt{10N}$	$1/N$ .00
400	160 000	20.00000	63.24555	2500000	450	202 500	21.21320	67.08204	2222222
401	160 801	20.02498	63.32456	2493766	451	203 401	21.23676	67.15653	2217295
402	161 604	20.04994	63.40347	2487562	452	204 304	21.26029	67.23095	2212389
403	162 409	20.07486	63.48228	2481390	453	205 209	21.28380	67.30527	2207506
404	163 216	20.09975	63.56099	2475248	454	206 116	21.30728	67.37952	2202643
405	164 025	20.12461	63.63961	2469136	455	207 025	21.33073	67.45369	2197802
406	164 836	20.14944	63.71813	2463054	456	207 936	21.35416	67.52777	2192982
407	165 649	20.17424	63.79655	2457002	457	208 849	21.37756	67.60178	2188184
408	166 464	20.19901	63.87488	2450980	458	209 764	21.40093	67.67570	2183406
409	167 281	20.22375	63.95311	2444988	459	210 681	21.42429	67.74954	2178649
410	168 100	20.24846	64.03124	2439024	460	211 600	21.44761	67.82330	2173913
411	168 921	20.27313	64.10928	2433090	461	212 521	21.47091	67.89698	2169197
412	169 744	20.29778	64.18723	2427184	462	213 444	21.49419	67.97058	2164502
413	170 569	20.32240	64.26508	2421308	463	214 369	21.51743	68.04410	2159827
414	171 396	20.34699	64.34283	2415459	464	215 296	21.54066	68.11755	2155172
415	172 225	20.37155	64.42049	2409639	465	216 225	21.56386	68.19091	2150538
416	173 056	20.39608	64.49806	2403846	466	217 156	21.58703	68.26419	2145923
417	173 889	20.42058	64.57554	2398082	467	218 089	21.61018	68.33740	2141328
418	174 724	20.44505	64.65292	2392344	468	219 024	21.63331	68.41053	2136752
419	175 561	20.46949	64.73021	2386635	469	219 961	21.65641	68.48357	2132196
420	176 400	20.49390	64.80741	2380952	470	220 900	21.67948	68.55655	2127660
421	177 241	20.51828	64.88451	2375297	471	221 841	21.70253	68.62944	2123142
422	178 084	20.54264	64.96153	2369668	472	222 784	21.72556	68.70226	2118644
423	178 929	20.56696	65.03845	2364066	473	223 729	21.74856	68.77500	2114165
424	179 776	20.59126	65.11528	2358491	474	224 676	21.77154	68.84766	2109705
425	180 625	20.61553	65.19202	2352941	475	225 625	21.79449	68.92024	2105263
426	181 476	20.63977	65.26868	2347418	476	226 576	21.81742	68.99275	2100840
427	182 329	20.66398	65.34524	2341920	477	227 529	21.84033	69.06519	2096436
428	183 184	20.68816	65.42171	2336449	478	228 484	21.86321	69.13754	2092050
429	184 041	20.71232	65.49809	2331002	479	229 441	21.88607	69.20983	2087683
430	184 900	20.73644	65.57439	2325581	480	230 400	21.90890	69.28203	2083333
431	185 761	20.76054	65.65059	2320186	481	231 361	21.93171	69.35416	2079002
432	186 624	20.78461	65.72671	2314815	482	232 324	21.95450	69.42622	2074689
433	187 489	20.80865	65.80274	2309469	483	233 289	21.97726	69.49820	2070393
434	188 356	20.83267	65.87868	2304147	484	234 256	22.00000	69.57011	2066116
435	189 225	20.85665	65.95453	2298851	485	235 225	22.02272	69.64194	2061856
436	190 096	20.88061	66.03030	2293578	486	236 096	22.04541	69.71370	2057613
437	190 969	20.90454	66.10598	2288330	487	237 169	22.06808	69.78539	2053388
438	191 844	20.92845	66.18157	2283105	488	238 144	22.09072	69.85700	2049180
439	192 721	20.95233	66.25708	2277904	489	239 121	22.11334	69.92853	2044990
440	193 600	20.97618	66.33250	2272727	490	240 100	22.13594	70.00000	2040816
441	194 481	21.00000	66.40783	2267574	491	241 081	22.15852	70.07139	2036660
442	195 364	21.02380	66.48308	2262443	492	242 064	22.18107	70.14271	2032520
443	196 249	21.04757	66.55825	2257336	493	243 049	22.20360	70.21396	2028398
444	197 136	21.07131	66.63332	2252252	494	244 036	22.22611	70.28513	2024291
445	198 025	21.09502	66.70832	2247191	495	245 025	22.24860	70.35624	2020202
446	198 916	21.11871	66.78323	2242152	496	246 016	22.27106	70.42727	2016129
447	199 809	21.14237	66.85806	2237136	497	247 009	22.29350	70.49823	2012072
448	200 704	21.16601	66.93280	2232143	498	248 004	22.31591	70.56912	2008032
449	201 601	21.18962	67.00746	2227171	499	249 001	22.33831	70.63993	2004008
450	202 500	21.21320	67.08204	2222222	500	250 000	22.36068	70.71068	2000000

Table X SQUARES, SQUARE ROOTS, AND RECIPROCALS 1–1,000 (*Continued*)

N	N²	√N	√10N	1/N .00	N	N²	√N	√10N	1/N .00
500	250 000	22.36068	70.71068	2000000	550	302 500	23.45208	74.16198	1818182
501	251 001	22.38303	70.78135	1996008	551	303 601	23.47339	74.22937	1814882
502	252 004	22.40536	70.85196	1992032	552	304 704	23.49468	74.29670	1811594
503	253 009	22.42766	70.92249	1988072	553	305 809	23.51595	74.36397	1808318
504	254 016	22.44994	70.99296	1984127	554	306 916	23.53720	74.43118	1805054
505	255 025	22.47221	71.06335	1980198	555	308 025	23.55844	74.49832	1801802
506	256 036	22.49444	71.13368	1976285	556	309 136	23.57965	74.56541	1798561
507	257 049	22.51666	71.20393	1972387	557	310 249	23.60085	74.63243	1795332
508	258 064	22.53886	71.27412	1968504	558	311 364	23.62202	74.69940	1792115
509	259 081	22.56103	71.34424	1964637	559	312 481	23.64318	74.76630	1788909
510	260 100	22.58318	71.41428	1960784	560	313 600	23.66432	74.83315	1785714
511	261 121	22.60531	71.48426	1956947	561	314 721	23.68544	74.89993	1782531
512	262 144	22.62742	71.55418	1953125	562	315 844	23.70654	74.96666	1779359
513	263 169	22.64950	71.62402	1949318	563	316 969	23.72762	75.03333	1776199
514	264 196	22.67157	71.69379	1945525	564	318 096	23.74868	75.09993	1773050
515	265 225	22.69361	71.76350	1941748	565	319 225	23.76973	75.16648	1769912
516	266 256	22.71563	71.83314	1937984	566	320 356	23.79075	75.23297	1766784
517	267 289	22.73763	71.90271	1934236	567	321 489	23.81176	75.29940	1763668
518	268 324	22.75961	71.97222	1930502	568	322 624	23.83275	75.36577	1760563
519	269 361	22.78157	72.04165	1926782	569	323 761	23.85372	75.43209	1757469
520	270 400	22.80351	72.11103	1923077	570	324 900	23.87467	75.49834	1754386
521	271 441	22.82542	72.18033	1919386	571	326 041	23.89561	75.56454	1751313
522	272 484	22.84732	72.24957	1915709	572	327 184	23.91652	75.63068	1748252
523	273 529	22.86919	72.31874	1912046	573	328 329	23.93742	75.69676	1745201
524	274 576	22.89105	72.38784	1908397	574	329 476	23.95830	75.76279	1742160
525	275 625	22.91288	72.45688	1904762	575	330 625	23.97916	75.82875	1739130
526	276 676	22.93469	72.52586	1901141	576	331 776	24.00000	75.89466	1736111
527	277 729	22.95648	72.59477	1897533	577	332 929	24.02082	75.96052	1733102
528	278 784	22.97825	72.66361	1893939	578	334 084	24.04163	76.02631	1730104
529	279 841	23.00000	72.73239	1890359	579	335 241	24.06242	76.09205	1727116
530	280 900	23.02173	72.80110	1886792	580	336 400	24.08319	76.15773	1724138
531	281 961	23.04344	72.86975	1883239	581	337 561	24.10394	76.22336	1721170
532	283 024	23.06513	72.93833	1879699	582	338 724	24.12468	76.28892	1718213
533	284 089	23.08679	73.00685	1876173	583	339 889	24.14539	76.35444	1715266
534	285 156	23.10844	73.07530	1872659	584	341 056	24.16609	76.41989	1712329
535	286 225	23.13007	73.14369	1869159	585	342 225	24.18677	76.48529	1709402
536	287 296	23.15167	73.21202	1865672	586	343 396	24.20744	76.55064	1706485
537	288 369	23.17326	73.28028	1862197	587	344 569	24.22808	76.61593	1703578
538	289 444	23.19483	73.34848	1858736	588	345 744	24.24871	76.68116	1700680
539	290 521	23.21637	73.41662	1855288	589	346 921	24.26932	76.74634	1697793
540	291 600	23.23790	73.48469	1851852	590	348 100	24.28992	76.81146	1694915
541	292 681	23.25941	73.55270	1848429	591	349 281	24.31049	76.87652	1692047
542	293 764	23.28089	73.62065	1845018	592	350 464	24.33105	76.94154	1689189
543	294 849	23.30236	73.68853	1841621	593	351 649	24.35159	77.00649	1686341
544	295 936	23.32381	73.75636	1838235	594	352 836	24.37212	77.07140	1683502
545	297 025	23.34524	73.82412	1834862	595	354 025	24.39262	77.13624	1680672
546	298 116	23.36664	73.89181	1831502	596	355 216	24.41311	77.20104	1677852
547	299 209	23.38803	73.95945	1828154	597	356 409	24.43358	77.26578	1675042
548	300 304	23.40940	74.02702	1824818	598	357 604	24.45404	77.33046	1672241
549	301 401	23.43075	74.09453	1821494	599	358 801	24.47448	77.39509	1669449
550	302 500	23.45208	74.16198	1818182	600	360 000	24.49490	77.45967	1666667

Table X SQUARES, SQUARE ROOTS, AND RECIPROCALS 1–1,000 (*Continued*)

N	N²	√N̄	√1̄0̄N̄	1/N .00	N	N²	√N̄	√1̄0̄N̄	1/N .00
600	360 000	24.49490	77.45967	1666667	650	422 500	25.49510	80.62258	1538462
601	361 201	24.51530	77.52419	1663894	651	423 801	25.51470	80.68457	1536098
602	362 404	24.53569	77.58866	1661130	652	425 104	25.53429	80.74652	1533742
603	363 609	24.55606	77.65307	1658375	653	426 409	25.55386	80.80842	1531394
604	364 816	24.57641	77.71744	1655629	654	427 716	25.57342	80.87027	1529052
605	366 025	24.59675	77.78175	1652893	655	429 025	25.59297	80.93207	1526718
606	367 236	24.61707	77.84600	1650165	656	430 336	25.61250	80.99383	1524390
607	368 449	24.63737	77.91020	1647446	657	431 649	25.63201	81.05554	1522070
608	369 664	24.65766	77.97435	1644737	658	432 964	25.65151	81.11720	1519757
609	370 881	24.67793	78.03845	1642036	659	434 281	25.67100	81.17881	1517451
610	372 100	24.69818	78.10250	1639344	660	435 600	25.69047	81.24038	1515152
611	373 321	24.71841	78.16649	1636661	661	436 921	25.70992	81.30191	1512859
612	374 544	24.73863	78.23043	1633987	662	438 244	25.72936	81.36338	1510574
613	375 769	24.75884	78.29432	1631321	663	439 569	25.74879	81.42481	1508296
614	376 996	24.77902	78.35815	1628664	664	440 896	25.76820	81.48620	1506024
615	378 225	24.79919	78.42194	1626016	665	442 225	25.78759	81.54753	1503759
616	379 456	24.81935	78.48567	1623377	666	443 556	25.80698	81.60882	1501502
617	380 689	24.83948	78.54935	1620746	667	444 889	25.82634	81.67007	1499250
618	381 924	24.85961	78.61298	1618123	668	446 224	25.84570	81.73127	1497006
619	383 161	24.87971	78.67655	1615509	669	447 561	25.86503	81.79242	1494768
620	384 400	24.89980	78.74008	1612903	670	448 900	25.88436	81.85353	1492537
621	385 641	24.91987	78.80355	1610306	671	450 241	25.90367	81.91459	1490313
622	386 884	24.93993	78.86698	1607717	672	451 584	25.92296	81.97561	1488095
623	388 129	24.95997	78.93035	1605136	673	452 929	25.94224	82.03658	1485884
624	389 376	24.97999	78.99367	1602564	674	454 276	25.96151	82.09750	1483680
625	390 625	25.00000	79.05694	1600000	675	455 625	25.98076	82.15838	1481481
626	391 876	25.01999	79.12016	1597444	676	456 976	26.00000	82.21922	1479290
627	393 129	25.03997	79.18333	1594896	677	458 329	26.01922	82.28001	1477105
628	394 384	25.05993	79.24645	1592357	678	459 684	26.03843	82.34076	1474926
629	395 641	25.07987	79.30952	1589825	679	461 041	26.05763	82.40146	1472754
630	396 900	25.09980	79.37254	1587302	680	462 400	26.07681	82.46211	1470588
631	398 161	25.11971	79.43551	1584786	681	463 761	26.09598	82.42272	1468429
632	399 424	25.13961	79.49843	1582278	682	465 124	26.11513	82.58329	1466276
633	400 689	25.15949	79.56130	1579779	683	466 489	26.13427	82.64381	1464129
634	401 956	25.17936	79.62412	1577287	684	467 856	26.15339	82.70429	1461988
635	403 225	25.19921	79.68689	1574803	685	469 225	26.17250	82.76473	1459854
636	404 496	25.21904	79.74961	1572327	686	470 596	26.19160	82.82512	1457726
637	405 769	25.23886	79.81228	1569859	687	471 969	26.21068	82.88546	1455604
638	407 044	25.25866	79.87490	1567398	688	473 344	26.22975	82.94577	1453488
639	408 321	25.27845	79.93748	1564945	689	474 721	26.24881	83.00602	1451379
640	409 600	25.29822	80.00000	1562500	690	476 100	26.26785	83.06624	1449275
641	410 881	25.31798	80.06248	1560062	691	477 481	26.28688	83.12641	1447178
642	412 164	25.33772	80.12490	1557632	692	478 864	26.30589	83.18654	1445087
643	413 449	25.35744	80.18728	1555210	693	480 249	26.32489	83.24662	1443001
644	414 736	25.37716	80.24961	1552795	694	481 636	26.34388	83.30666	1440922
645	416 025	25.39685	80.31189	1550388	695	483 025	26.36285	83.36666	1438849
646	417 316	25.41653	80.37413	1547988	696	484 416	26.38181	83.42661	1436782
647	418 609	25.43619	80.43631	1545595	697	485 809	26.40076	83.48653	1434720
648	419 904	25.45584	80.49845	1543210	698	487 204	26.41969	83.54639	1432665
649	421 201	25.47548	80.56054	1540832	699	488 601	26.43861	83.60622	1430615
650	422 500	25.49510	80.62258	1538462	700	490 000	26.45751	83.66600	1428571

Table X SQUARES, SQUARE ROOTS, AND RECIPROCALS 1–1,000 (*Continued*)

N	N²	√N	√10N	1/N .00	N	N²	√N	√10N	1/N .00
700	490 000	26.45751	83.66600	1428571	750	562 500	27.38613	86.60254	1333333
701	491 401	26.47640	83.72574	1426534	751	564 001	27.40438	86.66026	1331558
702	492 804	26.49528	83.78544	1424501	752	565 504	27.42262	86.71793	1329787
703	494 209	26.51415	83.84510	1422475	753	567 009	27.44085	86.77557	1328021
704	495 616	26.53300	83.90471	1420455	754	568 516	27.45906	86.83317	1326260
705	497 025	26.55184	83.96428	1418440	755	570 025	27.47726	86.89074	1324503
706	498 436	26.57066	84.02381	1416431	756	571 536	27.49545	86.94826	1322751
707	499 849	26.58947	84.08329	1414427	757	573 049	27.51363	87.00575	1321004
708	501 264	26.60827	84.14274	1412429	758	574 564	27.53180	87.06320	1319261
709	502 681	26.62705	84.20214	1410437	759	576 081	27.54995	87.12061	1317523
710	504 100	26.64583	84.26150	1408451	760	577 600	27.56810	87.17798	1315789
711	505 521	26.66458	84.32082	1406470	761	579 121	27.58623	87.23531	1314060
712	506 944	26.68333	84.38009	1404494	762	580 644	27.60435	87.29261	1312336
713	508 369	26.70206	84.43933	1402525	763	582 169	27.62245	87.34987	1310616
714	509 796	26.72078	84.49852	1400560	764	583 696	27.64055	87.40709	1308901
715	511 225	26.73948	84.55767	1398601	765	585 225	27.65863	87.46428	1307190
716	512 656	26.75818	84.61678	1396648	766	586 756	27.67671	87.52143	1305483
717	514 089	26.77686	84.67585	1394700	767	588 289	27.69476	87.57854	1303781
718	515 524	26.79552	84.73488	1392758	768	589 824	27.71281	87.63561	1302083
719	516 961	26.81418	84.79387	1390821	769	591 361	27.73085	87.69265	1300390
720	518 400	26.83282	84.85281	1388889	770	592 900	27.74887	87.74964	1298701
721	519 841	26.85144	84.91172	1386963	771	594 441	27.76689	87.80661	1297017
722	521 284	26.87006	84.97058	1385042	772	595 984	27.78489	87.86353	1295337
723	522 729	26.88866	85.02941	1383126	773	597 529	27.80288	87.92042	1293661
724	524 176	26.90725	85.08819	1381215	774	599 076	27.82086	87.97727	1291990
725	525 625	26.92582	85.14693	1379310	775	600 625	27.83882	88.03408	1290323
726	527 076	26.94439	85.20563	1377410	776	602 176	27.85678	88.09086	1288660
727	528 529	26.96294	85.26429	1375516	777	603 729	27.87472	88.14760	1287001
728	529 984	26.98148	85.32292	1373626	778	605 284	27.89265	88.20431	1285347
729	531 441	27.00000	85.38150	1371742	779	606 841	27.91057	88.26098	1283697
730	532 900	27.01851	85.44004	1369863	780	608 400	27.92848	88.31761	1282051
731	534 361	27.03701	85.49854	1367989	781	609 961	27.94638	88.37420	1280410
732	535 824	27.05550	85.55700	1366120	782	611 524	27.96426	88.43076	1278772
733	537 289	27.07397	85.61542	1364256	783	613 089	27.98214	88.48729	1277139
734	538 756	27.09243	85.67380	1362398	784	614 656	28.00000	88.54377	1275510
735	540 225	27.11088	85.73214	1360544	785	616 225	28.01785	88.60023	1273885
736	541 696	27.12932	85.79044	1358696	786	617 796	28.03569	88.65664	1272265
737	543 169	27.14774	85.84870	1356852	787	619 369	28.05352	88.71302	1270648
738	544 644	27.16616	85.90693	1355014	788	620 944	28.07134	88.76936	1269036
739	546 121	27.18455	85.96511	1353180	789	622 521	28.08914	88.82567	1267427
740	547 600	27.20294	86.02325	1351351	790	624 100	28.10694	88.88194	1265823
741	549 081	27.22132	86.08136	1349528	791	625 681	28.12472	88.93818	1264223
742	550 564	27.23968	86.13942	1347709	792	627 264	28.14249	88.99438	1262626
743	552 049	27.25803	86.19745	1345895	793	628 849	28.16026	89.05055	1261034
744	553 536	27.27636	86.25543	1344086	794	630 436	28.17801	89.10668	1259446
745	555 025	27.29469	86.31338	1342282	795	632 025	28.19574	89.16277	1257862
746	556 516	27.31300	86.37129	1340483	796	633 616	28.21347	89.21883	1256281
747	558 009	27.33130	86.42916	1338688	797	635 209	28.23119	89.27486	1254705
748	559 504	27.34959	86.48699	1336898	798	636 804	28.24889	89.33085	1253133
749	561 001	27.36786	86.54479	1335113	799	638 401	28.26659	89.38680	1251564
750	562 500	27.38613	86.60254	1333333	800	640 000	28.28427	89.44272	1250000

413

Table X SQUARES, SQUARE ROOTS, AND RECIPROCALS 1–1,000 (*Continued*)

N	N²	√N	√10N	1/N .00	N	N²	√N	√10N	1/N .00
800	640 000	28.28427	89.44272	1250000	850	722 500	29.15476	92.19544	1176471
801	641 601	28.30194	89.49860	1248439	851	724 201	29.17190	92.24966	1175088
802	643 204	28.31960	89.55445	1246883	852	725 904	29.18904	92.30385	1173709
803	644 809	28.33725	89.61027	1245330	853	727 609	29.20616	92.35800	1172333
804	646 416	28.35489	89.66605	1243781	854	729 316	29.22328	92.41212	1170960
805	648 025	28.37252	89.72179	1242236	855	731 025	29.24038	92.46621	1169591
806	649 636	28.39014	89.77750	1240695	856	732 736	29.25748	92.52027	1168224
807	651 249	28.40775	89.83318	1239157	857	734 449	29.27456	92.57429	1166861
808	652 864	28.42534	89.88882	1237624	858	736 164	29.29164	92.62829	1165501
809	654 481	28.44293	89.94443	1236094	859	737 881	29.30870	92.68225	1164144
810	656 100	28.46050	90.00000	1234568	860	739 600	29.32576	92.73618	1162791
811	657 721	28.47806	90.05554	1233046	861	741 321	29.34280	92.79009	1161440
812	659 344	28.49561	90.11104	1231527	862	743 044	29.35984	92.84396	1160093
813	660 969	28.51315	90.16651	1230012	863	744 769	29.37686	92.89779	1158749
814	662 596	28.53069	90.22195	1228501	864	746 496	29.39388	92.95160	1157407
815	664 225	28.54820	90.27735	1226994	865	748 225	29.41088	93.00538	1156069
816	665 856	28.56571	90.33272	1225490	866	749 956	29.42788	93.05912	1154734
817	667 489	28.58321	90.38805	1223990	867	751 689	29.44486	93.11283	1153403
818	669 124	28.60070	90.44335	1222494	868	753 424	29.46184	93.16652	1152074
819	670 761	28.61818	90.49862	1221001	869	755 161	29.47881	93.22017	1150748
820	672 400	28.63564	90.55385	1219512	870	756 900	29.49576	93.27379	1149425
821	674 041	28.65310	90.60905	1218027	871	758 641	29.51271	93.32738	1148106
822	675 684	28.67054	90.66422	1216545	872	760 384	29.52965	93.38094	1146789
823	677 329	28.68798	90.71935	1215067	873	762 129	29.54657	93.43447	1145475
824	678 976	28.70540	90.77445	1213592	874	763 876	29.56349	93.48797	1144165
825	680 625	28.72281	90.82951	1212121	875	765 625	29.58040	93.54143	1142857
826	682 276	28.74022	90.88454	1210654	876	767 376	29.59730	93.59487	1141553
827	683 929	28.75761	90.93954	1209190	877	769 129	29.61419	93.64828	1140251
828	685 584	28.77499	90.99451	1207729	878	770 884	29.63106	93.70165	1138952
829	687 241	28.79236	91.04944	1206273	879	772 641	29.64793	93.75500	1137656
830	688 900	28.80972	91.10434	1204819	880	774 400	29.66479	93.80832	1136364
831	690 561	28.82707	91.15920	1203369	881	776 161	29.68164	93.86160	1135074
832	692 224	28.84441	91.21403	1201923	882	777 924	29.69848	93.91486	1133787
833	693 889	28.86174	91.26883	1200480	883	779 689	29.71532	93.96808	1132503
834	695 556	28.87906	91.32360	1199041	884	781 456	29.73214	94.02127	1131222
835	697 225	28.89637	91.37833	1197605	885	783 225	29.74895	94.07444	1129944
836	698 896	28.91366	91.43304	1196172	886	784 996	29.76575	94.12757	1128668
837	700 569	28.93095	91.48770	1194743	887	786 769	29.78255	94.18068	1127396
838	702 244	28.94823	91.54234	1193317	888	788 544	29.79933	94.23375	1126126
839	703 921	28.96550	91.59694	1191895	889	790 321	29.81610	94.28680	1124859
840	705 600	28.98275	91.65151	1190476	890	792 100	29.83287	94.33981	1123596
841	707 281	29.00000	91.70605	1189061	891	793 881	29.84962	94.39280	1122334
842	708 964	29.01724	91.76056	1187648	892	795 664	29.86637	94.44575	1121076
843	710 649	29.03446	91.81503	1186240	893	797 449	29.88311	94.49868	1119821
844	712 336	29.05168	91.86947	1184834	894	799 236	29.89983	94.55157	1118568
845	714 025	29.06888	91.92388	1183432	895	801 025	29.91655	94.60444	1117318
846	715 716	29.08608	91.97826	1182033	896	802 816	29.93326	94.65728	1116071
847	717 409	29.10326	92.03260	1180638	897	804 609	29.94996	94.71008	1114827
848	719 104	29.12044	92.08692	1179245	898	806 404	29.96665	94.76286	1113586
849	720 801	29.13760	92.14120	1177856	899	808 201	29.98333	94.81561	1112347
850	722 500	29.15476	92.19544	1176471	900	810 000	30.00000	94.86833	1111111

Table X SQUARES, SQUARE ROOTS, AND RECIPROCALS 1–1,000 (*Continued*)

N	N²	√N	√10N	1/N .00	N	N²	√N	√10N	1/N .00
900	810 000	30.00000	94.86833	1111111	950	902 500	30.82207	97.46794	1052632
901	811 801	30.01666	94.92102	1109878	951	904 401	30.83829	97.51923	1051525
902	813 604	30.03331	94.97368	1108647	952	906 304	30.85450	97.57049	1050420
903	815 409	30.04996	95.02631	1107420	953	908 209	30.87070	97.62172	1049318
904	817 216	30.06659	95.07891	1106195	954	910.116	30.88689	97.67292	1048218
905	819 025	30.08322	95.13149	1104972	955	912 025	30.90307	97.72410	1047120
906	820 836	30.09983	95.18403	1103753	956	913 936	30.91925	97.77525	1046025
907	822 649	30.11644	95.23655	1102536	957	915 849	30.93542	97.82638	1044932
908	824 464	30.13304	95.28903	1101322	958	917 764	30.95158	97.87747	1043841
909	826 281	30.14963	95.34149	1100110	959	919 681	30.96773	97.92855	1042753
910	828 100	30.16621	95.39392	1098901	960	921 600	30.98387	97.97959	1041667
911	829 921	30.18278	95.44632	1097695	961	923 521	31.00000	98.03061	1040583
912	831 744	30.19934	95.49869	1096491	962	925 444	31.01612	98.08160	1039501
913	833 569	30.21589	95.55103	1095290	963	927 369	31.03224	98.13256	1038422
914	835 396	30.23243	95.60335	1094092	964	929 296	31.04835	98.18350	1037344
915	837 225	30.24897	95.65563	1092896	965	931 225	31.06445	98.23441	1036269
916	839 056	30.26549	95.70789	1091703	966	933 156	31.08054	98.28530	1035197
917	840 889	30.28201	95.76012	1090513	967	935 089	31.09662	98.33616	1034126
918	842 724	30.29851	95.81232	1089325	968	937 024	31.11270	98.38699	1033058
919	844 561	30.31501	95.86449	1088139	969	938 961	31.12876	98.43780	1031992
920	846 400	30.33150	95.91663	1086957	970	940 900	31.14482	98.48858	1030928
921	848 241	30.34798	95.96874	1085776	971	942 841	31.16087	98.53933	1029866
922	850 084	30.36445	96.02083	1084599	972	944 784	31.17691	98.59006	1028807
923	851 929	30.38092	96.07289	1083424	973	946 729	31.19295	98.64076	1027749
924	853 776	30.39737	96.12492	1082251	974	948 676	31.20897	98.69144	1026694
925	855 625	30.41381	96.17692	1081081	975	950 625	31.22499	98.74209	1025641
926	857 476	30.43025	96.22889	1079914	976	952 576	31.24100	98.79271	1024590
927	859 329	30.44667	96.28084	1078749	977	954 529	31.25700	98.84331	1023541
928	861 184	30.46309	96.33276	1077586	978	956 484	31.27299	98.89388	1022495
929	863 041	30.47950	96.38465	1076426	979	958 441	31.28898	98.94443	1021450
930	864 900	30.49590	96.43651	1075269	980	960 400	31.30495	98.99495	1020408
931	866 761	30.51229	96.48834	1074114	981	962 361	31.32092	99.04544	1019368
932	868 624	30.52868	96.54015	1072961	982	964 324	31.33688	99.09591	1018330
933	870 489	30.54505	96.59193	1071811	983	966 289	31.35283	99.14636	1017294
934	872 356	30.56141	96.64368	1070664	984	968 256	31.36877	99.19677	1016260
935	874 225	30.57777	96.69540	1069519	985	970 225	31.38471	99.24717	1015228
936	876 096	30.59412	96.74709	1068376	986	972 196	31.40064	99.29753	1014199
937	877 969	30.61046	96.79876	1067236	987	974 169	31.41656	99.34787	1013171
938	879 844	30.62679	96.85040	1066098	988	976 144	31.43247	99.39819	1012146
939	881 721	30.64311	96.90201	1064963	989	978 121	31.44837	99.44848	1011122
940	883 600	30.65942	96.95360	1063830	990	980 100	31.46427	99.49874	1010101
941	885 481	30.67572	97.00515	1062699	991	982 081	31.48015	99.54898	1009082
942	887 364	30.69202	97.05668	1061571	992	984 064	31.49603	99.59920	1008065
943	889 249	30.70831	97.10819	1060445	993	986 049	31.51190	99.64939	1007049
944	891 136	30.72458	97.15966	1059322	994	988 036	31.52777	99.69955	1006036
945	893 025	30.74085	97.21111	1058201	995	990 025	31.54362	99.74969	1005025
946	894 916	30.75711	97.26253	1057082	996	992 016	31.55947	99.79980	1004016
947	896 809	30.77337	97.31393	1055966	997	994 009	31.57531	99.84989	1003009
948	898 704	30.78961	97.36529	1054852	998	996 004	31.59114	99.89995	1002004
949	900 601	30.80584	97.41663	1053741	999	998 001	31.60696	99.94999	1001001
950	902 500	30.82207	97.46794	1052632	1000	1 000 000	31.62278	100.00000	1000000

Bibliography for Further Reading

The following list of books has been compiled for the reader who wishes to learn more about statistics. It is arranged by main topics, by and large in the same order in which they appear in the text:

A. Inference and Probability
B. Sampling
C. Quality Control
D. Index Numbers
E. Time Series and Correlation
F. Electronic Computers, Linear Programming, Input-Output Analysis, etc.

To help the reader, each book has been identified by two criteria—the nature of the book and its level of mathematics. To indicate the nature of the book the following numbers are used:

1. Theory and principles
2. Methods and applications
3. Related topics.

The following symbols identify its mathematical level:

Ar   Arithmetic
Al   Algebra
Ca   Calculus
PC   Postcalculus
SL   Symbolic Logic
NM   Non-mathematical.

A. INFERENCE AND PROBABILITY

1. David Blackwell and M. Girshick, *Theory of Games and Statistical Decisions* (New York, John Wiley & Sons, Inc., 1954). (1 PC)
2. Irwin D. J. Bross, *Design for Decision* (New York, The Macmillan Company, 1953). (1 NM)
3. Harald Cramér, *The Elements of Probability Theory and Some of Its Applications* (New York, John Wiley & Sons, Inc., 1955). (1,2 Al, Ca)
4. Wilfrid J. Dixon and Frank J. Massey, Jr., *Introduction to Statistical Analysis* (New York, McGraw-Hill Book Company, Inc., 1951). (2,3 Al)
5. William Feller, *An Introduction to Probability Theory and Its Applications* (New York, John Wiley & Sons, Inc., 1950). (1,2 Al, Ca)
6. Robert Ferber, *Statistical Techniques in Market Research* (New York, McGraw-Hill Book Company, Inc., 1949). (2,3 Al, Ar)

7. Ronald A. Fisher, *Statistical Methods for Research Workers*, 10th ed. (London, Oliver & Boyd Ltd., 1946). (2 Al)

8. John E. Freund, *Modern Elementary Statistics* (New York, Prentice-Hall, Inc., 1952). (2,3 Ar)

9. Paul G. Hoel, *Introduction to Modern Statistics*, 2d ed. (New York, John Wiley & Sons, Inc., 1954). (2 Ca)

10. Maurice Kendall, *The Advanced Theory of Statistics*, 3d ed., Vols. I and II (New York, Hafner Publishing Company, 1951). (2 Ca)

11. Richard E. von Mises, *Probability, Statistics, and Truth* (New York, The Macmillan Company, 1939). (1 NM)

12. Alexander M. Mood, *Introduction to the Theory of Statistics* (New York, McGraw-Hill Book Company, Inc., 1950). (2 Ca)

13. Jerzy Neyman, *First Course in Probability and Statistics* (New York, Henry Holt & Company, Inc., 1950). (1,2 Ca)

14. Donald W. Paden and E. F. Lindquist, *Statistics for Economics and Business*, 2d ed. (New York, McGraw-Hill Book Company, Inc., 1956). (2,3 Ar)

15. H. Reichenbach, *The Theory of Probability* (Berkeley, University of California Press, 1949). (1 SL)

16. Leonard J. Savage, *The Foundations of Statistics* (New York, John Wiley & Sons, Inc., 1954). (1 SL, Ca)

17. George W. Snedecor, *Statistical Methods*, 5th ed. (Ames, Iowa College Press, 1956). (2,3 Ar)

18. R. Clay Sprowls, *Elementary Statistics for Students of Social Science and Business* (New York, McGraw-Hill Book Company, Inc., 1955). (2,3 Al, Ar)

19. Abraham Wald, *Statistical Decision Functions* (New York, John Wiley & Sons, Inc., 1950). (1,2 PC)

20. Helen M. Walker and Joseph Lev, *Statistical Inference* (New York, Henry Holt and Company, Inc., 1953). (2,3 Ar)

21. W. Allen Wallis and H. V. Roberts, *Statistics: A New Approach* (Glencoe, Illinois, The Free Press, 1956). (2,3 Ar)

22. G. U. Yule and Maurice G. Kendall, *An Introduction to the Theory of Statistics*, 14th ed. (New York, Hafner Publishing Company, 1950). (1,2 Ar, Ca)

B. SAMPLING

23. William G. Cochran, *Sampling Techniques* (New York, John Wiley & Sons, Inc., 1953). (1,2 Ca)

24. William E. Deming, *Some Theory of Sampling* (New York, John Wiley & Sons, Inc., 1950). (1,2 Ca)

25. Leon Festinger and Daniel Katz, *Research Methods in the Behavioral Sciences* (New York, Dryden Press, 1953). (2,3 NM)

26. Morris H. Hansen, William N. Hurwitz and William G. Madow, *Sample Survey Methods and Theory* (New York, John Wiley & Sons, Inc., 1953) (1,2 Ca)

27. Mildred Parten, *Surveys, Polls and Samples: Practical Procedures* (New York, Harper & Brothers, 1950). (2,3 NM)

28. S. Payne, *The Art of Asking Questions* (Princeton, Princeton University Press, 1951). (2,3 NM)

29. U.S. Department of Commerce Special Advisory Committee on Employment Statistics, *The Measurement of Employment and Unemployment Statistics* (Washington D.C., Bureau of the Census, August, 1954).   (2,3 NM)
30. Frank Yates, *Sampling Methods for Censuses and Surveys* (New York, Hafner Publishing Company, 1953).   (2 Ar)

C. QUALITY CONTROL

31. Irving W. Burr, *Engineering Statistics and Quality Control* (New York, McGraw-Hill Book Company, Inc., 1953).   (2 Al)
32. Acheson J. Duncan, *Quality Control and Industrial Statistics* (Homewood, Ill., Richard D. Irwin, Inc., 1952).   (2,3 Al)
33. Eugene L. Grant, *Statistical Quality Control* (New York, McGraw-Hill Book Company, Inc., 1952).   (2 Al)
34. Abraham Wald, *Sequential Analysis* (New York, John Wiley & Sons, Inc., 1947).   (1,2 PC)

D. INDEX NUMBERS

35. Charles F. Carter, W. B. Reddaway and Richard J. N. Stone, *The Measurement of Production Movements* (Cambridge, The University Press, 1948).   (NM)
36. Arthur H. Cole, *Measures of Business Change* (Chicago, Richard D. Irwin Inc., 1952).   (2 NM)
37. Frederick E. Croxton and Dudley J. Cowden, *Practical Business Statistics* (New York, Prentice-Hall, Inc., 1948).   (2,3 Ar)
38. Irving Fisher, *The Making of Index Numbers* (New York, Houghton Mifflin Company, 1923).   (1,2 NM)
39. Wesley C. Mitchell, *The Making and Using of Index Numbers* U.S. Bureau of Labor Statistics Bulletin No. 656 (Washington D.C., U.S. Government Printing Office, 1938).   (1,2 NM)
40. Bruce D. Mudgett, *Index Numbers* (New York, John Wiley & Sons, Inc., 1951).   (2 Al)
41. William A. Neiswanger, *Elementary Statistical Method as Applied to Economic and Business Data*, 2d ed. (New York, The Macmillan Company, 1956).   (2,3 Ar)
42. Richard M. Snyder, *Measuring Business Changes* (New York, John Wiley & Sons, Inc., 1955).   (2,3 NM)
43. M. J. Ulmer, *The Economic Theory of Cost of Living Index Numbers* (New York, Columbia University Press, 1949).   (1,2 NM)
44. United States Congress Joint Committee on the Economic Report, *Consumers' Price Index* 80th Cong. 2nd Sess. Joint committee print.   Robert A. Taft, Chairman (Washington D.C., U.S. Government Printing Office, 1949).   (2,3 NM)
45. United States Congress House Committee on Education and Labor, *Consumers' Price Index* 82nd. Cong., 1st Sess. House.   Subcommittee report No. 2 (Wash., D.C., U.S. Government Printing Office, 1951).   (2,3 Ar)

E. TIME SERIES AND CORRELATION

46. H. C. Barton, Jr., "Adjusting for Seasonal Variation," *Federal Reserve Bulletin*, June, 1941. (2 Ar)
47. Arthur F. Burns and Wesley C. Mitchell, *Measuring Business Cycles* (New York, National Bureau of Economic Research, 1946). (1,2 NM)
48. Frederick E. Croxton and Dudley J. Cowden, *Practical Business Statistics*, 2d ed. (New York, Prentice-Hall, Inc., 1948). (2,3 Ar)
49. Harold T. Davis, *The Analysis of Economic Time Series* (Bloomington, Principia Press, 1941). (2 Ca)
50. Mordecai Ezekiel, *Methods of Correlation Analysis* (New York, John Wiley & Sons, Inc., 1941). (2 Al)
51. E. Frickey, *Economic Fluctuations in the United States: A Systematic Analysis of Long-run Trends and Business Cycles* (Cambridge, Harvard University Press, 1942). (2 NM)
52. Ragnar Frisch, *Pitfalls in the Statistical Construction of Demand and Supply Curves* (Leipzig, Hans Buske, 1933). (2,3 Al)
53. Trygve Haavelmo, *The Probability Approach in Econometrics*, *Econometrica*, Vol. 12, Supplement (Chicago, Econometric Society, University of Chicago, 1944). (1,2 Ca)
54. Anders Hald, *The Decomposition of a Series of Observations* (Copenhagen, G.E.C. Gads, 1948). (2 PC)
55. William C. Hood and Tjalling C. Koopmans, *Studies in Econometric Method*, Cowles Commission Monograph No. 14 (New York, John Wiley & Sons, Inc., 1953). (1,2 PC)
56. Lawrence R. Klein, *Economic Fluctuations in the United States 1921–41*, Cowles Commission Monograph No. 11 (New York, John Wiley & Sons, Inc., 1950). (1,2 Ca)
57. Lawrence R. Klein, *Econometrics* (Evanston, Row Peterson, 1953). (1,2 Ca, Al)
58. Tjalling C. Koopmans, *Linear Regression Analysis of Economic Time Series* (Haarlem, Erven F. Bohn, 1937). (1,2 PC)
59. Tjalling C. Koopmans, *Statistical Inference in Dynamic Economic Models*, Cowles Commission Monograph No. 10 (New York, John Wiley & Sons, Inc., 1950). (1,2 PC)
60. Frederick R. Macaulay, *The Smoothing of Time Series* (New York, National Bureau of Economic Research, 1931). (2 NM)
61. Lewis A. Maverick, *Time Series Analysis: Smoothing by Stages* (San Antonio, Paul Anderson Company, 1945). (2 Ar)
62. William A. Neiswanger, *Elementary Statistical Methods*, 2d ed. (New York, The Macmillan Company, 1956). (2,3 Ar)
63. Fred H. Sanderson, *Methods of Crop Forecasting* (Cambridge, Harvard University Press, 1954). (2 Al)
64. Max Sasuly, *Trend Analysis of Statistics: Theory and Technique* (Washington, D.C., Brookings Institution, 1934). (2 Ca)
65. Henry Schultz, *Theory and Measurement of Demand* (Chicago, University of Chicago Press, 1938). (2,3 Ca, Al)

66. Richard N. J. Stone, *The Measurement of Consumers' Expenditure and Behaviour in the United Kingdom, 1920–1938* (Cambridge, Cambridge University Press, 1954). (2,3 Ca, Al)
67. Jan Tinbergen, *Statistical Testing of Business-cycle Theories.* Vol. I: *A Method and its Application to Investment Activity.* Vol. II: *Business Cycles in the United States of America, 1919–1932* (Geneva, League of Nations, 1939). (1,2 Al)
68. Gerhard Tintner, *Econometrics* (New York, John Wiley & Sons, Inc., 1952). (1,2 Ca, Al)
69. W. Allen Wallis and Geoffrey H. Moore, *A Significance Test for Time Series and Other Ordered Observations.* National Bureau of Economic Research, Technical Paper No. 1 (New York, NBER, 1941). (1,2 Al)
70. Peter Whittle, *Hypothesis Testing in Time Series Analysis* (New York, Hafner, Publishing Company, 1951). (1,2 Al, Ca)
71. Herman Wold and Lars Jureen, *Demand Analysis: A Study in Econometrics* (New York, John Wiley & Sons, Inc., 1953). (1,2 PC)

F. ELECTRONIC COMPUTERS, LINEAR PROGRAMMING, INPUT-OUTPUT ANALYSIS, etc.

72. Tibor Barna, *The Structural Interdependence of the Economy* (New York, John Wiley & Sons, Inc., 1956). (1,2 Ca)
73. Richard G. Canning, *Electronic Data Processing for Business and Industry* (New York, John Wiley & Sons, Inc., 1956). (2 NM)
74. Ned Chapin, *An Introduction to Automatic Computers* (Chicago, Technology Center, 1955). (2 NM)
75. A. Charnes, W. W. Cooper and A. Henderson, *An Introduction to Linear Programming* (New York, John Wiley & Sons, Inc., 1953). (2,3 Al, Ca)
76. Robert Dorfman, *Applications of Linear Programming to the Theory of the Firm* (Berkeley, University of California Press, 1951). (2 Al)
77. W. J. Eckert and Rebecca Jones, *Faster, Faster* (New York, McGraw-Hill Book Company, Inc., 1956). (2,3 NM)
78. Haskins & Sells, *Data Processing by Electronics* (New York, Haskins & Sells, 1955). (2 NM)
79. Tjalling C. Koopmans (ed.), *Activity Analysis of Production and Allocation,* Cowles Commission Monograph No. 13 (New York, John Wiley & Sons, Inc., 1951). (1,2 PC)
80. George Kozmetsky and Paul Kircher, *Electronic Computers and Management Control* (New York, McGraw-Hill Book Company, Inc., 1956). (2,3 NM)
81. Wassily Leontief, *The Structure of the American Economy,* 2d ed. (New York, Oxford University Press, Inc., 1951). (1,2 Al)
82. Wassily Leontief and others, *Studies in the Structure of the American Economy* (New York, Oxford University Press, Inc., 1953). (1,2 Al)
83. Joseph F. McCloskey and Florence N. Trefethen (ed.), *Operations Research for Management.* Volume I (Baltimore, The Johns Hopkins Press, 1945). (2,3 Al)

84. Joseph F. McCloskey and John M. Coppinger (ed.), *Operations Research for Management.* Volume II (Baltimore, The Johns Hopkins Press, 1956). (2,3 Al)

85. Philip M. Morse and George E. Kimball, *Methods of Operations Research* (New York, John Wiley & Sons, Inc., 1951). (2,3 Al)

86. J. D. Williams, *The Compleat Strategyst* (New York, McGraw-Hill Book Company, Inc., 1954). (2,3 NM)

Index